WINNING FRENCH MINDS

Radio Propaganda in Occupied France 1940–42

BY DENIS COURTOIS

CASEMATE

Philadelphia & Oxford

Published in the United States of America and Great Britain in 2023 by
CASEMATE PUBLISHERS
1950 Lawrence Road, Havertown, PA 19083, USA
and
The Old Music Hall, 106–108 Cowley Road, Oxford OX4 1JE, UK

Hardback Edition: ISBN 978-1-63624-146-3
Digital Edition: ISBN 978-1-63624-147-0

A CIP record for this book is available from the British Library

Printed and bound in the United Kingdom by CPI Group (UK) Ltd, Croydon, CR0 4YY

Typeset in India by Lapiz Digital Services, Chennai.

For a complete list of Casemate titles, please contact:

CASEMATE PUBLISHERS (US)
Telephone (610) 853-9131
Fax (610) 853-9146
Email: casemate@casematepublishers.com
www.casematepublishers.com

CASEMATE PUBLISHERS (UK)
Telephone (01226) 734350
Email: casemate-uk@casematepublishers.co.uk
www.casematepublishers.co.uk

Contents

Acknowledgements

First and foremost, I am indebted to Ruth Sheppard at Casemate Publishers for having given me the opportunity of a lifetime to bring the fascinating story of radio propaganda during World War II in France to readers beyond academia – this book is largely based on my PhD thesis on the same topic. I would like also to thank Els Boonen, archivist at the BBC Written Archives Centre (WAC), Caversham, who – with the other staff – was most helpful during my research. She gave me insightful information on the letters and the BBC Monthly Report, and her expertise and guidance were of great help during my time spent at the BBC WAC. I would like also to thank Tom Hercock, archivist at the BBC Archives, who was very helpful in answering my queries and providing me with the required documents.

I would like to thank all the staff members at The National Archives at Kew who helped me, including Lynn Swyny, copyright manager; Juliette Desplat and Daniel Gosling, remote enquiries duty officers for their invaluable help regarding the publication of National Archive material. I would like also to thank Hannah James, records manager and college archivist and Katharine Thomson, archivist from the Churchill Archives Centre for their patience regarding my numerous queries; M. Randall Bytwerk from the German Archives, Calvin University, for allowing me to use invaluable materials about German propaganda that had been translated from German to English.

I would like to thank Ms Aurélie Zbos, assistant to the head, and the staff at the Collections du Service Archives écrites et Musée de Radio France (CSA); Ms Cécile de David-Beauregard, head of the Department for Written Archives and Museum, General Secretariat, Radio France for granting me the right to use the documents necessary to illustrate this book; and M. Jacques Polacco Angerie, secretary general of the Radio History Committee, for allowing me to use materials from the journal, the *Cahiers d'Histoire de la Radiodiffusion*, which are available in this archive. I would like to thank the archivists of the Archives Nationales de Pierrefittes in Saint-Denis, and Geneviève Profit, chief curator at the Archives Nationales for her help when discussing copyright of French archival material.

My thanks also extend to Ms Valérie Thépault, documentalist at the Institut national de l'audiovisuel (INA) for helping me understand the archival system; Ms Christine Barbier-Bouvet (responsable Inathèque), Anne Paris and Corinne

Gauthier for helping me gain access to the indexed narratives of the numerous broadcasts I listened to during my visit; and Ms Sophie Morel, assistant to the director of Dissemination, for being my contact and providing me with the necessary information to move this project forward. I cannot forget all the other staff members who were extremely kind to me and supported me in my research during the long months I spent at the INA.

I would like to thank the staff of the Archives de la Préfecture de police de Paris, who guided me in searching for information relevant to my research and, in particular, Nathalie Minart, head of the Images department.

Last but not least, I would like to thank my wife Echo for her unconditional support during my years of research in archives and the writing of this book.

Translations and Terminology

This book makes extensive use of material translated from French, in particular published broadcasts and its digitised version, including correspondence from the BBC Written Archives Centre, Caversham and police reports from France, as well as secondary literature. I have used published English translations where available. In all other examples, the translations are my own, including those in quotation.

When referring to Pétain as the head of the state, the French term 'chef' is used rather than its direct English translation of 'chief' to preserve the authenticity of this respectable title ('chef' means both a leader and the head of a kitchen in French).

I noticed some common discrepancies when citing the names of radio programmes, both in French and English literature, including in archival documents. For example, for *Les enfants chantent* (the title of a radio programme), I found three different ways of capitalisation in publications and archival documents: *Les Enfants Chantent*, *Les Enfants chantent*, and *Les enfants chantent*. Inconsistency in capitalisation is a common occurrence with almost all the radio programme titles mentioned in this book. I adopted the standard terminology used in French publications when introducing these names to the readers, unless it is used in a direct quotation.

French spelling is used in the book for French cities, towns, regions, *arrondissements* and *départements*, unless quoted from an English source.

Where there is an abbreviation in text, I have included the English translation of that term in the Abbreviations section. Where the French terminology closely resembles the English, I have not included an English translation. Otherwise, the English translation is provided in text in brackets.

I have used the terminology employed at the time when referring to *départements* and *détachements*. Several *départements* have since been renamed: for example, Loire-Inférieure is known today as Loire-Atlantique, and Charente-Inférieure is now Charente-Maritime.

Abbreviations

AA	Anti-aircraft
AFIP	Agence française d'information de presse (French Agency Press Information)
ATS	Agence télégraphique suisse (Swiss telegraph agency)
BBC	British Broadcasting Corporation
BDIC	La bibliothèque de documentation internationale contemporaine (The International Contemporary Documentation Library)
BSP	Brevet Sportif Populaire (Popular Sports Patent)
CAP	Certificat d'aptitude professionnelle (certificate of professional competence)
CGEGS	Commissariat général à l'Éducation générale et aux Sports (General Commission for General and Sports Education)
CICR	Comité international de la Croix-Rouge (International Committee of the Red Cross)
CIS	Centre d'Initiatives Sociales de Radio Paris (Social Initiative Centre of Radio Paris)
COSI	Comité ouvrier de secours immédiat (immediate relief workers' committee)
DDWB	Daily Digest of World Broadcasts
DDD	Deutsche Drahtlose Dienste (German wireless services)
DES	Deutsche Europa Sender (German Europe Channels)
DNB	Deutsches Nachrichtenbüro (German news office)
FFM	Fédération Française de la Montagne (French Federation of Mountaineering and Climbing)
HONAFU	Höhere Nachrichtenführer (Higher News Leader)
INA	Institut national de l'audiovisuel (National Broadcasting Institute)
INBEL	Office belge d'information et de documentation (Belgian Information and Documentation Office)
INR	Institut national belge de radiodiffusion (Belgian National Broadcasting Institute)
JM	Jeunesse et Montagne (Youth and Mountain)
JPF	Jeunesses Populaires Françaises (French Popular Youth movement)

LVF	Légion des volontaires français contre le bolchevisme (Legion of French Volunteers against Bolshevism)
MOI	Ministry of Information
PPF	Parti Populaire Français (French Popular Party)
PTT	Postes, Télégraphes et Téléphones (Postal, Telegraph and Telephones)
PWE	Political Warfare Executive
RAF	Royal Air Force
RCA	Radio Corporation of America
RN	Radiodiffusion Nationale (national broadcasting)
RNB	Radiodiffusion Nationale Belge (Belgian National Radio)
RNP	Rassemblement national populaire (National Popular Rally)
RVPS	Royal Victoria Patriotic School
SGJ	Secrétariat général de la Jeunesse (General Secretariat for Youth)
SNCF	Société nationale des chemins de fer français (French national railway company)
SNI	Syndicat national des instituteurs (National Union of Teachers)
SO1	SOE propaganda section
SOE	Special Operations Executive
SR	Service de la radiodiffusion suisse (Swiss Broadcasting Service)
SSR	Société suisse de radiodiffusion (Swiss Broadcasting Corporation)
STO	Service du travail obligatoire (compulsory work service)
TFA	Travailleurs français en Allemagne (French workers in Germany)

Introduction

The beginning of radio broadcasting

Radio broadcasting was a technology new to the 20th century, although experiments in wireless transmission had begun decades earlier. The first radio news programme was broadcast in the USA in the early 1920s, pioneering national news broadcasting, various cultural genres and commercial sponsorship, and acquainting the Americans with this mode of communication. American society during this period cannot fully be understood without considering the impact of radio on society and culture, not least because no other medium changed everyday lives so quickly and profoundly.[1] Indeed, it has been argued that radio was 'the most important electronic invention of the century'[2] because it changed the habits of Americans, blurring the boundaries between the private and public spheres,[3] shaping not only individual but also collective identities, as well as cultural and political history.[4]

In Britain and France, the technology of wireless similarly transformed societies once both countries had started radio broadcasting from 1922. The British Broadcasting Company (BBC) was formed in October that year and the first programmes were broadcast on 14 November 1922.[5] John Reith became the first general manager of the BBC. He advocated the change of the BBC from a company to a corporation on 1 January 1927.[6]

However, it was not until World War II that radio became one of the primary modes of communication that was used on an unprecedented scale by both the Allied and Axis powers. Then, radio emerged as a new weapon that could be used to direct messages with clear political objectives to a mass audience, and to fight psychological battles. It was also the first time in history, apart from the Spanish Civil War (1936–39),[7] that the radio was used in a total war – when countries mobilised all their available resources, including the civilian population.

Today, we consider World War II as having been a visual war, thanks to newsreels and films, when in fact it was first and foremost a radio war.[8] Radio penetrated the homes of millions and narrated the war to the listeners,[9] broadcasting news, government ideology and propaganda. It also played a crucial role in steering public opinion and propagating a strong sense of patriotism.[10] Listening to the radio became a national habit and a symbol of national unity,[11] bringing together the public behind the war effort. On the other hand, radio could also be associated with the dangers of mass-mediated politics, hypnotising its listeners 'under the sway of irrational forces like fascism, communism'.[12]

Propaganda in 1940–42 – the three radio stations

This book focuses on the three main radio stations with the largest audience in France during this period: the BBC, the Radiodiffusion Nationale (RN – the radio station of the Vichy government)), and Radio Paris (RP – the radio station controlled by the German occupier). They broadcast from three different localities and with distinct political perspectives, but all claimed to represent the 'true' voice of the French. The book will attempt to give them the recognition they deserve in the historiography of wartime France by presenting the narratives of their broadcasting that lie at the heart of their politics, motivation, propaganda, and interaction with the population at large. The potential audience of these stations was impressive. In France, it is estimated that 6.5 million wireless radio sets[13] were in use during the war, and an estimated 47–58% of French households had a wireless,[14] meaning that 19–24 million people might have listened to the radio regularly (in 1939, the estimated total population in France was 41.2 million).[15] Radio emerged as one of the main channels through which millions of people received news about the war and current affairs.

The period between 1940 and 1942 marked the defeat of France, the division of France into two zones, and the creation and evolution of Vichy. At the time, there were a few main players in the business of radio broadcasting: the three mentioned above and Radio Sottens (from Switzerland). There were also other radios that had fewer listeners, such as Radio Moscow, the Voice of America (WRUL Boston Radio) and Radio Belgique.[16] In addition to these official channels, there were also 'black' (clandestine) radio stations broadcasting to France.[17]

World War II is a difficult topic in French historiography; the rapid capitulation to Germany was a major blow to the confidence and self-perception of the French nation. For many decades, historiography of French wartime experiences focused on the French resistance, de Gaulle's government-in-exile, the *débâcle* (or rout) in 1940, Vichy's political role, the National Revolution with its implications for the population, and collaboration. Collaboration and Vichy are seen as a stain on French history, something 'un-French' and often marginalised. The reality, however,

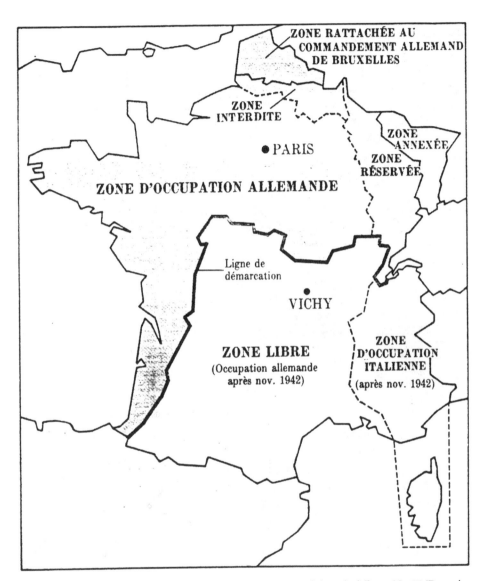

Map of France during the occupation. From CSA, *Cahiers d'Histoire de la Radiodiffusion*, No. 27 (December 1990), 48.

is somewhat different, especially during the first two years of the French defeat since resistance did not play an important role at that time.

This book will focus on the first half of the war, from 25 June 1940, the date of the signing of the Armistice that marked the defeat of France, to 11 November 1942, when Germany invaded Vichy. In this period, France was divided into two main zones:[18] the occupied zone and the unoccupied zone (Vichy). The division of territory had a profound impact on the beliefs and experiences of the French in a time of severe material shortage and moral distress. The sway of public opinion was most apparent in the first two years of the war and could easily have gone either way, as we will see.

During this period, the intensity of broadcasting within and to France increased significantly as the various powers sought to influence, control and manipulate the minds and hearts of the French, who were disoriented and unsettled following the unexpected and rapid defeat of the French army in 1940. Radio propaganda in France during World War II was not researched in earnest until the 1970s, and then most publications were linked to the BBC. For example, a book was written by Asa Briggs,[19] a BBC historian; Tim Brooks[20] wrote about British propaganda effort towards the French including the use of BBC broadcasts and the secret broadcasting stations; Martyn Cornick[21] wrote a paper giving information on how the BBC used letters from listeners to compile intelligence reports throughout the war years in France; and Crémieux-Brilhac[22] wrote a few papers about how the BBC French Service was perceived by the French, the role of the Free French who were exiled to the UK, and radio propaganda during the war.

Compared to the BBC, relatively little is known about RN and Radio Paris and only a handful of writers have offered a comparative view of the operation of different radio stations. These include E. Tangye Lean, who gave a useful account of the technical aspects (jamming, transmitters etc.) of radio broadcasting and the operation of Radio Paris until 1942;[23] Hélène Eck, who edited a book that contains a lot of factual and background information about the BBC, RN and Radio Paris in broad strokes from before the war through to its end in 1945;[24] and Cécile Méadel, who wrote about Radio Paris's music features and the relationship between music and propaganda.[25] Despite this, among the existing historiography of radio propaganda, the actual narratives of the broadcasts remain unknown.

The BBC was a powerful voice that became instrumental in the psychological battle against the Axis power: this 'transnational broadcasting' enabled the French to hear news and opinions regarding the conflict from the British point of view,[26] counterbalancing the effect of the messages broadcast on RN and Radio Paris. Indeed, with technological progress, the radio became the best means of communication as radio airwaves could traverse borders, and the jamming of the BBC programmes by the Germans and Vichy authorities did not completely prevent them from reaching France due to the various concurrent wavelengths used.[27] However, RN and Radio Paris did have the advantage of broadcasting from within France and reception was unrestricted within its own territory for the targeted audience. While the BBC undoubtedly moulded public attitudes and led public debate with its broadcasts to France, RN and Radio Paris also worked hard to influence people's opinion by attracting listeners with a wide variety of programmes containing both open and hidden political messages.

People's war – psychological warfare

World War II was often called the 'people's war'. One of the BBC's preferred ways of contributing to the war effort was to represent the concerns of the people and put them in a wider context. Listeners' responses to the BBC's wartime broadcasting not only enabled ordinary people's concerns, hopes, fears and aspirations to be voiced publicly, but they were also heard by the British government, thus influencing the subsequent evolution of propaganda policy.[28] In contrast, RN and Radio Paris were more concerned with projecting legitimacy and disseminating information using the voices of authorities and ordinary people. In so doing, they actively sought the participation of the public and constructed their preferred realities through the responses and voices of these participants.

Before turning to the narratives of the different radio stations it is necessary to reflect on the role of radio in psychological warfare and propaganda. The study of propaganda in occupied France and Vichy as conveyed in the narratives of the broadcasts is the main focus of this book. 'Propaganda' as a term had historically been associated with lies and falsehood, and this was particularly prevalent during the Great War of 1914–18.[29] Contemporary propaganda in the more technologically advanced society of the 1930s, however, was not just about lies and falsehood. Instead, it could encompass many levels of truth.[30]

During World War II, both the Germans and the British recognised that lying must be avoided and facts must be accurate in their messages to the public. Joseph Goebbels, the Reich Minister of Propaganda, wanted the communiqués of the Wehrmacht to be as accurate as possible.[31] There is, however, a distinction between the facts – which must stay true – and the intention and interpretation of the moral elements of those facts, which could be manipulated to serve the political purpose of the propagandists. This distinction is key to understanding propaganda[32] and the role played by the three radio stations.

The European Services of the BBC enjoyed a reputation of truthfulness among its listeners. The BBC report of 21 February 1941 cited evidence originating from Northern France praising the BBC, saying that 'we hear the voice of truth, **our** France – you are "the voice of the Frank".'[33] Similar evidence was cited in subsequent reports that the French listeners had great faith in the veracity of the BBC. However, it is the interpretation of 'true facts' that reveals the political aim of the radio propagandists. As established in the report of 8 July 1940, the future role of the BBC lay in keeping the French on the British side, giving something more than 'straight news' if the BBC wanted to be an effective weapon.[34]

For example, when the British bombed Paris and its suburbs in 1942, all three radio stations reported this fact, which was true. However, it was the intention and interpretation of this fact that marked the difference in the narratives of their broadcasts, which served different propaganda aims and political purposes: while the BBC interpreted the event as a necessity for the greater good, Radio Paris interpreted it as a murderous act, causing unnecessary suffering and loss of civilian life, whereas RN started reporting on it in a matter-of-fact manner, in an attempt to preserve the station's perceived 'neutrality', although this stance soon changed as the war progressed.

In terms of the effects of propaganda and how far it serves the purpose of changing attitudes and ideas, it is more limited than is widely believed. Instead, propaganda plays a more prominent role in reinforcing, sharpening and focusing existing trends and beliefs.[35] Propaganda needs to appeal to the rational element in humans as 'attitudes and behaviour are also the products of rational decisions',[36] and should be viewed as an integral part of the whole political process. There is also an argument that propaganda should be viewed as a sociological phenomenon 'rather than as something *made* by certain people for certain purposes'.[37] Propaganda can be categorised into 'propaganda of agitation', which is subversive propaganda, and 'propaganda of integration', which is often more subtle and complex and aims at stabilising and unifying society.[38] These two types of propaganda could both be observed in all the narratives of the three radio stations to a varied extent.

The effects of propaganda cannot really be measured using experiments involving small groups, nor can they be replicated in a test tube.[39] This is because propaganda, especially that of wartime, is a unique phenomenon that results from 'the totality of forces pressing in upon an individual in his society'.[40] Therefore, this book aims to present and evaluate the narratives of each radio station in the context of the totality of forces imposed on the French during the period of occupation.

Propaganda has its limitations, of course. For example, it relies on pre-existing attitudes, which can only be modified very slowly; it cannot reverse or change the central psychological or sociological trends in that society; and it must be compatible with facts or at least appear to be compatible with facts, rather than being solely based on ideas. Goebbels cleverly shifted his propaganda focus to the heroism of the German soldiers when reporting the battle of Stalingrad, rather than emphasising military merits, because it was a major military defeat.[41] Moreover, the psychological effect of propaganda is largely time-bound: 'the psychological action must be lasting and continuous'.[42] Propaganda directed at foreign countries is inevitably much less effective because of the propagandist's psychological ignorance of the attitudes, interests and beliefs of their target audience, who in return commonly display a spontaneous suspicion of anything that comes from the outside.[43]

For these reasons, the BBC was facing an uphill battle from the outset: the broadcasts came from outside of France and were therefore subject to this additional limitation. The BBC attempted to address this by using mainly French speakers and tapping into the practical concerns of the public, making far greater efforts to collect intelligence and monitor public opinion than did RN or Radio Paris. In contrast, RN and Radio Paris were both broadcasting from within France and claimed to represent the voice of France, albeit somewhat controversially, especially in the case of Radio Paris.

Radio propaganda played a crucial role in the execution of the psychological warfare targeted at the French during this period. This is because radio has a number of unique advantages. One of these is immediacy, which meant the listeners could be made believe that they were participating in and bearing witness to events of great importance.[44] For example, appeals for food and clothing via radio broadcasting could be shown to be very successful in helping people who had lost their homes after the bombing of Paris.

By July 1940, the BBC had come to realise that radio broadcasting was their only means of rapidly and effectively addressing France and most of the rest of Europe.[45] It had several advantages over other conventional methods of communication. Leaflet-dropping by air, for example, was not considered cost-effective due to factors such as the weight of the paper to be dropped, the number of sorties and aircraft needed for the operation, the navigation skills that were required to drop the leaflets accurately, the experience of the aircrew, the possibility of adverse weather, the fuel cost, the wear and tear of the aircraft and the risks for the crew members.[46]

RN was the flagship radio station of the Vichy administration, whose first priority was to seek legitimation. As soon as the Armistice was signed on 22 June 1940, RN started to act as the voice of Vichy authority. The latter had the difficult task of presenting itself as an independent French State in the context of limited political sovereignty, a controlled environment and restricted freedom as imposed by the German authorities. The very nature of Vichy meant that it depended on radio as one of its main propaganda tools. Pétain's heavy involvement with RN meant that he was able to establish a personal relationship with the public and impose his political vision on the audience. '*Travail, Famille, Patrie*' became the tripartite motto used by its radio propaganda to convince the French of the superiority of the new moral order and the movement of National Revolution, which sought the revival and reconstruction of France and to revert to its days of glory.[47]

Goebbels, the mastermind of the Nazi propaganda machine, also saw radio as an effective means to persuade those who had already been partially converted to the German cause.[48] He maintained that to be successful, the propagandist must know the individuals and their social groups well and possess the ability to unite people for the National Socialist movement:

> The propagandist must understand not only how to speak to the people in their totality but also to individual sections of the population: to the worker, the peasant, the middle class … he must be able to speak to different professions and to different faiths. The propagandist must always be in a position to speak to people in the language that they understand. These capacities are the essential preconditions for success.[49]

Goebbels's aim was reflected in both the organisation of Radio Paris and its choice of speakers. Radio Paris presented itself as a French radio, using mainly French speakers with a variety of good-quality programmes to keep its listeners tuned in. Radio Paris was a German managed station in terms of its organisation and control but was disguised as a voice for the French. There was a good balance between its propaganda message, news services, entertainment, and cultural programmes.[50] Radio Paris would have had more success in making the French believe in the new ideology of Collaboration and the concept of New Europe if only Hitler's policy towards France had been different. For the ideology of Collaboration and of a united Europe to have the slightest chance of succeeding, the Germans would have to stop crushing France under their boots, which they never stopped doing during the war years. If it transpires that radio propaganda reflects the policy of the enemy or a policy of hypocrisy, its credibility vanishes – Hitler's mistake was the revenge he inflicted upon the French which people then had to live through.[51]

Sources of the radio narratives

This book presents the narratives of the broadcasts that were selected from those available in written form and in audio recording. Both these and the voices of the listeners reveal the political rhetoric and the perceived social norms during the German occupation, and the exercise of power that may be taken for granted. For each of the three radio stations, I have selected a key theme as well as several sub-themes that have common features that link the various narratives to the particular social and political context of the specific period.

The narratives of the broadcasts of the BBC mainly come from two sources. The first is the original transcripts from the BBC Written Archives, where the work of official censorship remains visible. For example, words, group of words or entire passages are crossed out and appropriate corrections have been made to the original text. The transcripts are also accompanied by the speaker's name, the date and time of broadcasting,[52] and occasionally, the number of days since France fell.[53] From 1942, a stamp, 'BBC Passed for Security' appears on some of the transcripts.[54] The benefit of using archival transcripts is that the information retrieved is not hindered by the quality of recording, although the narratives are limited to written words, which are cut and dried. The second source is the published transcripts collated by Jacques Pessis, which are organised in chronological order but with very limited accompanying information; for example, the name of the presenter is sometimes missing, as is the time of the broadcast and the name of the programme. I have also used some transcripts from Maurice Schumann's book, which focuses solely on the narratives of the Free French as broadcast by the BBC.[55] The length of a BBC broadcasts varies from a few lines (six lines minimum) to a total of eight typed pages depending on the topic being debated on the day,[56] although the average size of a broadcast ranges from one to three pages.[57] As written materials are abundant, there was no need to search for the audio recording, which was anyway very limited.[58]

For RN and Radio Paris, on the other hand, written materials are much more limited. Therefore, a lot of the narratives came from my transcriptions of audio recordings that are available at the Institut national de l'audiovisuel (INA), an archive in Paris.

For RN, some of Pétain's speeches via the wireless or otherwise are readily available in Jean-Claude Barbas's book.[59] Pétain's speeches vary in length from a few lines to a transcribed text of more than 250 lines.[60] There is virtually no written record of the broadcast narratives of Radio Paris, although a pamphlet published during the war was uncovered, which contains a small collection of Dr. Friedrich's speeches from 20 April to 6 July 1941.[61]

Both RN and Radio Paris have preserved a sizeable number of audio broadcasts, which makes it possible to study and compare the narratives as well as their evolution surrounding the themes and sub-themes I identify below; however, it is impossible to gauge the percentage of these broadcasts against the actual number of broadcasts during the period covered. The radio magazines have certainly helped in providing useful background information about the various programmes, the speakers, the key concerns of a certain period, and the style of propaganda and broadcasting hours, but there are limitations here too. The radio magazines started much later than radio broadcasting: *Radio National* was first published in May 1941 while *Les Ondes* was first published in April 1941 (although the first issue available in the archives of Radio France was dated 1942 and is only available on a disc). The schedule includes detailed information for cultural programmes; for example, the name of a play or a list of the songs and artists for a concert, but for other programmes, only the title of the programme is listed.

In terms of the audio recordings of RN and Radio Paris, each digital recording of the indexed broadcast is accompanied by a printed page or fact sheet including the 'title' of the broadcast; the broadcasting date (a common feature for RN but one that appears only 16 times for Radio Paris); the duration of the recording; the themes of each individual broadcast (politics, teaching, the social question, sports, etc.); the type of broadcast (reportage, interview, etc.); the speakers (if known); a description comprising a few key words about the broadcast; the production company that created the programme; the date of the recording; and a summary of the content, among other key factors. Information about the name of the programme from which the broadcasts originate and the time of broadcasting, however, are largely missing, making it very difficult to map the broadcast to the programme schedule published in the radio magazines.

The depth of the summary of the content on the fact sheets differs significantly between RN and Radio Paris. For RN's broadcasts, detailed summaries are available, giving background information about a reportage. These are broken down into segments with a clear start and end time and a description for each segment, making it easier to locate a particular segment of narrative once that indexed broadcast has been identified among all the unindexed broadcasts in the clip. However, in the case of Radio Paris, the summary is considerably less informative, with much shorter descriptions (three to five lines maximum), making it harder to identify the indexed broadcast; in most cases, the whole broadcast audio recording must be listened to before one can be certain that the correct segment has been included.

Moreover, the information provided on the printed summaries of RN and Radio Paris broadcasts does not always match the information on the audio recording. Where this is the case, an explanation is provided on the fact sheet; for example, the digitised version might have been produced from the inventory disc and certain segments of the audio recording may have been lost due to the disc being too degraded, but the fact sheet might not have been reproduced, resulting in the mismatch of information.[62]

The narratives transcribed from the audio recordings of the broadcasts are 'real-world data' that are authentic in format and content, neither edited nor sanitised.[63] The audio recordings also capture the emotion of the moment, the concerns of both the authorities and the people, and thus the evolution of radio propaganda in the context of historical events.

There were, however, many challenges in making sense and use of the audio recordings – in fact, it was this challenge that motivated me to do a PhD on this topic in the first place. Crucial historical information on radio propaganda is largely hidden away in French archives and in resources only available in French. This data may be less accessible to non-French speaking researchers with limited access to translation.

As radio historians in the USA have stated, radio messages are 'one of the spottiest, most ephemeral historical records in all of the mass media',[64] and the same is true for the recordings for these three radio stations. Study of the recordings and narratives of wartime radio is hindered by the lack of primary material, especially recordings and transcripts, and the difficulties in accessing relevant information. This was a time when radio programmes were not consistently recorded and preserved; as a result, there are now only a few recordings available, which are often incomplete or of poor sound quality. The speed and accent of the speakers (for example, when pronouncing a name or place) and the environment in which the recording was made (for example, when it was a live reportage in a public place) add another layer of difficulty to the correct understanding of the broadcasts,[65] even to a native speaker of French like myself.

Most of the surviving digitised recordings of RN focus on Pétain's speeches, ideology and the events in which he was involved. In fact, there are only a handful of surviving radio programmes in which Pétain did not participate. There exists a total of 199 available recordings of RN covering the period 1940–42, though as explained, we cannot know what proportion of the total broadcasts made during this period this represents. Each indexed broadcast contains recordings of varying lengths, with an average duration of two to three hours, and with multiple clips of messages mingled together. The two main types of broadcasts available for public listening are live broadcasts – some of which may have been recorded for re-broadcasting at a later date – and broadcasts that were pre-recorded in studios and then put on air.[66]

I identified some 14 major themes among the available audio recordings for RN, covering a wide range of topics, such as the youth, prisoners of war (POWs), government, National Revolution, charity, the French Empire, etc., in a variety of genres, including news, interviews and reportage. These were recorded in the studio of RN or else in a public or business place. These themes recur; however, the intensity and focus of coverage of each theme changes over time depending on the priorities of the respective government behind the radio stations. There are also other ad hoc themes that appeared throughout, though sparsely. Due to the limited and selective nature of the digital recording of the available broadcasts, the recordings were reviewed in conjunction with the information available in *Radio National*, RN's radio magazine.

Regarding Radio Paris, a total of 468 indexed broadcasts are listed, each containing multiple clips of messages of varying length, with an average duration of two to three hours, except for art and music programmes, whose length could run up to six hours. Among Radio Paris's available audio recordings of broadcasts there are many art, cultural and music programmes, such as extracts of theatre plays, interviews with artists, live concerts, etc. From the available digital recordings, I identified eight major recurring themes, including anti-British/anti-American propaganda, collaboration, the youth, workers, Communism and Bolshevism, alongside a large number of other themes that appeared occasionally, in a variety of forms such as news, interview, reportage and sketches taking place both within and outside of the studio of Radio Paris. I have also used *Les Ondes,* Radio Paris's magazine, to supplement the information available on the recordings.

Discrepancies over the date of a broadcast occur frequently, which adds to the difficulties experienced in identifying the correct date of the broadcast. While the majority of the audio records were recorded and broadcast on the same day, some have a different date for recording and broadcasting.[67] As mentioned, RN displayed both the recording and broadcasting dates on the archival fact sheet, whereas, by and large, Radio Paris only preserved the date of recording (the date of broadcasting only appeared 16 times). Given the inconsistent level of information, I decided to use the 'date of recording' when referring to a radio broadcast, as this information appears in the archival fact sheet of both RN and Radio Paris.

To make matters even more complicated, there are many broadcasts from both RN and Radio Paris dated 1 January 1941 and 1 January 1942, which does not reflect the actual date of recording or broadcasting. Rather, this is an indicator that the date of recording and broadcasting was unknown to the archivist when they were indexed. The only way to estimate a more accurate date of broadcasting is by listening to the content and looking for information contained within the broadcast itself. If the date of the recording is identified solely from the context of the audio recording, I have put a note in the relevant endnote.

Moreover, there are occasional errors in the dates recorded by the archivist. For example, INA indexed on RN *Après la visite de Pétain à l'école de cadres de Gannat* shows a 'date of recording' as 20.10.1941, when it was in fact recorded a year earlier.[68] The indexed *Voyage du Maréchal Pétain à Chambéry (Savoie)* shows a 'date of recording' of 01.01.1941 but it was in fact recorded in September 1941.[69] Where these are identified, I explain the discrepancy in the endnote.[70]

The structure of the book

There are key differences between the themes of the BBC, RN and Radio Paris. While the BBC tended to focus more on giving timely news and airing the various aspects of the daily concerns of the French, the two radio stations broadcasting within France were much more concerned with French youth and the future of France.

Each chapter is structured chronologically as I show how the focus of the broadcasts and the themes change, depending on the priorities of the respective station's government, the course of war and the general situation in wartime France and Europe.

Chapter 1 gives an overview of each of the three radio stations; their historical context, the various challenges encountered by these radios, information on their programmes and presenters, their respective magazines and how they maintained contact with their target audience and the general public, etc.

Chapter 2 gives an overview of other international radio stations in Europe, America and Africa that could be heard in France. This is so that the radio war in France can be better understood within the context of a world war: there was a continuous war of waves between foreign stations broadcasting to or within France, including its colonies, and to the francophones during 1940–42.

Chapters 3, 4 and 5 focus on the BBC, RN and Radio Paris broadcasts respectively, each covering the same period of 1940–42. Within each chapter, radio broadcasts are presented chronologically, grouped by year.

In Chapter 3, on the BBC, the overarching theme is 'food', since this was one of the main preoccupations of the BBC's messages to the French public. This theme also encompasses the discussion of the British blockade, restrictions on food (rationing, black market, family parcels), and their social and political consequences (the housewives' demonstrations, lack of calories for children, starvation, mortality rate and weight loss). By choosing 'food' as a leitmotif, the BBC demonstrated good knowledge of the popular concerns of the French during this period and used it as a lever to empathise with the French, raise patriotic feelings and put pressure on Vichy and German authorities.

In Chapter 4, the key theme is 'the youth' – one of the main preoccupations of Vichy. It also encompasses the expectations and social responsibility of French youth: giving birth as a patriotic duty, rejuvenation of the youth via the various youth movements, and the role of education and sports in youth development. The preoccupation of RN was to seek legitimacy for the Vichy government and to inspire the regeneration of the nation through the transformation of the youth.

In Chapter 5, 'the youth' is again the overarching theme, but the focus differs considerably. Unlike RN, Radio Paris expressed the German expectation of French youth (rural service, the future of the youth, charity work, collaboration), youth events, public service (employment placements), and depicted French youth as victims of the Allied actions. 'The youth' was a crucial aspect of German propaganda, as the occupiers were looking for a supply of labour for the German war effort, hence using young people to influence public perception of the future of France in a Europe dominated by Nazi Germany.

The final chapter concludes the book, outlining how the narratives conveyed through these media evolved between 1940 and 1942, and how the focus of the propaganda shifted; how the radio stations interacted; how the tone and emphasis in the narratives evolved; and how listeners and the public were involved in the production of these broadcasts.

CHAPTER I

The main players in the space of radio propaganda

The foreign-language service of the BBC

Historical context

From December 1932, the BBC, located at Bush House in London, began to broadcast a new service, the British Empire Service, in English and on short wave addressed to the British Empire, including Australia, New Zealand, India, East and Southern Africa, Canada and the West Indies. The purpose was to bring together the scattered parts of the British Empire. By the late 1930s, the BBC had to consider broadcasting in foreign languages as a desperate response to the imminent threat posed by anti-British propaganda aired across borders by German and Italian radio stations. The top priority was to broadcast in Arabic, in order to counter the anti-British propaganda being spread by Radio Bari, an Italian radio station broadcasting in Arabic in North Africa and Palestine. This was achieved in January 1938. Shortly afterwards, in March, the BBC added broadcasting services in Spanish and Portuguese because Britain's commercial and diplomatic interests in Latin America were being threatened by German radio stations in South America. Broadcasting in French, German and Italian began in September 1938 during the Munich crisis.[1] At that time, the BBC was facing a lack of both transmitters and competent staff to broadcast news bulletins in more than a few languages, and more importantly, the matter of whether propaganda was 'a good thing' was being discussed both within and outside the BBC.[2]

Prior to the outbreak of the war, due to the uncertainty of the situation, neither the BBC nor the government was clear about how their relationship would work. On 28 July 1939, a statement was made in the House of Commons that the government did not intend 'to take over the BBC in war time', but 'would treat broadcasting as we treat the Press and other methods of publicity, the Press and the films, and … leave the BBC to carry on … with a very close liaison between the Ministry of Information and the Broadcasting Corporation, with definite regulations as to how the work should be carried on.'[3]

In the meantime, a Memorandum of the Ministry of Information (MOI) indicated that it intended to have a 'Director of Radio' in the ministry, implying that the government *did* intend to take over the BBC. This confusion was later clarified but the post of Director of Radio Relations was nonetheless created to oversee the tempo and content of radio broadcasting.[4]

On 1 September 1939, when Germany attacked Poland, the question of why there was only one home radio programme, first posed as early as spring 1938, remained unresolved.[5] The British government was reluctant to communicate news through radio waves. Harold Macmillan, the first Minister of Information,[6] expected the BBC to broadcast only the authoritative information given by the ministry, 'implying that the BBC was "independent" only as to … the lighter parts of its programmes'.[7] The MOI was particularly concerned that the BBC should not be allowed to harm the interest of the press by making early announcements ahead of them. Despite assurance from the BBC that its desire to provide constant news coverage throughout the day was based on the national interest rather than to compete with the press, their reassurance to Macmillan and the press was brushed aside. Thanks to these government reservations, during this period BBC news releases were delayed, and broadcasting was held up on several occasions. This improved in October 1939, but it was not until December that the pattern of wartime broadcasting in Britain took shape.[8]

As to the BBC's overseas services to France, from September 1939 there was an expressed demand from French listeners to provide them with the time and wavelengths of BBC broadcasts to France, because the French station, RN, had failed to broadcast proper news. Indeed, in November 1939, the British consul in Nantes stated that the BBC broadcast at 21h00 had become more popular among the French as the BBC news bulletins were found to be more interesting and more thorough than those of RN. The good reputation of the BBC French Service soon began to spread.[9] At the same time, the BBC Empire Service became the BBC Overseas Service.[10]

Noel Newsome, former employee at the *Daily Telegraph*, joined the BBC in September 1939 as an assistant at the Overseas News Desk. In December, he became the European News Editor, responsible for the Central News Desk. In December 1941, he was appointed director of European broadcasts.[11] France and Germany were the two 'giants' at the BBC foreign-language section at this time. Each foreign-language section had its own editor and its own staff. The French team was headed by Darsie Gillie, former correspondent at the *Morning Post* in Paris, who was genuinely keen to look at France in an unbiased way.

All foreign-language sections were dependent on the supply of news coming from the Central News Desk,[12] the role of which was to gather and prepare stories in English for the regional news editors. Within the limits prescribed by the directives, each foreign-language section was free to produce its own programmes in the way it wanted. Once the news had been received by the regional news editors, they would make news bulletins, which had to be approved by the Central News Desk prior to broadcast, and were subject to censorship. This approach was set up to ensure consistency and to avoid having identical regional news bulletins or conflicting stories. This practice was not entirely foolproof, though, as it did not prevent the broadcasting of news that would later be proven inaccurate, although it is remarkable that there were few complaints relating to the inaccuracy of the BBC European News.[13]

The invasion of Norway on 9 April 1940 marked a turning point for the BBC. The MOI did not engage much during the Norwegian campaign, and rumour started spreading due to the lack of official information from both the MOI and the Admiralty. When the Supreme War Council decided to withdraw from Norway on 27 April, the information was not communicated to the BBC, nor was the BBC invited to the special briefing attended by the editors of national newspapers a few days later. After the event, the BBC was left to face criticism that should have rightly been directed elsewhere. Newsome complained on 5 May that the government had tried, in the last stages of the campaign,[14] to use the European News Service to 'throw dust in the eyes of the enemy'[15] while totally disregarding the importance of telling the truth to the listeners:

> Owing to the fact that our treatment of the campaign was based on the assumption that it would be carried on, a false picture of the true situation was inevitably created and as inevitably has had a damaging effect on our reputation abroad for reliability … I cannot but resent most strongly … that we were used as a blind tool.[16]

In this instance, the BBC didn't have a chance to defend its position to tell the truth as it never had a full picture of the situation. The BBC might have seen itself as 'the entirely innocent victim of strategic needs',[17] but this was not the conclusion drawn by the government from the campaign in Norway. Some Cabinet members saw the BBC as 'an enemy within the gates'.[18] For this reason, the lack of leadership and planning on the behalf of the government led the BBC to become the scapegoat for the failure for news coverage of the campaign of Norway. Shortly after, the political landscape changed further when Germany invaded the Low Countries on 10 May 1940.[19] That same month, Winston Churchill replaced Neville Chamberlain as the wartime prime minister and a government of national unity was created.[20]

The Blitzkrieg in the Low Countries and France brought another blow to the reputation of the BBC. This was in part due to the fast movement of German troops, which meant the situation changed rapidly, but also to the censorship system that was in place within the BBC. As a result, Germany was often able to provide more up-to-date news in its propaganda regarding the progress of the war by simply telling the truth.[21] As the BBC intelligence report of 8 July 1940 stated: 'Lately, however, Hitler's predictions have come true while those of the Allies have not, and this has greatly damaged the prestige of British news.'[22]

The report also recommended that, following the events of Norway and France, the BBC would need more than 'straight news' if it wanted to win the propaganda war in Europe.[23] Colonel Buckmaster, future leader of the French section of the Special Operations Executive (SOE), wrote: 'We needed to establish full confidence in the BBC so that when the time comes, the French patriots would accept without question or murmur any directive which would be launched on its wavelength.'[24] A consensus emerged that the best propaganda would be that which appeared the most sincere and truthful. A similar view was shared by Charles de Gaulle, leader of Free France.[25]

The BBC's reputation regarding veracity was again called into question during the Battle of Britain in the summer and autumn of 1940, since the British communiqués were not always truthful in reporting the number of planes that had been shot down on both sides. However, they were more accurate than the German communiqués. The BBC, at least, did not avoid conveying bad news by hiding the truth.[26] As Pierre Bourdan – an editor at Havas Agency in London in June 1940[27] who later became one of the most prominent speakers at the BBC – stated, 'the news tonight is bad, this is a bad period to pass, but all will end well, the German victory is impossible'.[28]

The first French listeners probably turned to the BBC partly because of their patriotic obstinacy, but more often out of curiosity. However, it very quickly became evident to these French listeners that the British would survive the Battle of Britain and that the war would go on.[29] As Jean Marin, former reporter at *Le Journal* in London,[30] said, 'during the first 6 or 8 months, it probably mattered little what we said at the microphone, the essential [thing] was that a voice is heard: it was enough to prove that England still existed'.[31]

Despite the issues and constraints, it was estimated by the Vichy radio monitor in early 1941 that the BBC had a daily audience of 300,000 listeners, a figure thought to be a low estimate. As the war progressed, the estimation at the end of 1942 showed that the daily audience had grown tenfold.[32] Throughout this period, the BBC took a huge risk by insisting on news integrity despite the repeated military failures and setbacks faced by the Allies up until the end of 1942. Both France and Britain believed that final victory could only be achieved if trust in their own veracity was maintained – and they were proven right in the end.[33]

Further organisational changes were made at the BBC from late 1941. Ivone Kirkpatrick was appointed as Controller of European Services in October 1941, which triggered a full separation of the BBC's foreign services into two distinct groups: European and Overseas.[34] In March 1942, Bruce Lockhart was appointed the new Director-General of the Political Warfare Executive (PWE). He subsequently moved to Bush House and set up his office on the floor above that of Kirkpatrick, Newsome and the BBC's European Services. Kirkpatrick joined Lockhart's Executive Committee in March 1942[35] and, in his own words, 'had successfully changed the whole situation'[36] in June 1942 at the BBC by strengthening internal communication, improving liaison procedures with formal and informal talks, and managing to remove 'the whole cumbrous and highly paid Programme staff appointed by Salt',[37] the then Director of European Services.[38]

Kirkpatrick was the middleman between Lockhart and Newsome. He continued working on propaganda but cared very little about the PWE. Led by Newsome, the Director of European Broadcasts, there was now a substantial degree of independence in the BBC's selection and presentation of news. This was not always well perceived: some of the news items broadcast by the BBC led to protests by the PWE or the Foreign Office after the event, with orders for future prohibition, although these were not very effective. The directives were prepared solely by Newsome in daily news conferences attended by a wide range of staff, and this resulted in a sense of immediacy and speedy broadcast of daily news operation. It was a matter of pride for all BBC personnel to put the news on the air in the shortest possible time once it had been collected from the Central News Desk.[39]

'Weapon of action'

From 1941, the BBC acted as a 'weapon of action' in terms of giving on air the full names and addresses of collaborators and denunciators. The BBC did this because it knew that it was in accord with most of the public opinion in France, as expressed in anonymous listeners' letters.[40] With the changes implemented by the new management of the BBC, it became even more active, especially when Pierre Laval, prime minister of France, declared on Radio Paris on 22 June 1942 that he wished for a German victory. Maurice Schumann's response on the BBC was unambiguous: 'Even before he uttered this sentence, Laval expelled himself from France. Even before he uttered this sentence, Laval sentenced himself to death.'[41]

Other events were orchestrated by the BBC, for example the demonstrations of 1 May and 14 July 1942.[42] The latter was prompted by an incident that took place on the French national holiday, 14 July 1942, when several people were shot dead by machine guns and another six or so were injured, including a 15-year-old boy whose thigh was pierced by a bullet. The BBC launched another appeal on 16 July 1942, calling for the people of Marseille to attend the funeral of the two women who had been shot dead, Mrs. Simon and Mrs. Krebs. The BBC announced that the funeral would be held on Friday at 14h00 and called the population to attend the funeral with 'silence and dignity!'[43] As the prefect of Marseille stated in his report of 22 July 1942, the BBC had become both a very formidable and highly responsive tool: 'The calls by the English radio heighten; they broadcast more and more specific watchwords executable within hours and, in these circumstances, affect the opinion for sure'.[44]

The BBC also referred to German atrocities in its radio broadcasts on numerous occasions, reporting the execution of French hostages and the persecution of Jews.[45] It did not hesitate to report such incidents as these served as a reminder to the French of the cruelty of the occupiers. By contrast, among the surviving broadcasts by RN, very few were of such a nature.[46] In a broadcast following the execution of 50 Frenchmen as the result of the murder of two German officers, Maréchal Pétain, head of the Vichy government, expressed his frustration at the situation, and stressed that no fighting against the occupiers was allowed following the Armistice. He then stated that foreign powers were responsible for radicalising the French and encouraging them to kill the German officers and called for the population to denounce the criminals.[47] French lives would be at risk if they followed the advice of foreign powers, including that transmitted via the wireless.

As for Radio Paris, the emphasis of their broadcast regarding the execution of the French was on the German authorities' 'unwillingness' to subject the peaceful French population to further summary executions for crimes they had not committed or approved of; their justification for carrying out these executions – which were deemed lawful according to the Hague Convention outlining the Laws and Customs of War on Land – and their condemnation of the Jews speaking on the French and American radio stations for encouraging such reckless actions.[48] The purpose was to appease the French while giving a stern warning of the consequences of following the instructions of foreign powers.

Despite these warnings, the actions and advice of the BBC against the occupiers would increase exponentially until Operation *Torch* in November 1942 and the Allied landing in North Africa. In response to that, the Germans executed Operation *Anton*, resulting in the German invasion and occupation of the unoccupied zone in France.[49] Now, for the first time since the Armistice, the whole of France was reunited. As Schumann declared on the BBC the same day: 'by breaking the monstrous border which he had built in the vain hope of dividing, against itself, the indivisible France, the enemy accomplishes a lunatic but symbolic gesture; he decrees, against himself, total union for total war'.[50]

Propaganda to France after June 1940

The BBC had made no plans for propaganda in advance of the war because no one had expected the rapid defeat of France and hence the need to engage in subsequent events. As a result, the propagandists had to wait until the Armistice on 22 June 1940 to prepare themselves for further actions.[51] As Goebbels stated the day after the Armistice, 'future historians will have to take especially into account the 4th weapon, the weapon of propaganda'.[52]

Following the Armistice, the propagandists at the BBC had a difficult task when targeting France as they had to differentiate their approach towards the occupied and unoccupied zones. For the occupied zone, they could attack the authorities without any restraint but in the case of the unoccupied zone, they had to deal with the fact that Pétain – a hero of Verdun in 1916 – was widely perceived as a father figure by the French. Apparently, he wanted to save France again. Discrediting Pétain could therefore backfire.[53]

Following the fall of France, it became apparent that a France controlled by Germany could become a threat to Britain and had to be neutralised as soon as possible.[54] The BBC's intelligence report of 8 July 1940 stated:

> The weight of anti-British propaganda in France will henceforth be enormous. The long-term effectiveness of volume in propaganda has been repeatedly emphasised in these reports … and it will require a skilful and determined use of all British propaganda resources to create an effective fifth column on our side in France.[55]

The propagandists understood that any attempt to eliminate this threat without the French population's consent for British actions in France was doomed to fail. Britain's military actions in France would inevitably cause material destruction and death among civilians. Propaganda would need to explain and justify the actions of the British and provide accurate news on the progress of the war and the British war effort. The French had to be reassured that Britain would not surrender and that victory would finally be attained. Helping the Allies would be beneficial to the French as well, as independent France would be restored. Finally, British propaganda had to promote de Gaulle and the Free French as an independent body representing the 'true' France against Hitler and Vichy. British propaganda would have to appeal to French goodwill and understanding in order to achieve this objective.[56]

From the very first day, the British leaders had the idea of creating a fifth column in France[57] to oppose the Germans when the time was right, because France was viewed as 'the most important British propaganda target in Europe'.[58] The urgent need for propaganda directed towards the French was again highlighted in a BBC report dated 5 August 1940, which stated that if British policy as conveyed by the BBC did not effectively present to Europe a more attractive and convincing picture than Hitler's New Order, the British propaganda front would turn into another 'Sedan gap'.[59] This was the battle in May 1940 that sealed the fate of France in a matter of days as the German Blitzkrieg smashed French defences with impunity. This disaster for the French army led to the Armistice shortly after. The message was clear – if the British propaganda didn't change, France's defeatist fate could be sealed the same way and the BBC would lose some credibility to the German propaganda machine.

During the summer and autumn of 1940, the reorganisation of the BBC's service to France was part of the larger reorganisation of its Overseas Service, which was still incomplete at the time. In this period of German advance in Europe, Newsome had inspired his team with his strong, forward-looking views and feelings, and adopted an aggressive approach rather than a defensive one in broadcasting.[60] The need for such propaganda was highlighted again in a BBC report dated 30 September 1940, which pinpointed the French sense of betrayal:

> Great Britain is still accused of indifference to French sufferings, of 'stabbing France in the back' at Oran; she is taken to task for her unpreparedness, for her past leniency towards Germany, for having 'wished that Frenchmen should be killed in her defence'.[61]

The role of the BBC was now to counter this sentiment by presenting a more positive image of Britain[62] in their daily broadcast to France.

Challenges

During the first months of the war, the BBC's development of its foreign broadcasting was slow, largely because of a shortage of transmitters.[63] Given the scarcity of men and materials, building transmitters proved to be an essential but difficult task, especially since there was 'a war of transmitters' with Germany. In September 1939, Germany had a total of eight transmitters of 100 kilowatts, whereas Britain operated a total of 24 transmitters, of which five were of 100 kilowatts or more and 13 were short-wave transmitters. As additional transmitters were built, there was a steady increase in broadcasting time to France, from 17.5 hours weekly in September 1940 to 28 hours by September 1941, and 35.5 hours by September 1942.[64]

The synchronisation of the transmitters was another issue faced by the BBC. There were concerns regarding the sole long-wave transmitter from Droitwich, which was suspended between September 1939 and November 1941 for fear of it being used by the Luftwaffe as a homing beacon, although its operations finally resumed[65] when 'three additional transmitters were built'.[66]

During the bombing of Britain, some of the programmes broadcast on the BBC's medium waves were 'off the air most evenings for part of the time',[67] and two simultaneous programmes of the European Services were reduced to one.[68] However, with the subsequent increase of power and the number of transmitters being built, 'the BBC could be heard across France'.[69] By 1945, the BBC operated 121 transmitters, while the Germans had only 50.[70]

The jamming of the BBC's foreign-language programmes represented a serious threat to the BBC broadcasts to France. Both the Germans and Vichy authorities used jamming to prevent listening. Jamming stations were set up in both the occupied and unoccupied zones, using either high-powered jamming transmitters or control centres with a network of small jamming stations.[71] To solve this problem, the BBC resorted to broadcasting 'each programme on half a dozen wavelengths simultaneously'.[72] The listener's job was to choose the wavelength that was least affected by jamming.[73] As an enthusiastic listener of the BBC stated, '*Quand les Allemands nous brouillent, les Français se débrouillent*' (When the German jam us, the French manage), and this was proven accurate in the end.[74]

Another challenge was the decline in working radio sets in private possession in France. In 1940, approximately 6.5 million radio sets were owned by the population including unlicensed ones.[75] Buying radio sets certainly cost money. According to a British resident in Nice, the price of radio sets of different quality available on the market in June 1940 were as follows:

> the cheapest set capable of being tuned in to England on the short waves costs Frs. 1400 [£8]. To be moderately sure of results one must run to Frs. 2000 or over. The price of a first class set is round about Frs. 3000. But there are many models capable of picking up practically any continental station in the middle waves at well under four figures in France.[76]

Many radio sets were taken from private households. The Advisory Board for Damages and Repairs estimated in 1947 that during the period 1940–45, the Germans requisitioned a minimum of 200,000 radio sets belonging to individuals. Some 100,000 sets were taken for the use of German civilians or soldiers; about 50,000 were confiscated from Israelites, and about 50,000 were taken by the Germans while retreating.[77]

Amongst those who had a radio set, a failure or breakdown was not unexpected. Official radio repairers had a licence, and they were the only ones to have access to spare parts, thus avoiding the black market, unlike the rest of the population. Nonetheless, finding spares for and repairing existing radio sets proved difficult. As short-wave radio sets became increasingly popular, many wanted to convert their existing sets into this type. However, the component needed for such a conversion became in short supply. New sets could be expensive and second-hand ones became rarer in the market, as spare parts were both lacking and in general of poor quality.

The German and Vichy authorities also showed an interest in the control and supply of radio sets and spare parts according to a plan that was first announced on Radio Paris and later implemented in the summer of 1941. In the occupied zone, there was evidence that a ban existed on the sale of sets and spare parts, and a ban on the manufacture of new sets by October 1942.

As the war progressed, keeping the radio in working order became a constant problem for listeners. This restricted the ability of the French to have direct access to the BBC. It was estimated that an average of seven to 11 people would have had to gather around a single radio set to directly listen to BBC's live broadcasts. Nevertheless, a large proportion of the French population had regular access to second-hand information from the BBC as they learned about broadcasts from family, colleagues, neighbours and friends.[78]

Development of broadcasting

Darsie Gillie, the BBC French Regional Editor, was 'instrumental in shaping the French service, selecting its broadcasters, promoting its independence and helping it become capable of challenging German propaganda'.[79] Most broadcasters were

French and used pseudonyms to avoid reprisal against family members in France, whereas the administrative staff were mainly British.[80]

The BBC aired several programmes that became popular during the war years. *Ici la France* was created on 19 June 1940 on the orders of Churchill to serve as a programme that would speak the truth. It was first broadcast at 20h30 for 15 minutes, its duration increasing to 30 minutes from 30 June 1940. *Ici la France* was renamed to *Les Français parlent aux Français* on 6 September 1940.[81] The team of *Les Français parlent aux Français* largely comprised reporters, not professional broadcasters; however, they were inspired by pre-war French private radio stations and included serious comment, reports, songs and slogans in the programme.[82] Wit, pace and humour were used to win the hearts of their audience in France.[83]

Concurrently, Churchill decided to give voice to de Gaulle in the aftermath of Mers-el-Kébir by providing him with a five-minute slot in which to broadcast to France each day, which he could use as he saw fit. Mers-el-Kébir was a controversial incident on 3 July 1940 where the British navy opened fire and destroyed the French fleet anchored along the Algerian coast, killing almost 1,300 French sailors.[84] Even though those warships could have been used eventually to promote German military objectives, the aggressive British naval action caused consternation in France. De Gaulle's radio programme, *Honneur et Patrie,* was launched on 18 July 1940 with Schumann as spokesman and was aired for the duration of the war.[85] In 1941, this programme received five additional minutes at noon. This was not much considering that the total output of daily broadcast by BBC French Services reached two and half hours per day in September 1940 and five hours in September 1942.[86]

The evening structure of French broadcast was renewed on 18 July 1940 and remained practically the same until 1944. The evening broadcast now started at 20h15, with the *BBC French Service news* for 10 minutes, followed by *Honneur et Patrie* for five minutes, during which de Gaulle spoke 67 times and Schumann more than a thousand times. René Cassin,[87] professor at the Faculty of Law of Paris and legal adviser to Général de Gaulle, also spoke more than 100 times at the BBC before leaving for Algiers in 1943.[88] The programme was followed by *Les Français parlent aux Français*, which became the flagship show of the BBC French Service during the war.[89] This was created and led by Michel Saint-Denis, known by the pseudonym Jacques Duchesne, for four years.[90] He was joined by Pierre Maillaud, aka Pierre Bourdan, who spoke three to four times per week, commenting on political and military affairs from 1940 to July 1944.[91] *Les Français parlent aux Français* became so popular that in 1942 eight daily broadcasts were made available to the listeners using eight short wavelengths, a medium wave and a long wave as powerful as that of Radio Paris.[92] *Les Trois Amis,* hosted by Bourdan, Jean Marin and Jean Oberlé, was also a very popular talk show in France because listeners could hear several views on a specific topic.[93]

Les Trois Amis and *La Petite Académie* were both satirical programmes that were firm favourites among the French youth. Long after the *Petite Académie* ceased to exist, young listeners were still asking for its return on the air. These programmes were viewed as stimulating, constructive and entertaining. A young girl from the unoccupied zone wrote to the BBC stating that the *Trois Amis* programme 'cleverly combine[s] the useful with the pleasant',[94] so much so that she formed her own Three Friends group to comment on the news of the day as best they could (letter dated 9 June 1941).[95]

Jean Marin, aka Yves Morvan, was a reporter for the newspaper *Le Journal*. He was in the corridor next to de Gaulle's studio when de Gaulle recorded his message on 18 June 1940. The following day, he volunteered to work for the BBC French section and became, on the same evening, the first editor at the microphone. He worked there until June 1943. Jean Oberlé, who decided to join the Free French, wrote editorials and sketches but also the slogan '*Radio-Paris ment, Radio-Paris ment, Radio-Paris est allemand*' ('Radio Paris lies, Radio Paris lies, Radio Paris is German'), which was broadcast on 6 September 1940.[96] The BBC monthly report of 8 April 1941 reported a statement from an Englishman who had left France in February that this slogan had 'practically knocked out Radio Paris for a year'.[97] Finally, Georges Boris rejoined de Gaulle on 19 June 1940[98] and was one of the main speakers to talk about the food situation in France.

From 1941, a weekly programme called *Courrier de France* started with Brunius, aka Jacques Cottance, a poet and cineaste, as its speaker.[99] His programme consisted of reading letters from listeners sent from France 'to build up a sense of contact with the audience'.[100] Letters from listeners were used in the broadcasts to encourage others to continue listening to the BBC in case their letter was acknowledged on air. More importantly, it showed that the listeners' voices were being heard and that the BBC valued their opinion.[101]

The BBC French Service had two principal English speakers during the war. One was William Pickles, a professor at the London School of Economics and specialist in French affairs, who was associated with Henri Hauck[102] – a socialist union member and director of Labour of Fighting France – who hosted the daily broadcasts at 06h15 for three years.[103] The other was Ernest Bevin, the Minister of Labour.[104] Popular programmes were repeated throughout the day. Shortly after noon, there was a rebroadcast of *Honneur et Patrie* from the previous evening, including extracts from *Les Français parlent aux Français*, which was repeated at 16h15, 18h15 and 00h30.[105] The increase in the number of broadcasting hours gave the French more opportunities to pick up BBC programmes. Listening at night at home was probably most favoured by the French as there was a reduced risk of them being caught.

As we shall see, the BBC's programmes did not target French youth in a similar way as RN and Radio Paris. However, by the beginning of 1942, the BBC felt the need to monitor the response of French youth to its programmes. A report was subsequently compiled using feedback from young French listeners. It seemed that satirical songs and slogans were particularly popular amongst the French youth under the age of 25. The teenagers at high schools were particularly interested in songs and several of them requested that a printed copy of the lyrics be dropped over France by air, according to a Frenchwoman who arrived in England from Cannes in August 1941. 'C'est le père Musso' was a particular favourite, as was 'La Flotte Tarantine' (a song celebrating the British victory in Taranto, Italy, in November 1940).

In the occupied zone, French children were delighted to 'sing under the very noses of the Germans the songs which we hear on the radio', according to a letter sent to the BBC dated 9 February 1941. A young man from Brittany who arrived in England in early 1941 also stated that since the BBC programmes had started to use songs and slogans, the programmes had been favourably commented upon and repeated by Breton children.[106]

True stories were also popular. 'Young listeners are often inspired to write to the BBC by broadcasts in which youthful recruits to the Free French Forces have described their adventures.'[107] For example, on 15 September 1941, Major Billotte was invited to tell the story of how he and 185 other French soldiers escaped a German POW camp in Pomerania and subsequently travelled to Russia before arriving in England.[108]

According to the BBC's report, the only types of broadcasts that elicited a strong response from the French youth audience were programmes that were either entertaining or featured exciting broadcasters. In the spring of 1941, the programme *Le quart d'heure français du soir* was temporarily put together into a 'Radio News-Reel', a programme comprising 'news flashes, songs, slogans and resistance stories'.[109] People listened to it at 19h30. This programme evoked an enthusiastic response from a young listener in Remiremont, Lorraine, who stated that listening to this kind of programme made the young people and others want to resist (letter dated March 1940).[110]

Sources of information

It soon became clear that in order to influence the situation in France and keep a finger on the pulse of public opinion, the British needed to obtain a constant flow of information. The BBC's European Intelligence Department, which was set up by Sir John Lawrence, was tasked with analysing and assessing all forms of evidence regarding the listening conditions and the various reactions of listeners in Europe, with Emile Delavenay as its Assistant Director of European Intelligence throughout the war. Intelligence was gathered mainly from four different sources: French newspapers obtained via the British embassy in Lisbon, extensive listening to radio broadcasts by Radio Paris and RN in Caversham and Evesham, correspondence arriving at the BBC, and interviews with people arriving from France. The information was then compiled into the BBC Monthly Intelligence Report and communicated to the BBC's news and programme staff.[111]

Correspondence from listeners was an important source of information for the BBC, as it originated from various parts of France and came from different segments of the French population. Letters were written by teenagers, women, veterans, well-educated professionals and other groups.[112] That being said, most correspondence from the occupied zone came from the *départements* along the demarcation line or from Paris and its surrounding areas. Once in the unoccupied zone, the letters could finally be sent out through the French postal system.[113] However, Vichy had imposed postal censorship, which opened between 320,000 and 370,000 letters a week to monitor people's opinion in France.[114] On average, around 80 to 120 letters reached the BBC each month until November 1942. The number fell considerably thereafter and never recovered. Despite the postal censorship imposed by Vichy, not all letters were opened. After all, it was the censors' decision as to what to do with the letter, if intercepted. Letters were also smuggled out of the country,[115] given to acquaintances, or passed on to British embassies in neutral countries.[116] Nevertheless, the majority of the letters came from the unoccupied zone.[117]

The views expressed in the letters may have been both genuine and shared by a large number of people who were unwilling or unable to write their views or, if they did, perhaps their letters never reached the BBC. Those who wrote the letters must have belonged to the most vocal group, knowing that their letters might incriminate them. It would also seem unlikely that those who took the risk of writing these letters would falsify their content voluntarily; however, it is possible that, at times, some writers exaggerated the information given without having any intention of deceiving the reader.[118]

The BBC's approach to airing feedback from listeners also had its limitations. The conclusion drawn from their correspondence always had to struggle with a time lag as it could take months for a letter to arrive. This posed a dilemma for the BBC as it had to decide whether the issues and opinions expressed in the letters remained newsworthy by the time the letters arrived or whether they were outdated. Regardless, from these letters and other sources of information, the BBC gathered intelligence about local events that may not have been reported by the press or other media – for example, the spontaneous housewives' demonstration described later – and in this was stayed somewhat relevant to the concerns of the French.

The majority of the letters came from friendly listeners, although there were examples of unfriendly ones.[119] In one anonymous letter, for instance, the writer questioned the BBC speakers about the risks they incurred in their studio compared to the risks facing all those in a place where the population suffered enormously. The writer concluded that the jingles and songs were not enough to make the French feel better.[120] The discontent displayed in the letter does not necessarily indicate that the writer was against the Allies; rather it was an expression of deep frustration about the situation in which people had to live in France.

Another piece of evidence is provided by interviews with people arriving from Europe who were vetted at the Royal Victoria Patriotic School (RVPS) by the British intelligence services. A wide range of people were interviewed, among them politicians, journalists, experts in problems of broadcasting, military personnel of all ranks, scholars, writers, diplomats, bankers and businessmen, British or Franco-British repatriates, Breton and Norman fishermen, Irish priests and English female students, French people returning to London after their release from an *Oflag* (a POW camp for officers), some Special Operations Executive (SOE) agents and Intelligence Service agents.[121] After the interview, information regarding the situation in Europe was passed on to different bodies, including the BBC, for their broadcast.[122] Names were also communicated to Delavenay and his staff, who would then make contact and ask sources whether they would be interested in being interviewed again by the BBC's Intelligence Department. At least 511 interviews were conducted by the BBC's Intelligence Department between 1940 and 1944, with each interviewee invited to complete a questionnaire.

These interviews offered a more balanced view than the other sources of public opinion in France.[123] The report compiled by Delavenay in June and July 1940 showed the British government that the French were listening to the BBC, despite the jamming, and that there existed an independent French opinion that could be studied. This convinced the British government to invest in more transmitters.[124] Delavenay also believed that his department had helped to give the British government a more realistic and balanced view of the changes in French public opinion since the Armistice, including how the Vichy regime was perceived and the attitudes towards the British.[125]

Radiodiffusion Nationale (RN)

Historical context

The modernisation of the radio network in France was initiated by Georges Mandel, the Minister for Post, between 1934 and 1936 and was then continued from 1938 onwards.[126] With increasing international tensions following the Munich crisis, the government of Édouard Daladier was compelled to reconsider its views on the power of the radio: RN, which became commonly known as Radio Vichy, was to be reorganised and developed within a larger structure that would include both news and propaganda.[127]

During the 1930s, there were about 5 million radio licence holders in France, a quarter of whom were registered in Paris and its immediate suburbs. The listeners were mainly located in Paris, the north, Normandy and important towns in other

French regions. In rural areas, radios were virtually unknown.[128] The approximate number of wireless sets was 6.5 million if undeclared ones were included.[129]

During the inter-war period, French listeners had the choice between two networks: the public network and the private network. The former operated with state funding and tax on radio sets, and the latter financed their programmes solely with commercial income.[130] The predecessor of RN was the public network, the French equivalent of the BBC, and hosted a varied albeit elitist schedule, including plays, classical concerts and serious but – according to listeners' accounts – boring talks. The private network was, on the other hand, more spontaneous and imaginative in the presentation of their programmes. Their reports and interviews were mixed with light music and commercials, as well as improvisation when reading from scripts. This was in stark contrast to the public network where improvisation was not permitted and the speakers were expected to merely read out what was written on the pre-approved scripts.[131]

The public network had at its disposal 14 stations. Three of these were in Paris: Radio Paris, Paris PTT and Paris-Tour Eiffel. The long-wave transmitter was located in Allouis[132] and attributed to Radio Paris, making it the only station that could broadcast to the whole of France. The 11 remaining radio stations were situated in the main provincial towns and broadcast regional news and programmes, in addition to political commentaries from the public network. The private network had 12 radio stations, four of which were in Paris: Le Poste Parisien, Radio 37, Radio-Cité and le Poste de l'Île-de-France, with the remainder in major French provinces.[133]

Centre permanent de l'information générale and Radio-Journal de France

In February 1939, a Centre permanent de l'information générale was created under the direct authority of the *président du Conseil*, Édouard Daladier. Emile Lohner, former editor of the socialist weekly *Vendredi*, became the director of the centre, whose purpose was to control the distribution of all official news, including '*Radio-Journal de France*, the various columns and press reviews, the radio broadcastings in foreign languages and the listening centre of the Fort de Bicêtre'.[134]

On 29 July 1939, five weeks before the outbreak of war, RN was created by grouping all the services of the public network under its sole authority. It was given a status under a statutory order, which acted as 'armour' during and beyond the war (this framework governing French radio and television network remained in place for another 30 years after the war).[135] The radio stations in the public network were linked with a common mode of funding, provision of infrastructure and common programming, but they were largely self-managed and autonomous. When Daladier created this unified administration of RN, he also changed its reporting structure: rather than the Ministry of Postes, Télégraphes et Téléphones (PTT), it would now report directly to the *présidence du Conseil*. Léon Brillouin, physicist and professor

ETAT DES RESEAUX METROPOLITAINS AU DEBUT DE 1940

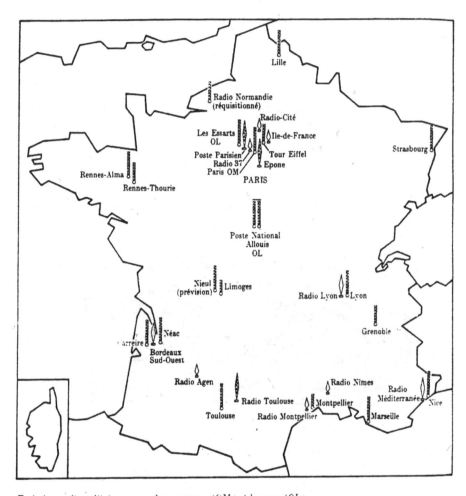

Extrait de : Hélène ECK (sous la direction de)
- La guerre des ondes - Armand Colin, Paris, 1985, p.40

State of metropolitan networks at the beginning of 1940. From CSA, *Cahiers d'Histoire de la Radiodiffusion*, No. 27 (December 1990), 32.

RÉSEAU D'ÉMETTEURS

A. - ZONE NON OCCUPEE — 1) Ondes moyennes

RESEAU D'ETAT	PUISSANCE KW	ONDE mètres	FREQUENCE Kc/s
GRENOBLE NATIONAL	20	514,60	583
LYON NATIONAL	100	463	648
MARSEILLE NATIONAL	100	400,50	749
TOULOUSE NATIONAL	120	386,60	776
LIMOGES NATIONAL	2 (1)	335,20	895
NICE NATIONAL	60	253,20	1.185
MONTPELLIER NATIONAL	2	224	1.339
Après 18 h. 45 jusqu'à minuit EMISSION NATIONALE à grande puissance (1) 100 kw. à partir de mars 1942.		386,60	776

RESEAU PRIVE (Fédération Française de Radiodiffusion)	PUISSANCE KW	ONDE mètres	FREQUENCE Kc/s
RADIO TOULOUSE	60	328,60	913
RADIO MONTPELLIER	20	269,10	1.158
RADIO AGEN	1	235,10	1.276
RADIO MEDITERRANEE	25	227,10	1.321
RADIO LYON	25	215,30	1.393
RADIO NIMES	1	202	1.483

B. - ZONE OCCUPEE

POSTES	PUISSANCE KW	POSTES	PUISSANCE KW
POSTE PARISIEN	60	RADIO NORMANDIE	60
EPONES (près Paris)	100	BORDEAUX NATIONAL	40
LILLE	60	BORDEAUX NATIONAL (Nme) (Mise prochaine en service)	120
RENNES NATIONAL	120	RADIO CITE	20
RENNES ALMA	40	RADIO NATIONAL (ondes longues)	450

A. - ZONE NON OCCUPEE — 2) Ondes courtes — B. - ZONE OCCUPEE

EN SERVICE

TOULOUSE .... 2 émetteurs de 1 KW

EN SERVICE

ALLOUIS .... 1 émetteur de 100 KW

EN CONSTRUCTION

TOULOUSE .... 1 émetteur de 30 KW
.... 2 émetteurs de 25 KW
MARSEILLE .... 2 émetteurs de 25 KW
ISSOUDUN .... 12 émetteurs de 100 KW

EN CONSTRUCTION

ALLOUIS .... 3 émetteurs de 100 KW

(Les Documents Français, janvier 1942)

Transmitters network. From CSA, *Cahiers d'Histoire de la Radiodiffusion*, No. 34 (September–November 1992), 79.

at the Collège de France, became the general manager of RN, responsible for administrative and technical matters. The political and news programmes relied on the Lohner Centre. All the literary, artistic and music programmes were managed by Georges Duhamel, novelist and member of the Académie française, who did not accept any undue interference from his boss.[136]

Meanwhile, under a separate statutory order, Daladier created a new post, a Commissariat général à l'Information 'to organise, lead and coordinate all news departments and French propaganda'.[137] Jean Giraudoux, a famous writer, was appointed to this post. The head office of RN would not be subordinated to the Commissariat général as stipulated in the statutory order of 1 September 1939. Rather, both organisations would work in parallel. The sole responsibility of the Commissariat général for the radio was to oversee the broadcasts aimed at overseas listeners, including news and information that the Lohner Centre produced. Giraudoux would also chair a daily coordination meeting with Emile Lohner, Martinaud-Déplat, the director of censorship, and Colonel Thomas as the representative of the General Secretariat of National Defence. Under this new structure, RN now had four directors for the various aspects of its service: Brillouin, Lohner, Duhamel and Giraudoux. Daladier was later reproached for creating such a complicated organisation, leading to the conclusion that 'the overlapping of responsibilities and the conflict of powers hamper the effective implementation of the war radio'.[138]

As a democratic state, France had two major concerns about propaganda. First, it had been reluctant to subject its citizens to attempts to control their minds as Hitler had done in Germany.[139] Second, the new propaganda structures were inherited directly from those of 1918,[140] a period prior to the arrival of radio as a medium of wireless communication for the general public. Although radio broadcasting had already existed for a few years by then, no one yet knew how to use it efficiently. As a result, RN was not prepared for war. Nevertheless, as it turned out during World War II, radio would become a privileged medium of communication and for psychological manipulation, particularly for the population in occupied countries such as France.[141]

In 1939, *Radio-Journal de France* became the sole programme transmitting news and political commentaries on the radio. The news broadcasts were hosted by men who mainly came from private stations, such as Jean Guignebert, the director of Radio-Cité; Maurice Bourdet, one of the chief editors of Poste Parisien along with its administrator Roger Sallard; Jean Antoine, the head of the reporting service of Radio 37; Jean Masson, reporter at Radio Luxembourg and Louis Gautier-Chaumet, reporter at Radio-Cité; Pierre Crénesse and Alex Surchamp, the former being one of the pioneers of radio reportage at Paris PTT and the latter a correspondent for the army. The written press also provided collaborators, for example, Jean Piot, editor in chief of *l'Oeuvre*. *Radio-Journal* also produced edited programmes with themes devoted to the empire, the provinces and magazines that were usually broadcast during off-peak time at 14h30 and 22h00. There was also a series of six talks themed as follows: '*Le sens de l'humain*', '*France d'hier et d'aujourd'hui*', '*Contes populaires et littérature*', '*Comment l'Angleterre est gouvernée*', '*France-Angleterre*' and '*Connaissance de l'ennemi*'.[142] (Translations, respectively: 'The sense of humanity', 'France of yesterday and today', 'Folk tales and literature', 'How England is governed', 'France-England' and 'Knowledge of the enemy').

The status of the private stations changed after the war had begun. From September 1939, their independence and influence was reduced for four fundamental reasons: many of their popular radio presenters were mobilised; their advertising revenues decreased considerably; their own news broadcasts were replaced by the *Radio-Journal de France* and by the columns and reports provided by the Lohner Centre; the specialised weekly radio magazines that mainly featured the more diversified programmes of the private stations ceased to be published from the summer of 1939 and were replaced by a brief mention of their programmes in the daily papers.[143]

RN was not immune to some of the problems experienced by the private stations. On 24 August 1939, mobilisation day, the French army refused to exclude radio specialists from conscription, resulting in 387 out of 694 staff members being mobilised.[144] Moreover, the staff of Germanic origin who were working for Pascal Copeau, head of foreign broadcasting, were imprisoned, resulting in tremendous efforts to have them released several weeks later.[145]

The elitist nature of RN programming alienated its listeners, including the soldiers in their quarters or on the Maginot Line, the extensive defensive fortifications along the German-French border. For example, in December 1939, Radio Paris and Paris PTT broadcast 75 concerts, including those by orchestras, soloists and operas, in a total of 52 variety show programmes. There was a retrospective of the French Comic Opera, which was broadcast on Saturdays at 19h45. There were also drama plays that belonged to the repertoire of classics performed by the troop of the Comédie-Française and the Cartel des Quatres, including Louis Jouvet, Gaston Baty, Charles Dullin and Georges Pitoëff.[146] In contrast, Radio Stuttgart, Germany's French-speaking radio, disseminated its propaganda in cleverly disguised form between pieces of lively music and could be received by the weakest radio receivers at the border due to the location of its transmitters.[147]

There were critiques of RN programmes. For example, the Minister de Monzie dubbed Giraudoux the 'Marivaux of the abstraction' because of the subtlety of his editorials.[148] The playwright Armand Salacrou told Daladier: 'We have lost the first battle, the one of the radio!'[149] In addition, there were broadcasting issues regarding airtime: RN remained silent from 09h00 to 12h00 and from 15h00 to 18h00,[150] which made listeners tune in to other radio stations, including Radio Stuttgart.

Resolving the inter-governmental conflicts and developing a clear and consistent propaganda strategy proved to be a difficult task, since the people in charge of the

Commissariat général à l'Information never truly understood the problems facing them.[151] The dissatisfaction with RN programming led to a long parliamentary debate in February 1940. However, the return to the '*gaudriole*', an informal and fun-style programme desired by the French troops, was ruled out as it did not suit the taste of the various leaders of the Information Services and French propaganda. The dithering stopped on 10 May 1940 when the German offensive began. The radio stations stopped broadcasting one after the other as the German troops advanced quickly across the land and captured them.[152] As no news was circulating in France, the public was unaware of the unfolding situation, resulting in a general panic; hence the welcoming of Pétain's messages by the population, because at least it meant that news was finally reaching them.[153]

The Armistice had a significant impact on radio broadcasting. It was at that time that all RN correspondents in London were ordered to return to France.[154] France was split into two main zones, one was occupied by Germany, the other controlled by the new collaborationist French government located in Vichy. The Germans were quick to put restrictions on wireless communication. Article 14 of the Armistice settlement focused on the immediate role of the radio stations: 'All wireless transmitters located in French territory must stop immediately their broadcasts. The resumption of wireless transmissions in the part of non-occupied territory will be subject to special regulations.'[155]

The Vichy regime

From 25 June, only Radio Stuttgart, Radio Sottens Suisse Romande and the BBC could be heard in France.[156] It was not until 5 July that the new RN resumed broadcasting after relocating to a studio at the Casino de Vichy.[157]

During the first weeks following the Armistice, RN mainly broadcast the *Radio-Journal* programmes from its studio in Vichy. Under the direction of the journalist Paul Édouard Decharme, the previous editors were replaced by a group of far-right men from the weekly *Je suis partout*, a collaborationist newspaper.[158]

In July 1940, the Vichy regime banned commercial programmes on the private network. This meant that private stations were now cut off from their financial resources. The Vichy state, which was interested in keeping the private stations' wavelengths and maintaining a certain continuity of the regional programmes, decided to offer a monthly sum to more or less cover the operating costs of the private stations from August 1940. Being deprived of their financial independence, the private stations had only limited programming freedom and were controlled tightly by the state. The private radios had to transmit news bulletins and any other programmes deemed important at the request of the government of Vichy. However, the government did not take advantage of this situation to group private and public stations into one national network.[159]

After the Armistice, RN was in a paradoxical situation. The principle of sovereignty of the state over the airwaves was consistently asserted by the PTT administration. However, now that the German authorities were in control of a large part of the infrastructure of French broadcasting, they were in a position to decide how the programmes should be organised, leaving very little room for the French State (Vichy) to make decisions.[160] No Vichy laws were to be applied in the occupied zone without German consent, whereas the Vichy government tried to maintain a sense of unity that no longer existed in France.[161]

To tackle this problem, the Vichy government decided to control the news disseminated by the press through the Havas agency, 'in the same way as the Radiodiffusion Nationale in the general system of the state services responsible to inform the public, under the leadership of the responsible authorities to the country'.[162] To carry out effective propaganda, media such as film production, press and radio transmissions needed to be controlled centrally.[163] This is precisely what Vichy wanted to achieve. Under the Vichy regime, the new role of the press would be to deal with the '"disciplined renewal of French thought", by taking as model Hitler's Germany, Franco's Spain and Mussolini's Italy'.[164] RN thus became the voice of the Vichy government. By December 1940, an order was given by the *secrétaire d'État à la présidence du Conseil* to all the prefects to take control of the private stations (Radio-Lyon, Radio Nîmes, Radio-Montpellier, Radio-Toulouse, Radio-Agen, Radio-Méditerranée) so that they would broadcast only the programmes of RN and cease any other unrelated activities.[165] Naturally, no fair assessment of RN's reorganisation is possible without considering the context of its limited sovereignty and its controlled environment, which was largely dependent on the whims of the German authorities.[166]

With this renewed recognition of the role of radio broadcasting as a propaganda tool, the reorganisation of radio broadcasting became all the more urgent for Vichy. A personal relationship between Pétain and the public had to be established; this personal relationship was in fact well depicted in the various broadcasts of RN. Vichy's motto, '*Travail, Famille, Patrie*', was created to encourage the French to adhere to the new moral order of the National Revolution and to reconstruct France, steering it away from the old Republican values.[167] Pétain's policy was 'ideologically retrogressive; anti-industrial, rural, pro-Church, family, and the values of the past'.[168] Pétain was aware of the important role radio played in society and from September 1940, RN broadcast nearly 80 hours of monthly news.[169]

Once in Vichy, the government quickly took possession of the transmitters located in the unoccupied zone, possibly because Goebbels was conscious that French propaganda would be better suited to influencing French public opinion than German propaganda. The demarcation line corresponded exactly with the split of the network of transmitters between the Germans and the Vichy government.[170]

Pierre Laval, the vice prime minister, and Jean-Louis Tixier-Vignancour, a conservative deputy,[171] were directly responsible for RN, and they were to use it to the benefit of Germany's New Order. At that point in time, French morale was low and the alleged elites were ready to give in to the occupier.[172] Under Laval's leadership, pro-Nazi journalists and politicians penetrated RN staff and came into conflict with those who wanted to preserve France's 'neutrality'. As a result, a struggle ensued over the control of RN until Laval's eviction on 13 December 1940, when many of the pro-Nazis left and joined Radio Paris.[173] As Antoine Lefébure, a French historian, pointed out, 'after a flying start towards collaboration under the influence of Laval, "the radio resumed, after 13 December, a tone always oriented [towards the Vichy cause] but more moderate."'[174]

The requisition of private stations also gradually eased. According to a letter dated 5 February 1941 to the *ministre secrétaire d'État aux Affaires étrangères* (Secrétariat général de l'Information), the Vichy government confirmed the lifting of the requisition over Radio-Méditerranée and the possibility of resuming their own broadcasting programme, under certain conditions. These included the following obligations: to follow the fixed schedule set up by the National Broadcasting Administration; to broadcast the news programmes of the *Radio-Journal de France* and not any other news unless otherwise agreed upon; to broadcast anything deemed important by RN; and to seek pre-approval of all the programmes they intend to broadcast at least eight days in advance.[175]

Challenges

The distribution of transmitters in France prior to the war did not correspond with the number of people in a region or the number of radio sets, largely due to the political and electoral agenda at the time. While the northern and eastern regions were more densely populated and had a larger number of radio sets, there only were two transmitters located in Lille and Strasbourg, and none in Normandy. The southern region, which had a smaller population and a very low density of radio sets, however, had a total of 13 transmitters, among them several powerful ones.[176] Following the Armistice, the transmitters of the state-run stations located in the unoccupied zone, including those in Lyon, Grenoble, Nice, Marseille, Montpellier, Toulouse and Limoges, were under Vichy's control. Vichy also had legal control of the transmitters of private stations such as 'Radio Toulouse, Radio Montpellier, Radio Agen, Radio Nîmes, Radio Méditerranée and Radio Lyon'.[177]

Following the move to Vichy, the new RN faced various technical challenges. There was a lack of sufficiently powerful relays to carry their transmissions in the north and in Brittany, resulting in poor reception of its broadcasts in these areas. Some regions of the unoccupied zone also remained badly covered due to the hilly terrains.[178] The network of short- or medium-wave stations, which were required to broadcast to the entirety of the empire, needed improvement. The quality of programmes was viewed as a matter of national prestige; however, any investment in producing an excellent programme would be pointless if the listeners were thwarted by the low quality of transmission and reception of the broadcasts.[179]

There were issues with the synchronisation of the transmitters. Prior to the war, the operations of both private and public stations were based on the autonomy of each radio station, which meant that each would almost exclusively broadcast its own programmes using the designated wavelength of their allocated transmitter. The state network was built piecemeal as each station was connected to the other stations in an episodic manner. Therefore, to achieve a true national network, it would be necessary to obtain a national wavelength linking all the stations, enabling each to broadcast the same programme at the same time. This national wavelength would also resolve a crucial military security weakness and prevent enemy pilots from using various wavelengths as a beacon to identify their locations. The national synchronisation of December 1941 was later explained by Raymond Braillard, director of the technical services of RN, in an article published in *Radio National* in January 1942.[180]

Making synchronisation harder was the fact that the weekly *Radio National* showed an inconsistent end-of-broadcasting time in the evening. For example, the programmes ended at 22h15 in the last week of May 1941,[181] at 23h15 in the second week of July 1941[182] and at 21h15 in the first week of October 1941.[183] Once the national synchronisation of the network had eventually been achieved, however, RN was able to extend the broadcasting time until midnight.[184] This schedule would remain in force until November 1942 and beyond.[185] It is also worth noting that synchronisation was a common problem encountered by the BBC and Radio Paris as well.

In addition to its technical challenges, RN also lacked popularity. The '*Exposé d'ensemble de la situation de la Radiodiffusion Nationale*' report released in early 1941 highlights the apparent causes for the disaffection of the public with RN. First, there was a lack of public interest in the artistic and musical programmes and variety shows, which were seen as mediocre. The public expected to hear well-known, gifted and beloved artists as opposed to mediocre ones or understudies, and considered the programmes put on air to be below their expectations.

Second, RN aired too many propaganda programmes on the themes of youth, agriculture and school, etc., and these were often broadcast at the most popular hours of the day. They were mediocre in their presentation and the public soon became irritated by hearing constant propaganda. The schedule of these programmes was disjointed, uncoordinated and lacked organisation in the overall programming. More importantly, RN failed to meet the expectation of listeners who wanted to hear timely news because they would only report news 24 hours after the morning papers so as not to compete with the press. This put RN at a disadvantage.[186] The BBC had a similar arrangement in terms of the press and its news before the war,

REPARTITION GEOPOLITIQUE
DES CHAINES ET/OU PROGRAMMES (au 19.10.41)
A DESTINATION DES AUDITEURS METROPOLITAINS

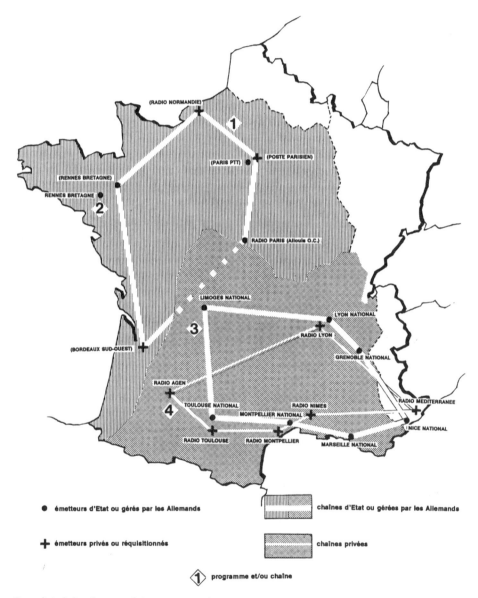

Geopolitical distribution of the stations and/or programmes (at 19.10.41) to metropolitan listeners. From CSA, *Cahiers d'Histoire de la Radiodiffusion*, No. 30 (September 1991), 41.

but the restrictions were removed after the outbreak of the war, making their news programmes much timelier and more attractive.[187] RN news was also presented in a monotonous way. So, listeners overall found it incorrect, outdated and uninteresting. This report concluded that RN would benefit from having its programmes monitored properly, making them more appealing and better presented in the overall schedule.[188]

The same report highlighted the underlying structural issues behind staffing. The legal status of the various staff members at RN was not clear. The regulations were written such that the executives did not know where they were going or what was the limit of their authority. Confusion reigned at the top of the hierarchy. There were also frequent changes of responsibilities in senior management. Political interventions happened often and prevented the improvement of RN's programmes. Moreover, staff lacked homogeneity because the employees came from very different backgrounds. RN was, in major part, composed of technicians from the PTT, but they were not trained in broadcasting, nor was there any interest in helping them develop knowledge or expertise in the technicalities of broadcasting.[189] All this created confusion, which hindered the operations of the various departments of RN.

Changes at Radiodiffusion Nationale *from 1941 onwards*

The first changes took place in May 1941, when the news programme was reorganised and divided to specialised services, such as the foreign service, domestic policy and general information, supplemented by a sports service and a media service. RN stimulated the 'good people's' simplicity, courage and good humour when it discussed regions and history. From June 1941, the number of hours for variety shows increased from 16 to 20 hours per week for information, communiqués and official broadcasts of all sorts. As RN was broadcasting a great deal of music, it was decided in the autumn of 1941 that the artistic programme office in Marseille would acquire a proper studio that was suitable for broadcasting lyrical and symphonic pieces.[190]

Unfortunately, the politics of the Vichy government were undermined by the success of Radio Paris, which was threatening to divide public opinion in the two zones. Radio Paris also attacked the Vichy leaders on several occasions. RN would need to have been heard by the whole of France to advocate, instil and persuade the French to believe in the ideology of the National Revolution. However, the Vichy government was aware that RN had very limited access to the occupied zone. Therefore, it was necessary for the province to renew links with Paris. Then, in September 1941, a major success was achieved by Vichy when it secured access to broadcasting from Paris twice a week to the unoccupied zone via the modulation centre of Lyon, enabling its listeners to hear once again about the shows in Paris and other sports events held in the occupied zone.[191]

With Laval's return to power in April 1942, the political environment in which RN was operating had shifted further from preaching for the ideology of National Revolution and New France to an overt acceptance of collaboration. To Laval, propaganda was less about seducing French public opinion, and more about avoiding antagonising or hampering the current negotiations that he was involved in with the occupier.[192] As Laval said to Paul Creyssel, the Director of Propaganda Services in the unoccupied zone: 'The president had made me understand that my role, in his eyes, was not so much to make his government popular but to allow it to remain effective.'[193] He made further substantial changes to RN by forming a new team and appointed André Demaison as the new director[194] in order to ensure his vision for RN's role in propaganda was implemented.

The substantial changes made in the programmes and politics of RN resulted in a more positive perception by the public. By the end of 1942, RN's programme was filled with music, plays, poetry, sports, literary programmes, and magazine and news articles, among other things, throughout the day.[195] In fact, RN benefited immensely from the involvement of experienced entertainment presenters from private stations. For example, its entertainment programme was run by the Radio-Cité team in 1941–42.[196] Thus, RN succeeded in attracting the greatest artists, as did Radio Paris. It also managed to deliver an extremely serious yet also light programme.[197] The improvements made by RN did not go unnoticed by the BBC. The intelligence report of 17 August 1942 stated:

> Word-weariness makes many also turn to Vichy's radio … not jammed and not forbidden; and the authorities of Vichy are taking great pains to see that the programmes reach a high standard. (…) A letter written from Lyons … says: 'In our house the radio is on, if not all day (except on Sundays) at least practically all the evening. The programmes are really French and very well done. (…) A lot of singing, operas, operettas, (with an excellent cast); light and classical songs; a lot of symphony concerts … concertos, chamber music. It is a real feast. Comedies and classical dramas, reportages from Marseilles, Nice, Toulouse and even music and Montmartre cabarets from Paris' (Lyons, 6.1).[198]

A further change took place on 7 November 1942, when a new law was enacted. This clearly defined the new role of RN as a propaganda tool at the disposal of the government and increased the level of centralisation and control. In the meantime, it also gave RN more flexibility in terms of its funding, allowing it to distance itself from a very restrictive financial administrative system. As a result, RN would now receive an extra budget, allowing it to proceed with additional operations for development purposes.[199]

The programmes

At the end of 1940, RN had developed a system of 'themed programmes' addressing different interest groups. For example, *Radio-Travail* targeted workers, peasants, craftsmen, employees and business-owners; and *Radio Révolution* led a counter-propaganda campaign against the BBC and Radio Brazzaville (Free French radio in Africa) with *les Français de France répondent aux émigrés*.[200]

Radio Légion was a five-minute programme hosted by the Légion Française des Combattants, an association for veterans that was created in August 1940 as a major propaganda arm of Vichy. Anti-Semitic comments appeared openly from October 1940, when anti-Jewish laws came into force, and intensified as the laws were renewed in June 1941. *Radio Légion* became a daily programme from May 1941.[201] From autumn 1942, to counter the BBC's attack on Vichy's round-up of Jews in the summer of that year, *Radio Légion* portrayed the Jews as the enemy of the National Revolution from a racial and biological perspective. Airings of anti-Semitic programmes also intensified with *La question juive* being broadcast three times a week from that point on.[202]

Radio Jeunesse, which was launched on 15 August 1940 under the leadership of the Youth Commissariat, had the aim of restoring young people's courage.[203] Pierre Schaeffer, Claude Roy and Pierre Barbier were among the first presenters.[204] *Radio Jeunesse* broadcasts always featured a boys' choir singing the Youth anthem at the beginning and end of the programme. The recordings of visits to youth camps were often used, with both men and women as speakers in the broadcast. The purpose of this programme was 'to approach in concrete fashion the questions facing young workmen, peasants and all young Frenchmen; to inculcate into the youth of France the ideals inspiring the reconstruction policy of the Pétain government' (10.9.40).[205] There was a different topic on each day of the week: Mondays: peasants; Tuesdays: youth associations; Wednesdays: Entr'aide social service; Thursdays: young people at work; Fridays: young workmen; Saturdays: students.[206]

This programme soon became a concern for the British, as highlighted in the BBC intelligence report of 4 June 1941. According to the feedback given in a letter dated 8 April from the occupied zone, 'Radio Jeunesse "is presented in a lively and attractive form". It also makes constant and constructive propaganda for Fascist youth organisations'.[207] In November 1941, *Radio Jeunesse* expanded its broadcast to two sets of news bulletins: one at 07h20 and the other at 13h40. It also collaborated with some cultural programmes. For example, there was a show called *Radio Jeunesse magazine* at 18h30 on Tuesdays,[208] which included musical, topical and cultural elements, such as group visits to a cinema and the recordings of young artists, etc. There was also *L'heure des jeunes* at 17h00 on Thursdays, which featured plays and songs.[209] These programmes were relayed by the private stations in the unoccupied zone as well as on the Algiers and Rabat network twice a week to the French colonies.[210] *Radio Jeunesse* wanted the participation of new listeners who would bring new ideas about interpretations of the past, travel and imaginative content.[211] *Radio Jeunesse* was one of RN's leading programmes, which demonstrated how far RN had gone to attract the youth of France and the French Empire to the ideal of National Revolution. However, according to the newspaper *Figaro* on 23 October 1941, it was criticised for being too serious for the youth.[212]

Other programmes included *Les enfants chantent*, which was run by an excellent broadcaster, Jean Nohain, for very young children. This was essentially a singing competition in which the children performed in a French or North African theatre or cinema each week. *L'heure scolaire* was an educational programme that ran up until December 1941. The daily show included two languages lessons, including 'Latin, Greek, English, German, Spanish and Italian';[213] science, which covered maths, chemistry and physics; humanities, which included geography and history; and two talks that focused on philosophy and ethics. There was perhaps some infiltration of totalitarian ideas in these talks, which had titles such as 'The Spirit of Sacrifice', 'Liberty is the fruit of discipline' and 'Moral education in the family'.[214] However, there was equally some apparent encouragement for pupils to think for themselves in shows titled, for example, 'Structure of Rational Thought'. The literature aspects covered international as well as French authors, such as Shelley, Browning, Dante, Nietzche, Schiller, Goethe, Baudelaire, Montesquieu and La Fontaine. Regular speakers of both sexes would read from a script that had been given to them. These talks had a high cultural standard and a large proportion of them were devoted to American civilisation, particularly the educational system. There was no apparent propaganda purpose to these programmes and controversial topics such as 'Collaboration' were avoided.[215]

From 9 January 1942, there was a change in the format of *L'heure scolaire*. The broadcast was heralded by a trumpet call and a drum roll and became *L'Heure de l'Éducation Nationale*. The regular lessons were replaced by '"a word of advice to young people concerning their duty towards society", a travel talk, a talk on Knights in the Middle Ages and a literary talk'.[216] M. Jean Masson, ex-director of the RDN, introduced some of these items. The programme was generally made more lively and less academic in tone by the insertion of stimulating musical items between talks, or introductory remarks.[217]

Radio Révolution – the Vichy secret station – was set up by the Vichy authorities and broadcast from Vichy. It was first monitored by the British in December 1941 and was a direct response to *Radio Inconnue,* a British secret 'black' propaganda radio station. *Radio Révolution* suggested that de Gaulle wrote the script of *Radio Inconnue* and blamed him personally for encouraging acts of resistance. It also attacked *Radio Gaulle*'s broadcasts after February 1942 and discredited *Radio Patrie*,[218] both of which were British black radio stations.

The private network had, on the other hand, brought in new programmes that had a higher amusement content. Radio Toulouse offered a variety of programmes for the youth, such as *Informations régionales sur la jeunesse* or local youth news. This programme was a mixture of sports, instruction and advice to the youth, interspersed with music. *La Voix des jeunes*, sometimes subtitled *Le tréteau des jeunes*, was another programme in which boys and girls would perform. A new Sunday broadcast called *La chronique du dimanche* aimed to engage a number of young people to discuss topics such as 'how youth can best collaborate in common task of national recovery'.[219] A promise was made that questions sent in would be debated on air. There was also a children's programme in which 'Auntie' and 'Uncle' would encourage children to participate in competitions and poems etc. A programme titled *Radio Scolaire* was broadcast from Toulouse only and lasted for 10 minutes per week. It 'was devoted to discussion of the educational reform authorising the teaching of the Langue d'Oc in schools.'[220]

Both RN and Radio Paris had a similar vision and concentrated on the same themes – work, family and the youth – in their daily propaganda.[221] Compared to the intensity with which these French stations targeted the French youth, the BBC's effort in this respect was low. As exemplified in the BBC report of 23 January 1942, between August 1940 and January 1942 the combined regular output of broadcasts relating to the youth from RN and Radio Paris rose from 4 hours 15 minutes per week to 13 hours 55 minutes per week, while that of the BBC remained at half an hour per week. The report also highlighted that among the correspondence received at the BBC, not a single letter referred to its youth programme, for three possible reasons: it was more difficult for French youth to get their letters to the BBC; the programme itself might not have been interesting enough for French youth; or poor coverage may have resulted in a lack of awareness of the programme.[222]

From September 1940, the various Vichy ministries were given a daily timeslot from 19h20 to 20h30, during which they presented their achievements and projects. The topics covered were: sport and hygiene on Sundays, fine arts on Mondays, communications on Tuesdays, news on Wednesdays, agriculture on Thursdays, the Navy on Fridays, and work and education on Saturdays. At the start of these programmes, a representative of the Ministry of Family gave a brief talk. In addition to the ministry's propaganda, it was decided that RN would increase the number of broadcasts of the *Journal Parlé* to eight times a day from February 1941.[223]

Despite the fact that Vichy had no control over the content of Radio Paris's programmes, the latter did broadcast two daily RN news bulletins,[224] at 08h00 and at 11h45 for a quarter of an hour from 10 November 1940.[225] This enabled the French population living in the occupied zone to follow what was happening in the unoccupied zone.

From the end of July 1941, RN developed a routine of concluding its daily programme with the national anthem, 'La Marseillaise'.[226] This was banned in the occupied zone (the aim being to eradicate this key national symbol, under which rebellion might be fostered), but it was performed routinely during Pétain's travels in the unoccupied zone.[227] RN tried to unite the French around the national anthem, to reinforce the idea that RN was the French national radio, and to reassure listeners that RN's programmes represented the Vichy government as the legitimate national government.

Radio National *magazine*

To increase its audience, RN developed *Radio National*, a weekly magazine listing detailed daily schedules of the radio programme. Its editorial office was in Marseille at 3, rue Méry.[228] *Radio National* also acted as a visual supplement to the radio, using every opportunity to instil patriotism in the French. The magazine was an effective propaganda tool as it could also reach those members of the general public who were not necessarily listeners of RN programmes. It was presented as an illustrated magazine that offered the readers reportages, portraits of artists, gossip columns, radio reviews and a women's page.[229]

The first issue of *Radio National* came out on 25 May 1941, costing 2.50 fr. and containing 28 pages.[230] The two issues on 12 July 1942 and 19 July 1942 shrank to 12 pages for unknown reasons but it was restored to the original extent afterwards.[231]

The magazine also included schedules of Radio Suisse Romande,[232] as well as overseas stations (Radio PTT Alger, Radio Maroc).[233] *Radio National* introduced the detailed schedule of *La Voix de la France*,[234] a programme that started on 1 August 1941 and enabled France to renew contact with its empire thanks to a powerful short-wave transmitter.[235] As for the programmes of Radio Paris, they appeared in *Radio National* from 9 August 1942 onwards.[236]

The special issue marking *Radio National*'s first anniversary included an article celebrating its success by reviewing the first year of operation. It stated that as news archives were centrally kept in Paris, the journalists of *Radio National*, whose offices were in Marseille, had difficulty gaining access to them. It had taken a great deal of ingenuity for these journalists to deliver the very first issues of the magazine to the public. They managed to obtain sufficient material from the archives of the Marseille Press (*Le Petit Marseillais*), the library of the city of Marseille, the Chamber of Commerce, the Academy of Arts and booksellers. The success of the magazine was also attributed to its innovative presentation and design, which took three months to develop, and a year to reach its final form. All this work paid off, as *Radio National* was read by 150,000 people in its first year, with 13,000 subscribers, and its publication was viewed by the journalists as a success story.[237]

The content of the magazine varied, with articles covering various aspects of French people's daily lives and their concerns. There was a section on the French POWs in Germany, '*Boîte aux lettres pour nos prisonniers*', which aimed to inform, update and interpret the latest policies regarding POWs, to give practical guidance on specific issues faced by the families of POWs and to publish excerpts from listeners' letters expressing their gratitude to the programme, their emotions, or any specific difficulties.[238] Another section, '*Images des Stalag*', contained photos of POWs in the *Stalags* (POW camps for non-commissioned officers and other ranks) and *Oflags* (officers' POW camps).[239]

From 31 August 1941, *Radio National* added a new section titled '*Votre poste vous a parlé de ...*' This section was made up of five or six short articles giving historical or background information about a topic or event that the radio had covered in the previous week.[240] From 10 August 1941, there was a page called '*La Vie Parisienne*' in which the realities and memories of Paris were portrayed. There was also a section for women, '*Ecoutez Madame*', in which the main topics discussed were those thought to be of interest to women: health, food, children's education, family values, solidarity between women, fashion, etc.[241] The last issue of *Radio National* in December 1941 published a list of about 200 names of artists who had appeared at the microphone of RN.[242]

Following a survey entitled '*Comment concevez-vous la RADIO?*' seeking the opinions of the general public regarding the role of radio, a selection of public feedback was published in *Radio National* from 16 November to 13 December 1941, reflecting the views of various intellectuals regarding the present and the future role of the radio.[243] For example, Maître Henri Ripert, dean of the Faculty of Law of Marseille, stated that 'if we want to grow our country, we must bathe the soul and spirit of our people, especially our young people, in greatness and heroism. The radio must and can realise this magnificent work'.[244] Francis Carco of the Académie Goncourt considered that 'the radio must inspire us to get back on our feet'.[245] These excerpts indicate one of the commonalities between *Radio National* and RN: the use of 'authoritative voices' in their reportage to convey important messages and achieve their propaganda objectives. They tend to quote officials or professionals whose 'voices' could not be easily contested or questioned.

Correspondence

The '*Exposé d'ensemble*' report demonstrates that, as with the BBC, RN also sought its listeners' opinions through correspondence. When the report was published, the disaffection among the French public for RN was reflected in some ways by the small number of listeners' letters received, which fell to less than 500 a month during the last months of 1940, although the number of letters received would not necessarily correlate with the actual number of radio listeners.[246]

There was, however, ample evidence that people were listening to RN. The BBC's intelligence report of 8 April 1941 pointed out that RN profited from the distrust of Radio Paris and successfully presented itself as the 'Voice of France', despite a general feeling that both radio stations were viewed with disgust. A letter from the English wife of a French doctor residing in the Gironde region wrote to the BBC stating that 'we can no longer bear to listen to the lies of Radio Paris, we only take the French radio now (Arcachon, January)'.[247] This excerpt demonstrates that educated French people listened to RN despite their feeling of distrust. One of the most successful programmes, *Bonjour la France*, featuring

Jean Nohain, aka Jaboune[248] as the presenter, received thousands of 'friendship' letters during the Easter period because of its pleasant content[249] – it encompassed an 'almanac of various sorts, recipes, simple poesy and physical education'.[250] However, despite its popularity, *Bonjour la France* disappeared from the schedule in the autumn of 1941.[251]

It remains unclear whether any of the letters received at RN have survived. As it stands, the only evidence of listeners' responses to RN were those expressed in the '*Exposé d'ensemble*' report, some highly selective letters from 'authoritative voices' published in *Radio National,* and excerpts of correspondence from the BBC official reports or correspondence obtained at the BBC Written Archives. The available correspondence from the BBC offers a glimpse on RN programmes as well as listeners' responses but one must bear in mind that the French writers to the BBC was biased against Vichy's ideology and the German occupier in France; therefore, it is impossible to compare views other than those expressed at the BBC from 1940 to November 1942.

The rebirth of Radio Paris

Propaganda Abteilung

Prior to the war, Radio Paris was part of the French public network.[252] Once the Armistice had been signed on 25 June 1940, Radio Paris followed a different path of development to RN. Hitler made a serious mistake by suppressing French radio in the Armistice clause,[253] a mistake that he quickly realised when Général de Gaulle declared on the BBC the same night that a French National Committee would be formed in London, because the new government in France would be subject to the control of Germany and Italy. Orders were thus given for French radio to resume transmission 10 days later.[254] The period of radio silence from 25 June at 00h30 to 5 July heralded the end of the Third Republic and the beginning of a new era in France. The Germans could now use Radio Paris to influence French public opinion thanks to the almost intact network of French transmitters that fell into their hands after the campaign of May–June 1940.[255]

Propaganda Abteilung was a Nazi propaganda service under German military command in occupied France. It was created on 18 July 1940 and remained in service until the end of the occupation in August 1944, operating from their offices at the Hôtel Majestic in Paris.[256] Propaganda Abteilung implemented the guidelines of the propaganda ministry, headed by Goebbels.[257] The political agenda was twofold: to break the morale of the French population so they would comply with German directives, and to convince the French of the superiority of German culture.[258] Propaganda Abteilung established a '"tool of ideological repression" in all fields of thoughts and culture, such as cinema, fine arts, publishing and the radio'.[259] Its budget was over 1 billion Reichsmarks, with 1,000 people employed to work in its six divisions, radio being one of them. Dr. Bofinger, former head of Radio Stuttgart, was put in charge of Radio Paris,[260] which was under the direct control of Propaganda Abteilung, headed by Major Heinz Schmidtke.[261] The studios of Radio Paris were located at 116, avenue des Champs-Elysées and their technical facilities were considered the most modern in the city.[262]

The radio programmes were divided into three sections: music, talks and variety shows, and news and information. To monitor these, a 'censorship and control service' was set up. The recruitment of artists, musicians, lecturers and comedians was subject to the policy of cordon sanitaire, which required that those working on culture and entertainment programmes should have no involvement in politics – that was exclusively reserved for those working on news and propaganda. Propaganda Abteilung also used a combination of bonuses, praise, threat and manipulation to attract employees. Indeed, Radio Paris had a distinct advantage over RN because it offered higher wages.[263] Although it is impossible to determine today the total amount of money spent by the Germans on radio propaganda in the occupied zone during the occupation, it was calculated that Radio Paris alone spent a total of 3,435,915 Reichsmarks (the equivalent to 69,078,300 francs using the exchange rate of 1943) for fees and salaries paid to artists, journalists and speakers throughout the occupation.[264]

Transmitters and broadcasting hours

Following the Armistice, Radio Paris became the legal term given to all radio stations attached to Propaganda Abteilung, private or public. Collectively, these stations enabled the Germans to start and sustain an extremely active and direct propaganda in the occupied zone.[265]

An official assessment of the war damages report stated that the transmitters used for radio broadcasting in the occupied zone could be broadly divided into three categories. At the time of occupation, the transmitters at the disposal of Propaganda Abteilung were used by the public stations of Rennes-Alma, Allouis ondes courtes I, and Radio-Normandie, as well as the private stations of Poste Parisien and Bordeaux Sud-Ouest. All these stations broadcast programmes in French and the operating staff were paid by RN.[266] Their broadcasts could reach almost the whole of France.[267] The second category of transmitters was those available to Höhere Nachrichtenführer (HO.NA.FU.), which included the public stations of Rennes-Thourie, Bordeaux-Néac, Allouis ondes courtes II, Bordeaux Lafayette, and Allouis National (long waves), as well as the private station of Radio-Cité. These stations broadcast programmes in German and their operating staff were paid by the Germans. The last category of transmitters was those either detached from the network – for example, the station of Lille Camphin, which was attached to HO.NA.FU. Belgium – or destroyed, such as the transmitters of Paris-Villebon and Strasbourg Brumath, which had not been rebuilt at the time of the report.[268]

One constant battle between Radio Paris and the BBC was over reaching the French audience. The Germans made great efforts to block the reception of BBC broadcasting using jamming as the main technical measure. Due to security concerns, the military dictated that Radio Paris's broadcasting would stop after 20h00,[269] giving the BBC the monopoly on the airwaves after this time. Otto Abetz, a renowned specialist of French opinion, noted this disadvantage and brought Dr. Grimm, a diplomat and academic, to Paris in September 1940. Dr. Grimm advocated fighting on an equal footing with the BBC by extending Radio Paris's broadcasting time late into the night[270] – something that was achieved progressively.

In 1940, Radio Paris's logbook indicates a stable schedule time ending at 22h20, until 15 September, when a new timetable came into effect, ending the programmes at 21h00. This schedule remained in place until November. Between 4 November and March 1941, the programmes ended at 19h15 except for the three days during Christmas and New Year of 1940–41, when the programmes ended at midnight and 01h00 respectively. From March 1941 until mid-1942, there was a steady increase in broadcasting time: from 20h15 on 2 March 1941, to 21h00 on 2 June,[271] 22h15 on 9 November,[272] and eventually to 02h00 on 22 June 1942, increasing the number of the *Radio-Journal de Paris* (a news programme advocating Nazi propaganda) shows to nine broadcasts per day at 07h00, 08h00, 09h00, 13h00, 14h00, 15h00, 20h00, 22h00 and 24h00.[273]

Management and programmes

The Germans made an almost clean sweep of the staff and programmes after they took over Radio Paris and, as a result, they did not encounter any of the problems or qualms experienced by RN.[274] Radio Paris had clearly become a German radio station in terms of its organisation and control, but remained a French station for its staff, the listeners and its programmes.[275]

Radio Paris mainly targeted the occupied zone, especially residents in and around Paris. The German leadership set up a realistic and efficient schedule that would remain in place during the four years of occupation, and which served a dual purpose of propaganda and appealing to the general public.[276] The station made good use of the services of its extensive pool of actors, singers and musicians from the capital. Indeed, many of the contemporary songs played were popularised by Radio Paris. Apart from broadcasting views from officials,[277] writers[278] and artists,[279] the reporters also developed new types of broadcasts, for example, interviewing people on the street, playing a mixture of music, hosting variety shows and giving running commentaries.[280]

Radio Paris's management was headed by Dr. Bofinger and supported by Friedrich Dambman (a speaker known as Dr. Friedrich), Lieutenant Morenschild (the director of the *Radio-Journal de Paris*), Sonderführer Joseph Haëfs (editor in chief),[281] Karl Kopf and Kurt Georg Kiesinger, the latter of whom in 1966 became the chancellor of the Federal Republic of Germany.[282] Morenschild appointed Gabriel du Chastain, a former member of Action Française, an extreme-right organisation, to recruit collaborators from members of several institutions. Among these recruits, some were defectors from RN who considered Vichy policies too 'soft' in their path of collaboration.[283]

The *service politique* (political services) department was responsible for ensuring that broadcasting followed the strict directives from the *section Pays étrangers* (foreign countries section) of the Ministry of Propaganda in Berlin. Haëfs would brief the French editorial writers and the leaders of the news teams about the directives and make 'suggestions' to them about what could be put on air to facilitate German propaganda and counter that of unfriendly news agencies, such as the BBC.[284]

In terms of its programmes, almost all of Radio Paris's output was broadcast in French. Only a 15-minute programme entitled *Informations pour les soldats allemands* and a 60-minute programme entitled *L'heure du soldat allemand* were broadcast in German. These were aimed at German soldiers but were short-lived, ending in October 1940.[285] In reality, this date may not be quite this clear-cut. Four broadcasts presented in German were found in the archives after this date: two were recorded in November 1940, one in December 1940 and one in August 1941. It is, however, unclear whether these recordings were ever broadcast.[286]

The artistic programmes of Radio Paris seemed to have fulfilled their mission as they were popular, of good quality and interesting for a wide audience. French programmes occupied an important part of its schedule and were among the most interesting and the best made in the history of radio until the 1950s. The French team was built around a handful of musicians and radio presenters.[287] For example, Radio Paris gave Jean Fournet, a 29-year-old musician, the task of building the Grand Orchestre de Radio Paris, which consisted of 90 musicians.[288] The orchestra boasted that between 20 April and 31 July 1941, it 'did not play the same piece twice, despite having two or three weekly concerts', and made 'a huge effort in the research, study and execution of new pieces or forgotten ones'.[289]

Another important musician was Raymond Legrand, whose orchestra was founded in 1934, and who had his golden age during the occupation, when his orchestra featured regularly on Radio Paris from August 1940 to 1943. Between August 1940 and March 1942, the band was involved in 520 broadcasts[290] and performed with guest singers such as Tino Rossi, Maurice Chevalier and Mistinguett.[291] Legrand was arrested in September 1944 for having worked for Radio Paris but was given a light sentence of six months in prison by the Comité national d'épuration des professions d'artistes dramatiques, lyriques et de musiciens exécutants (National Committee for the Purification of the Professions of Dramatic, Lyrical Artists and Performing Musicians). This is a post-war committee which punished artists who were seen as collaborators during the war. His six-month sentence was light because he had helped the resistance from 1943 onwards.[292]

Richard Blareau, who founded an orchestra that grew to as many as 50 musicians, also performed at least two concerts a week on Radio Paris and participated in major galas at the Théâtre des Champs-Elysées, where he performed with Maurice Chevalier and Charles Trenet. His orchestra was well suited to the style of Radio Paris and radio broadcasting. He became conductor at the Opéra de Paris after the war.[293]

An activity report published on 23 May 1941 gave detailed information about the programmes from July 1940 to May 1941, shedding light on the types of programmes, their aims and their impact as evaluated by the propagandist. The report divided the programmes into two categories: general news and political news.

The report stated that the development of 'general news' was initially hindered due to the lack of French collaborators. Since the beginning of August, a reportage service had been created with Laporte, the chief reporter, as its speaker, presenting the most important moments of Parisian life as it returned to normal,[294] resulting in the programmes being more varied. This was the reason why on 1 January 1941, under the supervision of Radio Paris, the broadcasting company Radio-Actualités reopened. Its director, Jules Ferry, was given the monopoly of reportage production. By the time this report was written, 10 reportage programmes were being broadcast per week, allowing the listeners to participate in the most important Parisian events via the radio.

Another subsidiary company of Radio-Actualités had been in development in Bordeaux since 15 April, as a result of Radio Paris's initiative. In 1941, in addition to reportage, there were programmes presented as discussions of special interest to professionals in various fields and certain categories of the population, for example, *Jardin d'enfants* for children (from 16 July), *Le micro est à vous, Mesdames* for women (from 30 October), *Le fermier à l'écoute* for farmers (daily from 30 October) and *Pour l'ouvrier* for workers (from 1 May). Entertainment programmes such as *La revue de cinéma* for film lovers (from 4 August), *Le feuilleton théatral* for radio plays (from 15 March) and cultural reportage discussing places of interest or historical events were also put into this category.[295]

The non-political programmes had 'the purpose to sweeten the radicalisation of the content of the news.'[296] From 29 September 1940, the management of Radio Paris issued a statement highlighting the artistic vision for the next season: 'The programmes must be such that all French may follow with pleasure, even if they do not have the musical or literary culture. They will be constituted in such a way that they will appeal to the dilettante.'[297]

Music programmes occupied more than two-thirds of the broadcasting schedule, covering a diverse range of music, singers, composers and orchestras.[298] It is possible that many listeners turned to Radio Paris for this reason. The German censorship of music programmes (*Rundfunksgruppe*) did not interfere too much with the choice of the producers and this meant Radio Paris's music programmes were largely authentically French.[299]

Both 'general news' and 'political news' programmes had a political significance and the transition between the two types was imperceptible.[300] Within 'political news', there were five sub-groups of programmes. The first were political programmes disguised as non-political programmes: for example, *Grands Français et grands Allemands* (from 1 January 1941) and *Interview d'artistes et de savants* (from December 1940).

The second group were programmes about 'crisis', focusing on the magnitude of the existing misery in France as well as the efforts of Radio Paris in fulfilling a social function and alleviating the plight of the population. These programmes had a high social and propaganda value; for example, *Du travail pour les jeunes* for the employment of young people (from 7 December 1940) and *Le Trait d'Union du Travail* for the unemployed (from 1 January 1941) had both been highly successful as they had already provided jobs to 1,500 unemployed Frenchmen. The aim of the programme *Grand concours social* was to find solutions to local unemployment.[301] Thanks to this, the Centre d'initiatives contre le chômage was created under the leadership of M. Raymond Froideval, the trade unionist,[302] facilitating the employment of more than 2,000 people.[303] A separate report by the same writer highlighted the value of these altruistic programmes in attracting listeners: they had a great effect on the public because they attempted to alleviate the social difficulties caused by the military chaos, and encouraged listeners' participation by asking them to propose local solutions to counter unemployment, promising to forward these to the Commissariat général français à la lutte contre le chômage (French General Commission for the fight against unemployment) to consider.[304] Other programmes, such as *Où sont-ils?* (from 7 July to 9 October, sometimes three times a week), *Recherches par la Croix-Rouge* (from 31 January 1941) and *À la recherche des enfants perdus* (from 1 February 1941)[305] all had an aim of searching for missing or lost people.

Through these programmes tackling social crisis, Radio Paris presented itself as a station for the public good that helped the unemployed, the injured and the missing. However, there was a hidden agenda: to attract the listeners to tune into their programmes and to disseminate the covert propaganda that was cleverly slotted in between shows or intertwined with the programme. A separate report dated April 1941 stated that the social programmes occupied a large part of Radio Paris's output, including shows specifically targeting women and young people.[306]

The third group of programmes were political talks and sketches. Various campaigns were organised under different themes; for example, *Une parodie de Radio Londres* from 3 September to December 1940, and *Sketch-Surprise*, a political satire, from 28 September to December 1940. From 18 October 1940, a new programme, *Tribune*, was created in which pro-Nazi collaborators would present a discussion on the air every evening. Radio Paris gathered a panel of collaborators, knowledgeable in specific fields, whose talk would follow a specific area of interest for the public. More than a hundred collaborators participated in these discussions, including Marcel Déat, a politician; Georges Oltramare aka Dieudonné, a Swiss journalist;

and Eugène Schueller,[307] an industrialist and founder of L'Oréal,[308] to name just a few. One of the themes discussed in *Tribune* was anti-British propaganda. In fact, this featured heavily in the broadcasting schedule during the first 10 weeks. From 15 December 1940, this anti-British programme doubled its output and was aired at noon and in the evening through *Tribune de Midi* and *Tribune du Soir*. Following the anti-British propaganda campaigns and the *Tribune* programmes, there was a considerable increase in public participation and the number of letters received at Radio Paris. It was hoped that this would bring new listeners.[309]

La Rose des Vents is another example of a very successful programme under this third category. It was created on 1 December 1940[310] under the leadership of Robert Peyronnet, a rare idealist among Radio Paris's collaborators, and was dedicated to the problems of the moment and social issues,[311] often with the participation of French comedians.[312] It was so popular among French listeners that Radio Paris received approximately 20,000 letters about it. A special service, *Contact avec les auditeurs*, was created around the same time to deal with the letters,[313] presumably sent in about various popular programmes. A report stated that among the 6,250 letters received from 28 February to 30 April 1941, 83.5 per cent were in favour of collaboration, and that this programme had an estimated total of 18,000 followers.[314] This success was noted in the BBC's Monthly Surveys of European Audiences of 4 June 1941, in which a listener stated in his letter dated 12 May 1941 that 'Radio Paris has adopted a new technique. A transmission called "La Rose des Vents" claims to have "met with enormous success because it expressed the sentiments of every true Frenchman"'.[315] Another letter sent on 21 May declared that:

> Although there are constant boasts of heavy mail bags full of listeners' letters, bribery in the form of competitions with 1,000 francs prizes seems to have been found necessary in order to obtain such letters. These are then read out at the microphone to the accompaniment of laborious attempts ('oh dear, this one **is** so badly written') to prove their genuineness.[316]

Monitoring was not a characteristic of Radio Paris as it preferred speaking to listening;[317] however, *La Rose des Vents* was one of the exceptions, whereby correspondence was used to air the opinions of their listeners.[318] It is unclear whether they were all from genuine listeners or whether some letters were fabricated.

The fourth group of programmes were those with a focus on 'special actions', which were aimed at supporting the politics of the day. For example, there was *Action anti-anglaise* from 13 October to 31 December 1940, for which a contest was organised by the news department that encouraged listeners' participation by asking them to work out *De qui est-ce* (Who is…) the person, using information provided in short anti-British historical sketches or quotes originating from a famous person. With this contest, Radio Paris successfully achieved two goals: the active participation of the public[319] and the gathering of 'the first extensive address list of the listeners of political programmes of Radio Paris'.[320]

There was also action regarding the National Revolution,[321] which started from 15 April 1941. Representatives of each trade discussed the Revolution and its impact on their field, and the public was encouraged to respond and propose contradictory suggestions. Radio Paris would select the public response that represented the desired view of the propagandists as the voice of the people.[322] As the report states: 'The purpose of this programme is to influence listeners in the way we desire, for the inevitable establishment of a new French State doctrine and social (mentality)'.[323]

The last 'special action' programme focused on anti-Semitic activities from 11 May 1941. In all the news services of Radio Paris, there was a focus aimed at destroying the influence of Jews in both zones. These programmes were presented to the public in a variety of forms: reportage, interview, sketches, slogans, etc.[324] After June 1941, Radio Paris attacked the Bolsheviks virulently, as Operation Barbarossa was viewed as a '"liberating" conflict to rid Europe of "the Bolshevik nightmare which has hunted it for twenty years"'.[325]

The last group of programmes was concerned with contact with the listeners of Radio Paris. The report stated that a large number of letters arrived at Radio Paris, which made the management reconsider how the political views of the radio could better reach their sympathisers. What came out of this consideration was the creation of *Les Ondes*, a new weekly news magazine that reached a circulation of 100,000 from its fifth issue. The purpose of both the radio and its magazine was to reinforce German leadership and European collaboration.[326] Two brochures, '*Ici Radio Paris*' and '*La Rose des Vents*', which were sent by post, were hugely successful, as was demonstrated by the high volume of thank-you letters received by Radio Paris; they helped increase the station's contact with its sympathisers.[327]

The report itself is biased in its evaluation of Radio Paris and may have exaggerated its success or presented an overly positive impression of its listeners, but it nevertheless provides a useful overview of the station's various programmes and their underlying political aims, which is lacking in most existing literature about Radio Paris. Radio Paris also targeted children with programmes such as *Tante Simone*, an attractive programme featuring a woman of Austrian origin and filled with songs, stories and soap operas. The competence of programme directors and the talent of renowned comedians helped to bring quality and popularity to *Tante Simone*,[328] which may not be considered a political programme per se yet reflected the occupiers' policy towards French youth.

There were two further programmes on Radio Paris that focused on work for French youth: *Du travail pour les jeunes* and *Des vacances pour les jeunes*, the latter being a temporary programme that was broadcast only during the summer months in 1941. These were presented by Max Vignan, who read out lists of vacancies for manual labour. The programme also contained a weekly description of a trade, such as dressmaking or electrical work, both of which were considered trades of practical value. The aim was 'to serve as a link between employers of labour and youth and to furnish advice to those finishing school'.[329] In addition, there was an adult labour-focused programme, called *L'Éphéméride du travail*, which incorporated interviews.

The numbers of letters received at Radio Paris showed youth's interest in such programmes. *Des vacances* received about 7,000 letters between 29 January and 19 August 1941 and *Du travail* received 14,324 letters on 6 September 1941. These two youth shows were prime examples of explicit propaganda to attract young French people to return to the land and perform manual labour. There were plenty of vacancies; no one had applied for jobs as joiners and carpenters, whereas 300 letters had been received in response to jobs in retail and offices. Vignan warned young listeners that 'only those who could work with their hands now had a chance of getting a job'.[330] Girls were frequently reminded that there was a chief demand 'for farm workers, general domestics, dressmakers and darners'.[331] The BBC report declared that this programme was a 'well-presented, efficient, but not encouraging broadcast.'[332]

Les jeunes copains, by contrast, was a bright programme during which careful impromptu discussions were held between boys and girls in the studio of Radio Paris. From time to time, the listeners were reassured that the discussions were truly held by the young people debating in the studio. The last three minutes of the programme were accompanied by a moment of gaiety. At first, the programme focused on collaboration and Europe; antiquated and out-of-date nationalistic ideas, which were viewed as suitable for the older generation. Later, this broadcast became more practical. In May 1941, the broadcast and the station associated itself with children at risk. Each week, an 'urgent social case' was brought up at listeners' request. There were also useful weekly quizzes and surveys, such as 'How can the life of young folks in the country be made more agreeable?', and 'Is there any case of young folks in your district taking to drink?',[333] with prizes offered to participants.[334]

For the very young children, there were two programmes: *Pour nos jeunes* and *Jardin d'enfants*. These apparently served as pure entertainment and saw children coming into the studio to enjoy singing and listening to stories, playing games, etc. The general atmosphere in the studio was one of fun and enjoyment. Individual children would perform and there were rhymes and musical interludes. Indeed, all performers were children and any child could audition to be chosen to participate in the broadcast.[335]

Les Ondes

The weekly magazine of Radio Paris, *Les Ondes,* was first published on 27 April 1941, although the first available issue was dated 11 January 1942. Its editorial office first settled at 82, boulevard des Batignolles in Paris before moving to 55, avenue des Champs-Elysées two months later. Its price was 3 francs, which was comparable to other magazines. The cover of the magazine exclusively featured

- 20 -

Appendix A

Schedule of BROADCASTS TO FRENCH YOUTH as at 15th January, 1942

BST	Monday	Tuesday	Wednesday	Thursday	Friday	Saturday	Sunday
0720-0725	Radio Jeunesse (RDN)	Radio Jeunesse (RDN)	Radio Jeunesse (RDN)	Radio Jeunesse (RDN)	Radio Jeunesse (RDN)	Radio Jeunesse (RDN)	
0850-0900	Radio Scolaire (HPN)	Radio Scolaire (RDN)	Radio Scolaire (RDN)	Radio Scolaire (FFR: Toulouse only).	Radio Scolaire (FFR: Toulouse only).	Radio Scolaire (RDN)	
0900-0915				Radio Scolaire (RDN)	Radio Scolaire (RDN)	Du Travail pour les Jeunes (R.Paris)	
1030-1045							La Voix des Jeunes: (FFR: Toulouse only)
1130-1200				Catéchisme des Petits et des Grands (RDN)			
1200-1205				Les Enfants chantent (RDN)			
1205-1215		Informations Rég. (FFR: Toulouse only)	Informations Rég. (FFR: Toulouse only)	Informations Rég. (FFR: Toulouse only)	Informations Rég. (FFR:Toulouse only)	Informations Rég. (FFR:Toulouse only)	Informations Régionales:(FFR: Toulouse only)
1215-1225	Informations Régionales sur la Jeunesse (FFR: Toulouse only).						
1300-1330				Emission Enfantine (FFR: Lyons only)			
1330-1400			À des Enfants (Rennes)	Jardin d'Enfants (RDN)			
1605-1610				Les Copains (R.Paris)			Pour les Jeunes (R.Paris)
1615-1630				BBC - Children		BBC - Youth	
1700-1800		Radio Jeunesse Magazine (RDN)		L'Heure des Jeunes (RDN)			
1715-1725				La Voix des Jeunes (FFR)		La Voix des Jeunes (FFR)	
1740-1750		L'Orientation Pratique de la Jeunesse (RDN)			L'Orientation Pratique de la Jeunesse (RDN)		
1800-1815				Emission Enfantine (FFR)			
1820-1830			Pour les Chantiers de la Jeunesse (RDN)				

Schedule of broadcasts to French youth on 15 January 1942. From BBC WAC, E2/188/1, 23 January 1942 (European Intelligence Papers).

- 21 -

Appendix B

Schedule showing increase in output of BROADCASTS TO FRENCH YOUTH FROM OCCUPIED & UNOCCUPIED FRANCE from Franco-German Armistice to January 1942

			August 1940			November 1940			February 1941			May 1941			August 1941			January 1942		
			Time	Duration	Days	Time	Durtn.	Days	Time	Durtn.	Days	Time	Durtn.	Days	Time	Durtn.	Days	Time	Durtn.	Days
UNOCCUPIED FRANCE	RDN	Radio Jeunesse	1245	¼-hr.	Sundays only (R.Méd. only up to Oct.)	1215	¼-hr.	Daily ex.Sun.	1215 1845	½-hr. ¼-hr.	Daily ex.Sun. Thurs. & Sat. only	0655 1220	5 min. 10 min.	Daily ex.Sun. Daily ex.Sun.	0655 1220	5 min. 10min.	Daily ex.Sun Daily ex.Sun.	0720 1700 1820	5 min. 1 hr. 10 min.	Daily ex.Sun. Tues.) Thurs.) Wed.
		Radio Scolaire	1030	½-hr.	Daily ex. Sun.	0900	½-hr.	Daily ex.Sun.	0850	1 hr.	Daily ex.Sun.	0850	1 hr.	Daily ex.Sun.	0850	1 hr.	Daily ex.Sun.	0850	1 hr.	Daily ex.Sun.
		Catéchisme des Petits et des Grands													2145	½-hr.	Tues.	1130	½-hr.	Tues.
	FFR	Radio Scolaire (Toulouse only)																0850	10min.	Thurs.
		L'Orientation Pratique de la Jeunesse (Toulouse only)																1740	10 min.	Tues.) Fri.)
		Informations Régionales pour la Jeunesse (Toulouse only)													1100	30 min.	Daily ex.Sun.	1215 1205	10 min 10 min.	Daily Sun.only
		La Voix des Jeunes																1030 1715	½-hr. 10 min.	Sun. Tues. & Fri.
	RDN	Les Enfants chantent													1200	25 min.	Thurs.	1200	25 min.	Thurs.
	FFR	Emission Enfantine													1115	¼-hr.	Thurs.	1800	¼-hr.	Thurs.
		Emission Enfantine (Lyons only)																1800	20 min.	Thurs.
OCCUPIED FRANCE	Paris	Les Jeunes Copains	1330	½-hr.	Sun. & Thurs.	1330	½-hr.	Sun. & Thurs.	1530	¼-hr.	Thurs.	1815	¼-hr.	Wed.	1630	¼-hr.	Wed.	1600	¼-hr.	Thurs.
		Du Travail pour les Jeunes							1635	¼-hr.	Sat.	1030	¼-hr.	Sat.	1030	¼-hr.	Sat.	0900	¼-hr.	Sat.
		Des Vacances pour les Jeunes													1235	¼-hr.	Tues.			
	Rennes	Quart d'Heure des Enfants																1545	¼-hr.	Wed.
	R. Paris	Pour nos Jeunes							1315	½-hr.	Sun.	1315	½-hr.	Sun.	1300	½-hr.	Sun.	1330	½-hr.	Sun.
		Jardin d'Enfants										1315	½-hr.	Thurs.	1330	½-hr.	Thurs.	1330	½-hr.	Thurs.

Schedule showing the increase in output of broadcasts to French youth from both zones from the Armistice to January 1942. From BBC WAC, E2/188/1, 23 January 1942 (European Intelligence Papers).

celebrities at the microphone, such as Yvonne Printemps, singer and actress, Tino Rossi or Madeleine Renaud.[336]

Les Ondes primarily provided a detailed weekly schedule of Radio Paris's programmes, but also those of Rennes-Bretagne, RN, Paris-Mondial, Radiodiffusion Allemande[337] and, later, Poste Européen Téléradio (a station of European news and opinion broadcasting news, talks and sketches,[338] which was replaced by Poste 'Métropole' from June 1942).[339] The schedule of '*La Voix du Reich*' was added in the summer of 1942, focusing on news and *L'Heure française*.[340]

The number of pages initially varied considerably between 16 and 36; however, from 17 May 1942 it stabilised at 20 pages per issue,[341] which may have been the result of a shortage of paper.[342] Half of the magazine was dedicated to the detailed schedules for the various stations, organised by day. The layout of the magazine meant that there was less space for supplementary articles as compared to *Radio National*.

Among the articles published, the editorials of Roland Tessier, the chief editor and columnist, mainly addressed unemployment, social problems and the difficulties of daily life.[343] His articles always featured on the third or fourth page – a prominent place before the schedules. In these articles, he rigorously defended the merit of the social order.[344] There were other articles in *Les Ondes* as well: '*L'heure de la femme*' by Françoise Laudès focused on fashion;[345] '*Tante Simone vous parle*' told stories for children,[346] supplementing the same programme on Radio Paris; and Pierre Hiégel spoke about the various aspects of music: composers, performers, interpretation of music, recording, etc;[347] Pierre Aubertin was the presenter of *Le fermier à l'écoute*, a weekly talk show that became a daily programme in the summer of 1942 and offered advice from fellow farmers. Aubertin also wrote articles to supplement the radio broadcast. The hundreds of letters received every day asking for additional information demonstrated the popularity of this programme among farmers.[348]

Each week, several pages were reserved for promoting the Franco-German collaboration and the ideology of National Revolution. For example, the article '*Le Secours Rapide de Radio-Paris*' called for French solidarity in helping and giving donations to the victims of the bombing of Paris by the Royal Air Force (RAF).[349] Articles promoting collaboration were written by Jacques de Lesdain, a columnist of *Illustration* (a weekly French newspaper), Raymond Froideval, Schueller and Dr. Friedrich etc.[350]

Although *Les Ondes* reflected the political and ideological vision of Radio Paris, the articles served various purposes. For example, some were to give a flavour of an event or topic to raise the listener's curiosity, such as an article providing background information about a cycling event due to take place shortly.[351] Others had a clear political agenda; for example, Jean Brun Damase's article criticised the messages of the 'ex-general' de Gaulle.[352] *Les Ondes* was essentially a written representation of Radio Paris, propagating the ideology of collaboration, with anti-British and anti-Semitic sentiments featuring in many articles.

Indeed, Radio Paris openly promoted its anti-Semitic stance from as early as October 1940. Among surviving broadcasts, there are three such in 1940, 17 in 1941 and 14 in 1942. Anti-Semitism is one of the key and recurring themes in both the broadcasts and in *Les Ondes*. Radio Paris was known for advocating aggressively anti-Semitic rhetoric. It would seem that attacks on Jews started in May 1941, when sketches, clever talks that manipulated facts and figures, and historical details were used to reinforce anti-Semitic emotion. For example, Radio Paris used reports of exhibitions such as *Le Juif et la France* to illustrate its policies on Jews, and historic references to justify the order for Jews to wear the yellow star, thereby implying that this sanction should not be taken as demeaning.[353]

Popular speakers

The presenters of Radio Paris played a major role in the diffusion of German propaganda on air. Dr. Bofinger used a team of young, inventive, and intolerant Frenchmen who were encouraged to criticise Vichy's policies and neutrality and were allowed to develop the most provocative views as long as they supported German policy.[354] They were extreme-right French collaborationists who intended to transform the defeat into revolution. They wanted to 'take revenge on the old order … to establish a regime certainly as authoritarian and hierarchised as that of the French State, but which would no longer be controlled by "reactionary" and "clerical" gerontocracy'.[355]

The French team for the artistic programmes was built on a handful of presenters, such as Pierre Hiégel, who came from Radio-Cité before the war and worked at Radio Paris from the summer of 1940 until the liberation in 1944. He tried to reach out to all music lovers and to the public at large.[356] Hiégel said in a letter dated 3 February 1949 to the *Inspection générale de la Radiodiffusion française* that he was, 'the only Frenchman participating in the committee of music programming of the station', and that by his 'patient and repeated action', he could impose a maximum of French music on air: Debussy, Ravel, Fauré, Duparc, Roussel, Messager … and not – 'as the Germanic taste wanted – Lortzing, Lehar, Strauss'.[357]

After the war, Hiégel was suspended from all professional activities for a nine-month period by the Comité d'épuration des professions artistiques. He later found a job at a private radio station, Radio Luxembourg, where he continued his career in 1950.[358]

Luc Bérimont, who often worked with Pierre Hiégel, hosted literary and poetic programmes. His main show was *Le film invisible,* the idea being to offer rich and vivid sound pictures so that the listeners' imaginations would enable them to recreate the scenes. Comedian guests would be assisted by a residential team to deliver the programme every week.[359]

André Alléhaut, who came from the Poste Parisien, was very interested in radiophonic theatre. He wrote and directed numerous adaptations of literary works, which he produced and presented on Sunday evening each week. He provided quality radio programmes at a time when the radio occupied an important place in Parisian life.[360]

André Claveau, meanwhile, was a talented singer and radio presenter who held a special place in the world of entertainment, especially among the female audience of Radio Paris, who enjoyed his *Cette heure est à vous,* a music programme using the title of one of his songs. He had a crooner's voice that was well suited for radio, and this contributed to his popularity – Radio Paris really started his career.[361] After the war, Claveau was permitted to return to work at *Radio National* in 1948.[362]

Jean Hérold-Paquis was one of the most virulent presenters of Radio Paris in his attacks against the British and the Gaullists.[363] He was appointed by Paul Marion, Secretary General of Information, as delegate for Propaganda in the Hautes-Alpes after the Armistice. By the end of 1941, he had become disappointed with the Vichy's National Revolution, and decided to join Jacques Doriot's party, the Parti Populaire Français (PPF). The Germans had been interested in the PPF since the beginning of the conflict in Russia in June 1941, and were seeking a leader from the French collaboration movement in occupied Paris to work for them at Radio Paris. This was when Paquis met Lieutenant Morenschild, the number two in the political section of Radio Paris, who arranged for him to work as an editor at Radio Paris from January 1942. During the summer of 1942 and for the next two years, Jean-Hérold-Paquis became 'the voice' of Radio Paris.[364] He also worked as a journalist at the *Radio-Journal de Paris*, where he said: *L'Angleterre, comme Carthage, doit être détruite* ('England, like Carthage, must be destroyed').[365] He was executed for treason on 13 October 1945.[366]

Radio Paris was often perceived as a radio station that offered high-quality entertainment programmes that might have been enjoyed both by those in Paris and beyond. However, less evidence could be found in terms of its presenters and how many people actively listened to its programmes. Unfortunately, following the defeat of the Germans in 1944 and successive transfer of responsibilities to diverse administrations, many documents were destroyed.[367] Moreover, until 1942, the Germans were winning the war and Radio Paris's programmes and styles more or less reflected this fact: its remit was to provide entertainment and laughter, normalise the Parisian way of life and glorify collaboration and the New Order in Europe.

CHAPTER 2

Other international radios broadcasting in French

There were, of course, other international radio stations based in Europe, America and Africa, which broadcast in French and could be heard in France. Despite perhaps not being as influential as the BBC, RN and Radio Paris, these radio stations nonetheless formed part of the omnipresent radio war between foreign stations. They too featured news and stories that perpetuated their own political agenda: they were either pro-German or pro-Allied forces and provided either an affiliated or an independent view. Interestingly, some news features or stories that were deemed inappropriate for broadcast by the main stations found their way to the public via these alternative stations.

Radio stations based in Britain

Radio Belgique

The Institut national belge de radiodiffusion (INR) was created in 1930 in Belgium and did not have a monopoly – until 1940, there were also another 16 local stations. A certain amount of airtime was given to the organisations representing the main political and ideological currents of the country. As bilingualism had been a consideration since 1936, two general directorates coexisted within the INR: one French-speaking (Théo Fleischman) and the other Dutch-speaking (Boon).[1]

The presidency of the INR was subordinate to the ministry of the PTT, as part of the public service. In 1939, the INR's links with the government were strengthened by the creation of a new Ministry of Information, headed by Arthur Wauters, former director of *Le Peuple*, a socialist daily newspaper.[2] However, on 5 January 1940, due to the growing tension in the west, the Ministry of Information was scrapped, resulting in the return of INR to the ministry of the PTT headed by Antoine Delfosse, a member of the Liberal Party.

A German attack of Belgium was believed to be imminent in early 1940, although nothing happened until 10 May. During this 'Phoney War' period, an adaptation of the programmes ensued to prepare for the feared imminent German attack. For example, a programme for soldiers, *La demi-heure du soldat*, was introduced. This effort was complicated by the mobilisation of some of the INR's personnel. The plan was to set up new and more powerful transmitters but this failed to materialise. The INR did, however, manage somehow to set up a studio in Boitsfort, in the Brussels suburbs. It was from this 'secret' studio that news was broadcast during the first days of the German invasion of Belgium. The station also broadcast from the Belgian House of Representatives the verbal report that Paul Henry Spaak, Minister of Foreign Affairs, made when he met the German ambassador on 10 May.[3]

The Belgian troops had a huge morale setback during the 'Phoney War', largely due to the severe weather conditions during the winter of 1939-40. Life on the front was dreary and drab, and there was not much activity on the front. Once the invasion began on Belgian soil, the troops had to confront the tactical superiority of the Germans troops, with their optimal use of aviation and armoured divisions. The exodus of populations on the roads also made it difficult for the Allied forces to fight back. Thus, the surprise crossing of the Ardennes, which had until now been deemed an insurmountable obstacle by the Allied powers, meant that Belgium fell within a fortnight.

Following this, differences quickly arose between the king, Leopold III (and his military advisers), and the government. On 25 May, the king believed that it was time to declare the end of the war to avoid unnecessary deaths, however, it was not until 28 May that he declared the capitulation of Belgium alone. The king's declaration and subsequent refusal to go into exile with his government meant he was reproached by both Paris and his government, headed by the Belgian prime minister, Hubert Pierlot.[4] In October, the new Belgian government in exile in London was formed with the arrival of Spaak and Pierlot.[5]

The technical installations of the Belgian radio stations were sabotaged by order of the government and some staff opted for voluntary evacuation, making Belgium the only occupied country where radio broadcasting was provided by the German army's mobile transmitters throughout the war. Scattered INR staff met in Paris as early as 17 May, prior to being evacuated further away from the front.

In response to the impossibility of Belgian radio being transmitted on home soil, the French authorities suggested that Montpellier station be made available for use. However, between 21 and 25 May, negotiations failed to bring cables to link Paris to Montpellier for communication. The Veltem transmitter that had been dismantled and brought from Belgium was therefore transported to Poitiers instead of Montpellier. On 27 May, Fleishman went to Paris to find a solution for the future of Belgian radio in France. The next day, he decided to go to Poitiers, where numerous meetings were held between the Belgian ministers and those who had an interest in resuming broadcasting. Eventually, Belgian radio successfully transmitted five bulletins through the Paris transmitter on 11 and 12 June. However, Paris was taken on the 14 June, bringing the short-lived period of Belgian radio broadcasting in France to an end.[6]

However, it soon found its voice again, this time in London, from 28 September 1940. The station was renamed Radio Belgique and managed by Victor de Laveleye for the French programme, while Radio België was managed by his Flemish counterpart, Jan Moetwil.[7]

Radio Belgique and, later, Radio Nationale Belge, benefitted from the Office belge d'information et de documentation (INBEL) – the Belgian press agency now based in London. From 1940, INBEL provided all the useful information regarding the activities of Belgians in Belgium and abroad, including the 'R' service, which monitored, reproduced and analysed what was said on Radio Bruxelles,[8] the pro-German radio based in Brussels.

Born in 1894, Laveleye was the son of a Brussels banker. He had volunteered in World War I and was a successful lawyer and politician in Brussels. His appearance in the press as a specialist in diplomatic news earned him the position of *rapporteur* of the Foreign Affairs Committee of the Liberal Party. In 1939, he was elected to the House of Representatives, where he spent very little time working as a Member of Parliament. In May 1940, he followed the Belgian government to France, but following the agreement concluded by Maréchal Pétain, he left France and arrived in London on 24 June.[9]

Laveleye became involved with Radio Belgique largely thanks to Cecil de Sausmarez, officially the cultural advisor of the British embassy in Brussels before the invasion of Belgium. He admitted after the war that he had been in contact with British Secret Service before May 1940. While in Brussels, he established multiple contacts with Belgian politicians, including Laveleye. The two men harboured no illusions about the real chances of Belgian neutrality being respected. Between May and June, Sausmarez was the head of the Anti-rumour Bureau of the Ministry of Information, then he became the regional expert for the Netherlands and Belgium. Upon Laveleye's arrival in London, Sausmarez heard him speak in a meeting and was immediately impressed; he knew that he had found the right person to take on the task of speaking to the Belgian francophones and cheering them up in the difficult times to come.[10]

During the months of August and September, Sausmarez attempted to convince the various authorities 'that a Belgian radio station was needed, independent from the government and under the control of the BBC and the Special Services'[11] (of various Allied countries). This eventually led to the revival of the pro-Allied radio station speaking to francophones in Belgium, and it could also be heard in France.

The radio station had to follow certain guidelines. First, King Leopold was a taboo subject as he was now a prisoner. Second, the '18 Days' Campaign' during which Belgium was crushed by the advancing German troops was not to be discussed as it would divide the Belgians. Third, programmes were to discuss as much as possible the British war effort, both in terms of its failures and its successes. Fourth, presenters were to underline the work achieved by the Belgian forces in the Congo and amplify the importance of Belgian forces in Tenby, the town in Wales where Belgian forces were assembled, as well as speaking of the contribution of the Belgian sailors and the Belgian navy. Fifth, they were to attempt to demoralise the Germans in Belgium and sow discord among the collaborators; in other words, scare them by talking of a future British victory. The speakers also had to follow two key principles: there had to be equality between French and Dutch on air, and only the truth could be told. No one should be misled.[12]

Once Belgium had been occupied, the Germans were quick to set up rules about listening to the radios. It was announced in a first decree that from 13 June 1940 it was illegal and punishable by law for those living in Belgium to listen to non-German transmitters in public or in groups, or to provide the opportunity for others to do so, unless approved by the German army. As the decree was vague – the punishment was not explained, and it excluded listening to radios in private – it in effect left Belgians with the choice and right to listen to whatever broadcast they wanted on their own. A further decree on 18 June 1940 restricted the transmitting stations, in particular the amateur ones, and the spare parts of such stations were ordered to be taken to the *Kommandantur* (military headquarters). The receiving sets owned by individuals, on the other hand, were not confiscated, meaning that anti-German propaganda on radio had to be controlled by the authorities. A new *ordonnance* (act), published on 27 July, prohibited the intentional listening to the English broadcasts. The punishment would be forced labour in the most serious cases and a prison sentence for the less serious cases. The 'intentional' character of the listening and the 'less severe cases' were, however, not clearly defined. This changed on 23 December, when it was clarified that all BBC broadcasts were included in the prohibition, not just news bulletins. Also, the population could only listen to the German stations and those affiliated with them.[13]

One of the most prominent campaigns organised by Radio Belgique is no doubt the 'V' campaign, launched by Laveleye on the evening of 14 January 1941, which subsequently spread to other BBC foreign services. Why? Because 'V' is the first letter of '*Victoire*' (victory) in French and '*Vrijheid*' (freedom) in Flemish. The two notions were thought to go together like Walloons and Flemings against the occupier; victory by the British would eventually lead to the return of freedom. What's more, the letter 'V' could be easily and quickly pencilled anywhere as a symbol.[14]

Radio Belgium brought the 'V' sound alive. 'It is the announcement of the musical theme of the BBC, the first notes of the *Fifth Symphony* by Beethoven, this Pom, which is also in Morse language, three short strokes and one long stroke (…-), the transcription of the letter "V"'.[15] This campaign was a great psychological success for the Allies, and the Germans were slow to respond to it.

Nevertheless, the Germans eventually recovered from the 'V' campaign, and to their benefit. During the period between 15 and 31 July 1941, mention of the 'V' appeared in a report of the Propaganda-Abteilung Belgien. This reveals that the 'V' for *Victoire-Vrijheid-Victory* can also be translated as *Viktoria* in German, signalling a German victory.[16] Thus, the Radio Bruxelles programme *Billet du jour* on 26 July 1941 was devoted to this German interpretation of 'V' of victory. 'There is only one "V", dear listeners, and it is that of the German Victory. It has been the case for two years on all the battlefields of Europe where England believed it could provoke the power of the Reich.'[17]

Radio Belgique continued broadcasting until the end of the war in 1945. From 1942, the Radiodiffusion Nationale Belge (RNB) started broadcasting from the Belgian Congo and from that point on, Radio Belgique was no longer alone.[18] An informant from Belgium, who was interviewed at RVPS, revealed on 19 February 1942 that the special broadcasts from Radio Belgique found many listeners, as they were not jammed.[19]

Black (secret) radio stations

There were five French Research Units (RUs, or British secret radio stations), which were given the identifying numbers F.1 to F.5. The French RUs used short wave as they were cheaper to operate, requiring less power. They were based in Britain, although they claimed to be operated by the resistance based in France. Most of their programmes were pre-recorded. The broadcast tended to be short – up to 12.5 minutes – due to the restriction of the discs, which was limited to 15 minutes, with the quality in the final 2.5 minutes being poor.[20] Each of these black stations would broadcast to a different audience, using both British and French broadcasters and scriptwriters.[21]

It is unclear how popular the RUs were in France; they were not frequently mentioned by those arriving to Britain from the country. They were perhaps heard only by a small number of people or else those interviewed did not listen to them. However, the fact that these stations were mentioned on even just a few occasions demonstrates that these black radios did sometimes reach an audience. For instance, an informant declared that he 'occasionally heard "Le Poste Inconnu" on the short waves just before the BBC French programme at 1915 hrs. The programme was very pro-de Gaulle and the station was supposed to be in Toulouse'.[22] Another informant interviewed declared that he used to listen to black stations, such as France Catholique, on 20-metre band.[23]

Radio Inconnue (F.1) was one of the two stations that were set up first. However, by August 1941, they had swapped their identifying numbers. Radio Inconnue transmitted between 15 November 1940 and 10 January 1944, which made it the longest-running French RU. This clandestine station was operated exclusively by SO1 (SOE propaganda section)/PWE. It was kept secret from both the Free French and the American propagandists for security reasons.[24] Radio Inconnue would target the '*petite bourgeoisie*', regularly attacking Pétain and Vichy, sowing confusion, rumours and discord within the Vichy administration and the Germans. In June 1941, Radio Inconnue began advocating minor acts of resistance such as slashing the tyres of German vehicles, and created a fictitious organisation, *Les chevaliers du coup de balai* (the Knights of the Sweeping Broom), to harass the Germans in France.

Radio Inconnue also advocated for Admiral François Darlan and Fernand de Brinon's assassination.[25] Admiral Darlan had replaced Pierre-Étienne Flandin as the head of the Vichy government on 9 February 1941, a position he held until April 1942, when he was replaced by Laval.[26] Fernand de Brinon was the delegate of the Vichy government in the occupied zone.[27] When Laval returned to power in 1942, Radio Inconnue suggested that Laval should be eliminated, too. In addition, Jacques Doriot and his party, the PPF, were intensively targeted during a campaign. Some other important themes developed by Radio Inconnue included the exploitation of France by Germany, the dissuasion of French workers from going to Germany, food requisitions and queue riots.[28] The three main speakers were Brits who spoke excellent French.[29]

Radio Travail (F.2) was the other radio that was set up alongside Radio Inconnue. It first broadcast on 17 November 1940 and was shut down on 21 May 1942, having broadcast once a day in the interim. Radio Travail was also operated by SO1/PWE.[30] It was initially supposed to target the northern French industrial workers, but it increasingly targeted the conservative trade unionists.[31] 'It dissociated itself from the Free French and the Communists.'[32] Radio Travail was very well informed on internal French politics during its existence, regularly attacked the Germans and encouraged passive resistance following the invasion of Russia in June 1941. By early 1942, Radio Travail was urging transport workers to strike against German invaders as part of a wider campaign and mentally prepared them to take an active role in sabotage if there were an Allied invasion.[33] The station's original speaker was an ex-miner from Lille, who was later joined by a trade union official.[34] In May 1942, Radio Travail was forced to close because of a lack of current information on the French labour movement. However, for the two years during which Radio Travail operated, 'it had usefully filled a niche'.[35]

La France Catholique (F.3) broadcast daily between early July 1941 and May 1942 when it closed temporarily. It resumed broadcasting in June 1943 and continued until mid-May 1944.[36] The station targeted the clergy and the religious community in France. It was designed 'to assist priests there by providing materials for their sermons'.[37] There were two types of material given to the priests on the radio. One was purely religious, lending credibility to their programmes. However, twice a week, material of propagandist nature would be broadcast on the air, using themes such as starving children, POWs in captivity in Germany and comparing Hitler with Satan. They also urged French citizens working for the Germans to deliberately sabotage their work and threatened any collaborators that they would be sentenced as traitors. There were two broadcasters working at La France Catholique, both of whom were Free French priests. Initially, Lagrave was the sole speaker until the station closed in May 1942 because he wanted to become a pilot in the Free French air force. However, he later returned part time and was assisted by Florent, also a pilot, when the station reopened.[38]

Radio Gaulle (F.4) broadcast from 25 August 1941 until 15 November 1942, but not daily. It created a total of 426 programmes over a period of 447 operational days.[39] The themes discussed in the broadcasts were aligned with de Gaulle's ideology. For example, the notions that: 'France should re-enter the war on the Allied side';[40] the current problems of France were rooted in the signing of the Armistice; the whole of the French Empire should fight and not just metropolitan France; de Gaulle should be seen as the symbol of French resistance, etc. The staff of Radio Gaulle remained anonymous, but they were provided by the Free French and were subsequently replaced in June 1942, something that pleased the PWE.[41] One informant who listened to that station around lunchtime and in the evening on approximately 27m or 31m (metre band) stated that he had problems hearing what was said on the radio due to jamming.[42]

Honneur et Patrie (F. 5) was known as Radio Patrie, the '*Radio de la Résistance*'. It began to broadcast on 11 October 1942 and continued until 2 April 1944. It made two broadcasts a day and one repeat.[43] The early broadcasts represented the views of one resistance group and were initially hostile to the Free French. As the war progressed and resistance activities in France started to pick up, however, they acted as the official voice of the resistance, often leading and guiding their actions.[44]

Radio stations based in France

There were a number of radio stations based in France that were overtly pro-German. Several of these were placed at the disposal of the Propaganda Abteilung although their staff were paid by RN. These included the state stations of Rennes-Alma, Paris Allouis ondes courtes I and Radio Normandie, as well as the private stations of the Poste Parisien and Bordeaux Sud-Ouest. They were at the service of Dr. Bofinger, who controlled the programmes broadcast by Radio Paris and made them 'available' for German propaganda.[45] Radio Normandie was requisitioned for the purpose of broadcasting Radio Paris programmes from 8 September 1940.[46]

An informant who arrived in England in September 1942 stated that the Germans had fully understood the propaganda value of music. For this reason, Radio Calais's broadcasting station was listened to by Parisians and those in the suburbs. Radio Calais played a lot of good English records and attracted a lot of listeners.[47]

Radio stations based in Belgium

After the fall of Belgium, the INR Standing Committee disappeared. However, some Belgian staff remained and resumed some of the functions of radio broadcasting. This allowed the military administration to organise the management of Radio Bruxelles,[48] which was set up in the building formerly occupied by INR.[49] On 31 July 1940, a managing commissioner was appointed with very broad powers; he could decide practically everything, except matters that could affect the legal status of the institute, which would require the prior authorisation of the military commander. The radio was financed by the Belgian administration with a budget of 41 million Belgian francs, rising to 45 million in 1943. The direction of the broadcasts depended on the managing commissioner, assisted by a chief of broadcasts for the French language, Lieutenant Sapper; a technical chief and a chief of musical broadcasts. All the chiefs were Germans, but some had a Belgian 'counterpart'. For Sapper, the counterpart was Gabriel Figeys.

The radio programmes were placed under the authority of the Militärverwaltung (military administration) and the Propaganda Abteilung.[50] Programmes were broadcast in the three official languages of Belgium – Dutch, French and German – and were alternated throughout the day. Broadcasting started at 07h00 and the last programme was aired at 20h15.[51]

The news mainly came from the agency Deutsches Nachrichtenbüro (DNB) and Belga-Press, as well as the two organisations specialising in radios: the Deutsche Drahtlose Dienste (DDD), which transmitted from Berlin, and the Deutsche Europa Sender (DES), which was based in Brussels. There was also a news service that wrote 'chronicles, theatrical and cinematographic news, reports, interviews and the Billet du jour'.[52] In the *Billet du jour* there were articles written by the speakers, which covered a wide variety of issues, such as the Secours d'Hiver, which sought to help people in dire situations, the need of solidarity in the country at the present time, etc.[53]

Let's take the programme broadcast on 15 September 1940 as an example. It was a Sunday morning. The first programme in French was the news, presented from 07h45 to 08h00 – this could be picked up in Vichy as well. This first news article was a direct attack on the Jews. It was followed by a justification for Germany declaring war. Reasons given were that the country had been forced to defend itself against its enemies, since Édouard Daladier had declared war on Germany on 3 September 1939. Britain had also organised a blockade against the women and children of Germany, resulting in starvation. Because of these actions, Germany asserted that it had the right to retaliate against Britain.[54]

After the news, there were two musical programmes of 30 minutes each from 09h00 to 10h00. A second French news programme came on at 13h15 to 13h30. From 14h15 to 14h30, there was a programme for children (*Le quart d'heure des petits*[55]). From 14h30 to 14h45, there was another musical programme and from 14h45 to 15h00, the third news programme. From 19h45 to 20h00, there was the last news programme of the day.[56]

The Jews were frequently mentioned in the broadcasts of Radio Bruxelles. There were several episodes of programmes devoted to the Jewish problem, for example, '*Le complot judéo-bolcheviste*' ('The Judeo-Bolshevik plan', 26 June 1941), '*La collusion judéo-bolchevique*' ('The Judeo-Bolshevik collusion', 11 July), '*La franc-maçonnerie et la juiverie internationale*' ('The freemason and international Jewery', 11 September), '*L'Angleterre juive*' ('The English Jew', 10 October), '*L'impuissance juive*' ('Jewish impotence', 30 October) and '*Les Juifs anglo-saxons*' ('The Anglo-Saxon Jews', 19 December)'.[57] There were also other prominent programmes that didn't focus solely on Jewish problems but nonetheless attacked the Jews on occasion. For example, the *Billet du jour* that was broadcast at 18h15 on 19 March 1941 was titled '*Qu'est-ce que le Juif?*' ('What is the Jew?') It stated that the Jewish problem needed to be tackled objectively. 'The racist's point of view is simple: (…) Is the Jew assimilable? Can he merge into a national community of white race? For any man of good faith, the answer leaves no doubt: No, the Jew is not assimilable.'[58]

During the first month of 1941, Radio Bruxelles emphasised the need to help organisations such as the Secours d'hiver, which had been created at the end of October 1940 to attempt to establish national solidarity.[59] During the freezing winter of 1940–41, a new problem arose in Belgium: famine. This threatened the fate of the Belgian population. Despite putting a ration system in place before the invasion, based on its experience of World War I, which allocated 450g of bread per person per day, the system as a whole did not work because of the disorganisation caused by the exodus. The daily ration of bread was reduced to 225g before the capitulation of 28 May. Thereafter, the situation worsened with the German requisitions and the birth of the black market.[60]

The response to the hungry population in Belgium was the encouragement of voluntary departure to Germany (compulsory labour, however, was not established until 1942 in Belgium). In 1941, this theme was picked up by the radio. On 24 January, the station discussed a letter from a 'former socialist activist', a trusted source, who talked about the welcome, the comfort and the 'abundant food' received while in Germany – a significant matter in these dire times.[61]

The radio tirelessly celebrated the benefits of being in the New Order. For example, there was a weekly Radio Bruxelles programme titled *Aujourd'hui et naguère* (Today and in the past), whose aim was to hold up all the mistakes and failures of the past against the imagined future with the New European Order. For those who remained hesitant to believe in the New Order, the campaigns of the Wehrmacht in the Mediterranean and in Russia soon provided new arguments in its favour.[62]

Radio Bruxelles also broadcast cultural programmes, such as the Saturday evening show *Trois chansonniers de chez nous* (Three singers of our house) on 21 June 1941. This was put on the air from 19h45 to 20h30, followed by a famous Belgian orchestra that played entertainment music from 20h30 to 21h00 hours.[63] On Sundays, there was the programme called *Notre lopin de terre* (Our patch of land) from 08h00 to 08h05, followed by a religious and secular music programme until the news at 09h30. After the news, the musical schedule resumed with *L'heure des auditeurs* (Listeners' hour). On the programme, which was launched and managed personally by Figeys, records were requested by listeners, who gave dedications for a birthday or shout-outs to a relative or friend. This programme was so successful that it went from being a weekly to a bi-weekly programme within three months of first airing. It also became a barometer of the listening figures for Radio Bruxelles, which had to apologise on many occasions because there simply wasn't time to share all the requests. It was said in Figeys's report of September 1941 that more than 10,000 letters had arrived at the station since the start of the programme in April. It was noted that prior to making a dedication, the listeners would voluntarily pay a small amount of money, mainly to the Secours d'hiver.[64]

An informant interviewed at the RVPS declared that Radio Paris, in collaboration with Radio Bruxelles, made every possible effort to provide the listeners with pleasant concerts. According to this source, people would listen to the *Radio-Journal* of Radio Paris simply because they had left their sets tuned in in order to listen to the concerts played on Radio Paris.[65]

The French-speaking programmes of Radio Bruxelles contained a good balance of literary and dramatic service. From 1 September 1940 to 31 August 1941, the station aired a total of '122 radiophonic games and plays. (…) 64 symphonic concerts, 25 lyric broadcasts and 597 recitals (…); the radio orchestra participated in 360 concerts, the dance orchestra organised some 122 and the Radio Bruxelles Choir performed in 94 occasions'.[66] We can thus see how the radio programme tried to attract listeners with a popular array of music and cultural programmes, slotting in disinformation and propaganda between the shows to normalise life under the German occupation and encourage allegiance to the Reich.

Radio stations based in Africa

Radio Brazzaville (Free French radio)

In October 1940, de Gaulle visited the French Congo because it had recently joined his authority. He decided that a centre for broadcasting and propaganda for the Free French needed to be created. De Gaulle's representatives found in Brazzaville, the capital of the new Free French Africa, a local station called Radio Club, the predecessor of Radio Brazzaville. This station was operated by a small group of amateurs who provided a limited news service. In addition, there was an 8kW station intended solely to communicate with France via the Morse code used by the PTT.

Shortly after de Gaulle's visit, Radio Brazzaville began broadcasting a regular service on short wave. On 16 December, de Gaulle received a message in London stating that seven daily programmes were now on the air: 'two in Morse, three to North Africa and Syria, and two programmes for the locals'.[67]

Philippe Desjardins, a young journalist, assisted by his half-brother, Michel Bréal, was appointed head of the information service. Desjardins foresaw that the radio had the ability to serve equatorial Africa and the bordering countries thanks to an increase of power.

However, to make Brazzaville a global station, Desjardins needed suitable equipment. De Gaulle agreed in March 1941 and the new station was renamed La Voix de la France libre.[68] The Radio Corporation of America (RCA) company was developing a 50kW transmitter at that time – the most powerful short-wave transmitter built in the USA. The Free French ordered it, with the understanding that the payment would be made directly to the Free French in dollars to avoid them owing anything to anyone in the future. During a conference in Brazzaville in May 1941, de Gaulle said that he wanted to install three 50kW transmitters to take into account future needs. This way, France would have three high-power stations after the war to broadcast to the metropolis, even if, as he foresaw, all short-wave stations in France were destroyed during the retreat.[69]

In the end, de Gaulle received one transmitter. Desjardins's Franco-African team, would succeed in:

> constructing a building 150 metres long to house the information and radio services, erect six oriented antennas supported by four pylons of 33 metres, laying kilometres of underground cables, carrying out complex electrical installations, mounting the transmitter, which involved the handling of hundreds of tons of delicate items, all that without workers, without technicians, without foremen.[70]

With this new station, Free France would make its voice heard worldwide but first and foremost in France. After the successful launch of French news, other languages were added, for example, 'English broadcasts for Great Britain, the United States and Canada, then in Spanish, in Italian and in Portuguese'.[71] Letters received from France confirmed that Radio Brazzaville was heard in Paris, albeit with difficulty.[72]

The editors of Brazzaville became passionately militant very quickly once it started its broadcasting service and this was something that de Gaulle encouraged. Using the new platform, they multiplied the appeals to the French of the empire. From the beginning of 1941, French West Africa jammed the broadcasts of Radio Club, 'while Radio Brazzaville jammed the shortwave broadcasts of Dakar'.[73] By December 1942, however, the Free French could still only use their old transmitter, whose power had been increased to 5kW. Using Radio Brazzaville, de Gaulle could at least broadcast messages when he was banned by Churchill from broadcasting from London,[74] during the period between the American invasion of North Africa (which belonged to Vichy) as part of Operation *Torch* in November 1942, and shortly after Darlan was assassinated on 24 December 1942 due to disagreement between Churchill/ the Americans, and de Gaulle on the decision of the appointment of Darlan as the High Commissioner in North Africa.[75]

Radiodiffusion Nationale Belge in Léopoldville

When Spaak and Pierlot got back together with the ministers already present in England, Albert de Vleeschauwer and Camille Gutt, they quickly realised the need to create an official station for the government to broadcast Belgian politics and showcase Belgium's war effort outside the restricted framework set up by the BBC, to which Radio Belgique was compelled to adhere. Delfosse, who had presided over the last meeting of the standing committee of the INR in Brussels on 29 July 1940, later joined the new Belgian government in London, where he was appointed Minister of Communications, making him an ideal candidate to oversee the creation of RNB.[76]

The purpose of having a Belgian radio in Congo was to give independent news about the contribution of Belgium to the final victory; the economy, which was geared towards the war effort to help Belgian allies; and the role of Belgian Congo, which provided a wide range of strategic products, including uranium. For that reason, it was logical that the new transmitter should be installed in Léopoldville (Kinshasa) in the Belgian Congo. This short-wave transmitter was purchased in the USA in 1941 and its assembly began early in 1942. On 13 October 1942, the Moniteur[77] officially announced the birth of the RNB – a new organisation whose headquarters would remain in London for an indefinite period until the end of the war.

The BBC offered a place for the RNB in the BBC grid schedule and promised that the content of RNB broadcasting would be considered independent of Radio Belgique. On 9 February 1943, the first broadcast of the RNB took place from London. The time was shared alternately between French and Flemish and the programme had 15 minutes of speaking time. The length of the RNB's programmes doubled on 29 March 1943, broadcasting at 13h15 and 22h30. On 13 May 1943, the Léopoldville transmitter was inaugurated with speeches from Pierlot, British Foreign Secretary Anthony Eden, and Pierre Ryckmans, the governor of the Belgian Congo.[78]

There were three different news programmes broadcast on RNB to occupied Belgium from London, New York and Congo: "*Les Belges vous parlent de Londres*", "*Les Belges vous parlent de New York*", and "*Les Belges vous parlent du Congo*".[79]

Radio stations based in Switzerland

From the first half of the 1930s, la Société suisse de radiodiffusion (SSR), the Swiss Broadcasting Company, was determined to "give to the radio a national character", to "explain the ideal and the development of the fundamental principles of our democracy", even to "develop good humour, but, if possible, a Swiss humour".[80]

By the late 1930s, a new threat called ideological infiltration appeared on the radio.[81] The Swiss authorities responded by introducing a proposal to the parliament on 9 December 1938 to protect the values of Switzerland in case their neighbours attempted to impose upon them the authoritarian doctrines of the north. The resulting official document enumerated the various aspects of cultural life and specified the tasks necessary for cultural defence, such as the protection of German-speaking writers and editors in Switzerland, theatre, popular shows, fine arts, cinema, scientific institutions, architecture and folklore. Special attention was given to the radio as it was viewed as the most powerful tool for propaganda because the airwaves could travel across borders.[82] The role of broadcasting was 'to make our national spirit known whilst embracing its regional characteristics; to show its scope, beauty and purpose; to ensure that the Swiss understand and always respect each other'.[83]

Before World War II, Swiss radio had a semi-private status and was placed under the jurisdiction of Département fédéral des postes et des chemins de fer (Federal Department of Post and Railways). For technical and administrative reasons, all the radio installations, including the transmitters and studios, were placed under the Direction générale des PTT (Directorate-General of PTT).

However, the development of the programmes had been entrusted to the SSR since its creation in 1931. Radio Lausanne and Radio Genève were local companies that produced and presented the programmes, but the state controlled the general orientation of the radio and their broadcasts. The Directorate-General of PTT was responsible for the supervision of the application of the concessions given to the SSR. The radio stations had to follow some general principles, such as defending the national interests, enshrining the spirit of impartiality, etc., which was not to the liking of everyone; some would have preferred to be under a department that was 'better qualified in artistic and intellectual matters'.[84] The SSR was only authorised to broadcast the news bulletins prepared by the Agence télégraphique suisse (ATS). The ATS was owned by the Swiss Association of Newspaper Publishers and was the sole news agency in Switzerland, which had the monopoly of news.[85]

On 29 August 1939, the day when the state of active military service became mandatory for the whole of Switzerland, Marcel Pilet-Golaz, head of the Federal Department of Post and Railways, requested that the government suspend the status of the SSR so that radios could be used as an instrument to disseminate government policies. Pilet-Golaz wanted the radio to become a special service of the federal postal administration. As a result, on 2 September, the SSR was renamed the Service de la radiodiffusion suisse (SR).[86]

It was also decided that until further notice, the responsibility for the programme would be assumed by a single radio station for each transmitter. For programmes transmitted via Sottens, Radio Lausanne was the choice, although this situation would remain for just a few months. Alfred Glogg, the former general manager of the SSR, was appointed the new head of the SR from 2 September. He instituted internal censorship, whereby spoken broadcasts had to be submitted to him in advance, and he could request to read any manuscript if he so wished. However, the instructions of Pilet-Golaz were not explicit. If the SR considered that it depended in this field directly on the PTT administration regarding administrative and technical matters, it was a different matter when it came to programmes. The radio broadcasters deemed it unthinkable to submit the content of the broadcasts, including their cultural characteristics to the officials responsible for operating technical installations. To do so would create an impoverishment of the programme and a setback in the quality of their work, as a certain degree of autonomy was needed to maintain a creative space at work.[87]

With the approach of hostilities, the general staff of the army showed an interest in the creation of a press and radio section in the event of war. They decided that when the time came, they would create a division in charge of press-related issues. This would be called La Division presse et radio. Colonel Kurt Schenker, director of the Bern radio station in civilian life, was appointed to run this new press and radio division. Schenker had planned to place all the radio activities under the control of the military, however, Pilet-Golaz did not like this idea and limited his division to military matters only. Schenker's main tasks now were to prepare news programmes about the life of the troops for the civilian population, and to put in place censorship that would apply to all broadcasts in relation to military questions. This resulted in conflicts of jurisdiction between Pilet-Golaz and Schenker.[88]

The Swiss radio sector was not militarised as Schenker had imagined[89] (although there were a few programmes dedicated to the soldiers, for example, *Pour nos soldats*, *Chez nos soldats* and military songs that were popularised following the creation of a military choir in March 1941[90]), nor was it a state radio put in the hands of a minister of culture, or a propaganda ministry. It was, however, closely controlled through internal censorship that was encouraged at all levels, and by official censorship.[91]

By 1941, 49 per cent of Radio Sottens's programmes were dedicated to music and 37 per cent to spoken programmes. The popular spoken programmes among the listeners were those that discussed political events or social developments. The SR wanted to keep its listeners informed about economic and social activities, artistic events taking place in the country, the latest scientific developments and the Swiss daily life in both the military and civilian spaces.

The French-speaking stations of Geneva and Lausanne supplied programmes alternately to the Sottens transmitter. Radio Geneva provided programmes called *Micro-Magazine* (started in 1936) and *Courrier du soir* (Evening Mail). Radio Lausanne provided the programmes *Echos d'ici et d'ailleurs (Echo from here and elsewhere)*, and *Micro dans la vie (Micro in life)*. *Micro-Magazine* presented a varied and rapid sequence of topics that listeners found attractive.[92] Indeed, the content of all these programmes was diverse. For example, there were countless reports on Swiss news, the issues of the day, songs and 'rhyming games', interviews of literary men, recipes and practical advice, sketches, and sports news. Sottens showcased Switzerland in the best light and displayed its national heritage in all its forms. Regarding the principles of objectivity and prudence demanded by the authorities, Sottens followed the path of neutrality, putting itself at the service of the Swiss State, even if that sometimes meant the listeners did not necessarily like what they heard on the radio.

Not all the spoken programmes had the same success. Some were on the air for months and years, while others did not last that long. Conversely, some topics became so popular that they were later developed into programmes of their own. For instance, the programme *Courrier de la Croix-Rouge internationale* started out as a topic of interest with *Courrier du soir* but was later, in 1941, given its own broadcasting time on one evening every two weeks by the Geneva station.[93] There were also programmes about the Comité international de la Croix-Rouge (CICR), whose aim was to appeal to the generosity of the listeners and who used the radio as a tool to enable it to promote its activities and support humanitarian efforts. Brief communiqués would be issued in several languages, growing to seven by the end of the war.[94]

Another example of a popular programme was René Payot and his show about major political events, *La Situation internationale*. This programme began from 24 October 1941 at the Geneva Station. Thanks to this weekly programme, Payot gained an extraordinary reputation in Switzerland, France and Belgium. He commented on news about military operations and diplomatic developments and spoke every Friday for 10 minutes at 19h30. He had multiple sources: he received official communiqués, confidential reports from all over the world, handwritten notes and letters. He then filtered and analysed the information he had received as he was concerned with the truth.[95] If Payot's words had a liberating effect and his listeners drew great moral support and hope from them, it was due to the wealth of information and the honesty of his comments provided on the air. For example, in October 1941, he discussed the execution of hostages, which he considered harsh but in accordance with the law of war.[96]

Radio stations based in the USA

Walter S. Lemmon, a young naval radio engineer, founded WRUL Boston radio largely with his own funds in order to foster international understanding, having foreseen the advantages of short-wave radio. He christened it the World Radio University or WRUL. This was a non-commercialised radio station and counted on the support of American citizens' contributions to help win the war. Before 1939, this university of the airwaves introduced language courses such as basic English and occasionally broadcast in several foreign languages. Yet WRUL's schedule encompassed a wide variety of cultural elements, of which language teaching was just one dimension.

With the looming of the war in Europe in 1939 and the Axis forces spreading propaganda by transmitting on both long and short waves, WRUL took the initiative to counteract this negative influence with honest broadcasts using dominant languages as well as some minor ones. In fact, WRUL became the largest non-commercial station in the USA that went 'all out' in the defence of democracy, incorporating messages of encouragement and sympathy to the dominated peoples of the world in its programmes. Transmitters of over 50,000 watts were located in Scituate, Massachusetts. The radio station was leased by the US government for the duration of the war. Many programmes originated from the Office of War Information in New York City, and it operated on a 24-hour schedule using the same channels.[97]

The first foreign languages on the air were French and Spanish, and these occupied a large portion of the daily schedule. This was followed by Italian and German. The subsequent languages showed how WRUL had successfully covered the world's linguistic atlas; it was broadcasting in many foreign languages, including 'Albanian, Alsatian, Arabic, Austrian, Czechoslovak, Danish, Dutch, Finnish, French, German, Greek, Hungarian, Italian, Norwegian, Persian, Polish, Portuguese, Spanish, Swedish, Thai, Turkish, and Yugoslav (Serbo-Croatian)'.[98] A programme in Arabic was broadcast to the Near East when it became the focus of attention in the battle zone. The Alsatian language was included in the French programme. Some of the minor languages had their allotted schedules increased or decreased depending on the changes in the political and military events. For example, when the Germans threatened the Balkans, WRUL increased the number of programmes in Serbo-Croatian. It was thought that WRUL was influential in Yugoslavia's decision to resist the German invasion.[99]

The workforce at WRUL was polyglot and included many people with PhDs working as volunteers, alongside college professors, instructors, exiled patriots and foreign students. Some had radio experience, but others didn't. Harvard University supplied the station with speakers who not only knew the language, but also the temperaments, tastes and interests of the people speaking that language. Several of these exiled speakers also worked as writers, public speakers and editors. Each speaker had to know at least one other language in addition to English. There were also guest speakers, who came from a variety of backgrounds – for example, statesmen, authors, scientists and scholars. Many speakers, including the most regular ones, remained anonymous or used fictitious names for fear of endangering their future chances of returning home or endangering the lives of their family members who remained in the home country.[100]

Most listeners abroad incurred greater danger because the German government in occupied territories and the puppet governments in place had decreed punitive measures such as fines and imprisonment for listening to American broadcasts. Yet the listeners remained faithful to the Boston station. WRUL believed that 'truth makes the best propaganda when one's cause is just'.[101] As a Polish informant interviewed on 20 October 1942 stated, he often 'listened to an American broadcast direct on 19.45m'. He also listened to French, Polish, or English programmes in the mornings and at night. He enjoyed these programmes as they were not jammed and there were more news programmes, although he did not think it was as reliable as the BBC.[102]

Here is a testimony from the Pyrénées, in non-occupied France, that was received at WRUL:

> I don't know what we would do without the WRUL station of Boston. Imagine how impatiently we await the hour of the programme every evening, since it is really the only one that, with some exceptions, we hear with perfect clarity. Without your station we would be almost without

news, because all attempts to hear anything other than broadcasts for propaganda purposes are in vain; they are intentionally scrambled. So far yours seems to escape the rule and we hope that it will remain so in the future. I wanted to tell you with what interest you are listened to, and to express my gratitude to you and that of my friends and neighbours.[103]

In the BBC report of 8 April 1941, a further comment was made by a Pau engineer, who stated that:

in his experience the stations listened to were 'first the BBC, second WRUL at 9.30 and third Brazzaville'. He had found that WRUL was more popular than any other American station largely because it has only recently come to the notice of the public and is regarded as a real 'war station'. He himself had never met anyone who listened systematically to any station other than our own, WRUL and Brazzaville.[104]

The BBC report of 1 July 1942 observed that American broadcasts were becoming increasingly popular thanks to their perceived impartiality in dealing with French affairs.[105] An informant mentioned in the same year that he heard on WRUL about one of the raids before the BBC reported it.[106]

It would seem that WRUL suffered some local jamming but to a much lesser degree than other pro-Allied stations. Due to an increase in confiscation of letters and other interdictions, WRUL saw a drop of direct mail coming from Europe. However, more letters were received indirectly, forwarded via friends and other correspondents residing in America.[107]

Radio-Brazzaville sometimes coordinated its schedule with that of Boston and urged its listeners to listen to WRUL programmes at a specific time. Many European black stations also used WRUL as a news source. Even the BBC recorded many of the WRUL programmes in London and rebroadcasted them. The BBC-WRUL relationship was a traditional one. The BBC, prior to entering the war, had rebroadcasted several of Radio-Boston's English language transmissions. The two programmes *Friendship Bridge* and *Namesake Towns* were most popular among the listeners and created a bridge between British and American people.[108]

Radio stations based in Russia

'Soon after the creation of the Soviet Government in Moscow, the Department of Agitation and Propaganda was setup [sic] to coordinate and control all the media outlets in the nation.'[109] The Russian government took in its stride the radio, a new technology that would spread the word more effectively than newspapers and magazines over the vast land. Indeed, the radio soon became the way to disseminate information, including messages from the central government in Moscow and broadcasts about health, agriculture, etc. Under Lenin's leadership, radio spread messages across Europe and Africa.

Ten stations were operating in the Soviet Union within two years of the founding of a Moscow radio laboratory in 1922. Radio broadcasting remained firmly in the hands of the Soviet government, although organisations and collective farms were allowed to operate radio stations. Recognising the important role of international radio broadcasting, the Soviet leadership decided to establish Radio Moscow, which was set up in 1929, initially in three languages: French, English and German.

Subsequently, the foreign language department grew further and offered 'Swedish, Turkish, Portuguese, Spanish, Italian, Hungarian, Czech, and Russian services by 1932'.[110] Radio Moscow, like the domestic radio stations, highlighted both the success of the 1917 Revolution and the attainments of the Soviet government.[111]

From 1938 onwards, Hitler's territorial expansion into Austria and Czechoslovakia made the Soviet leadership nervous and presented them with new challenges on their western borders. The signing of the Molotov–Ribbentrop Pact in August 1939, a non-aggression pact between Nazi Germany and the Soviet Union, kept the Germans away from the Soviet Union until the invasion on 22 June 1941. When the German troops invaded Soviet territory, there had already been a great building up of radio stations and there were now more than 100 stations in the Soviet Union. The invasion caught the Soviet leadership by surprise, which meant they had little time to put Radio Moscow on a war footing. However, Radio Moscow still managed to put on broadcasts in the language of those living in German-occupied territory during this early stage of the war, and increased broadcasting time with the newly constructed powerful stations as the Soviet leadership acknowledged the need to counteract German radio broadcasting.[112]

Radio Moscow's initial messages were of 'premature declarations of victory, reports of atrocities on the opposing side, and accounts of conditions on the enemy's home front'.[113] It was not until 1942 that Radio Moscow managed to gain the trust of its listeners when it changed strategy so that the messages were more reliable and allowed listeners to reach their own conclusions.[114]

During wartime broadcasting, there were 13 native broadcasters who enabled Radio Moscow to produce programmes in most European languages. Among them was a strong German-language department, which became particularly useful in the post-war occupation of Germany. Technology was also upgraded, which allowed Radio Moscow to broadcast to most of the Eurasian continent and speak in 29 different languages by 1945.[115]

According to a report by the BBC monitoring service dated 27 July 1941, during 1940 and 1941, the daily total duration of Moscow's broadcasts in French averaged three to three hours and 20 minutes. Radio Moscow broadcast to Canada, Europe and West Africa. The broadcast to France happened from 14h00 before 17 July 1941 and at 13h40 after 17 July 1941, except for during the German invasion when an additional 30-minute broadcast at 05h30 to France was slotted in. For several days after 17 July 1941, violent appeals were made to the French colonies of North Africa (Morocco, Algeria and Tunisia) and the whole African continent that Radio Moscow would tell them the truth every day in a 20-minute bulletin. The early evening and night-time broadcasts always happened at the same time and kept their wavelengths during this period. The broadcast from 18h45 to 19h15 used two wavelengths. The following transmission was from 20h30 to 21h30. The one-hour long broadcast at 20h30 was the most important one of the day. The last transmission was from 23h00 to 23h30.

The Russian anthem, the 'Internationale', was usually played twice every day with the French programme, first at 13h40, followed by the news in other languages (Romanian, Italian, Bulgarian and Serbian), and again at 23h00. The reason for playing the 'Internationale' at certain times during the day was technical: it was used to introduce the first sequence of foreign language broadcasts of the day.[116] Frequent reminders were made during the bulletins to remind people of the identity of the station they were listening to, such as *Ici Moscou*. The bulletins were divided into topical sections and an announcement was made prior to the start of such a topic using the stock phrase '*Veuillez écouter maintenant, chers auditeurs...*'[117]

A regular news broadcast would follow a set structure. First, there would be 'the reading of an official communiqué from the Soviet Information Bureau (usually signed by its deputy chairman Lozovskii) or with a review of that day's Soviet press.'[118] Then, it would be *Nos informations*, which would focus on the Russian war effort. Too many Russian names and places were mentioned in this broadcast – French listeners would have cared more about Russian views on world events. *Quelques informations internationales* was the next item focusing on foreign news, which consisted mainly of summaries of foreign press reports and accounts of German brutalities on the local population in occupied territories.[119]

After the invasion of Russia on 22 June, a major shift took place in its programmes. First, the space given to music, such as folk songs, military marches or classical pieces in French bulletins decreased significantly, resulting in more direct calls for resistance and more regular political talks. These appeals were placed in between various items in the bulletin, without prior notice, and would sometimes last several minutes on special occasions such as 14 July. The tone and content of these calls to action were very 'French', as if a Frenchman had written them. They would usually come on during the 20h30 bulletin, using personalities such a writer, a journalist, an author or a general who had lived in Paris during the inter-war years. By using such a variety of speakers, Radio Moscow attempted to appeal to the largest possible base of French listeners.[120] At the end of the broadcast, a reminder of the transmission times was given in GMT as well as their respective wavelengths.[121]

There were usually two broadcasters for each broadcast, a man and a woman. From time to time, the woman would read the bulletin on her own. The BBC monitor, who transcribed and translated the bulletins, felt that both presenters were without doubt French:

> Her delivery is measured and forceful, for a French person she speaks rather slowly and always succeeds in keeping her voice completely flat without making it sound dull; her announcing suggests cold, cast iron determination and a fanatical belief in the Soviet cause – a belief which is prompted by reason and logic, not by sentiment.[122]

The announcement to introduce the bulletins was made in the same way: 'Proletarians from all countries! Unite! Here is Moscow. Here is Moscow on the (-) meter strip. Here is Moscow. Here is Moscow on the (-) meter strip. Warning! We start our transmission.'[123]

Radio Moscow's broadcast to France from the end of May to the beginning of June 1940 were pessimistic in nature: the predicament and defeat of France were inevitable. For example, according to the BBC's Daily Digest of World Broadcasts (DDWB) on 31 May 1940, the following comments were made by Radio Moscow:

> By reaching the Channel ports the bulk of the German Armies are directly threatening England. It is therefore unlikely that large English reinforcements will be sent to France. On the contrary, it is more than likely that units hastily formed by the British Government will remain in Britain to defend the Mother-Country. Consequently, the French Army will be left to itself much more than in 1914–1918.[124]

From December 1940 to 21 June 1941, Radio Moscow presented programmes about the international situation in general. However, when the relations between Russia and Germany became spiteful, more talks on political matters were broadcast in French. The Vichy regime was, for the first time, condemned by Radio Moscow on 1 July 1941. It was not until 5 July, four days later, that Moscow made its first direct appeal to the French resistance. The DDWB of 6 July 1941 noted this message: 'Frenchmen, do not follow Pétain and Darlan any longer. Oppose Hitler and his gang by all means in your power. Now is the time for France to start the real battle for her freedom, on all fronts and by all means.'[125] From that point on, Radio Moscow's messages became more frequent, detailed and specific.

Radio Moscow succeeded in setting up a steady propaganda line for both before and after 22 June 1941, targeting the people of Vichy and those from the previous government.[126] As noted by the DDWB of 11 July 1941: 'German Fascism would never have conquered France if it had not been allied with the Lavals, the Daladiers, the Weygands and other agents of the German Fascists.'[127]

Radio Moscow's broadcasts to France after 22 June 1941 targeted the spirit of nationalism in its listeners and appealed for unity and support for men like de Gaulle and the Allies, even though they had previously been called capitalists and imperialists. The ideological conflict was now put aside in the face of the greater common enemy, and Moscow's broadcasts in French reflected the necessities of the time.[128]

CHAPTER 3

BBC broadcasts

Among the wide variety of French topics discussed by the BBC, this book focuses on the coverage of food provision and food shortages. Getting hold of food was a daily challenge in France. Talking about food raised interest as it addressed the concerns of BBC listeners, making the BBC's broadcast 'personal' and relevant. Furthermore, the raw materials, finished products and food resources from France played a key role in supporting Germany's war effort, so German needs took priority over those of the French population – a fact that many French resented bitterly. Discussions about food, food shortages and the French love of food could thus be used as a psychological weapon to counteract German propaganda.

It is widely acknowledged that the provision of food was one of the primary concerns of the French during the war years as food became scarce in the markets, towns and cities. The lack of food itself was a significant factor in the perception of the occupation as the French population believed they knew who was responsible for the food shortage. The Ravitaillement général (or 'general supply'),[1] an institution responsible for setting up the overall plan for the collection and distribution of food and coupons and monitoring offences, was introduced in France in September 1940 and remained in place until towards the end of the decade. It was unpopular among the public from the beginning and throughout the occupation period. The provisional governments and the first governments of the Fourth Republic failed to reconcile the French with it because their policy was closely linked to the politics of the Vichy regime and German occupation.[2]

Germany's policy towards food in France was unambiguous. Hitler's vision as expressed in *Mein Kampf* shaped his policy towards France:[3] he viewed France as the foremost military power on the European continent, having no serious rival to oppose it and, therefore, he thought that a powerful France would be a danger to Germany.[4] He considered that France's political aim was to Balkanise Germany – an action that was necessary to safeguard her dominant position in Europe and to prevent the establishment of a unified power in Germany.[5] Hitler therefore believed that Germany would be in a stronger position to win the war if it requisitioned most of France's raw materials and finished products, including food and wine. His vision was rigorously implemented by the German authorities in France. For example, on 5 and 6 August 1942, Field Marshal Hermann Göring, Hitler's right-hand man, summoned the *Reichskommissars* for the occupied territories as well as the military commanders to the Air Ministry in Berlin to discuss the food situation in France.[6] Göring's declaration at this meeting was a strong testimony to the political climate at that time:

> Moreover, the French population is so stuffed with food that it is really a disgrace. I saw villages where they paraded with their long white bread under their arms. In small villages, I saw baskets full of oranges, dates from North Africa. Yesterday someone said. 'This is true, the normal food of these people comes from the black market and barter, the ration card is only an extra.' That is the secret of the cheerfulness of the people in France. Without it, they would not be so cheerful.[7]

Göring continued by expressing his view of collaboration between the Germans and the French, declaring:

> Collaboration, it's only M. Abetz who does that, not me. The collaboration of the French, I see it this way: that they hand over all they can until they can give no more: if they do so voluntarily, I will say that I collaborate; if they eat up everything themselves, then they do not collaborate. We need the French to realise it.[8]

Given Göring's policy concerning food and collaboration, which he vividly expressed at a time when there was a severe food shortage in French towns and cities, it is not surprising that hunger and suffering dominated the lives of urban French people throughout the war.

Thus, the German authorities tried to systematically exploit the food resources in France. Food was undoubtedly important for military purposes. The military strategy of Blitzkrieg did not always allow sufficient food to be brought forward for the troops on the field. As a result, the troops had no other option but to live off the land. People in the rural areas of both Normandy and Brittany in particular suffered from the occupiers' need for food as the Germans had a significant presence there. As was common practice throughout the occupation, the Germans made their purchases without rationing cards.[9]

The occupation of France was a recurring theme in BBC broadcasts. Maurice Schumann spoke on 3 September 1940 in the name of the Free French in London, blaming Hitler as the sole person responsible for the loss of their land, freedom and liberties. He declared:

> We only had the choice between dishonour, the road to servitude, and the struggle for the defence of our land, our homes, and our liberties. And this terrible dilemma is imposed by Hitler himself on to us, by carrying out what he wrote in Mein Kampf, the great confession that he has always refused to deny: 'My main aim is to isolate and to crush our mortal enemy, France'.[10]

Food supply, food shortage and the black market were also discussed on numerous occasions in BBC broadcasts, acknowledging the concerns and discontent of the French, instilling pro-British sentiments, giving information on the broader picture of the food supply situation in various parts of France, and calling for passive and, later, active resistance towards the occupier. To assert the credibility of the broadcasts, the BBC used a number of sources originating from neutral countries as well as from Vichy and Germany. It is impossible to say how many broadcasts overall discussed this topic as many have not survived the war or are still buried in the BBC Written Archives, which are catalogued in chronological order and are not topic specific.

The discussions on the subject of food did not take place at a regular time or occur in a specific programme. It all came down to the subjects to be debated on a particular day, as well as whether the radio presenters had received information from France – letters, for example – or whether the BBC Monthly Intelligence Report had reported on food shortages. Nevertheless, what recordings there are provide valuable information about how the BBC viewed food as a link to people's hearts and minds, especially to the youth and families.

1940

Economic exploitation and food shortages

Food shortage in France had become an issue of interest as soon as the Armistice was signed in June 1940. In the police report of 22 July, food supply was a major topic. The report noted that there were some signs of improvement; a week earlier, railway services had partly resumed and the supply of food to wholesale businesses at the *halles centrales* (main markets) had improved. These factors contributed to a more regular supply for retailers, easing the long queues of buyers near the shops. Some retailers who had previously closed their shops had now reopened: nearly 50 per cent of commercial establishments, including Félix Potin and Julien Damoy, were now open for business in the Paris area, with more retailers requesting to reopen. However, they had tremendous difficulties replenishing the stock, largely due to the lack of rolling stock and restrictions on fuel supply. Consequently, horse-drawn carriages had to be put back into service, only partly making up for the lack of motor transport. The report also detailed the difficulties of businesses in obtaining certain food products in Paris and its suburbs due to the lack of an adequate commercial transport system.[11]

Towards the beginning of August 1940, transport gradually recovered, especially by rail. But there were many problems remaining, such as the destruction of railway lines, bridges, train stations, roads and canals. The Germans used the French railways for its military transport for the war, but also to transport the levies of agricultural and food products bound for Germany.[12] The supply of large distribution centres in big cities such as Paris, Lyon, Marseille, Bordeaux, etc. for the French population was particularly affected.[13] The Société nationale des chemins de fer français (SNCF) saw its fleet of usable locomotives going to Germany but not returning to France.

The number of usable locomotives fell from 13,675 in 1940 to 11,423 in 1943. The number of usable wagons fell from 245,200 in 1940 to 198,300 in 1943.[14]

The year 1940 was marked by German requisitions, the implementation of food ration cards and food priority cards, a ban on hunting, the progressive deterioration of food supply, and hunger. 'Integrating France into their war economy meant the systematic requisition of agricultural as well as industrial goods'.[15] There is evidence that the German policy of exploiting French economic resources was executed in the following order: looting and pillaging executed by Göring, the seizing of stock, and finally the purchasing of all the goods available on the market with their strong Reichsmark.[16]

Monetary policy was part of the economic exploitation, particularly with the severe inflation of the French franc. As Göring revealed during a conference in Berlin about the food situation in August 1942, 'The franc does not need to have more value than some paper reserved for a certain usage. Only then will France be hit as we want.'[17] It is likely that Göring, who was in charge of economic policies for all occupied territories, would have had this in mind as early as 1940. The French franc was devaluated significantly to merely a third of what it was worth prior to the war.[18] The Armistice also meant the French were responsible for the upkeep of the German army, the cost of which was estimated by the Germans at 20 million marks per day, with a fixed exchange rate that represented a significant over-evaluation of the mark.[19]

The exploitative German occupation policy was taken up by the BBC. François Quilici, a speaker there, pointed out to his listeners that collaboration would eventually lead to the destruction of France. He quoted from Hitler's *Mein Kampf*: 'When I want to destroy a country, I will use its nationals who, by ambition and cowardice, will act more doggedly than my army and my police.'[20]

Quilici explained on 1 August that the systematic looting and attempts to starve the French were part of the Nazis' aim to destroy France, but he also claimed that the German authorities would, in time, facilitate the return of refugees to the occupied zone in order to save the harvest.[21] This was proven true, as reflected in the police report of 26 August that highlighted that the tonnage of food arrivals had not increased in Paris, despite an increase in the number of refugees arriving. The police report also noted two further issues affecting the availability of food for sale: the occupation authorities requisitioned significant amounts and the regional centres purchased food at the production centres at a higher price than those on the Parisian market, causing a further reduction of available supplies intended for the French population. Already, large queues of consumers formed early in the morning near the shops selling farm produce, groceries and meat of all kinds. There were also considerable queues in front of establishments that sold limited quantities of rarer products,[22] such as 'sugar, coffee, chocolate, tea, pasta, butter, eggs, fresh pork, as well as certain cleaning items such as soap, bleach and laundry detergent'.[23]

In the same broadcast, Quilici declared that a strong mark would create difficulties for French families and inevitably lead to food price increases. Food products would become less and less affordable. This would lead families to despair and people to revolt against such an unbearable situation. Quilici predicted that the authorities would suppress the rebellion in a bloody fashion. The Germans hoped, continued Quilici, that the French would have no other choice but to turn to the foreign leader (Hitler) for help as no one else would be there to lead them. However, the French nation would eventually thwart the German plot because Hitler did not understand the tenacity of the French people when it came to suffering. Moreover, Vichy would soon appoint judges to the Supreme Court who would work for the benefit of the occupiers rather than the patriotism of the French.[24]

Price hikes were, indeed, already happening in France. The 22 July police report indicated that the control of prices and sales surveillance were stepped up in all areas. The various services of the Préfecture de police carried out price verifications on a massive scale. On the other hand, the Supply Department regulated the distribution of stored products to maintain the level of stocks in reserve, thus limiting the amount released for retail distribution to customers. To prevent retail traders from taking advantage of the current situation, the authorities immediately set up measures to prevent retailers from making unjustified or abusive price increases for customers.

However, despite the decree, food shortages were soon driving up prices beyond the cap imposed by the authorities. During the police investigation, a total of 263 dossiers on illegal price increases was compiled, involving shops selling fruit and vegetables, cheese, butter, meat and other foodstuffs.[25] From 16 August, the Criminal Court of the Seine pronounced 19 convictions for illegal price increases with penalties of up to three months in prison and a fine of 500 francs.[26] Within a month, and from 6 September, the number of convictions went up significantly: 83 were convicted in total, and they were given a higher penalty of six months in prison and a fine of up to 1,000 francs.[27] This would become a common feature in subsequent police reports. There was clearly aggravation as the situation worsened as people railed against the daily queues in front of shops and the requisitioning. The latter was a significant issue. For example, on 17 October, at the Marché de la Villette in Paris, out of 3,824 cows put on sale, 1,065 were taken by the Germans; out of 389 calves, 96 were taken; and out of 74 pigs, 74 were taken (none was taken out of the 3,605 sheep as this was not the meat of choice of the Germans).[28]

Quilici's technique of using a dramatic ending to his broadcast as well as repeating the key message during the broadcast would soon become the common feature of motivational speeches by BBC speakers. These aimed to keep the momentum alive among the ever-increasing number of BBC listeners, stressing the French final victory over the oppressors and their allies, and that any act of collaboration would be detrimental to the French people.

British blockade and the risk of famine

Following the intensive German propaganda surrounding the British blockade against France, there was a spike of BBC broadcasts countering these efforts and justifying the blockade. The broadcasts reveal how the BBC responded to the attack on the British by Radio Paris, the collaborators and the 'fools' who blamed the British for the blockade and believed that food shortages in France were a result of it.

On 16 September, Georges Boris spoke positively of the blockade to the French population. He drew a parallel between the current war and the Great War, explaining that during the Great War, the blockade had been imposed upon their elders and themselves in the north and east regions of France. The French had accepted the blockade then because they had understood that it could act as a powerful weapon against the enemy and would eventually lead France to victory. Now, when the Germans, their agents or those 'fools' spoke to the French about the blockade, their purpose was to turn the French against the blockade and in doing so, repudiate their chance for freedom. The French were as courageous as the heroic people of Norway and the Netherlands, whose governments had not capitulated. Norway and the Netherlands also suffered from the blockade as much as France, but the population had accepted it, understanding that this was the price of freedom.[29]

Not only did Boris use patriotic appeals and historical arguments to persuade his audience, but he also defended the British blockade rigorously as a military action that had proven effective in the last war. Those French who believed that the British blockade was an action against France to prevent the French from having access to food were 'fools'. Boris's broadcast was inspired by the BBC Monthly Intelligence Report of 2 September, which concluded that Radio Paris was disconcerted by the number of people who would not hide their support for the British blockade. Even those who had to collaborate because they felt they had no other choice might have been secretly hoping for a British victory.[30] So, this intelligence report, written in the early years of the war, revealed signs that the French supported the British blockade. As expressed by a listener from St. Gervais les Bains in his letter on 17 September to the BBC: 'We must suffer in order to get rid of the Boches, that all Frenchmen realise. We suffer a hundred times more through what is taken from us by the Germans than from the lack of the few provisions that cannot come to us by sea'.[31]

In the same broadcast, Boris asserted that the Germans had created a smart and barbaric plan to starve France, steal its wealth and reduce it to misery regardless of what German propaganda might be saying. The split in France between the wealthy northern and western areas and the poor regions of the south was evidence of how the Germans wanted to prevent the wealthy regions that produced an agrarian surplus from supplying the poor regions. Throughout the centuries, the northern and western regions of France had provided seven-eighths of agricultural production to the Midi.[32]

Boris's statement was not made without evidence. The Nord and the Pas-de-Calais were two of the richest *départements* from an agricultural point of view. Both were attached to the German administration in Brussels to enable the agricultural production of rich crops and choice cattle to be sent to Germany. However, this did not happen in reality as local consumption was quite high among the German services operating from there, such as the army, the organisation *Todt* (German organisation responsible for engineering work in occupied territories), etc., as well as the 3 million inhabitants. The latter represented 7.14 per cent of the total French population, many of whom were miners and metallurgists and needed a solid ration to avoid disruption and enable manufacturing to continue at full productivity.[33] Moreover, the implementation of the demarcation line enabled the Germans to have total control over the movement of people, food and goods between the two zones of France. In effect, the demarcation line became 'the Great Wall of China in modern times.'[34]

Boris continued his broadcast by identifying the real reason behind the food shortage. Food had become scarce, he asserted, because the Germans seized it and kept it for themselves. They appropriated the harvest from the farmers and purchased it in shops with their artificially over-valued marks. Defending the blockade, Boris stressed that there was no doubt that the French knew the truth regarding the blockade. It was dangerous, he warned his audience, to listen to those who claimed or promised that the products coming from overseas would not end up in the hands of Germany. It was because of Germany that the French were being condemned to famine and despair. He also reminded his listeners of Hitler's *Mein Kampf*. The only salvation for France was the defeat of Germany; a defeat that the courageous British had heralded.[35]

Boris was a persuasive speaker, using simple and clear language and developing his arguments logically and progressively. There could be little doubt, after listening to his broadcasts, that Germany wanted to bring down France. His listeners could link the broadcast to their daily experiences with the shortages of certain foods in their local shops. It was credible that foodstuffs from French colonies might have been diverted towards Germany. Boris stressed repeatedly that the French had Britain as their strong ally and this alliance would bring the defeat of Germany in the end. Backing up this claim, this broadcast took place the day after the end of the Battle of Britain, which had culminated with a decisive victory for the RAF. Boris used this victory to demonstrate the determination of Britain to continue the fight against the Axis powers. France should therefore have faith in the British.

Another example of a broadcast discussing the British blockade was the one made by Jean Marin on 25 October 1940 – the day after Pétain's meeting with Hitler in Montoire-sur-le-Loir, at a time when Pétain's prestige was at its highest.[36] Until then, the listeners of the BBC had denounced Vichy and their inability to tackle food shortages, but Pétain was largely left out of any criticism. Therefore, the BBC had to be careful when attacking Vichy and its policies to avoid any negative repercussions for criticising Pétain. As one listener wrote:

> Food scarcity and other difficulties are blamed on the Government; food queues, those ideal 'grumbling centres', indulge in dangerous comparisons between the plenty of the good old days of Blum and the severe rationing under the Marshal. (*L'Avenir*, quoted by *France*, 2.11)[37]

In his broadcast, Marin spoke of a rumour suggesting that one of the arguments that had persuaded Maréchal Pétain to meet with Hitler was the prospect of famine in France, an argument cleverly presented by Laval, who was described as a 'corrupted politician'. Marin admitted that famine was an impending threat; however, he asserted that Germany was exclusively to blame. Germany had stolen France's stocks and harvests and imposed a rigorous blockade between the two zones. Germany had knowingly created the current state of affairs by keeping hundreds of thousands of French peasants as prisoners of war so that they could continue to blackmail France. Defending the British blockade, he said, 'Contrary to Germany, England does not impose its blockade against France for the purposes of conquest and oppression; it is a lesser evil for the greater good: the liberation of France.'[38]

Marin had cleverly separated Pétain from his Vichy administration. He blamed Laval for tricking Pétain into meeting Hitler by using the prospect of famine as a lever. This way, the French would not feel that any personal attack had been made on the hero of Verdun. Meanwhile, the BBC had collected much evidence of French support for the British blockade. Most of the letters from the listeners were very similar in nature, accepting the British blockade as a means to defeat Germany. For example, one listener wrote, 'In my village the people are almost glad to go hungry. "It means the British blockade is working", they say, "and that is what really matters. Let the English win first, we will eat afterwards"' (South-West France, 15.9).[39]

The BBC concluded that these listeners who chose to write to them to express their support for the British blockade may not be numerous, but they could be potential leaders of opinion, through whom ordinary Frenchmen's irritation and frustration over food shortages could be diverted against the occupier.[40]

Food rationing

Prior to the war, France was considered a self-sufficient country in terms of agriculture, but this changed following the occupation.[41] An early warning sign of hard times to come was heralded by Albert Chichery, the Minister of Agriculture and Supply, as early as 8 July when he announced that all French people would have to accept rationing at some point.[42]

When the ration card system was rolled out on 23 September 1940,[43] the civilian population resented the quantity of foodstuffs allocated to them by rationing, especially daily essentials such as bread and meat, which were both in short supply. The BBC made a number of broadcasts explaining to the French population the situation in each zone and how the unification of food rationing in both zones worked to the advantage of the Germans, making the Vichy government the scapegoat of their policy.

On 27 September, Boris stated that, in response to the dissatisfaction voiced by the people, the press and the government of Vichy that those in the unoccupied zone were given less rations as compared to those in the occupied zone, the Germans had agreed that a limited amount of meat and sugar could be transported across the demarcation line so that a unified rationing system would apply to both zones. This would appear to be the right thing to do but, in fact, it had the consequence of making the Vichy government the scapegoat for cuts in food rationing. The Germans had restored to Vichy its authority to oversee the rationing in both zones. Instead of increasing the food rationing, though, Vichy had to reduce the amount of food rationing in both zones in order to achieve a unified rationing system, inflicting new hardships on the population everywhere.[44]

Through analysing and rationalising the situation of food rationing in both zones, Boris conveyed the message that although the Vichy government appeared to be in charge of the rationing system in the whole of France, they had no real authority in determining the amount of food available. It was the German occupiers who had total control over the amount of food that they took for their war effort and what remained was not sufficient to feed the French population. This was the real reason why the French were subject to rationing and starvation. By collaborating with the Germans, a large quantity of foodstuffs such as wheat, vegetables, butter and live animals such as cattle were requisitioned by the Germans, resulting in less food being available to the French. It was similar story with the supplies arriving regularly from the colonies to Marseille,[45] the meeting place between two worlds: metropolitan France and its empire.[46]

In the meantime, the stocks of grocery products were dwindling. In the police report dated 23 September, the decrease was already noticeable and was attributed to a number of factors: the frequent and heavy requisitioning imposed by the occupying authority; the inadequacies and inefficiency in the means of transportation; and the difficulties of bringing food from one *département* to another, making it harder to replenish the stocks in the stores. The shortage in food supply was exacerbated by the pricing policy, as there was less incentive for the provincial producers to supply Paris.[47] For example, French eggs had become scarce on the markets due to the season. Prior to the war, French eggs would have been supplemented by Moroccan ones, which would have been shipped to Marseille. Unfortunately, the quantity arriving in Marseille was not enough to resupply the market. Moreover, with the capped price for eggs in Paris and the transportation costs, the traders would have made a loss by transporting the eggs to Paris.[48] As a result, it was not financially viable for the traders to sell on the Paris market. In fact, it was anticipated that all colonial products would be lacking in the capital in the near future.[49]

In the same broadcast, Boris went on to discuss in detail the rationing of some essential foods, and why it was inadequate. Boris argued that a daily ration of 325g of bread was low for the French, because 'bread is much more the staple food for the French than it is for the Germans'.[50] The French were entitled to buy 420g of meat per week while the Germans were entitled to 500g; 500g of sugar per month as opposed to 1kg for the Germans; and 100g of fat per week as opposed to 285g for the Germans.[51]

The figures that Boris quoted were largely in line with the information from other sources, although there were slight deviations; for example, the ration for bread was reported as 350g per day elsewhere rather than 325g.[52] The ration rate for a person in category A, which covered anyone aged 12 to 70 years, was established in September 1940 as follows:

> bread, 350 grams per day; pasta, 250 grams per month; cheese, 50 grams per week; fat, 200 grams per month; margarine, 200 grams per month; meat with bone, 300 grams per week, which in fact corresponds to 240 grams; sugar, 500 grams per month; rice, 50 grams per month. This ration is equivalent to 1,327 calories per day (against 3000 before the war), which is insufficient.[53]

It had also been noted that despite the quantity of food available, the quality of food was another area of discontent. For example, when bread was available in shops, 'it was always of poor quality and there was never enough of it'.[54]

Boris interpreted in his broadcast the provision of food rationing as a representation of what Hitler had often expressed: France was an inferior country, hence its citizens would receive less food as they were inferior to the Germans. Vichy had boasted that they had received certain assurances from the Germans that they would only draw the necessary amount of grain from the occupied zone to make bread for their troops, and likewise the necessary amount of meat. The reminder would come from Germany. If that were true, how could a country like France, which had been self-sufficient, suddenly be reduced to such a level of deprivation? Only German atrocities and looting could account for the food shortages. The Vichy government had given various reasons to explain it – such as the destruction of war, foot and mouth disease, poor harvests, etc. – but these were not satisfactory. If there was a food shortage in France, it was due to the German occupation, which emptied the resources from the country. Their sinister task was accomplished when they ordered the French to settle with and share among themselves what was left.[55]

In this broadcast, Boris accused Germany and the Vichy government openly and firmly of causing the food shortage and encouraged the French not to believe in the explanations of either the German or Vichy authorities. The amount of food rationing was decided by Dr. Reinhardt, head of the agricultural section, who made sure that the French rations were lower than those received in Germany. Under this rationing system, the French were entitled to only 1,500 calories a day when 2,500 were needed to sustain a normal life.[56]

A further broadcast made by Boris in October demonstrated a deepening in the debate about the real cause of food shortages in France. It covered a range of topics, but the section relevant to food scarcity was made in response to the statement of Dr. Walther Darré, the Minister of Agriculture in Germany, who blamed it on the French's mishandling of food supply.

Boris stated that Darré was said to have congratulated himself for the food situation in Germany because the German had 'potatoes … sugar, and even more butter than last year'.[57] Darré did not explain where this new abundance had come from; however, there were millions of people in France who knew. Darré positioned himself as an agricultural specialist and blamed the food shortages in France on the poor organisation of French agriculture, stating that it would be the fault of France alone if it were not able to feed its population during the coming winter.[58]

Boris's point is that the Germans were feeding on France, looting its rich resources and showing no remorse, compassion or empathy. Boris presented Darré's statement as facts, thus creating a powerful rhetoric to instigate hostility among the listeners towards the Germans. He did not state to whom Darré's message was addressed, not the time, the date or the medium used to communicate it. From the context of the broadcast, it would seem that the statement was addressed to Germany, to showcase the success of his department in securing food for the Germans, and it is conceivable that this information may have been obtained through monitoring radio broadcasts in Germany.[59] However, from 1941, the BBC became more conscious and consistent when it came to supplying the source of their information so that the listeners could judge the veracity of it for themselves.

In December 1940, shortly after Laval was removed from the Vichy government, Boris revisited the topic of price control and made a measured criticism of Pétain. He stated that Maréchal Pétain, who had always acted and thought for the French, had made the mistake of trusting a crook. Vichy told the people that everything was under control; however, this was contrary to the truth. Vichy had made the mistake of hiding the true economic and financial situation ever since the government had taken power six months previously. It had rejected the risk of inflation and asserted that the franc would remain strong and prices would not fluctuate, but it had been mistaken. Certain food items that were subject to price control became scarce in France, and this was because if any of these products were to be sold at the fixed price, they would be sold at a loss. Boris quoted an example from a week-old newspaper from Marseille stating that no meat was available because the maximum price imposed was too low; a price increase was finally authorised to rectify this situation.[60] In fact, M. Spinasse, a Vichy collaborationist, explained that the industrialists were offered three choices: they could either 'go to jail for illegal price hikes, or sell at a loss, or close their factories.'[61]

The meat situation in Marseille was one that was replicated in other regions of France. In fact, the situation was gloomy at the end of the year, although hope for a better future remained. According to a letter from a listener in Paris that was read out on the BBC on 21 December: 'The machine crushed us. But God will not abandon us. We hope everything from England, from America, from you especially. We do not consider France as vanquished, but as sold.'[62]

To put this into context, in the early stages of the war, reporting about supply problems was not the priority of BBC broadcasts to France, nor did it dominate the scheduling of the broadcasts. The BBC did not yet consider food supply a key issue and the main aim of their programmes was to inform the listeners of military news and to denounce Vichy as an illegitimate government.[63] This situation would change with the introduction of *Courrier de France,* a weekly programme that first appeared in January 1941,[64] highlighting the disastrous consequences of the Vichy policy of food supply. Intelligence regarding the food situation was collected diligently from letters sent by French listeners to the BBC.[65] Subsequently, the BBC broadcasters devoted several of their programmes to the issue of rationing, looting, requisitioning and levies imposed by the occupiers, as well as the despair and suffering of the French. As Léon Werth, a refugee in the Vosges region, wrote in his diary on 26 March 1941: 'Some French do not even expect anything at all except that tomorrow would succeed today and that the meat and the bread would miraculously come back in abundance on the table.'[66]

As the war progressed, it became more difficult to find food in France as the Germans needed to requisition ever greater quantities to sustain their military advance. From 1941, the BBC became more determined to keep the French informed about the situation of food supply as well as the distribution of food, using it as a psychological weapon against the occupier and Vichy administration.

1941

British blockade and public health

The discussion of food shortages in France became one of the BBC's main preoccupations in 1941. In January, William Pickles spoke about the delivery of vitamins, condensed milk and baby clothes from the American Red Cross to the French in the unoccupied zone, easing the pressure on food supply, which had worsened due to the British blockade.

Pickles stressed that the British blockade was not intended as a means to wage war on civilians, but to prevent the German government from using raw materials and extracting them for their war effort. In fact, the British government had tried its best to alleviate the situation: it permitted the entry of a cargo sent by the USA loaded with concentrated vitamins, so that it could be distributed in the unoccupied zone by the American Red Cross. Pickles asked the French to help the American Red Cross distribute the vitamins, and not to let this valuable cargo fall into the hands of the enemy. If, and only if, French children were receiving these vitamins, the French would have the assurance that other ships would follow suit. The vitamins from the Red Cross, he continued, were different to the ersatz or artificial vitamins given by the Germans to replace the real food that they had requisitioned. Compared to the vitamins from the Red Cross, the *ersatz* vitamins had no real value for children because they were fabricated in chemical factories and were not extracted from plants or animals.[67]

The distribution of goods from the American Red Cross featured prominently in the letters received from the unoccupied zone, especially regarding the distribution of bread made with American flour. Writers expressed their gratitude to the Americans with the hope that more relief would come soon. According to a correspondent from La Seyne-sur-Mer (Var) on 1 June:

> There were so many people round the truck, so many little children whose eyes were shining with anticipation as they looked at the sacks on which was marked a big Red Cross and the words 'From the people of America to the people of France', I cried like a child, my heart was deeply touched and everyone felt as I did – none of us will ever forget what America has done for us.[68]

Meanwhile, the debate on air regarding the British blockade intensified and the focus shifted. The German authorities and the Vichy government continued to blame food shortages on the British blockade for preventing commodities, particularly those from the French colonies, from reaching France. The British wanted to prevent any foodstuffs from being diverted to Germany, but the blockade had not completely stopped trade between North Africa and Marseille[69] because the British lacked the resources to do so. It was noted that during the first three months of 1941, 'only eight out of 108 French ships passing through the Straits of Gibraltar were intercepted'.[70] Moreover, the American government had decided that supplies to France would transit via French North Africa, which meant that ships should not be blocked by the British if Vichy gave an assurance that the supplies would reach the French population. Roosevelt's idea was to show British and American goodwill to Vichy, in order to bring it back to the Allied side and fight Germany. Admiral Leahy, the American ambassador to Vichy France, was in charge of building a consensus between Pétain and Roosevelt against Germany,[71] using Général Weygand, who had been appointed Vichy's proconsul in North Africa in September 1940,[72] as 'a cornerstone around which to build a policy of resistance towards Germany'.[73] The British were not convinced of Roosevelt's strategy; however, they could not prevent it.[74]

A written report dated 13 June concluded that the French public was unanimous in criticising the government for being responsible for the hard times they were facing due to a complete lack of meat, fish and wine and insufficient bread. Many people complained that they were undernourished, that their physical strength was diminished and that they had great difficulties carrying out their daily routine. Mothers foresaw with anguish the time when their children would become anaemic or sick because of insufficient nourishment. On 14 June, two incidents were recorded of women who abandoned their children, a seven-month-old in one instance and a two-month-old in the other. Both children had a note attached to their clothes explaining that their mother had no other choice because they could no longer feed them.[75] According to a letter sent by a mother on 14 May from Le Cannet:

> All parents are terribly anxious for the health of their young children. I, with my Alain, am terribly worried again… He has not been able to stand the strain of prolonged undernourishment and total lack of vitamins. The doctor has forbidden him all intellectual work, so his exam is sunk.[76]

By the end of August, with the approach of winter, many mothers became increasingly worried about their children entering this difficult period in a poor physical state. They also foresaw the difficulties of acquiring shoes and warm clothing for their children, making it impossible for them to attend schools.[77] As winter approached, the approval of new charcoal ration coupons was welcomed, although its value was generally judged to be clearly insufficient for the urgent needs of the population.[78]

It was important to stress relentlessly on the radio that the British government's decision to permit certain cargo shipments to arrive in France was made to help the vulnerable people in France. The hope was that the listeners would have the impression that the British cared for their well-being and would thus be more inclined to develop faith and trust in them rather than in those who 'stole their steak'.

The mothers were correct in their predictions. Malnutrition was a major concern for the French from 1941, leading to an increased number of tuberculosis and diphtheria cases, higher mortality rates for infants and the elderly,[79] 'anemia and vitamin deficiencies, weight loss and stunted growth for children and adolescents'.[80] The mortality rate in the hard-hit regions soared: 'Mortality rates increased by as much as 50 per cent in the period 1941-43; infant mortality increased significantly, from 63 per thousand in 1939 to 91 per thousand in 1940 and 109 per thousand in 1945'.[81]

Pickles also acknowledged in his broadcast the suffering of German civilians during the preparation for war as the result of Nazi leadership. Göring had told the German people that they had the choice between butter and guns. In the end, Göring decided for them. Butter and fat almost completely disappeared from German households – they were used to feed the German war industries instead of German children. The Allies, by contrast, had no intention of exposing either German children or the children of the Allies to famine.[82]

Pickles was well aware of the autarky policy that the Nazis attempted to implement in Germany in the 1930s. One of Goebbels's main propaganda targets was the control of consumption to prevent severe shortages.[83] The ultimate aim of Nazi autarky policy was to achieve self-sufficiency to counter the memory of the 'hunger blockade' imposed on the nation during the Great War.[84] Therefore, during the pre-war years, the German civilian population, including children, had to endure wartime propaganda. Nonetheless, this policy was doomed to fail as there was no rationing in force and imported goods were available on a large scale. This showed the limitations of the Third Reich's control over its population: propaganda was powerless when its message became unpalatable.[85]

Pickles drew a parallel between the 'hunger blockade' of Germany during the Great War and the current British blockade of France. The purpose of both was to prevent Germany from having access to resources that could aid its war efforts. The ultimate goal was to defeat Nazi Germany, but without hurting any children. Using this example, he stressed his argument again, that the British government was permitting the entry of Red Cross cargos to help the children of the unoccupied zone, and it would now be up to Vichy and the people to stand up and help the Red Cross distribute the goods to the people and prevent them from being directed to the Germans.

The day after Pickles's broadcast in January 1941, Boris spoke on the air about the blockade and called for French action. The blockade was at that time being imposed on four countries: Norway, Denmark, Holland and France. All these countries had been wealthy and well fed prior to the war but since the German occupation the people had all been suffering from food shortages due to German requisitioning. German propaganda had itself announced that the German population was better fed this year than last.[86] Dr. Robert Ley, the head of the Reichs Labour Front,[87] repeated a claim that an inferior race needed less food.

As the French already knew to their cost, Germany took control of French rail and road transport, preventing necessary foodstuffs from reaching urban areas. Once goods were unloaded from a ship in Mediterranean ports, both the Germans and Italians were on hand to requisition the supplies.[88] Despite the clear evidence that food shortages in France were caused by Germany, German propaganda continued to insist that the British blockade was responsible. The French, Boris continued, now needed to put pressure on the Vichy government not to agree to any further concessions or demands made by Germany.[89]

Mme. Paris, another speaker at the BBC, then stressed in February 1941 that the French knew what was happening. They were aware that boats originating from North Africa were searched by the German and Italian commissions as soon as they arrived in the port. Barely 20 per cent of their cargos were released to the French. France had the ability to feed her 40 million people, thanks to her rich soil, something that the Germans envied, but now France had lost control of its wealth.[90] As she put it:

> I saw these German soldiers rushing into shops taking everything that could be eaten. I saw the empty shops after the passage of these locusts: God, the Germans had long lost the habit of such purchases, of seeing such abundance of meat, fruit! Here is the sole victory that Hitler has offered to his people. This 'colossal' booty offers to the winners. Then, afterwards, the leitmotif that attempt to justify their pre-emptive right: 'the race of the conquered countries and the inferior, they need less food'.[91]

The two broadcasts were made about a month apart, delivering a clear message based on evidence. It was not difficult for Boris to prove that the British blockade was not to blame for the food shortage: he referred to the misery of all countries under German occupation; the heavy requisitioning and looting; the racial justification that France was an inferior race to Germany and therefore needed less food; the German control of the transport system, which resulted in uneven access to essential foodstuffs; and the Axis's seizure of cargos upon their arrival in Mediterranean ports. He challenged the French population of the unoccupied zone to put pressure on the Vichy government as this was the only way to prevent any further erosion of living conditions. He called on the French to resist German demands.

Mme. Paris complemented the argument by presenting a witness account that contained both figures and emotions. The wartime BBC had always presented its broadcasts with figures, when available, to reinforce the validity of its statements and to support its arguments. Doing so served a dual purpose: it emphasised the facts and had a more dramatic effect on the listeners. In this broadcast, the figure of 20 per cent was in fact an estimate provided by a listener, which might have been highly subjective, although not necessarily so. The reliability of such figures would largely depend on where the information came from; for example, a worker at the port might give a more accurate estimate than a casual observer.

The issue of superior and inferior races was highlighted consistently in these broadcasts. It became the new leitmotif of the BBC to refer to German racial ideas to explain why the French received less food than the Germans. Given the reputation of the Nazis for their anti-Semitic policy, an easy link could be made by the listeners and they might ask themselves whether any inferior race would eventually be subject to a similar fate, and what choices they would have.

The narratives of these three broadcasts made in early 1941 demonstrate a unified message from the BBC speakers: the British blockade was for the benefit of the French population and the real enemy was the Germans, regardless of their propaganda. In fact, the British blockade was further eased in March when the British government decided to grant 'navicerts' to enable American ships to sail to French Mediterranean ports and Algeria. The Rockefeller Foundation duly started to ship condensed milk and vitamins to provide essential nutrition to French children.[92] However, this additional supply was not sufficient to reverse the trend of malnutrition. A report of the Institut de Recherches d'Hygiène in Marseille concluded that 'in the first half of 1941, it was estimated that 40 per cent of adolescents aged between twelve and nineteen had lost three kilogrammes in weight'.[93] Dr. Bézançon,[94] specialist in public health, stated that 'the mortality rate of children between the ages of one and nine years has increased by 29 per cent in Paris'.[95] The medical and healthcare professionals also highlighted the disturbing progression of tuberculosis due to malnutrition and to the worsening of basic hygiene, such as lack of soap and water heaters.[96]

This public health crisis was fuelled by the explicit German policy. Both Göring and Abetz considered that the French should have a lower standard of living and less to eat than the Germans. Vichy was therefore incapable of bargaining with the German authorities about food delivery quotas or of preventing France from experiencing localised malnutrition.[97]

Apart from the British blockade, there were other factors contributing to the lack of calories in France. Insufficient wages was one of them. A French economist reported in June that the minimum wage needed for a worker to buy sufficient food for his family to live on for a month was 1,200 francs. Many French workers earned less than 1,000 francs a month, only part of which could be used to purchase food as they had to meet other essential costs such as 'rent, coal, clothing and footwear'.[98]

As an unnamed speaker of the BBC asserted on air, the daily ration of intake in calories decreased from 1,307 calories in November 1940 to 1,134 in June 1941, and the calorie intake had continued declining since that date. The speaker acknowledged that the figures were theoretical because full rations were impossible to obtain due to the lack of supply in the shops. Even the equivalent of 1,000 calories per day on ration cards was impossible to get. To supplement the diet, it became necessary to find non-rationed products. The quantities of food arriving on the markets were insufficient, stock levels were poor, and from the little left to the French, the Germans would still help themselves before everybody else was served. Only the well-off could afford the luxury of buying on the black market because it would cost an additional 30 to 40 francs per day to obtain enough food to reach 2,400 calories per day – money that the vast majority of the French people did not have.[99]

The winter of 1940–41 marked the beginning of difficult times for housewives, who had to start looking at other ways to buy the much-needed food for survival. By the spring of 1941, food had become so expensive that in the occupied zone, a growing number of leaflets condemned the anti-social Vichy policy, whereby 'the rich will always find ways to shop on the black market, while workers are condemned to the most appalling misery', and the looting policy carried out by the occupier.[100] However, this situation did not draw much sympathy from the occupier. An article published in September 1941 in the *Zeitschriften-Dienst,* a weekly newsletter for magazine editors that was distributed to the German soldiers, reminded them how much better their lives were now as compared to in the past. German people had suffered just as much hardship in the 1920s in terms of child malnutrition, and a scarcity of food and the income required for living. German soldiers were urged to remember the situation in Germany when the enemy took away the dairy cattle, causing the deaths of hundreds of thousands of German babies; the amount of food rationing soldiers' families had to live on from 1914 to 1932, which was much inferior to the ration they received today; and the fact that the purchasing power of an unemployed family in 1932 was much less than the purchasing power today.[101] This article shed light on how German propaganda sought to make German soldiers appreciate the 'good life' they now experienced, and how food shortages outside of Germany were to be viewed as a natural result of the occupation, something Germany had had to endure when it was defeated in the last war. The sentiment of revenge was apparent and was consistent with Hitler's view that the French deserved no sympathy as they had supposedly looted Germany by imposing huge reparations on Germany and had illegally occupied the Ruhr region in 1923.[102]

Military incidents and the psychological battle

The BBC was well aware of the impact of food shortages on public opinion, especially on the poor and the hungry, and it feared that these groups would be more prone to German and Vichy propaganda. The British blockade was thus a key psychological battlefield of German and British propaganda.

The Nemours incident of 31 March 1941 marked a period of heightened military tension between Vichy and the British. According to an official statement issued by the British, four merchant vessels had left Africa for Europe, escorted by a French destroyer. The British navy wanted to search the French vessels as intelligence indicated that they were carrying war material and equipment for Germany. However, the search request was declined by the French, even though their vessels had entered the open water. The merchant vessels then retreated along the coast and the French batteries in Algeria (which were under the control of Vichy) opened fire on the British navy. The British navy returned fire at the French batteries, where hits were noticed. The British could have fired upon the French merchant vessels and their escorts at this point but for humanitarian reasons, they decided not to do so. The French vessels then found refuge in the port of Nemours.[103]

Jacques Duchesne spoke on the BBC the day after the incident. He argued that Darlan was attempting to use this incident to restore the sovereignty of the French fleet in the Mediterranean by protecting the French merchant fleet using French warships to safeguard the sending of supplies to France. Intelligence indicated that the British had abstained from attacking any merchant ships and that the British blockade had not stopped trade between Algeria, Tunisia and Marseille. According to the French press, a total of 68 French merchant vessels reached Marseille from Algeria and Tunisia, carrying vegetables and fruit.[104]

This incident presented a golden opportunity for both the BBC and Vichy propagandists to sway French public opinion towards the British. Darlan's accusation that the British had opened fire at French batteries worsened the Franco-British relationship, casting another shadow following the attack on Mers-el-Kébir in July 1940 and the battle of Dakar in September 1940. Duchesne defended the British vigorously, accusing Darlan of not telling the truth about his real intention. He stated that the British navy never opened fire on the merchant vessels, nor did they did attack the French batteries; it was an act of self-defence. The British remained sympathetic towards the suffering of the French population, but the searches of merchant vessels were essential to prevent valuable resources from falling into the hands of the enemy. The British knew what would happen when the merchant vessels arrived at the French ports: they would be inventoried and requisitioned by the Germans.

The BBC propagandists defended the legitimacy of the blockade and placed the responsibility of the conflict solely on the ambition of Darlan to break free from British control in the Mediterranean. Nonetheless, the efficiency of the British blockade was never a topic of the BBC broadcast; when speaking on air, it was better to show empathy than to discuss efficiency. The situation was soon to change, however, when the Lend-Lease proposal was finally enacted on 11 March 1941 in the US Congress, providing more American goods and weapons for the British.[105]

Apart from military incidents, the BBC fought the psychological battle for French public opinion using a number of sources, as evidenced in its broadcasts. These were intended to divert criticism from the British blockade and to reveal the complacency of Vichy to German demands, and included personal testimonies, interviews and excerpts from Vichy, German and third-country newspapers.

Listeners' reactions to the BBC broadcasts were carefully analysed. As stated in the BBC Monthly Intelligence Report in March, there was a fair amount of correspondence expressing French acceptance of the blockade with no complaints coming from the occupied zone. Some of the letters originated in the port cities, where the witnesses spoke of their experiences of German pillage. The report concluded that the BBC broadcasts played an important role in persuading the French that the British blockade was in fact a battle of the French.[106]

A letter read by Bonifas, a speaker at the BBC, in the programme *Courrier de France* on 4 July gives a flavour of the experiences of an informant reporting looting in the port of Marseille. This informant from Paris, who had recently arrived in Marseille, stated that every day the inhabitants of Marseille saw boats loaded with oranges, but not a single one was on sale in Marseille. He continued by stating that among all the cargos arriving in Marseille for the supply of the French population, 40 per cent went to Germany, 40 per cent to Italy, 12 per cent were put in storage by the French government and only 8 per cent went on the market. It was a very real raid on food products.[107]

Personal testimonies such as this could serve as a powerful psychological weapon to reinforce the BBC's argument that German requisitioning was responsible for the lack of food. The percentages quoted represented a personal estimation, which required no accuracy check. Nevertheless, the BBC collected intelligence from other sources to obtain and provide a more complete picture; for example, Robert Rasumny, a French silk merchant interviewed at the RVPS on 31 July, stated that a German major in the Anti-Aircraft unit (AA) said that 80 per cent of all the cargo that was unloaded in a French port was taken by them because they had priority of purchase. It was not done openly, though; French middlemen were appointed to do the job.[108] The report contains no information about the context in which the German officer said this, or whether the informant heard it personally or from hearsay, so his reliability could not be confirmed. However, if there were enough letters and sources painting a similar picture, and Vichy was known to have been made to pay hefty reparations, why not use such dramatic figures to help the British cause?

That said, official statistics could be just as efficient as personal testimonies. Boris announced in his broadcast in April that he was in possession of a list of foodstuffs and other raw materials sent from both zones to Germany during the period from 15 December 1940 to 15 January 1941 – a list that would stir up emotions in Washington and London. It included 300 cars loaded with coffee; 1,220 tons of pork; 28,000 heads of cattle; 6,750 tons of whale oil; 900,000 quintals of oats; over a million quintals of hay and straw; and raw materials that included 45,000 tons of lead, 9,300 tons of aluminium, 6,300 tons of manganese and iron, and coal. The list was kept secret because Vichy wanted to hide it from the public at all costs.[109] Boris did not reveal the source of this official list, but the French people were already very aware of Germany's requisitions and its consequences for their daily life.

Articles published in the press in Vichy were also used as evidence to support the BBC's reports about food shortage. On 17 April, Schumann read an excerpt of an article published in *Temps*, the official newspaper of Vichy, which stated that:

> The food imported by our ships … should be exclusively used for feeding the French population. However, at the present time, it is not. The best proof is that in the unoccupied zone, it is impossible to obtain fruit, despite them arriving regularly from North Africa. To obtain butter, one must be queuing from 4 or 5 o'clock in the morning until 9am or later.[110]

Schumann used this excerpt from the official voice of Vichy to demonstrate that German requisitions, rather than the British blockade, were responsible for the worsening of the food situation in France.[111] This was one of the rare occasions when the press of Vichy had inadvertently reported something that could be used against them. Another later example, which we will come on to, was RN unintentionally reporting the housewives' movement in January 1942 and giving unexpected publicity to such undesirable events.[112] The 'mishandling' of such vital information provided the BBC with an excellent opportunity to sustain its psychological battle without having to worry about the credibility of this 'official' source.

In addition to information from official sources in Vichy, the BBC used sources from German press as evidence. Ernest Bevin, Britain's Minister of Labour, spoke on the BBC on 2 May about the whereabouts of wheat using evidence obtained this way. Bevin asserted that everything that had been taken, eaten or stocked by the Germans to consume later would not be returned to France. The scarcity of bread in the whole of France was due to the theft and looting carried out by the Germans. Those who saw the trains loaded with French wheat going to Germany knew this to be so, just as the BBC knew this.

The propaganda of Paris had attempted to blame the wheat shortage on the British blockade, and to show the generosity of the Germans for sharing a little of the French wheat and flour with the unoccupied zone by opening up the demarcation line at their discretion. The BBC, however, could now prove that French wheat was being taken by the Germans to Germany, because the fact had been published in the German press. The *Gazette de Cologne* (*Kölnische Zeitung*) dated 20 February stated that a number of mills currently had at their disposal French wheat and that the wheat supply in the region of Mannheim had improved. The BBC used this fact to demonstrate that the French needed to question more, and to ask Darlan and his ministers whether this is what Collaboration and a New European Order meant.[113]

The statements made in the German newspaper allowed Bevin to argue that if German mills in the Rhineland had French wheat at their disposal, this was due to the organised theft orchestrated in France, which was also the reason for the shortage of bread and other staple foods in the country. Bevin used this undisputable evidence not only to instil discontent towards Vichy but also to call for French action: the French should now question Vichy authorities about Germany's restitution of French wheat before talking more about collaboration and any improvement of French lives; they should remind the Vichy authorities that Germans had a 25 per cent higher bread ration than the French, whereas French children had had their rations further reduced; they should also question whether this was what the New European Order actually meant for the French.

A further broadcast about German requisition of wheat was made by an unnamed speaker at the BBC on 5 September. They warned the French about another massive levy on the French wheat harvest and a further reduction in their daily ration as a result of the German invasion of Russia that had taken place in June. A radio station controlled by Goebbels had declared on a programme recently that 'food shortage is impossible in Germany, because Germany has Europe at its disposal, and [that] she can draw supplies of all kinds'.[114] As stated in an article written by the Germans and published in a Dutch newspaper the previous July, the speaker at the BBC asserted, 'in the German economic system, the occupied countries must naturally supply to the Reich the products which are necessary to him, without regard to the form of payment'.[115]

Germany had completely failed to benefit from the harvest in Ukraine, which meant the troops would have to be fed with supplies from Germany. However, the cereal harvest in Germany had been poor for the first time in years, despite all the past bragging. The French peasants who made a fantastic effort to feed France would thus now in fact be working for Germany. The wheat was in the barn, but the French ration of bread was not going to increase as most of the wheat production was reserved for the Germans.[116] On 4 September, it was announced on a Dutch radio station controlled by the Germans what the BBC had always maintained from the beginning: 'thanks to the French harvest, the supply of Europe would be facilitated'.[117]

The BBC very clearly stated facts that originated from 'official' sources used by the Germans, such as the Dutch newspaper and the Dutch radio station, as well as German radio. By doing so, the BBC protected itself against any possible attack by either RN or Radio Paris over the veracity of their claims. Their broadcasts served as a blend of factual information and advance warning to the French, highlighting the complacency of Vichy and its inability to stand up to the German demands.

Housewives' demonstrations

The first housewives' demonstrations in France during the war years were recorded in December 1940 in the underground press and police reports.[118] The main purpose of the housewives' protests was to complain about the increasing difficulties of obtaining supplies.[119] They spontaneously took collective action, going out on to the streets or gathering around town halls to claim bread and milk for their children.[120]

However, there is evidence that the housewives' demonstrations started earlier than this. In November 1940, they had protested about the potato shortage in Carcassonne, Marseille and Béziers. The women succeeded in Carcassonne and Marseille, obtaining more potatoes. The one in Béziers failed, with the protesters being locked up, although they were freed shortly after. Following the initial success, 43 further demonstrations took place until May 1941, all occurring in the occupied zone. The demonstrations returned in force during the winter of 1941–42 for the second wave. This time, they spread from six *départements* to 24 and moved away from the communist fiefdoms in which they had initially been quartered.[121]

These demonstrations were viewed as a novelty when they first happened because they concerned the housewives and the working class alike living in towns and localities where protests on the street were rare or completely unheard of. These demonstrations also had political implications because these women openly and directly challenged the authorities.[122] During the first wave, the women often succeeded instantaneously. However, the authorities had a different response in 1941–42. At the end of January 1942, such demonstrations and riots caused enough concern in both zones for the authorities to consider taking preventive measures, although that did not succeed in suppressing them completely. In January 1942 in the Alpes-Maritimes, it was reported by intelligence that the demonstrations that took place in the *départements* had a disastrous effect on public opinion; housewives had declared that demonstrations were enough to bring about a rapid improvement in supplies, and this had paved the way for others to follow suit.[123]

The BBC became aware of the housewives' demonstrations in February 1941 and started reporting them on air. The narratives of these broadcasts shed light on what the BBC knew and how they portrayed these actions, which were otherwise largely under-reported.

Schumann spoke on 21 February, accusing the Germans of having created and used famine for their own benefit. A letter received by the BBC stated that a riot had broken out in Paris at Les Halles, where the Germans had requisitioned food in front of housewives who had queued up for hours just to witness all the potatoes they ardently coveted being taken by the occupiers. As a result of this riot, the potato supply to Paris was suspended for 40 days as a collective punishment. Another riot broke out at the Abattoirs de la Villette in Paris and as a result, Paris was deprived of meat for 40 days. Moreover, a quota meant milk was only available sparingly to children and the sick, yet it was openly distributed to German soldiers in the railway stations by German nurses.[124]

As Boris noted, there was an acute shortage of potatoes, sometimes for weeks. There was no butter at all and not enough milk for the children. Housewives had to get up early and queue sometimes for hours without being certain what they would be able to bring back home because the ration cards did not guarantee they would be able to obtain what they were entitled to. The necessary extra food had to come from the black market and was purchased at exorbitant prices. The dire situation led to increasing anxiety and unhappiness. The housewives had to live in constant worry, not knowing whether they would find enough food for their families.[125] All these factors might have motivated the housewives to take matters into their own hands.

A further broadcast was made by Mme. Paris in March, announcing another demonstration that had taken place in front of a few city halls in various *arrondissements* of Paris the previous week. This had seen numerous housewives holding their children in their arms demanding milk. Mme. Paris asked why these housewives had suddenly unleashed their fury, and concluded that it was due to the open distribution of milk to German soldiers. The Germans liked drinking milk, as much as the French liked drinking wine. France was a dairy country par excellence and a big producer of milk; therefore, the shortage of milk could not have been the result of the British blockade.[126] 'We must feed these gentlemen, the German soldiers, the guests, the tourists. We must shower them with milk while mothers do not have any for their little ones,' she said.[127] It should come as no surprise that the housewives, despite all their calm and dignity, decided to revolt. She called for the responsible authorities to make better provision in milk rationing. What would Radio Paris say? she asked; perhaps their response would be only lies and insolence as the speakers were commonly known to support the enemy.[128]

Mme. Paris expressed assertively, as much as other speakers, that there would be no hope for any significant improvement in the status quo as long as Vichy agreed to supply the German army with milk and other essential food. Demonstrations were the result of these empty markets and irregular, delayed or reduced food supplies. She warned that housewives would assemble in a spontaneous and angry crowd marching towards city hall when they were desperate. Moreover, housewives would not be satisfied with the explanations given by the authorities. This dissatisfaction and desperation subsequently turned into a conflict that would often evolve into verbal violence, insults, physical violence (for example, pushing), forced entry into a building and attempted pillaging in stores. Clashes were not uncommon, and the only way to calm the housewives down was to give them what they wanted.[129] A stark contrast was presented by Mme. Paris between the 'normal' calm and dignified French housewife and the 'crazy' crowd of housewives revolting in public against the scandalous behaviour displayed by the authorities. This unusual nature of the housewives' behaviour could only be explained by the food shortage. Only through revolt could the housewives get what they needed most: milk and bread for their children. To show her contempt for the occupier, Mme. Paris expressed clear sarcasm in her broadcast as she described the German soldiers as 'gentlemen', 'guests' and 'tourists'. Listeners knew that they were nothing of the sort.

The BBC was known to organise passive resistance during the war years; for example, by calling on the French to remain indoors on 1 January. However, on this occasion, there was no evidence that the BBC was in any way involved in the organisation of the demonstrations. Housewives acted mostly of their own accord. The BBC merely reported the incidents; however, in reporting them when they were not reported elsewhere, it also served the purpose of igniting and inspiring women in similar situations to resort to resistance.

In June and the subsequent months, the housewives continued to express their dissatisfaction (although not necessarily via demonstration) with the inadequate supply and the high cost of living, blaming the occupying authorities for the food shortage.[130] This formed a recurring feature in the police reports of the year.

This idealised *image d'Épinal*,[131] the image of a nation freeing itself, was used throughout the war years in BBC broadcasts as a means to encourage the French to take action against the occupier. By the end of 1941, the BBC had finally entered a more active phase in its broadcasts in calling for the French public to act against the occupier. Boris's first explicit call on air was made on 9 September, when he urged the French to make a choice between slavery and freedom.[132] It was followed by another broadcast on 25 September, when he urged all French, including the peasants, workers, farmers and city dwellers, to stop French products from reaching Germany. These more explicit messages were overt in nature and served to encourage the French to think of themselves as being part of something bigger. Hampering food transport to Germany was now part of the required action led by the BBC to save both French lives and France as a nation.[133]

The effect of such calls was, however, limited, as the reality was more nuanced. As the prefect of Jura observed, as much as the French did not want to supply the occupier, the farmers willingly agreed to sell to the German soldiers if they let them ignore taxes and regulations.[134] Therefore, it was the Vichy policies that were to blame as these made it impossible for the farmers to be both patriotic and make a living at the same time.

From 1942, the reports of the prefects and inspectors of food supply highlighted the peasants' egoistic attitude – they wanted to ensure that their families had sufficient food and so would naturally orient themselves towards productions that would yield maximum profit for minimum trouble. The peasant acted as he saw fit and did not care about the National Revolution. Because of the restrictions in place, he held power as he never had before and he used this to his benefit. The peasant would come to the aid of his relatives; his prices could fluctuate from the 'grey market' for friends to the black market for the others. This highlighted the growing hostility between the city dwellers and the farmers that was due in part to the discrepancies in their ability to access food. The situation was exacerbated by the black market, which favoured direct purchases by individuals on the farms. However, while enrichment was the primary goal for some, others did not hesitate to help the resistance by feeding or sheltering them or harbouring Jewish families.[135]

Farmers had to declare their produce to officials who knew little about farming, and price ceilings imposed at a local market would result in the disappearance of that produce in the market. The farmers saw the economic regulation imposed by the government as working against their interests and restricting their freedom, so evasion of economic and price controls became more common.[136]

In the winter of 1941–42, the housewives deeply deplored the shortage of shoes, slippers, woollens and textiles for young children.[137] They also deplored in particular the absence of essential textile articles for newborns.[138] Many anxious mothers wondered if it were possible to obtain clothes for their older children, too, and complained that the shortage of children's shoes meant their children would not be able to go to school.[139]

The housewives' demonstrations intensified at the beginning of 1942 in tandem with the worsening of food supply following a harsh winter, with a series of demonstrations taking place in cities in the south, such as Montpellier, Nîmes, Sète and Arles. These incidents were reported in Boris's broadcast, after this information had been obtained from a dispatch of Vichy's official news agency.[140] The nature of the protests had evolved from unorganised, spontaneous eruptions of discontent to organised actions, during which the housewives protested for additional rations of bread at town councils around Paris at Clamart, Bondy, Plessis-Robinson, Le Perreux-sur-Marne and the 20th *arrondissement*.[141] Given the nature and the increased intensity of such demonstrations, the attitude of the authorities also changed. During the winter of 1940–41, housewives often had their demands met on the spot. However, from 1942, to prevent a wave of new demonstrations from taking place, mayors were instructed not to grant any special distribution during or after a demonstration. Special distribution was to be given priority only in the most peaceful towns.[142]

The Germans' attitude to the housewives' demonstrations was significantly harsher in the occupied zone. The French authorities repeatedly questioned the housewives in the Paris region but hesitated to use violence. The Germans observed these demonstrations with a certain reserve as the demands being made were related to food supply and not the occupier directly. The worsening of the restrictions and the influx of refugees from the occupied zone to the unoccupied zone, however, caused an extension of housewife's demonstrations: the wave of demonstrations in the winter of 1941–42 began in the unoccupied zone and reached the occupied zone in January 1942.

It would have made authorities both unpopular and uneasy were they to reprimand such demonstrations overly harshly, taking into consideration the protesters' gender and the nature of their demands. The housewives were therefore able to publicly affirm the existence of dissatisfaction and demonstrate the possibility of expressing it in broad daylight. By this means, the demonstrations of the winter of 1941–42 helped to greatly undermine the popular consensus desired by Vichy and weakened its hold.[143]

1942

The mortality rate and deteriorating public health

From September 1941, a drought period began that extended to many French regions during the agricultural year of 1941–42. Local thunderstorms followed in the south in November, and in the north both in January and May 1942, resulting in a significant surplus of rainfall. From 3 January 1942, an intense period of cold weather started and remained until 4 March with 33 consecutive days of frost observed in Paris. The average temperature in the winter of 1941–42 was the coldest since the winter of 1894–95.[144] This excessive rainfall and the harsh winter contributed to the worsening of food supply in many French regions.

For the first time since the start of the war, numerous deaths 'by physiological misery' were reported in February 1942. The hardship had taken its toll and many men, women and children died of hunger.[145] Obtaining food to feed the family was normally the task of women who, in their testimonies, explained how they had to deal with their children's undernourishment and how they often deprived themselves of food to feed their families.[146] Despite all their efforts, mortality rates rose 'by 24 per cent in Paris, 29 per cent in Lyons and 57 per cent in Marseilles'.[147] Conversely, the mortality rate decreased in some agricultural areas, for example 'by 11 per cent in the Indre, 10.9 per cent in the Mayenne and 10.4 per cent in the Orne'.[148] The stark difference was partly the consequence of the rural area being much better off than urban areas in terms of food supply.

Police reports in January and February highlighted the seriousness of the situation for French families. The two main concerns for French families in early 1942 were the shortage of charcoal and the lack of food supplies. Already in January, there were diseases that spread among the old, the sick and the children who lived in unheated dwellings, resulting in a much higher mortality rate than during a normal year.[149] The lack of essential medicine in pharmacies exacerbated the problem.[150]

To the Vichy administration, the health of the population was a major priority – a policy that women benefitted from – as a variety of measures were put in place to keep a pulse on the well-being of nation. There was also an obsessive desire to protect childbirth levels. The health record book was introduced in 1942, along with the pregnancy record book, with the belief that mothers and children should be supervised closely by medical experts. This resulted in mothers being entitled to free visits by doctors.[151]

Vichy targeted women and family, which were considered 'the essential cell, the basis even of the social edifice, it is on this that we must build'.[152] This was because it partially blamed the defeat of France on the decline of birth rates and the diminishing role of the family. Women had failed the nation by not producing enough male children to replace those who had died in World War I and so they were to a large extent responsible for the defeat of France in 1940. Vichy's solution for a stronger France was thus to encourage peasant women to have many children,[153] hence the medical measures provided to protect women, children and the family.

One way to convey this important ideology to the population was to use, for example, *Radio National,* which offered advice to young people on how to stay healthy and strong for themselves and their children, and to be useful to the country and society. Health was considered the most precious capital a person could possess. It was with this idea in mind that *Radio-Santé* broadcast on Tuesdays, Thursdays and Saturdays at 07h40, giving brief advice on intoxication, food, dressing up, work and leisure, and maintaining self-control by using available natural resources, such as air, light, water and exercise. This information would later be published and available to purchase in bookstores.[154]

Good hygiene is the basis of sound health, but this was difficult during the war since soap was scarce. It was rationed at 100g a month before it disappeared altogether. Households found ways of making soap, but were hindered by the fact that there was also a restriction on the amount of fat,[155] an essential part of soap making, that was available in shops.[156]

This deterioration of health and the increase in the mortality rate did not go unnoticed by the BBC. On 7 October, an unknown speaker highlighted the increase of mortality rate in Paris, which may have had a dramatic effect on the listeners. The BBC reused the report written by Professor Besançon of the Academy of Sciences, whose figures had previously appeared in Schumann's broadcast on 12 November 1941.[157] Professor Besançon stated that 'since the German occupation began, the mortality rate increased by 9 per cent in Paris whereas the birth rate decreased by 18 per cent. The mortality rate of children aged 1 to 9 years of age increased by 29 per cent'.[158]

The same speaker reinforced his argument by quoting another report which was available from the Academy of Medicine, and compiled by authors, Gounelle, Vallette and Moine, who studied the physical examination reports of 1,075 schoolchildren from Paris.

The report noted that the index of development of young children was significantly down: boys of seven to 12 years of age showed a deficit of 1.5–2cm in height, and 1–2.28kg in weight as compared to the pre-war level. Two named doctors stated that 50 out of 115 blood donors were declared unfit because of their blood pressure or an insufficient number of red blood cells, due to a lack of food. A further testimony originated from a 12-year-old girl, Denise, who was asked to write a French composition about a fairy granting the pupils a wish. Denise wrote that her dearest wish was to have enough to eat during her life as she was starving. There were suggestions to the Academy of Medicine that the physical education programme should be taken off the school curriculum because it was too demanding for children who were undernourished.[159]

In this broadcast, a combination of evidence sources was used to support the argument. This ranged from authoritative figures in official reports and the opinion of medical professionals to the only wish of a child. The facts were stark: food shortages had caused a higher mortality rate and posed a significant threat to people's lives. 'If you must be hungry somewhere, Göring said, it will not be in Germany.'[160] This statement was repeated seven times by the speaker during this broadcast so that the message to the listeners was unequivocal: the Germans were responsible for the famine in France. The speaker highlighted that this part of the speech by Göring was intentionally omitted by Vichy to conceal the true opinion of the German authorities towards France.

Much of what the BBC reported was also reflected by officials' concerns about public health. In the police report of 21 September, the extent of the progression of the ravages caused by tuberculosis since late 1940 was highlighted. Tuberculosis became the largest cause of death among the 15–19 age group and mainly affected the malnourished youngsters during their years of growth, among other vulnerable people.[161] On 27 June, a letter was sent from Gidel, rector of the Academy of Paris, to Abel Bonnard, Minister of Education, reporting that 'students were abandoning their studies because of anaemia, general exhaustion, and lack of food, but above all because of tuberculosis, which was rapidly on the increase'.[162] Vitamin deficiencies were also seen as a major contributor to the deterioration of children's health.[163]

By October, there were many complaints from the population about the small quantity of combustible materials that had been allocated to each household, which were insufficient for the coming winter. Mothers who had not been able to provide warm clothes and shoes for their children were particularly worried, as their children's state of health was already precarious due to dietary restrictions.[164] These reports compiled by the police and a public figure confirmed that the authorities were well aware of the consequences of food shortages on the health of France's youth in particular – food shortages that were caused by excessive requisitioning by the German occupier.

The desperation of the French population was equally felt by the BBC as it received letters from listeners revealing increasing frustration. The BBC Monthly Intelligence Report of 21 October observed that what mattered most for the majority of correspondents was the immediate question regarding their suffering. As famine and despair descended on France, it became more and more difficult to remain positive about the future. As one listener wrote in a letter:

> You over there seem incapable of making anything but speeches about the post-war world and statements about the excellency of production. But that is all one sees or hears and you may well imagine that the bitterness of a rapidly starving Europe is rising (Lot, 25.7).[165]

This excerpt demonstrates how some French people felt at the end of 1942, when the situation became increasingly desperate. Food was lacking and there was no significant breakthrough in the Allied military efforts. Nothing seemed to have happened to give courage back to the French. Perhaps the French wondered whether there would ever be an improvement to this dire situation. However, while doubt may have settled in among some of the listeners of the BBC, solidarity towards children and the vulnerable continued to bring hope to the population. Many relief organisations' work in France sought to improve the lives of the vulnerable, and this should not be underestimated. Although Vichy's efforts to improve health among French youth were not without merit, despite their ulterior motives, the means available were insufficient for the task at hand. The situation would thus remain unchanged for as long as the Germans remained on French soil.[166]

Family parcels and black markets

As reported in an anonymous letter sent from Bâle on 27 July to the BBC, the situation of food supply in Lyon had become unbearable. Women would stand for hours in queues and sometimes still could not bring any food home. The Marché Saint-Antoine in Lyon had once offered a good quantity of fruit and vegetables, but now there was little available. On 9 July, only some 30 stalls opened, selling lots of peaches but no vegetables or salad. Large numbers of police officers were present in the market because mothers frequently manifested their outrage. Wholesalers blocked the sale of vegetables for the Germans as soon as they arrived. In the Rhône *département*, two tariffs coexisted: Tariff A (normal tariff) and Tariff B (black market).[167] This and other letters outlined the desperate situation in the unoccupied zone and provided the BBC with empirical evidence about the food situation, people's mood and opinion, as well as the intensified police control that was necessary to maintain peace. Correspondence such as this enabled the BBC speakers to discuss the local situation with confidence and use food shortages as a weapon to attack the Germans and Vichy.

Duchesne spoke on air about the dire food situation in France in a number of occasions in the run-up to winter. In his broadcast on 21 September, he acknowledged that the information originated from letters and stressed that it was in the cities that the French suffered the most. During the summer months, the population at least received a variety of green vegetables, such as salad, cabbage, chard and squash, although these vegetables were not really nourishing, and the actual quantity was minimal. For example, in Paris or Lyon, the residents only managed to obtain the equivalent of about 450g per month per person.[168] The reason was that the supply organisation prohibited 'the sale and circulation of nutritious vegetables'.[169] The same applied to 'family parcels' (see below): only greens and fruits were permitted but not butter, beans, potatoes or chestnuts. Any offenders who broke these rules would risk a heavy fine. Duchesne explained that France produced enough food for the whole population of France, but Berlin fixed the amount of food the French were entitled to have, and were aided mercilessly by Vichy in preventing the French from consuming their own products. He asserted that the BBC would continue to monitor and bring updates on the food supply so that all French people would be better informed of the situation and find ways to improve their food supply in anticipation of a tough winter.[170]

The informal practice of the family parcel was observed as early as 21 January 1941 although it was not formally regulated until 13 October 1941. The system permitted packages to be sent from family or friends who lived in the countryside to those in urban areas, in anticipation of another tough winter.[171] Although it mitigated the food supply situation, there were various limitations imposed on the transport of such packages, for example, the weight limit of 50kg and the restrictions on the contents of the package.[172] Nonetheless, family parcels made a positive impact as they contributed significantly to the supply of large cities, curbed the rising of illegal prices and reduced the number of intermediaries. Thanks to the family parcels, many urban families survived.[173] The system was so popular that 'for the year 1942 alone, a total of 13,547,000 parcels were shipped for a total weight of 279,000 tons'.[174]

Family parcels benefited most those who could afford them. According to the calculation of Sauvy, a historian of the French economy, the number of parcels received per capita in the wealthy *arrondissements* of 7, 8, 9 and 16 in Paris was 50 per cent higher than those going to poorer *arrondissements*.[175] Another issue was that the parcels took up precious space in the transport system. For example, it was noted that out of five wagons containing artichokes shipped from Brittany to Paris, three contained family parcels. Some of the shipments got diverted, too. For instance, there were parcels from Côtes-du-Nord that were diverted to Parisian restaurants in exchange for exorbitant prices.[176]

Despite acknowledging the family parcel system and its popularity, speakers such as Duchesne pointed out the limited content of the parcels and used this to attack Vichy. This shows that the BBC was very well informed of the situation in Paris and other urban areas, and of the rising costs of food, which meant only the better-off could lay their hands on a larger quantity of food. Speaking as the voice of the BBC, Duchesne showed clear commitment and devotion to the task of keeping the French informed and empathised with the French to remind them that the BBC would always be on their side.

In a different broadcast three days later, Duchesne raised the discussion of family parcels again, this time in comparison to the black market. He claimed that the French black market existed because of the German looting in France and the inability of the Vichy government to supply the French adequately and evenly. The black market only benefited the wealthy due to its exorbitant prices. The fact remained that Vichy created this fraudulent market and then pretended to fight against it without taking adequate measures to eliminate it. The black market could easily have been eradicated if Vichy had doubled the ration of bread and cheese and freed the trade of potatoes and beans so everyone could eat cheaply. France had the means to achieve this as the country produced enough. Why would Vichy not permit it?

Duchesne then answered his own question, repeating that family parcels were the best way to help the French feed themselves cheaply, and that this system could be one of the most efficient ways to fight against the black market. However, due to the restrictions imposed on the quantities and contents of parcels, it was not surprising that those who had the means still resorted to the black market, without which many more French would have starved. On the other hand, this dual system also condemned families on low incomes to famine.[177]

By 1942, the black market had to a certain extent become the lifeline of many French people. Furthermore, despite their negative connotations, not all black markets were the same. In a letter read out on the programme *Courrier de France*, Brunius explained how the French organised the *marché de solidarité* or 'solidarity market' between the city dwellers and the farmers to stand up to Vichy's chaos.[178] This type of information perhaps derived from an interview with an informant, such as Jean Abel Louis Poumeau de Lafforest, a French journalist at *L'Ouest-Éclair*, who explained the different kinds of black markets. He spoke about the *Marché Rose*,[179] which:

> covers all friendly transactions between townspeople and peasants whereby the small family rations are supplemented without having to pay the fabulous prices of the Black Market. The Black Market is a profit making racket, the Rose Market is the friendly self-help of the poor.[180]

The *marché de solidarité* is thought to have begun as early as the summer of 1941 when city dwellers visited the centres of production using their bicycles or trains. The real danger was the journey back to the Paris railway stations, where passengers were subject to controls. To avoid these, the 'shoppers' would throw the bags out of the windows of the train before arriving in Paris, or get off at a suburban station and continue their journey to Paris by bicycle at night. If they were checked, their goods could be confiscated, but sometimes a friendly police officer would let them go in exchange for some money or a portion of the smuggled goods.[181] This was not always the case, though. Sometimes the consequences could be dire for offenders caught in the act of smuggling food into the cities. A law was introduced on 15 March 1942 that enabled a greater repression of the black market with more severe punishment, meaning that people could be sanctioned with a heavy fine, or time spent in prison, just for devoting themselves to feeding their family. That said, some magistrates did not always follow the law to the letter and showed great leniency in cases of crimes related to buying on the black market, and there was a tendency to excuse a small amount of food trafficking.[182] In time, the Vichy government seemed to start treating food smuggling for self-consumption and that of the black market differently. Jean de Sailly, head of the service de Contrôle des prix (Price Control Service) since November 1940,[183] reminded its agents in the summer of 1942 that the essential goal of the economic control was not to bother those offenders who smuggled food just to supply their family – 'the father accused of some irregularities committed just for the sake of improving the supply of his family deserves leniency'.[184]

A Russian doctor who was a naturalised citizen of France stated that practically anything could be purchased for a good price on the black market. He stated that food came in bulk from the suburbs and was transported safely in German trucks by soldiers who were bribed into Paris, where it would be unloaded by them in an abandoned warehouse or garage. As soon as it had been unloaded, the buyer would collect it. The buyer, however, had to be there when the truck arrived or else the German soldiers would often go to their officers to report the 'illegal stores', and a German truck would be sent out immediately to requisition them.[185]

Although the *marché de solidarité* was encouraging, it was by no means the norm. Black markets, on the other hand, sold goods at significantly inflated prices. On 17 July, in the same broadcast, Brunius read out letters from listeners giving interesting insights on the local situations. In a letter from a Parisian, the writer stated that it was not humanly possible to live off the legal rations; the black market helped the French to survive and without it, 'they would be dead',[186] but it also brought exorbitant prices. The view was that freedom should be given back to the shopkeepers because that would bring prices down again. The black market was so widespread that the informant claimed that there was not one single family who had not purchased a few kilos of dried green beans or peas on it, or via friendly arrangements or from family. The average paid for these precious commodities was 20–40 francs per kilo. The correspondent highlighted that the harvest in 1941 had been so plentiful that the farmers could not possibly have sold all the green beans and peas. However, Vichy had ordered them to block the sale of the stock so that it could be used as a reserve for general supply and requisition for the Germans. This prevented the circulation of such goods among the general populace. The farmers also struggled to keep all the stock in their silos and barns. To free up space, they would either obtain a direct voucher of requisition from the Germans or make arrangements with a black-market trafficker to sell the stock.[187]

The priority of food supply was also mentioned by Alain Beauge, a French lawyer, who claimed in an interview to be conversant with the situation of farmers in the districts of Carantec, Morlaix and Rennes in Brittany. He stated that the director of rationing, who had worked hand in hand with the Germans in determining the rationing since about May 1942, was guided by the following considerations:[188]

> (a) To create stocks immediately available for German requirements and that in French requisitioned premises. (b) Then to create stocks officially for the French, distributed in small lots over an area, so that they can easily be requisitioned. These stocks are kept on unsuitable premises so that many of the foodstuffs perish. (c) To block commodities in such manner that their distribution and consumption is prevented. (d) No more non-rationed commodities.[189]

With such empirical evidence from listeners and interviews, the BBC could substantiate their claims more explicitly on the airwaves that the General Supply Service of Vichy was an agent of the Germans that was used to purchase foodstuffs. On 28 October, an unnamed speaker at the BBC announced to the French peasants that from 1 November, the surplus of their production beyond the quota of mandatory supply would not be available to their city friends. Half of that amount would go to the General Supply Service, which meant that it would most certainly be handed over to the Germans. Moreover, the city dwellers could no longer buy food from the farmers directly if they could not state the name of the farmers. The speaker encouraged the farmers to contact their potential buyers proactively either by phone or by travelling to the city in order to provide this information. The BBC also urged the farmers not to keep anything from their production beyond the mandatory quota of requisition; otherwise, they would see the General Supply Service wasting their harvest by letting the stock rot or freeze, as had happened in 1941. If the surplus disappeared, the Germans would not be able to take anything away from the farmers. The speaker accused Vichy of being the official purchaser of foodstuffs for the Germans and for blocking a large quantity of the food from reaching city dwellers.[190]

In reality, the Vichy authorities were hardly able to change the situation as their hands were tied: they were in no position to rebel against the German demands, and they had no will to do so, particularly after Laval's return to office in April 1942.[191] The BBC accused Vichy of being the puppet government of Germany and repeated this message again and again in its broadcasts. This served to convince many of its listeners who encountered day-to-day difficulties of food supply. The BBC accused Vichy of totally disregarding the interests of the French population, because it would rather let the stock rot or freeze than feed its people. They appealed to the patriotism and solidarity of the farmers and urged them to do more to help the urban population; however, it was questionable how realistic this course of action was.

Foodstuffs were made available to the French population only after German requirements had been met, and if it suited German military demand. As Z. J. S. Sieniewicz, a Polish industrialist, stated in the summer of 1942, there was a mass slaughter of sheep in France because the German army needed coats for their military campaign in Russia in the winter. This resulted in large quantities of mutton and lamb becoming available to the French in the butchers' shops,[192] because the Germans preferred beef. This was in line with the findings of Michel Cépède, a researcher and Professor in Economics and Rural Sociology, that requisitions of mutton was extremely low compared to beef: only 1,000 tons of mutton were requisitioned in 1941 and 1942 respectively, as compared to 116,000 tons of beef in 1941 and 163,000 tons in 1942.[193]

War of propaganda around food, Laval and the Dieppe landing

Food shortages in France could be used by both the Allies and the Axis powers as a psychological and economic weapon from 1940 to 1942 (and beyond), especially with the involvement of the USA in providing aid to the Allied cause from 1941. In a telegram sent to Churchill on 23 March 1942, Roosevelt stated that the United Nations should take advantage of the situation by resuming limited economic assistance to the North Africa bridgehead to Europe and by sending further Red Cross aid to children in France in order to hold off the Axis forces.[194] Further rumours were brought to light by the Agence française d'information de presse (AFIP), the Gaullist press agency in London, on 26 June 1942 that Anglo-American propaganda had intended to use a shipment of foodstuffs to France, with its risk of being intercepted or captured by the Axis powers, to win psychological points among the French population. The Americans would gain the support of the French population if the food shipment were successfully delivered to the population in France; on the other hand, if it were seized by the Germans, it would deepen anti-German sentiment.[195] This hypothetical shipment of food to help the French population, suggested by Roosevelt under a false pretence of humanity, shows that it was a war in which propaganda played a key role.

On 1 July 1942, BBC intelligence reported the concerns of several observers who stressed the importance of tackling food shortages in conjunction with an Allied landing: 'He who will bring enough to feed everybody will be followed and loved. There the Allies have a powerful trump card.'[196] The BBC also advised their staff to repeat the following message in their broadcasts: 'stocks of food in reserve are being built up in England for France once we know that the French and not the Germans will eat it'.[197] The purpose was to convince the French that by helping the Allies, food would definitely come to them. Between 1940 and 1942, talking about the food situation and requisitioning became one of the best propaganda tools of the BBC, providing it with ammunition to attract listeners, influence their opinion towards the occupier and Vichy, and gain their support.

On 21 June, a BBC broadcaster addressed French women, praising them for finding the impossible strength to try to make a home feel like home because they wanted their children to suffer as little as possible when they returned from work or school, despite the war that had now lasted for two years. The speaker told a story of a young woman he had met in the previous winter in Paris, whose husband was a prisoner of war. She had three children aged seven, five and three. In the absence of her husband, she only received the insufficient allowance of the wives of prisoners. To make a living, she did housework, sought out supplies outside her working hours, made everything shine in her house, and looked after her children, whom she took to school every morning. She clearly struggled so much: she said she would give anything for her husband to return home and for her children to eat plentifully, as they had before the war, even if that meant Germany won the war. To these words of desperation, the speaker responded with reason: with a German victory, the French would live perpetually reliant on coupons to buy food and other products. These food coupons could entail 10, 20 or even 50 years of miserable rations. France would be condemned to be the pantry of Germany forever and Germany could always take it all.[198] The message from this story is clear. What the speaker told the French woman was precisely the message he wanted to tell all the French women listening to the programme: giving up hope would not bring them what they were hoping for.

The return of Laval to power in April 1942 marked a closer collaboration between Vichy and Germany. When Laval made his '*Je souhaite la victoire de l'Allemagne*' ('I wish for a German victory') speech on 22 June 1942, there was a flurry of broadcasts from the BBC countering his speech with direct and open attack. For instance, Schumann responded on the same day:

> Even before having uttered this sentence, Laval had excluded himself from France. Even before having uttered this sentence, Laval had condemned himself to death. (…) One had never seen in history a Judas doubled of a blackmailer and tripled of a négrier [slave trader].[199]

On the next day, Marin added that:

> Hitler's Reich, exhausted by its Russian campaign and by the fabulous losses it suffered there, can no longer meet the demands of its production and the longer it goes on, the less it will be able to cope, and that will lead to a complete catastrophe. It is in this context that Laval's speech must be placed.[200]

This in turn was followed by the views of Jacques Borel, who denounced Laval's speech in these words: 'Pierre Laval had a crisis yesterday for being frank. He told us that Germany needs manpower. We've been telling you this for months.'[201] Pierre Bourdan, who listened to Laval's speech in the company of some friends, said in his broadcast what they felt: 'This is the first good news of the war in two weeks … Why? Because we did not expect such a clear, blatant admission of Germany's difficulties.'[202]

Boris picked up Schumann's invention of the new nickname 'Laval le négrier' ('Laval the slave trader'), stating that these two names were now inseparable.[203]

The BBC intelligence report of 26 August 1942 concluded that almost all the observers who wrote to the BBC agreed that if French morale had fallen so low, it was due to empty bellies (for example, the letter from Berne, 28.6).[204] The French were not very confident of the Allied victory, especially after their failure to open a second front during the Dieppe raid on 19 August, stating '*on n'a pas fini de crever de faim*' ('we are not done starving').[205] After the failure of Dieppe, André Labarthe declared on the BBC the reason Dieppe was chosen for the landing:

> In Dieppe (…), it was a question of proving. (…) It was necessary to test, to feel, to experience the solidity of the coastal fortress, and it is for this reason that we chose one of the most difficult strategic points, a heavily fortified city between two high cliffs that control it.[206]

A former Vichy correspondent wrote the following in the *Stockholms-Tidningen*, which was representative of how the French felt after the failure of Dieppe on 8 September: 'British retreats caused deep disappointment. So many scornful words even in Anglophile circles have never been heard before in France. Since then, not many have believed seriously in the Second Front in France this year'.[207] Now, French people foresaw another winter of deprivation and restrictions that would accentuate the general weariness of the population.

The failure of the Dieppe landing provided a golden opportunity for both Vichy and German propaganda. An article was published in *Radio National* with the title '*Raid de Luxe?*' It discussed the Dieppe landing and concluded that this British failure was a 'raid of luxury' – for which the blood of thousands were spilled for no reason – and that we must learn a lesson from this event and from the attitude of the French coastal populations who did not offer any help to the British, demonstrating magnificent discipline and courage.[208]

German propaganda followed suit in their radio magazine *Les Ondes*, which featured two pages showing nine photos of prisoners of war returning to France, titled 'Dieppe, 12 September 1942'. These were French prisoners in Germany who had lived in the Dieppe region before the war and who were being returned to France on the orders of the Führer to reward the good behaviour (discipline and calmness) displayed by the people of Dieppe during the Allied landing.[209]

As we have seen, throughout the period 1940–42, the narratives of the BBC broadcasts had a consistent focus on instilling hatred towards the German occupier and accusing Vichy of abandoning the interests of the French for the sake of the Germans, through passionate, patriotic and carefully crafted covert and overt messages. The supply problems and the hunger of the French population became one of the key propaganda tools against Germany and Vichy. As the war progressed, the narratives of the BBC broadcasts also evolved from stating the facts to building up discontent. Occasionally, it even encouraged passive and active resistance. For example, on 25 September 1941, a broadcast explicitly called for the French to use their own intelligence and ingenuity to help feed the French population with French produce. The message was clear: Vichy imposed a levy on food on behalf of the German authorities but there were things the French could do. Those who worked in the countryside could try to keep as much as possible for the French by preventing the Germans from getting hold of the stock; those working in the transport industry could complicate the transport of food, and encourage the farmers to provide food for the city dwellers.[210] The narratives of the BBC broadcasts became increasingly overt in their nature and this would soon develop into a period that advocated for resistance after the Allied landing in North Africa in November 1942.

CHAPTER 4

RN broadcasts

RN's broadcasts featured a number of recurring themes that were central to the political and propaganda aims of the Vichy government, most importantly education, youth, national unity and work.[1] In July 1940, Pétain confided to William Bullitt, the US ambassador, that 'France had lost the war because reserve officers had socialist teachers.'[2]

Pétain had already raised his concerns over the nation's education policy towards youth as early as 1927 during the inauguration of the Douaumont Ossuary – the memorial containing the bones of the 130,000 unknown soldiers who were killed in battle in 1916. On 5 April 1934, Gaston Doumergue, the newly elected prime minister of France, wrote a letter to the minister in charge of education outlining the new directives. It said: 'It is absolutely necessary for the country, both from the perspective of its defence and its moral recovery, that the teaching staff endeavour to form a resolute youth, virile and well prepared for the accomplishment of its military service.'[3]

Jules Ferry, who established the law offering free and mandatory laic (secular) education in the late 19th century, was seen as responsible for the poor functioning of the schools and the lowering of the level of studies, turning pupils into parasites and schools into 'a fighting machine' against Catholicism.[4] Ferry's other crimes were to have made the schools focus more on science and comprehensive learning at the cost of moral values.[5]

The retired *inspecteur général de l'Instruction publique,* Paul Crouzet, was in April 1940 the director of the Cabinet of the Minister of National Education of Albert Sarraut. One of the most outspoken critics and representatives of what would become Vichy's ideology on education, he vehemently denounced Ferry's education policy, accusing it of sacrificing moral culture in favour of scientific culture, and ultimately leading to the debasement of manual labour. Crouzet also blamed the Popular Front, which he said reduced working hours, introduced new methods of teaching through joy and freedom, and compromised the 'good old' education system, which valued hard work. He criticised doctors, too, for being overly generous in signing off school pupils on the basis of overwork. Crouzet concluded that generalised laxity had spread in schools and discipline had been the first thing to suffer. There was a lack of respect among the youth towards authority figures and this was becoming more visible.[6]

In terms of the structure of education, Vichy wanted to give priority to the reform of primary schools over secondary schools' classical education, which was perceived as the symbol of the 'bourgeois order'.[7] Primary schools' education programmes were perceived as 'the most aggressive secular activism'.[8] Since 1789, revolutionary ideas had been taught to pupils rather than the history of France itself. The modernism of the curriculum was particularly dangerous to the preservation of French traditions, as schools only covered the most recent period in the subjects of history and French. Crouzet declared that the French would find themselves uprooted because of this perceived encroachment of the present over the past and the new over old. Pétain would address this situation to ensure that the French would find their roots again.[9]

Teachers were also seen as responsible for this general deterioration. They fell under the control of the trade union, the Syndicat national des instituteurs (SNI)[10] in particular, as well as the Freemasons. The schools thus had become a failure. Teachers did not teach because they were too busy indoctrinating the pupils. This failure in education could be felt in the military[11] – 'the number of illiterates rose in military barracks from 2.12 per cent in 1914 to 4.29 per cent in 1931'.[12]

The idea that schools should follow a similar model to military training to address the imbalance and to physically harden the youth[13] was expressed in a well-known document entitled *L'école, antichambre de la caserne* (School, antechamber to the barracks)[14] after the defeat by the Prussians in 1870.[15] When Pétain spoke at the Cercle de l'Union Interallié (Circle of the Inter-allied Union) on 15 December 1934 in Paris, he expressed a similar view: that it would be necessary to strengthen 'the links between the school and the army'.[16] In essence:

> School executives and military officials have, in fact, a common mission: to develop the physical strength, to harden the hearts, and to forge the wills. While the army trains soldiers – the eventual instruments for National Defence, schools prepare citizens, permanent artisans for the grandeur of the country.[17]

Pétain also said that '"France has not acquired a true national education system" because the members of the teaching community openly allow themselves "to destroy the State and Society" by raising young people "in ignorance or contempt of the Fatherland"'.[18]

André Delmas, general secretary of the SNI, argued strongly against Pétain's speech and refuted his statement point by point in the Union's journal, *l'École libératrice*, of 15 December 1934. Delmas expressed that 'the army and the school do not have "a common mission"; what is true for fascists' countries is not for France'; and that schools are not bound 'to train the future soldier', but 'to train men and free citizens'.[19]

"Le Lit à colonnes". From CSA, *Les Ondes* (12 April 1942).

Radiodiffusion Nationale programmes. From CSA, *Cahiers d'Histoire de la Radiodiffusion*, No. 30 (September 1991), 55.

Radiodiffusion Nationale programmes. From CSA, *Cahiers d'Histoire de la Radiodiffusion*, No. 30 (September 1991), 58.

Cover of *Radio National* magazine featuring Maurice Chevalier. From CSA, *Radio National*, (4–10 January 1942).

On foreign airwaves. From CSA, *Radio National*, (24–30 August 1941).

La Voix de la France programmes. From CSA, *Cahiers d'Histoire de la Radiodiffusion*, No. 30 (September 1991), 59.

Radio Paris programmes in *Radio National*. From CSA, *Radio National* (30 August–5 September 1942).

Images of prisoners in "Stalag". From CSA, *Radio National* (24–30 August 1941).

"Listen Madam…" From CSA, *Radio National* (14–20 September 1941).

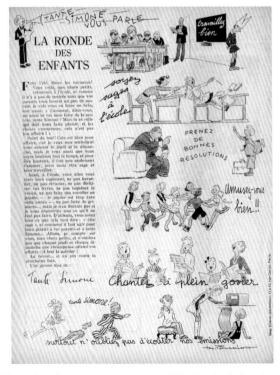

La Ronde des enfants by Tante Simone. From CSA, *Les Ondes* (18 October 1942).

Radio programmes from 18 to 24 October 1942. From CSA, *Les Ondes* (18 October 1942).

Dieppe, 12 September 1942. From CSA, *Les Ondes* (20 September 1942).

The athletes of the National College of Instructors of Antibes. From CSA, *Radio National* (7–13 September 1941).

Cover of *Radio National* magazine. From CSA, *Radio National* (26 October–1 November 1941).

Cover of *Radio National* magazine, Christmas edition. From CSA, *Radio National* (21–27 December 1941).

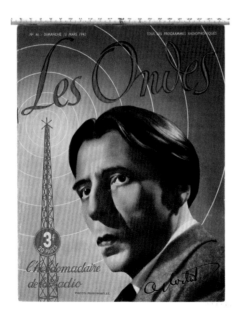

Cover of *Les Ondes* magazine with Alfred Cortot. From CSA, *Les Ondes* (15 March 1942).

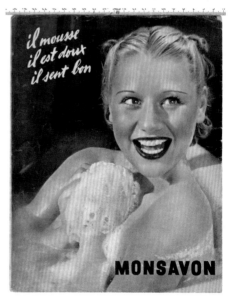

Advertisement for Monsavon soap. From CSA, *Les Ondes* (10 May 1942).

Advertisement for Imédia Oréal hair dye. From CSA, *Les Ondes* (24 May 1942).

Advertisement for Vibert Frères toothpaste. From CSA, *Les Ondes* (31 May 1942).

Advertisement for the Loterie Nationale. From CSA, *Les Ondes* (17 May 1942).

Rural Civic Service. From CSA, *Radio National* (10–16 August 1941).

Paris under the bombs. From CSA, *Radio National*, (15–21 March 1942).

Henri Becquart, the right-wing deputy, held similar views to Pétain regarding youth. As he announced at the École Saint-Joseph in Lille in 1936, pupils were witnessing the collapse of French society as individualism prevailed over the value of community. Young people had an obligation to restore the great traditions of every human society: '*Family*, Authority in the State, Liberty and Dignity of the individual, *Work*, Charity, *Country*.'[20] Becquart saw youth as the bearer of hope for French society. The right was now so close to the centre of power that it could influence education policies.[21]

Following the fall of France, the Vichy government's priority was to assert its power as the new 'legitimate' government of France. To achieve this goal, it had first to justify the capitulation and the Armistice, and to explain the reasons for the defeat. They could then begin to legitimise future collaboration with the occupier and to establish who would become the new enemies of France.[22] Once they had achieved this, RN, as the official wireless propaganda medium, could address Vichy's primary concerns, such as the transformation of youth and the regeneration of France.

To this end, there were extensive discussions surrounding multiple facets of the youth question on RN airwaves. First, Vichy promoted their ideal of family and motherhood. The French population was ageing because of the decline in the birth rate that had started at the beginning of the 19th century. This was followed shortly by the high number of casualties (1.3 million Frenchmen) during the Great War.[23] Between 1911 and 1931, France had approximately the same number of inhabitants. The birth rate, however, fell from 18.2 per cent in the period of 1926–30 to 14.8 per cent in the period of 1936–38.[24]

The role of women was to ensure the growth of the French race, and this needed to be understood by young women at school age.[25] Vichy multiplied laws to restrict women's activities in an attempt to reverse the decline in the birth rate and the lack of male children, which was seen as partially responsible for the defeat in 1940.[26]

Vichy also vigorously promoted family ideology and the virtues of motherhood. Several laws were created to protect families. On 11 October 1940, the employment of married women in the public sector was forbidden and in April 1941, it became more difficult to divorce.[27] Both birth control and abortion were illegal and as of February 1942, a new legislation made abortion punishable as a crime against the state and the French 'race'.[28] The aim was to restore the patriarchal family. The Conservatives stressed 'the harm female employment had done to the French moral fiber by creating delinquent children, alcoholic husbands, and flirtatious women. Women's work had also weakened France by lowering the birthrate.'[29]

Vichy's decision to make policies surrounding women and family a priority had a striking resemblance to that of the National Socialist Party in Germany when it first took power. Germany, too, had suffered a decline in its birth rate during the inter-war period. Goebbels stressed as early as 18 March 1933 that women's new role in German society was childbearing and the education of children, for the Fatherland's immortality.[30] He stated that 'If the nation once again has mothers who proudly and freely choose motherhood, it cannot perish. If the woman is healthy, the people will be healthy. Woe to the nation that neglects its women and mothers. It condemns itself.'[31]

Vichy viewed women as responsible for the family both as a wife and as a mother. The Vichy motto '*Travail, Famille, Patrie*' was forced on the French repeatedly through a variety of means, including the use of more advanced technology such as radio broadcasting and propaganda documentary clips. It became common practice in cinemas to show a short clip of news or documentary prior to the main feature, with images of cradles, babies and children to remind the audience that the family 'is the France of tomorrow'. Indeed, Vichy propaganda promoted childbearing as early as 1940 with its first short film *Première Valse*. A multitude of others followed suit. The most important one was made in 1942, *Le Jardin sans fleurs*, illustrating the decline of the birth rate in France during the inter-war period and stressing that French families needed to have more children to have a happy family life.[32]

The second theme was the crucial reform of education to mould French youth. Pétain publicly castigated primary school teachers 'as a major contributor to the defeat' in 1940 for not managing and not having the desire to teach moral and patriotic values to their pupils.[33] Teachers were accused of failing the youth by preaching for peace. For the teachers, the Great War was to be the last of all wars: many teachers who participated in the Great War never returned. They stood in the forefront of all pacifist demonstrations taking place between the two wars, urging the French not to accept that they had 'to die for Danzig'.[34] On 23 April 1939, J. Fontaine stated in the *l'École émancipée*, a union and educational magazine, that he would 'prefer servitude than war, because with servitude we return, whereas with war we do not'.[35] Such statements deeply offended the military.

Until Laval's dismissal in December 1940, teachers were ostracised by Vichy.[36] Moreover, the former education system was blamed: the teaching body needed to be purged; the curricula needed a complete makeover, including textbooks and teaching methods. As conscription no longer existed, youth organisations needed to fulfil their function in completing the school leaver's education using tradition, honour and high moral training.[37] This old education system was seen as too bookish, emphasising 'instruction' rather than 'education'. The new curricula included Vichy's elements of civic, social, moral education, artistic activities, physical training and games. It was adopted at all levels of the 'new' education system, and this new value was embraced by the youth groups as well.[38] Youth was to become a fundamental part of Vichy ideology as a guarantor for the future of the New France.[39] Children had to be made to believe in the New France, and in the vital role they would play as mothers, farmers, soldiers, etc. once they were adults. Education needed to be turned into indoctrination.[40]

The third theme of RN's broadcast was the new role of youth and the function of the various youth groups in the community. Vichy attempted to capture and train the minds of young individuals to be conditioned to Vichy's core values and ideology. It made a considerable commitment to ensure the prodigality of its support to youth movements and this resulted in a multitude of youth groups being created to serve this purpose. The number of young people enrolled in these groups more than doubled in 1941 and youth groups in different uniforms seemed to be omnipresent in the unoccupied zone, though not in the occupied zone.[41] Youth groups' participation in the daily lives of French households was considerable as they brought comfort and gave help to the community at large. Their actions improved the lives of many French citizens in need, especially their involvement with charitable organisations.

However, the German authorities quickly became suspicious of youth movements in Vichy, particularly their leaders and teachers, because some were led by French army officers. Any physical, moral or patriotic 'regeneration' of French youth was thought to pose a risk to Germany in the future. The Germans had applied a similar strategy with their own youth groups against the French when France had occupied the Rhineland after the defeat of Germany in the Great War. As a result, the youth movements were curbed in the occupied zone but continued to flourish in the unoccupied zone.[42]

The final theme focused on the role of sports in youth development, which featured much more heavily from 1941. For Drieu La Rochelle – writer, French nationalist and collaborationist[43] – only the '*révolution du corps*' ('health, dignity, development and harmony')[44] as proposed in fascism was capable of regenerating French youth.[45] Hitler believed that education should focus on German pupils being healthy and having a balanced body,[46] and Pétain had a similar vision, despite Vichy not being a fascist state.[47] Vichy wanted to regenerate its youth by questioning their values, their activities and their attitude; and reprimanding their materialistic spirit along with their spirit of insubordination and dilettantism – qualities that were inherited from the Third Republic.[48]

The physical recovery of youth became vital for the regeneration of the French race, and Vichy propaganda used the physical decline of French youth to explain the defeat of June 1940.[49] Sport, therefore, was placed at the heart of Vichy's educational reform. The Germans were opposed to the French participating in sport and outdoor activities because these nurtured youth's physical strength, promoted national sentiment and military prowess, and increased the risk of French youth becoming a threat to their position.[50] In an internal memorandum at German headquarters in Paris in 1941, the Germans learned that the Commissariat général à l'Éducation générale et aux Sports (CGEGS) had supplied 250 pairs of skis for use in the schools of the Hautes-Alpes to encourage primary school pupils to participate in skiing.[51] The memorandum asked, 'by giving instructions in skiing will not interests other than sporting ones [i.e. military ones] be pursued?'[52] Moreover in early 1941, the

Germans were horrified to discover that 'twelve out of the thirty-four inspectors and sports delegates for the occupied zone were ex-regular officers'.[53] The German authorities monitored the activities of the CGEGS closely as they were suspicious of the military characteristics of this ministry. They ordered a monthly report to be submitted to them with information about the commissariat's activities as well as a list of its key staff members, with particulars of their former employers.[54]

Vichy's actions could be understood as a logical response to the military defeat of 1940, which made physical preparation for a future liberation, national recovery or revenge its policy priority.[55] Vichy mobilised significant resources to convince teachers of the necessity of teaching physical education and creating this sporting faith in France,[56] resulting in physical education becoming deeply rooted in the life of all schools between 1940 and 1944.[57]

1940

Rejuvenation through a renewed commitment to family and birth

RN emphasised the need for the young generation to make a necessary return to the values lost during the Third Republic. Pétain, as the new *président du Conseil*, spoke on 25 June, three days after the Armistice had been signed on Radio Bordeaux Sud-Ouest, part of RN's public network, announcing that a New Order in France was to begin.[58]

During his speech, Pétain warned the French that life would be harsh from now on but said that people could count on him to hear the truth. France would be able to rely on its children in the future because of the way they would be brought up: they would be raised with a sense of duty towards France.[59] 'Our defeat was the result of our slackening. The spirit of enjoyment has destroyed what the spirit of sacrifice has built,' he stated. However, with intellectual and moral rejuvenation, a New France would rise from the ashes.[60]

The French suffered a shattering trauma in 1940 after being conquered in merely six weeks. It was against this backdrop that the French were relieved to greet the news that the Armistice had been signed.[61] Robert Gaillard, a French prisoner of war, wrote in his diary on 12 July 1940, expressing a feeling that was probably experienced by many French at that time: 'What is the point of revolting when we are nothing; what is the point of fighting when we are defeated?'[62] Pétain's broadcast made it clear that France needed shock treatment; its future would lie in the virtue of change, and the population needed to embrace the value of sacrifice and Vichy ideology to rejuvenate France.[63] The purpose of the National Revolution was 'to restore the essence of French grandeur by purging the causes of the Third Republic's supposed decadence and humiliating demise'.[64] To achieve that, a return to the values 'through a return to the earth, an embrace of regional culture and a restoration of the moral and physical vigor of French youth' became necessary.[65] The French would have to seize the defeat as an opportunity to change their behaviour. Only through change could they eventually forget their selfishness and individualism and embrace a new sense of 'community'. To Pétain, France then was no different from Spain in 1936, and Spain had been saved by its youth, its faith and its sacrifice.[66] '*Travail, Famille, Patrie*' was the centrepiece of the National Revolution, without which there would be no salvation.

Vichy's expectations of France and its youth were met with mixed responses, and Vichy was well aware of this fact. In a document originating from an official source, it was stated that despite all the indoctrination, Vichy did not have much hope that it could transform the French into believers in the New Order, because Vichy's preaching was so radically different to that which 'made the France of yesterday'. A real conversion of people's mentality would be necessary for the New Order to succeed. It would be naive to think that French adults would be converted that easily. It was for this reason that the Vichy government targeted the youth,[67] because 'they are not yet ossified in their values; they are powerful and not yet a fluid human being'.[68]

However, this expected transformation of the values of French youth demanded by Vichy, and by Pétain in particular, did not appeal to everyone, as Benoîte Groult, a 20-year-old wrote in her diary on 21 September 1940:

> This morning, we learned that it was no longer permitted to divorce. Mind your own business, Maréchal? We are already prisoners of the occupier; we will now be the prisoner of our spouse! … Because we enjoyed life too much under the Third Republic, as Pétain said; and pleasure debases us. The moralising, reactionary and petit-bourgeoisness in Pétain's doctrine is stinky. It is disgusting to be defeated.[69]

Vichy's policy regarding family and abortion had clearly engendered hostility as early as September 1940.

Pétain recorded the following broadcast on 11 July, speaking about the value of family and the expected role of the state, parents and young people, urging the French not to lose hope. He promised that French families would have the respect and protection of France. France would provide their children with education, confidence that had been lost over the years, and a bright future. French families were the custodians of a long history of honour, and they had a duty to safeguard and pass on to their offspring the ancient virtues that made them strong. Youth in modern times needed to fulfil its role by living with other young members of society and nurturing its strength through safe and friendly outdoor activities to prepare them for the future battle of life. The government would also make sure that the young enthusiasts would be united in a new momentum, which would define the new nature of the French race.[70] He concluded that France needed to be a place where '(a)ll the French are proud of France, and France proud of every French … Let us give ourselves to France. She has always led her people *to greatness*.'[71]

In his message, Pétain expressed his vision of what France would require for a brighter future and to regain this greatness. The state would nurture young people, allowing them to learn, develop and prepare themselves for future battles, all in a safe environment. These statements represent an overt declaration of Pétain's intention to revolutionise youth education, intensify youth movement and take a gender-specific approach to youth. This gender-discriminative social order had provoked resentment: as Groult wrote, 'freedom to the men, kitchen to the women'.[72] It became clear that women would pay the price for this new education system implemented by Vichy. Pétain's vision of a united youth in this New France was thus not necessarily to the taste of the youth themselves, especially young women.

In Paris and the *département* of the Seine, the timetable for girls in primary schools from 12 August to 15 September shows that their education was now focused on the making of lingerie pieces and mending, household tasks such as cleaning and ironing, and other practical courses on individual hygiene and childcare. This was very different to the timetable for boys, which included a much more varied range of activities, such as educational visits to museums or the zoo, teamwork activities, singing, PE, languages and technical skills required for apprenticeship.[73]

In a separate report broadcast by RN in November, Pétain spoke to a worker while visiting a construction site at the tunnel of the Croix-Rousse during his three-day visit to Lyon and Toulouse. The reporter explained that Pétain was having a walkabout with the workers. At one point, he spoke to a 62-year-old foreman, who told Pétain that he had one daughter. Pétain immediately expressed his regret that the foreman did not have more children, because he would otherwise have brought up more children beautifully, just like the foreman himself. A little while later, a young boy was brought to the site to raise the French flag with the help of a representative of the workers. Pétain praised him for a job well done, stating that the boy would remember this moment all his life.[74]

This broadcast was a typical example of overt propaganda for a higher birth rate. Although it remains unclear how a higher birth rate could be achieved without any obvious change in public perception regarding larger families, there could be no doubt that propaganda in its favour had a profound effect on the French population: a noticeable increase in birth rate not only in France but also in Nazi Germany and Fascist Italy was recorded from 1941.[75] The young boy and his actions represented Pétain's ideal for the youth, a revived generation bursting with vigour, strength and patriotism. The high-profile use of pre-adolescent children during Pétain's public appearance was also observed elsewhere, dominating the crowd scene, waving flags, surrounding Pétain. Every opportunity was used to win over the affections of the youth.[76]

From the surviving broadcasts, it seems that from 1941, the rhetoric about family values and the role of women subsided and the discussions about women shifted. However, it did not completely disappear from the airwaves. A further broadcast dated 19 June 1941 showed the contrast between the size of the families in cities and in rural areas. When Pétain visited the Limousin region, he stopped at the Richaud farm, where he met the peasants and discussed the situation on the farm. Pétain spoke to the sharecropper's wife, who had two children; both were prisoners of war. She pleaded with Pétain to bring them home.[77] He replied, 'your turn will come, have patience, patience is required for everyone including me. All the prisoners are my children. You have two; me, I have one and a half million'.[78]

During this visit to the farm, when talking to the residents, he often enquired about the make-up of the family as well as the numbers of prisoners of war. One of the families interviewed had eight children and another family six,[79] to which Pétain commented, 'happiness [belongs] to large families.'[80]

There is a striking contrast between his visit to Lyon in November 1940 and the one to the Richaud farm in June 1941. During the latter, Pétain expressed his satisfaction when the interviewees talked about their large families. During all his visits, the topics of family and children would usually occupy a prominent place, and this reinforced his image as a father figure of France. This broadcast was no exception, as Pétain repeatedly referred to all prisoners as his children.

The beginning of youth groups

The office of the Secrétariat général de la Jeunesse (SGJ) was created on 12 July 1940 as a priority in the national strategy to guide and moralise young people, with Georges Lamirand as its head. This office served a dual purpose: to provide a place at the government level to discuss specific issues concerning human, social and political aspects of youth, and to provide space for collective initiatives, such as the Chantiers de la Jeunesse, Compagnons de France, école des cadres (leadership schools), etc.[81]

Lamirand supported the creation of two new youth movements almost immediately after the instigation of the office, the Chantiers being one of them. The Chantiers was intended as a civil replacement for conscription; joining this work experience organisation was compulsory for any eligible young adult aged 20 or above.

After the Armistice, the Germans disbanded the French military forces except for a small army of 100,000 men to maintain internal order. The demobilisation had to be gradual and the youngest serving members were the last to go. It involved nearly 92,000 young men, many of whom had joined the army shortly before the Armistice.[82] The law of 1 August 1940 formalised the policy by creating the first youth group, the Chantiers de la Jeunesse. On 8 and 9 June, the Chantiers incorporated first those who had joined the army and demobilised a few weeks later.[83]

The Chantiers was led by Général de la Porte du Theil, who was familiar with both the military and the Scouting traditions. Their education focused on three areas: academic activities, which were aimed at correcting deficiencies in schooling; cultural activities, such as singing, dancing and visiting local communities in partnership; and vocational activities, which focused on learning technical processes in workshops and farms[84] 'to develop skill, order, precision, dexterity, and the ability to foresee practical difficulties'.[85] The recruits would also undertake a regime of vigorous outdoor physical activities to keep them fit. All this was done so they would embrace the community ideal.[86]

The first recruits were to spend six months doing work experience but a law of 18 January 1941 changed the duration to eight months,[87] and attached them to the State Secretariat for National Education and Youth. With this law, the organisation of the Chantiers extended to North Africa, whose territories were now participating in the recovery of France by focusing on the moral and physical rejuvenation of the French youth.[88]

The experience of the recruits, however, told a different story to what Vichy had hoped to achieve. According to Commissioner Fournols of group 23 (Hérault), 'if all are starting to comply with the discipline of the Chantiers, the fact remains that the large majority did not understand the purpose of their stay here. They always think of being on leave, their release, and their personal well-being.'[89] There were also criticism that this work experience was useless and a waste of time. By September 1942, these young men still did not understand what they were doing in this organisation. The notion of raising the country was too abstract. For them, the work experience was equivalent to military service, with the same obligations and constraints, such as living together, discipline, work, etc. They experienced a strong sense of confinement and captivity and felt hopeless and like they couldn't tolerate it, especially since they had to leave home and their family in these worrying times.[90]

Pétain's broadcast of 13 August was written by René Gillouin, Vichy's Minister of Education from 12 July to 6 September 1940.[91] It was the first time that Pétain had announced specific plans for youth of this age group as they were to become 'officially' full participants in the rebuilding of France. As such, it was an official endorsement of the fact that Vichy was determined to cultivate youth as future leaders who could realise the vision for a New France.

Part of the broadcast focused on the young soldiers who did not take part in the war but who would now contribute to new projects of national interest, which had been neglected for far too long;[92] their tasks would include the '*development of forests, camps, stadiums*, and construction of youth housing in villages'.[93] These projects were key to the rebuilding of France, and Pétain's message made it clear who would be at the forefront of the reconstruction. Vichy wanted the youth to contribute to all aspects of community life. On the other hand, it is conceivable that Vichy had no other choice but to take care of these young men, because many of them had lost their parents in the war, were homeless or could not return home at present.[94]

The other group of youth featured in this broadcast was the young 'demobilised'. These young Frenchmen were to be placed in long-term work, such as '*foster care, craft apprenticeship*, labour camps, and agricultural assistance'.[95] Regarding youth groups, Pétain declared that 'all the existing youth movements will be maintained; their originality will be respected; their action will be encouraged, extended and completed by new initiatives'.[96] These efforts were intended to create a 'strong youth, sound in body and mind, and prepared for the tasks which will raise *their souls* as Frenchmen'.[97]

From the broadcast, there could be little doubt that the government intended the young generation to adopt its ideology. A key feature of the youth movement was that army officers held leading positions in the SGJ as well as other various youth organisations.[98] These military men were experts in training young people both physically and mentally, and in instilling the values of discipline and order. From August, a decision was taken to promote a strong and healthy youth that would not only revive France, but also return France to its former splendour and glory. The potential military benefit of promoting sports and the youth movement was noted by an informant, Jean-Claude Fischoff, a French engineer who was interviewed at the RVPS on 21 May 1942. He stated that he had been connected to the Scout movement in France before being mobilised on 9 June 1940, hence his special interest in the youth movement. He considered that the best way to revive the French national spirit was for young people to receive training under rigid discipline. He argued that if the Ministry of War had had some influence on youth, military training could have been given to them and paramilitary organisations could have been formed more easily to fight the Germans when the time came.[99] There was also a series of broadcasts that were intended to appeal to French youth to help the community at large and to instil the value of solidarity towards those who were living in a precarious situation.

On 9 October, Pétain declared that *comités d'entraide nationale* (national mutual aid committees) had now been constituted in both zones. He appealed to the youth to become members of the committee, as he saw them as a prelude to the work of civic reconstruction and national efforts of social collaboration. Both young men and women should come to the aid of those who had been badly bruised by the war as well as those who had to face new and distressing ordeals in the harsh winter to come.[100]

Pétain reiterated this message on 10 November, pleading to the population as a whole but especially to the young people. He stated that pitying the population would not solve problems, but action would. He called for the population to give generously any blankets, shoes, clothes, underwear, sweaters and socks – i.e., any necessary personal effects that could still be used – to the teams of young people who would come to knock at doors and collect items for those in great need of help. Winter would not wait, so the response had to be quick if all the French were to be sheltered by the end of November. The Secours National would help the refugees, the unemployed and the needy, whereas the Service des prisonniers de guerre (Prisoner of War Service) in collaboration with both the Comité national d'assistance (National Assistance Committee) and the French Red Cross would send clothes to camps in France and Germany.[101]

The Secours National was a voluntary organisation that provided relief of all kinds to the civilian victims during the Great War.[102] It was revived by a decree of 19 October 1939 and subsequently placed under the authority of Pétain by a law of 4 October 1940.[103] These two broadcasts focused on Pétain's repeated plea to the population and for the youth's urgent support of these mutual assistance programmes. The donations of clothes, food, money and other items collected by the group were later announced on the radio to showcase this achievement. To encourage the French to donate, Pétain highlighted the seriousness of the situation in France, stating that in the coming months it would become a matter of life and death for hundreds of thousands of French who were living in difficult situations and who would not survive without the assistance provided by the youth. Their actions would help create a national effort for solidarity in France.

Jean Masson spoke on the radio on 15 November to reiterate the messages in Pétain's two broadcasts. Masson's speech was specifically intended to mobilise the youth and secure their continued support to help the Secours National. He discussed its important role for French society as a whole, especially for the elderly and victims of solitude, and how desirable it was that all youth movements supported the group. Masson appealed to the hearts of the French to play their parts in this collective relief effort. He stated that the government wanted the French to donate, but also to pay friendly visits, speak positive words and encourage more people to volunteer their time and effort as part of their community work to alleviate the suffering of the saddened and the bruised. The French population would have to act with confidence and tenacity in their fight against cold, hunger, misery, discouragement, sadness and despair in every town. Dedication would help the most deprived in the community to live through the winter and France would see better days.[104]

The Secours National was widely recognised as a significant force that participated in numerous generous mutual solidarity actions during the war.[105] Propaganda of such a nature appealed to the long tradition of 'mutual aid' in France and so the French population responded positively to Vichy's appeal to help, even though it was announced on RN, the voice that favoured collaboration. The French population seemed to take into consideration the purpose of the appeal when acting or ignoring the calls made on the radio station.

New education in France and 'La Marseillaise'

A further type of reportage concerned the *école des cadres*, which were created for the training of the new leaders of France. Vichy set up a total of six such schools, the idea being to prepare the leaders of youth movements through 'lived experience' instead of the old 'bookish' system.[106] The school at the Château de la Fauconnière at Gannat was relocated in October 1940 to Uriage, another castle near Grenoble,[107] and became the most celebrated youth leader training facility, operated under the leadership of Major Pierre Dunoyer de Segonzac.[108]

The purpose of Pétain's visit to Gannat was to demonstrate the impact of such education on young men, who, in turn, would become the new elite in charge of rebuilding France. A broadcast was recorded there and put on air the following day.[109] RN recorded the departure of Pétain after visiting the school to hear the reading of the oath of the future leaders of the National Revolution. The reportage began with the youth singing 'La Marseillaise' as Pétain and his officials drove away. The officials consisted of Marcel Peyrouton, Minister of the Interior; Georges Ripert, Minister of Education and Youth; and Georges Lamirand. The journalist then explained the purpose of the visit and briefly described what had happened during the ceremony: each youth team leader had turned towards the French flag and said, 'on behalf of my men, I pledge to work with all the strength of the mind and of my heart, with courage, perseverance, till death, for the salvation of France'.[110]

The journalist stated that the ceremony itself would be broadcast the following day at noon on the progamme *Radio Jeunesse*. He then conducted an interview with M. de la Chapelle, the director of Schools for Training of Youth Leaders, explaining that this school, which currently offered training to potential youth leaders, was in the near future going to be rapidly transformed into an elite school for youth leaders. De la Chapelle said that the network of schools and facilities were devoted to the training of youth and youth leaders. De Segonzac, the head of the School of the Youth, then commended all the young Frenchmen who aspired to become true leaders. While the interview was being conducted, the youth leaders were singing loudly in the background, finishing with 'La Marseillaise' once again. The journalist reported that the passion and enthusiasm of the youth leaders could be heard and felt throughout his report and that it was the wish of all French people to witness this renewed vigour of the youth.[111]

This broadcast served as a 'taster' for a ceremony that Pétain attended to raise interest in the listeners and to entice them to tune in the next day for the full report. The interviews conducted served a similar purpose, giving background information about the event and showcasing the enthusiasm of these youth leaders, who were presented as 'true' Frenchmen, fit to lead France to a bright future, devoted and united for a common ideal. These young men who seemed to have accepted the legitimacy and ideology of Vichy administration were presented as 'role models' for the French population and other youth to follow, who were taking control of their destiny by following the path of true leaders in the new Vichy France.

'La Marseillaise' was used as a tool to heighten French patriotism. In this case, it signified Pétain's departure after an activity that involved the youth. Vichy had the tradition of using 'La Marseillaise' because it was a part of the protocols that accompanied the head of state's travel. Both 'La Marseillaise' and the flag could be seen as political symbols, which evoked a set of common emotions among the French. 'La Marseillaise' has been found to have been played in 37 RN broadcasts from 24 July 1940 to 13 September 1942.[112] Despite being banned in the occupied zone, two broadcasts containing 'La Marseillaise' were produced by RN for Radio Paris: on 27 August 1941, Radio Paris aired a broadcast featuring the celebration in Versailles of the first French contingent of volunteers going to the Russian front to fight alongside the German soldiers;[113] on 24 January 1942, it aired another broadcast featuring a conference in Toulouse presented by Paul Marion, French Minister of Information, about the 'national revolution and social revolution'.[114] Both broadcasts clearly had German interests in mind.

Further broadcasts containing 'La Marseillaise' were produced and aired on Radio Paris from 1 January 1941 onwards on specific occasions: at a political rally during which the audience asked to sing 'La Marseillaise' to demonstrate against the Jews and Freemasons and for eternal France;[115] during a gospel concert, which Pétain attended, in Notre Dame de Paris dedicated to the French POWs currently in Germany;[116] during a follow-on reportage for the first French contingent of volunteers going to the Russian front, at which the reporter declared that for the first time since the Armistice, the French flag floated officially on the pediment of a barracks in the occupied zone;[117] and after a speech delivered by Fernand de Brinon (a delegate of the French government in the occupied zone) at the inauguration of the exhibition 'Bolshevism against Europe' in Paris.[118] Considering the context in which 'La Marseillaise' was performed in public in the occupied zone, its presence served to enhance German propaganda and their views on the future of France, and to direct the patriotism of the French to a France that existed within the framework of the German authorities. In such cases, it did not seem to matter that 'La Marseillaise' was played on Radio Paris – something that was normally forbidden.

As could be heard in the broadcasts, 'La Marseillaise' sung under Vichy rule was frequently truncated; this could be explained by the lack of time or the need to curtail the ceremonies.[119] There was also the fact that some stanzas probably had no place in a defeated and divided France, especially for a government that depended on the occupier. The shortened anthem would appear to resonate well with the desire of Vichy to nurture the sacred love of France through '*Travail, Famille, Patrie*'. Truncated, 'La Marseillaise' could be described as a 'touching anthem of love',[120] one that continued to stimulate nationalism and patriotism towards Vichy as France.

Moreover, the emphasis placed on the youth is evident both from Pétain's presence at the ceremony and by the subsequent flourishing of youth schools. The *école des cadres* became an important tool for training young people and potential leaders of young people. These students 'would be physically hardened, intellectually indoctrinated, and receive the civic and moral education necessary' for the accomplishment of their future responsibilities.[121] The oath was to be the cement that bound young people to become the leaders of the National Revolution but also to face their future responsibilities towards the state, to the death if necessary.

Another broadcast, which was recorded in November and featured Pétain's visit to an agricultural school in the Toulouse region, highlighted the role of education in Vichy. In this very short reportage, a student addressed Pétain and declared that all students wished to become educated and efficient farmers. Pétain expressed his gratitude and declared that he was extremely satisfied that the students had answered his call to 'the return to earth' and stated that their studies were interesting because of their practicality.[122]

Pétain advocated vocational education following primary school, and this agricultural school represented the ideal route, whereby the youth would pick their trade while at school. Moreover, the recovery of France could only be achieved with the National Revolution, and one of the aspects of recovery was agriculture. It meant a great deal to Vichy to motivate the youth to take up agriculture, not least because they participated actively in this sector during summertime.[123]

Despite the propaganda efforts of Vichy, however, it would appear that young people in France remained divided in their devotion to this new ideology. As revealed in a BBC intelligence report of 16 December 1940, a letter from the unoccupied zone dated 24 October described how some French youth saw the future of France: 'At the Lycée the opinion of the young ones does not change. We only live and feel for England and the French leaders, de Gaulle and Muselier.'[124] A subsequent report of 23 December concluded that Vichy had failed to capture the hearts of the youth as there was a high proportion of young people and schoolteachers writing to the BBC stating their attachment to 'the French traditions of free thought and national culture'.[125] Clearly, there was a discrepancy between Vichy propaganda broadcasts on RN and the testimonials reaching the BBC.

1941

Youth movements in full swing

The youth movement was well established by 1941, although this was not necessarily reflected proportionally in the number of surviving radio broadcasts. There were 13 broadcasts in the first half of 1941 concerning the various aspects of youth.[126] Broadcasts featuring youth movements seem to have picked up after spring, perhaps because the weather became more conducive for outdoor activities, and campaigns to encourage youth participation in areas where there was a labour shortage, for example, harvesting in the summer and charity work, were promoted more frequently on the radio. On the other hand, 1941 also saw the emergence of the image of a united youth following Pétain's ideal, which made for excellent propaganda.

Pétain's repeated calls for a youth united behind his vision were highlighted in the BBC report of 4 June 1941, commenting that Vichy spared no effort in its attempt to harness the patriotism of the youth to its own cause. As a letter from Marseille dated 19 March stated: 'The Marshal is trying to create a spiritual re-awakening based on youth. The Youth camps propaganda is done by fairly primitive means – the Marshal's words pinned on the walls, charcoal inscriptions on facades'.[127] This observation demonstrates that Vichy's efforts to rally the youth movements to his ailing cause were increasingly overt.

Achievements of different youth groups were advocated on the airwaves as well, particularly during Pétain's visits. During his visit to the Richaud farm in Limousin on 19 June, Pétain had also met with a priest who was in charge of the youth of the Chantiers de la Jeunesse. The priest explained that these young people were abandoned children or orphans from Limoges but that they were all now working as farmers.[128] The broadcast ended with a compliment from a young boy to Pétain, 'Our motto is the one you have given us, Maréchal: "Travail, Famille, Patrie"'.[129]

Vichy's encouragement for the youth movement gave a tremendous boost to the work of charitable organisations. It also enhanced the link between the city and rural areas as the victims of the war were taken care of, provided for and given the opportunity to obtain practical skills and work experience as farmers. The 'return to the earth' policy of Vichy included education as a core element. The ultimate purpose of this policy was to enable young people to learn practical skills. In the above broadcast, the learning of practical skills was led by a priest and supported by the Chantiers. To conclude the meeting, a young boy pledged his faith to Pétain's motto for the country most unreservedly in a cheerful and happy voice. Such a genuine and spontaneous pledge from young people through the radio was a common element of Pétain's reception during his visits, showcasing his popularity among the youth and the success of Vichy's indoctrination.

The next broadcast was recorded the next day, 20 June, and featured Pétain's visit to Valmatte.[130] This was a major public event involving a significant number of participants. As reported by *Radio National* shortly after the event,[131] 10,000 young people attended, including schoolchildren, students, workers, peasants and other groups.[132] As it is a typical representation of Pétain's visits, the event would be narrated as it unfolded on the airwaves to give a flavour of the ambience and public responses during such an event.

This broadcast is made up of two reels. The first contains four extracts but the first two segments are missing. The second reel contains one extract, featuring Lamirand's speech. The broadcast started with an address by a representative of the Légion des anciens combattants, or the Veterans Legion, a former Verdun veteran who expressed to the Maréchal his feelings of gratitude, loyalty and affection. This was followed by Pétain's address, which ended with the crowd shouting '*Vive le Maréchal*' and with 'La Marseillaise' being played by a brass band, accompanied by an overwhelming chorus from the crowd. The fourth segment of the first reel began with the youth rallying at the fairgrounds.

The second reel contains a reportage that began with repeated '*Vive le Maréchal*' calls from the crowd. A band played 'La Marseillaise' while the crowd sang, followed by a hymn to Pétain to the tune of 'Frère Jacques'. A young girl handed over 60,000 francs to Pétain, collected from all primary and secondary schools in the *département* of Haute-Vienne for less privileged children.

Lamirand's address followed shortly afterwards. He declared that the young people of Limousin were joined today by the delegates of all the provinces of the unoccupied zone. Moreover, the youth in the occupied zone had asked him in a previous meeting in Paris to represent them in this ceremony. Therefore, the youth from both zones were present today to show Pétain their unwavering confidence in the destiny of France and to swear their devotion with all their strength to its recovery. For eight months, Lamirand recalled, he had travelled and met young people in their towns and villages and he was deeply impressed that they understood the reasons and the extent of their deserved unhappiness. They also accepted the great mission to rebuild France and give it a new place in the world. They understood that this task would require renunciation, sacrifice and even heroism.

Lamirand concluded that the young people of France were ready because they were working hard to learn a trade and they had the ability to live tomorrow with joy and enthusiasm. Youth was resolutely united as young people of all youth movements stood side by side. Young people who did not belong to a youth movement, such as workers, peasants and students, were united in life by the creation of this social state that Pétain had designed and laid the foundation for, the National Revolution. They were united around the true leader whom they followed unconditionally and loved passionately.

Pétain then spoke again, announcing that he agreed with Lamirand because the largest share of the recovery of France would be accomplished by the youth. 'Youth, I trust in you!', he concluded. Again, his speech was greeted with calls of 'Vive le Maréchal'.[133]

For Vichy, there was a great need to show a sense of unity behind the regime as this was vital for its survival and to assert its authority over the people.[134] This gathering of youth in the symbolic ceremony in Valmatte showcased the mass support of French youth for Vichy. Such events were important as they allowed Vichy to demonstrate to the public the power of youth being united and their willingness to devote their energy to the cause of the National Revolution. Patriotism was frequently expressed among the crowd, who would sing along enthusiastically when 'La Marseillaise' was played.[135] Cries of 'Vive le Maréchal' to welcome Pétain were a common feature in all such broadcasts. These often originated from adults but they were taken up by children and adolescents, who occupied a prominent position during Pétain's travels. The presence of young people was highlighted by the participation of all the schools in the département and the collections that were presented as the fruit of their hard work to help the community. The young girl chosen to hand over the money represented the virtue and innocence of France, which was supposed to show the strength and devotion of youth to the course of the National Revolution. By 'deserved unhappiness', Lamirand meant the spirit of enjoyment that had prevailed during the Third Republic. He claimed that the French young people now understood that they had to go through a period of sacrifice and redemption to atone for this.[136] Lamirand's speech mirrored the message in Pétain's broadcast. Both leaders expressed their full confidence in French youth – a sentiment repeated at various occasions and in numerous broadcasts, creating a picture of national unity in their resolution to follow the calls of Vichy.

The details of Pétain's travel were also made available in the magazine *Radio National* so that those who missed the radio broadcast, or even those who listened to the broadcast, could learn more about his trip. For example, crew members from *Radio National* accompanied Pétain to Limousin and published a written account. The article focused on the people who met Pétain, especially children and young people. In particular, details of their age (usually in their teens and early twenties) were included to showcase the regeneration of France and their support for the head of state, and there were descriptions of traditional and regional people's clothes, the colour of the uniforms of the various youth groups, the adornment of towns and villages to showcase the local heritage, and gifts received by Pétain from the population as a symbol of warm welcome and affection for him. Pétain's successful completion of his travels, his extraordinary display of confidence and the close relationship between him and the people of France were also heavily featured.[137]

Winter campaign for solidarity and charity

From November onwards, RN intensified calls for young people to take action and to join the Secours National as winter was approaching fast and resources were becoming scarce again. There were at least four broadcasts on this topic.

A youth group, the Compagnons de France, responded to a call for help on 13 November 1941 to support the work of Secours National d'Hiver, an organisation that offered immediate relief for those in urgent need. The Compagnons was asked to collect clothes, blankets, woollens and cash donations and to participate in the sale of portraits of Pétain. A series of broadcast were made on RN to reach as many people as possible during this campaign. In addition, collections were organised in the evening in cinemas and theatres. A daily update was announced on air to showcase people's generosity and encourage further donations. Posters were put up and leaflets were given out. This was the first major propaganda event organised by the Vichy regime since the Armistice had been signed.[138]

Despite all the donations received from the empire, the Secours National still faced a significant shortage of funds and materials. On 17 November, Pétain made a second appeal on the airwaves for charity and solidarity.[139] He declared that in the previous year, he had asked the French to donate to the Secours National to help those in misfortune: 'In the course of one year, it has collected *three hundred and fifty million francs*, distributed *ten thousand* tons of clothes, more than one million food rations a day, sent a million children *to* summer camps.'[140] Now, he made another plea for a similar effort to be undertaken to help the Secours National in its attempt to alleviate misery in collaboration with the Croix-Rouge française (French Red Cross) and the Comité central d'assistance aux prisonniers de guerre (Central Committee for the Assistance of Prisoners of War). Answer the call, Pétain pleaded, so that they could feed those who were hungrier and clothe those who were colder. He asked his listeners to give whatever money and food they could spare, to search for spare clothes to bring happiness to those who had nothing. The schoolchildren would collect donations on Sundays. He asked his countrymen to donate in the spirit of mutual aid in anticipation of the dawn of the French resurrection.[141]

Shortly after Pétain's plea, Henri Champetier, a reporter at RN, repeated his message on 22 November, reinforcing and emphasising the urgency of helping those in distress in the spirit of dedication and solidarity. The spirit of 'mutual help' was presented as the only way to fight against the cold, hunger, misery, discouragement, sadness and despair, to pass the winter and to look forward to better days in the spring.[142]

Another broadcast with a similar message was transmitted through the radio the same day, featuring a speech by a teacher to his pupils. He spoke as a friend to the children because he knew them well and understood their current situation. He had been teaching for over 20 years in a village that was similar to many found across France. He said that the present situation had been caused by the defeat in 1940 and that there were French today who suffered more than before and they were not to be forgotten: the prisoners, the widows, the orphans and the refugees. He stated that all French people had a duty to renew their efforts this year. Quoting Pétain's message from a few days earlier, he reiterated that the youth was needed to rebuild France, and this involved youth action such as visiting people's houses to collect donations in their cities, towns, villages and neighbourhoods. They needed to be polite and courteous but also assertive and persistent in order to get results. The teacher concluded that he knew he could count on the children to do their duty because of their generous hearts.[143]

On 27 November, Lamirand made a further announcement on the airwaves. This speech was made on behalf of Pétain, addressing the youth of the occupied zone and the 'forbidden' zone at the Vélodrome d'Hiver in Paris. The youth in these zones were called to give three days of service to the French community, especially to those who suffered the most: the prisoners of war, the victims of war, the elderly and children less fortunate than themselves. By helping the efforts of organisations such as the Secours National, they would demonstrate great solidarity against the threat of the winter and faith for France.[144] Lamirand announced that 'this faith is matched only by the trust I have in you'.[145]

These four broadcasts were made by different people but within a short space of time and with striking similarities: they were presented by speakers who were clearly sympathisers and supported Pétain's political views and ideology; the messages were a clear signal that greater efforts had been put into urging both the youth and the general public to comply and to act; and the targeted audience were the French in both zones. It was through this continuous repetition that propaganda messages impregnated and convinced the public.[146] The results of the collection after four weeks were impressive. Seventy-five tons of clothing and a few tens of thousands of francs were collected during the winter campaign with the help of the Secours National and the Vichy government, supported by 30,000 posters and 50,000 leaflets.[147]

The youth was thus fundamental to Vichy's vision for a New France, both ideologically and at a practical level. It was, therefore, important to win the support of the teachers who had direct contact and great influence over young people, and a broadcast by a teacher was more effective than a generic news column. France had a long tradition of mutual aid and solidarity within the community but there were now clear signs of intensified efforts for nationwide voluntary actions by both the youth and the general public to combat the threat of winter, in multiple zones of France.

The 'moral renaissance' of pupils

Pétain visited schools on a number of occasions to preach about the 'moral renaissance' of pupils; reports of his visits were broadcast on RN. During these visits, he stressed the new moral values of honesty, integrity, loyalty and virtue to schoolchildren in person, and by broadcasting the visits, RN had become an effective tool of communication with all the children from the empire. This was part of a broader campaign to raise pupils' moral standards and encourage them to become intoxicated with the values of Vichy. Pupils were urged to form a 'League of Loyalty', and to display in their classes' 'honour codes', which they would undertake to follow.[148]

On 13 October, Masson presented a live news talk centred around Pétain's visits to a school in Périgny, a small village in the *département* of Allier. From his introduction, it became clear that RN broadcast his visit so that all the children of France could hear the Maréchal when he spoke to these pupils and would feel his presence. Périgny was chosen for a specific purpose; in Masson's words, it was because it had hardly changed over time, and possessed all the virtues of a traditional village.

Prior to Pétain's arrival, Masson interviewed M. Martel and his wife, both teachers, and learned that there were 47 children in the school aged from 5 to 13 years. Masson first met the children, who looked a bit frightened at the prospect of meeting the Maréchal, and explained that he loved disciplined children very much.

Once Pétain had arrived, he explained why he had chosen this village, and that the visit was to reward the pupils with his presence because the pupils had studied assiduously, and the teachers were very good. Pétain continued with a compelling speech to all the pupils of France to mark the start of the school year. The pupils needed to know that he counted on them to help him rebuild France and to make the French loyal and honest people. However, what mattered was not just words but acting on them. The pupils had obstacles in front of them and so he needed courageous boys and girls ready to take up the fight.

The first obstacle was the challenge of tenacity. Pupils may have made a lot of 'good resolutions' but some were forgotten very rapidly at the start of the school year. The challenge was to try to keep their word until their resolution had been achieved. Tenacity was a quality that Frenchmen somewhat lacked, but those who possessed it would be more successful than those who did not. The second obstacle was disloyalty. Pétain was aware that some pupils could not resist the temptation of cheating to get some extra points, although he wanted to believe that most of them did not do this. Pupils should have the courage not only to remain honest but also to prevent others from cheating. Pétain was aware that some pupils had organised multiple 'Leagues of Loyalty' and had a lot of success. He congratulated them for being proactive and said that he was sure that the teachers would advise and help them in this path. Even if you have cheated in the past, he said, you should redeem yourself by saying 'no' to it from now on.[149] The children sang 'La Marseillaise' at the end of his speech and at his departure from the school.[150]

This broadcast was an example of the close relationship between Masson and Pétain: in the pre-talk, Masson gave a touching speech about how proud the pupils should be about meeting Pétain, as if he were a 'quasi-divine figure'.[151] A few observations can be made from the narratives. First, the village of Périgny was significant. The fact that both Pétain and Masson explained the reasons for their visit gave away its symbolic importance: a small, rural, timeless place where people's lives remained little changed, and where good moral standing continued to flourish. The focus of the talk was pupils of primary age who had not come under the influence of the pursuit of 'unhealthy pleasure', which had started to dominate the slightly older youth located in urban areas – and some rural areas, albeit to a lesser extent.[152] Pétain was hoping to send a strong message to all school pupils that they must realise that they could be better than the adults because they were more adaptable, and they would play a more important role in the rebuilding of France.

He preached about tenacity and honesty and the creation of the league, reflecting both an idealised image of youth for Vichy and a brushing-over of the problems that had started emerging for young people: low morality, apathy and juvenile delinquency, the conviction rate for which increased at an alarming speed from 1940 to 1942.[153] 'Forgiveness' was preached as a given: as long as the pupils had corrected any misbehaviour voluntarily, it would all be forgotten and forgiven. As evidenced elsewhere, Vichy's 'moral renaissance' began to decline as early as 18 February 1941. For example, Micheline Bood, an adolescent, wrote in her diary, 'Nothing has changed, in spite of the so-called "moral revival". The same things are done as before, only they are done more hypocritically.' A month later, she added: 'God, how fed up I am with school and the Révolution Nationale'.[154]

Vichy's attempt at a moral renaissance of pupils was not restricted to the unoccupied zone. Algeria was part of the French Empire and to show its devotion to Vichy's policy, the oath of the pupils in Algeria to Pétain, the Head of State, was broadcast.[155] It began with an unidentified man's voice speaking to Pétain: 'you asked schoolchildren to be honest and loyal in the classroom. The schools of Algeria have listened and prove it'.[156] The children of Algiers then sang a song to the glory of the Maréchal and France, followed by an oath:

> I swear to be loyal, that is to say, honest, sincere, frank at all times and in all places, I swear it!
> I swear not to copy in class and not to defraud in composition and exams. I swear it!
> I swear to always tell the truth, the whole truth and nothing but the truth. I swear.
> Now you are bound by your oath, will you break it? No!'[157]

The schoolchildren recited the oath in a boisterous manner. At the conclusion of the ceremony, the pupils shouted out 'For France! Ready!', followed by a rendition of 'La Marseillaise'.[158]

Taking an oath was part of Vichy's attempt at moral revival, although it was an obsolete custom in France as Marcel Déat, the founder of the Rassemblement national populaire (RNP), a collaborationist party in early 1941, observed. Oaths were taken by schoolchildren, the Légion des volontaires français (LVF)[159] and athletes.[160] To what extent the oaths imposed on schoolchildren had achieved the desired 'moral renaissance' remained questionable, but for many it was nothing more than lip service. Attempts to set up 'moral codes' were doomed to fail at a time when cheating and lying to trick the Germans 'had almost become a patriotic duty'.[161] A headmaster of a school in Marseille declared that dishonesty continued unabated despite admonitions made to schoolchildren. Denunciation was encouraged outside school as well.[162]

If the pupils of the unoccupied zone were indoctrinated by this constant call of 'moral renaissance', the pupils of the occupied zone had a very different experience under German occupation and showed different perceptions of Pétain and Vichy as the legitimate government of France. The following broadcast features an interview with French young people and their teachers, when a group of boys were visiting the unoccupied zone for a summer camp after having met the Maréchal.[163]

The broadcast began with a reporter conducting an interview with a boy, whose parents lived in Lille, who said that he was happy to come to Vichy. There was, however, hardly any enthusiasm in his voice. The reporter then interviewed a PE teacher who accompanied the boys. The teacher explained that the pupils were very tired after a long journey to Vichy town, but they were satisfied with their stay because there was plenty of food: some young boys had gained 2–3kg. The children were distressed because they knew that food was plentiful in the summer camp but once they returned home, they would have to face food shortages again. One teacher said that he was prepared to give up his vacation to work in the summer camp with the children. Another teacher who was eating a cake said that she had been for a walk with the children and taught them some songs.

During the interviews, the reporter emphasised the importance of spending three weeks in the camp to find fitness, plenty of good food and various activities to entertain the children. The reporter then asked a 13-year-old boy if he was happy to have met Pétain. The boy responded in a soft voice. The reporter insisted that the boy repeat his answer with greater enthusiasm, to which the boy complied. However, it became apparent that despite all the efforts of the reporter to make the boys talk, he found them unwilling participants who left numerous long and awkward silences during the interviews. The most common answer from the children was 'yes sir'. In his last attempt, the reporter insisted that one boy should tell everyone that he had met Pétain up close and personal once he returned home, to which there was no audible response.[164] The broadcast ended with the reporter's frustrated voice, 'I have had enough, we will be able to do the editing'.[165]

This concluding comment made it unlikely that the report was used unedited on air; it would either be edited or was never aired at all because of the lack of enthusiasm demonstrated by the children during the interviews. There was thus a stark contrast in the responses of French youth to Pétain in the two zones. It would seem from this particular broadcast that the children from the occupied zone were much less impressed or enthusiastic than those from the unoccupied zone. One cannot rule out the possibility that the enthusiasm, behaviour and attitudes displayed by the children in the unoccupied zone in the broadcasts were staged for propaganda purposes, but no evidence of this could be found in the edited broadcasts available in the archives. In the unoccupied zone, by contrast, the young people were always very enthusiastic in their responses to Pétain; when interviewing them, the propagandists only aired what they wanted the public to hear. So, children's enthusiasm for Pétain as displayed in the broadcasts was not necessarily a reflection of how they felt about their participation in youth groups, sports or working in the fields as part of the regeneration of France.

Part of the reason for the discrepancy was that children living in the unoccupied zone viewed their lives very differently from those who lived in the occupied zone, where the occupier was present and the prospect of starvation, among other things, was much more acute. In the interview outlined above, the teachers appeared more than eager to participate in the interview and to express their enjoyment of the 'good' life of the camp; however, not all teachers were always so keen to take part in such events or liked engaging the children in the presence of the Maréchal.[166]

Despite the efforts of the Vichy propaganda to reinforce the benefits of the camps to the health and well-being of the children, by July 1942, with the worsening of the material shortage in France, children in the Paris region could no longer attend summer camps due to a lack of supplies such as shoes and clothing.[167]

Sports as a means to cultivate the strength of the youth

The idea that the regeneration of France could be achieved through sports was cultivated by political leaders at the end of the 1930s, and this marked the start of the sport movement.[168] From 1936, Léo Lagrange, the undersecretary of state for Leisure and Sports and a member of the Popular Front, revived the idea of regenerating the French youth through sport by eliminating commercialism and elitism in the participation of sporting activities. This was achieved through the Brevet Sportif Populaire (BSP), which had the objective of encouraging the mass French population to take care of their health by making sports facilities more accessible and investing in equipment.[169]

Vichy embraced this idea after the Armistice and sport became one of the pillars of Vichy's educational reform.[170] The promotion of sport was, on certain occasions, mixed with patriotic references: 'the sport movement would have provided the best soldiers of the Great War'.[171] Vichy turned sport into a 'body revolution', advocated by Drieu la Rochelle. The theme of 'reinvigoration of the race' was constantly cultivated with a strong connotation of authoritarianism. Sport was to be the way to make the masses 'a strong, courageous, tenacious, loyal race, with a sense of duty, a sense of discipline and the spirit of sacrifice'.[172]

The pedagogues of Vichy published in the journal *Éducation Générale* of March 1941 the new educational recommendations:

> A new Frenchman must free himself from the misfortunes of the present times. There is one condition for this: to rebuild a healthy and robust race, hardworking and joyful, disciplined and enterprising. That is, it is necessary to modernise our education, orient it towards action, towards effort and even towards a certain harshness exerted on oneself.[173]

These recommendations were inspired by the totalitarian educational model. Adopting a clear anti-intellectualist position where the bookish culture was condemned to foster only idleness, physical education was to occupy a prominent place in the school curricula. It was for this reason that the CGEGS was created on 7 August 1940 and attached to the Ministry of National Education a month later. This commissariat was tasked with organising the vast educational programme in the metropolis and its empire based around: 'General and Sports education, Sports, and Outdoor Activities and equipment'.[174] The budget of the CGEGS reflected the importance given to sports and physical education: it increased from 50 million francs in 1939 to 1.9 billion francs in 1940 (although the budget was subsequently halved to 960 million francs in 1942). Jean Borotra, a tennis champion, was responsible for the CGEGS from 13 July 1940 to 18 April 1942 before being replaced by Colonel Joseph Pascot, a former international rugby player.[175] Both bought into the German belief that sport is a means to achieve physical health and the British belief that sport enables character formation.[176]

The CGEGS implemented an intense propaganda programme to stress the moral and health virtues of sport and physical education, for example, *La Cité du muscle*, *Les Messagers du Sport en Afrique-du-Nord* and *Le Serment de l'Athlète* in 1941 and *Le Sport à l'école* in 1942. These propaganda documentaries had two aims: to publicise the policy of the CGEGS and to show the significance of sport in the education of young people. The CGEGS also organised propaganda campaigns in the countryside to show the documentaries, using a bus fitted with a projection booth.[177]

On 25 March 1941, the BSP was rebranded Brevet Sportif National to run the National Sport Certificate scheme. The certificate was mandatory for all boys and girls aged 12 to 18 years old who wished to join a club. Girls were included, even though to Vichy, the image of an athletic woman remained secondary to her social function of having children, being a housewife and being the guardian of the family home.[178]

Sport occupied an important place in RN programmes, as evidenced in *Radio National's* weekly schedule.[179] It is likely that major sporting events that featured heavily on *Radio National* were broadcast on RN, although very few such broadcasts survived.[180] The lack of narratives from broadcasts is compensated for by the printed articles in *Radio National*, which give a fuller picture of how sports were reported to inspire youth and to foster their physical and mental strength. It is possible to infer the content of the broadcasts from the *Radio National* magazine articles.

The organisation and broadcasting of major sporting events served as a testimony to Vichy's achievement in the pursuit of (what the regime called) national rejuvenation as it showed the sheer number of young people demonstrating their strength, patriotism and unity. Vichy's success in this area made the German occupiers suspicious. Military sports involved demanding physical training under strenuous conditions and was 'highly relevant to future military service'.[181]As one of the army officers who organised such an event said to the journalist, 'the charter of physical education, sports and sporting military training in the army has laid the principles of a new regulation in which the idea and the value of sports are no longer separated from the military idea and value'.[182]

In July 1941, Jacques Breteuil wrote an article about the story of the discovery of the caves of Aven d'Orgnac[183] to promote risk-taking, hard work, teamworking skills, courage and strength to young people. These were key qualities that were needed in the new youth for the rebuilding of France – qualities that Vichy was keen to foster and encourage.

In August, a full page article was written about a major event taking place at the Municipal Stadium of Vichy Town, which would be the first of a series of similar events, allowing the public to witness the renewal of the young French army. It was a display of muscle and youth in uniform in the presence of Pétain and former tennis player Borotra[184] from the CGEGS, among other VIP guests. Articles of such a nature were used extensively to demonstrate the renewed French youth in action, as a way to feature the idealised outcome of what was expected of youth.

A similar sporting event took place on 7 September at 14h45, also at the Municipal Stadium of Vichy town, when Borotra presented the Collège National de Moniteurs d'Antibes to Pétain. The purpose was to demonstrate the different activities taught during physical education, which would be applied to all the schools from the following October.[185] *Radio National* dedicated a full-page article to this event, with five photos of athletes throwing javelins, performing the high jump and hurdling, etc. The team had previously toured North Africa and was cheered on by spectators, the reporter wrote. The event began with a choir singing and was followed by a demonstration of various sports activities of an exceptional quality. There was then a friendly competition between the best athletes of the college and their counterparts from Paris, Marseille, Lyon, La Rochelle, Tarbes, Tourcoing, etc. All the proceeds were given to the Secours National on the last day of the *Croisade de l'Enfance* (Youth Crusade). The reporter explained that all these activities served only one goal: to train men who would put into practice what the commissioner-general had proposed: 'to be strong to serve better'.[186] This event also signified the first step towards 'sports days' that would later be organised in the main cities of the unoccupied zone.[187]

Using these sport events, Vichy wanted to promote sport and encourage people to join in the celebration. There were several overt messages in these articles: France remained united, with athletes from both the occupied and the unoccupied zones participating; and funding raised for the Secours National demonstrated the cohesion and unity of the New France. More importantly, these sport activities united youth, the public and those in need in one cause.

The oath taken by the athletes was another way to instil nationalist emotions towards Vichy. A short article was written about the ceremony, which took place in Marseille in the presence of Admiral Darlan and Borotra, and involved the participation of 16,000 young French people who paraded in a 'more or less' spectacular fashion.[188] The athlete Pau Peyre swore the oath: 'I swear on my honour to participate in sport with impartiality, discipline and loyalty, to better myself and better serve my country'.[189] The oath taken by the athletes was first pronounced on 29 April 1941 in Algiers during Borotra's tour of North Africa. Later, it was said that the athletes' oath became controversial because the athletes saluted the national colours in a way that was similar to Hitler's salute.

In fact, the Olympic salute had been codified in France for many years although it surprised the Germans when it was used during the opening parade of the Berlin Games in 1936.[190] The ceremony of the 'oath' taken by athletes was similar to that of school pupils, and both demonstrated that Vichy propaganda sought to portray the popularity of sports, fitness and strength among French youth, representing the image of a strong and fit nation.

1942

Pierre Pucheu, Secretary of State for the Interior,[191] made a comment to Colonel Groussard at the end of December 1941 that 'the more order reigns in a country, the stronger this country will be. The more strength Germany feels in us, the more she will respect us'.[192] It had now become clear that the Vichy regime would intensify its youth propaganda to ensure increased youth participation in the construction of the New France. As highlighted in the BBC report of January 1942, Vichy started targeting the disillusioned unemployed youth immediately after the Armistice. Their propaganda efforts increased shortly thereafter to promote the vision and the ideology of the new regime, using tools such as the radio, the press, the youth-led display of 'personal action'; flattery and the description of youth movement uniforms; and the activities in the camps and various youth rallies. This report also quoted the opinion of a French man who wrote to the BBC to say that 'the Ministry of Youth … has been the most efficiently organised (1.1.41)'.[193]

The USA joining the war on 6 December 1941 marked a milestone in World War II. This, coupled with Laval's return to power in April 1942, meant that French youth would be targeted even more by Vichy propaganda, not least because of the acute labour shortage, but also due to the renewed importance of luring young people into collaboration.

The Chantiers de la Jeunesse

Following Pétain's address on 13 October 1941 at Périgny, numerous letters were sent to him. A group of young people belonging to the Chantiers was involved in helping to sort and distribute the letters in a youth hostel in Hauterive, near Vichy. In January, Champetier accompanied Pétain to visit these young people and broadcast the reportage.

Prior to Pétain's arrival, Champetier explained that the refectory at the youth hostel had been divided into three areas, looking like a post office sorting room. There were huge piles of bags full of letters in each corner, and two long tables in the middle of the room around which sat a dozen young people from the Chantiers, in their forest-green uniform, busy sorting the mail.

Champetier then interviewed Maurien, the assistant commissioner and head of the *détachement,* who explained that the Chantiers of Châtel-Guyon had the responsibility of opening and sorting letters on behalf of Pétain. So far, 1,700,000 letters had been received since his address. M. Brisse, the foreman in charge of youth supervision, also explained that the young people were tasked with identifying the return address, so that each French child would receive a response, and sorting the letters according to their point of origin. There were also drawings, works of art, money and other items of value in the envelopes; all monetary donations were sent to the Secours National.[194]

This part of the reportage demonstrated Pétain's popularity among the French: the listeners would have been impressed by the number of letters (more than 1.7 million). Furthermore, the Chantiers who were chosen to perform this honourable task of opening the letters further emphasised the important role the youth occupied in the construction of New France.

The description of the green uniform of the Chantiers enabled the listeners to visualise the youth as symbols of growth, harmony, nature and hope – attributes with which the colour green is often associated. The Chantiers wore a uniform that belonged to a specific social and institutional group, and whose symbolism was linked to the values of discipline and duty – the young man had 'to recognise himself by the neatness of his outfit, to the cleanliness of his body, to the upkeep of his personal effects and to the correctness of his appearance'.[195] The uniform also served to standardise the different social classes. To this effect, a nationwide uniform scheme was introduced with the decree of 12 July.[196]

The message that these letters originated from all corners of France and its empire created an impression of the allegiance of the population to the head of the Vichy regime. The report about the donations was intended to show the faith and trust the French had in the Vichy government, which pledged to help the population in need.

Maurien then read a 'randomly picked' letter as an example of French youth's affection for the Maréchal. This letter was written by José, a 12-year-old boy, living in the Oise region:

> I have understood that it would mainly depend on the efforts of young French, that is to say, the schoolchildren of France. I, therefore, resolved to apply myself in my homework and learn my lessons seriously. I followed the advice, your advice and those of the mistress, and I will behave better. I have made efforts in mathematics, and especially I missed much fewer classes than the previous years. Your portrait is displayed at the school. It reminds me every moment that I have to be honest and I cannot say to you that I have always been. I am going to try to improve. The mistress repeats all the time that it is more meritorious to earn a point on its own than five points by copying a neighbour. I am going to strive to be more honest after acquiring greater love for my work. I express to you my gratitude for all that you do for us and I beg you to accept my respects.[197]

Champetier commended the boy for being so honest in his writing.[198] Maurien added that the letter had been chosen at random but was representative of the feelings of all the pupils across France and the empire.

We do not know whether the letter was randomly chosen or carefully selected; however, the content was in perfect harmony with Pétain's speech to all pupils in 1941, in which he instructed the pupils to be honest, not to cheat and to work hard. This letter represented an indoctrinated pupil who pledged to follow the politics of the Vichy regime. The voice of this young boy was essentially the voice Vichy hoped to hear from all French youth. But, the notion that this voice was unanimous nationwide, was nothing more than an idealistic illusion.

The second part of the reportage began with Pétain and Ménétrel's arrival at the youth hostel. Champetier explained that the sorting of the letters had started on 5 January, and many letters contained children's wishes to Pétain for a Happy New Year. Some letters were asking for help, and these would be referred to the Medical Service. The amount of money received so far amounted to 50,000 francs.[199]

So, as evidenced elsewhere, despite all the moral and material difficulties, children wrote letters from school to Pétain at Christmas. It was said that 'in 1940 some 200 post-bags arrived, accompanied by a million drawings on the theme of France',[200] which resulted in 10,000 of the best drawings being displayed in Vichy town. The large number of letters and offerings revealed the effect of a 'father figure' image that was built up by propagandists, and how the omnipresent propaganda served to draw children into this idolatry, particularly during the Christmas holidays of both 1940 and 1941.[201] Donations, particularly large sums, were always acknowledged in the broadcast and pledged to be redirected for charitable purposes.

In this reportage, a unique feature is the lack of input from the children themselves. As compared to earlier broadcasts, only the voices of the journalist, the authoritative figures and Pétain himself were heard, although this may be attributed to the quality of the disc, which is extremely deteriorated, rendering some parts inaudible.

To demonstrate the lived experience of the young people involved in youth groups, Pierre des Vallières wrote an article in *Radio National* about the Chantiers's camp in January, which merits closer examination. No one had tried harder than Général de La Porte du Theil to make the Chantiers something exceptional, he claimed. There was a total of 52 groups scattered around the unoccupied zone, each with their own special focus, depending on the geography and the needs of the locality, for example, grape-picking. The Chantiers would practise *Hébertisme* (see below) as a morning exercise, take care of the horses, cook, wash and sew, or write to their fiancées. Others listened to the radio or read books in the library. There was always a sense of rivalry as each group tried to outperform the others.

Des Vallières concluded that the camp was the place where youth could lead a healthy and active life with the entire community and where reluctant and hostile youth were transformed into real men. At the end of the day, the teams would gather around the flag as it was taken down.[202] This article illustrated the utopian lives of young people in a camp. This was where youth learned how to live in a community, work as a team and develop their physical skills. In reality, however, the conditions could be harsh and demanding, especially during the winter season.

Hébertisme is an activity named after Lieutenant Hébert, who invented it during the Great War for French soldiers. It was used extensively by both the Chantiers and the Compagnons. It consisted of 'walking, swimming, running, jumping, crawling, climbing, balancing, throwing, lifting, and self-defence'.[203] It was thought that these were simple but vigorous activities that everyone should be capable of doing, and that they would harden men to face the outdoor weather conditions and empower them to endure pain.[204] Hébert believed that there was a link between the body and the mind and they could not be dissociated as one influenced the other. The *Hébertisme* method was seen as a vital element of moral regeneration and character development by Vichy for the youth.[205] It remained the most practised type of activity during the war due to the low cost in terms of equipment and the ease of practice.[206]

Hébertisme was also fully in line with Vichy's educational aim, which was 'to train a new youth, active, hardworking, robust and athletic'.[207] Unsurprisingly, not all the youth enjoyed the harsh living conditions at the camp. As La Porte du Theil responded to a parent's complaint that life in the camp was too tough:

It's not by mollycoddling children, as has plainly been done in this case and, alas, in so many other French families, that character is forged...And it was a few tens of thousands of young men of this kind that we had to put up against hundreds of thousands of young Germans.[208]

Nonetheless, after a day of hard work, the various youth groups would all muster around the pole, where they were united under one symbol, the French flag, despite the living conditions.

A further broadcast was made about the Chantiers in July.[209] This reportage was presented by Champetier, who accompanied Pétain during his inspection of the Chantiers's facilities in the Forêt de Randan. Group 21, or Galliéni as it was called (each group of the Chantiers was given a name and a motto referring either to a national or a local hero)[210] would have the honour of Pétain's visit. There were also over a hundred young men and women who came from far away to meet him.

Boisterous acclamations from the young were heard repeatedly. The Maréchal appeared in his military uniform, which he habitually wore during official visits, accompanied by Général de La Porte du Theil and the commissioner of Group 21. After visiting the facilities, Pétain spoke briefly to the Chantiers, who greeted his speech with vibrant and disciplined enthusiasm. Pétain said that he would like to write a letter to tell them all the ideas and emotions that came to him while visiting their camp. They were making wonderful preparations for their personal development and reflection. Their current experience was the best training they could receive. The government would continue to seek fruitful ways to provide young people with the means to furnish their minds and body, and Randan was a perfect example of what he was looking for. The broadcast ended with the song 'Ce n'est qu'un au-revoir', which was sung in unison by the Chantiers at his departure.[211]

Everything about the all-male Chantiers was done to appeal to both nationalistic and patriotic feelings. A ceremony took place every morning and evening, when all these young men of different backgrounds gathered and united around the French flag, creating the feeling of belonging to the Fatherland. The singing or parading during commemorative ceremonies helped to perpetuate the memory of World War I, which symbolised courage and patriotism. The events organised after work by the chaplain or group leader helped to reinforce such an atmosphere. People would also gather around the fire to discuss the various aspects of the Maréchal's domestic and foreign policies regarding France and the empire.[212]

During the visit to Randan, Champetier spent a significant amount of time providing background information, all of which clearly served a political purpose. He described in some detail the uniform worn by Pétain and the Chantiers. The fact that Pétain was wearing his uniform for official visits highlighted the importance of the Chantiers: the facilities and activities they offered to youth played a crucial role in the rebuilding of the New France. Champetier next introduced Pétain as the hero of Verdun who had unity in mind and was totally devoted to France.

In his speech, Pétain emphasised the importance of practical training, which the youth were acquiring in the camp. This was in line with the ideology of the new education system, where practical skills and physical activities were seen as an integral part of both formal and skills-related education.

The Compagnons de France

The Compagnons was another important youth group. It was founded by Henry Dhavernas, a young inspector of finances, who was replaced in the autumn of 1941 by Colonel de Tournemire.[213] There was an urgent need to boost youth morale in France, and the term 'Compagnons' or 'Companions' was created to inspire 'friendship, work and service to the country'.[214] Dhavernas immediately received official financial support, allowing him to organise the first Compagnons's conference from 1 to 4 August 1940 at Randan, near Vichy.[215] Some 54 per cent of the participants were thought to be educators and were united, for the most part, by an urgent need for personal action and national recovery.

The Compagnons was born out of that gathering – the participants would have to supervise a total of 15,000 boys in five months, some of whom were not yet 15 years old.[216] The Compagnons was designed for young people from 14 to 19 years old,[217] and existed alongside other organisations for the same age group in the unoccupied zone, mostly church groups and Scouting organisations.[218]

On 4 October 1940 in Vichy, Pétain sent a personal message to Dhavernas, which constituted the first direct support for this movement. It read: 'A new generation is rising, ready to devote its forces to the recovery of the Country. May the *Compagnons de France* be the pioneers of this recovery through their work, their joyful ardour, their passion to serve.'[219] In September 1941, Pétain added that they were 'supposed to be the "avant-garde of the National Revolution"'.[220]

There were different kinds of 'companies' within the Compagnons group: rural companies, which put the young unemployed to farm work; city companies, which were charged with uniting all social classes; and itinerant companies, which were made up of eight companies of young artisans and one theatre company.[221]

A broadcast recorded in July 1942 on the second anniversary of the founding of the Compagnons explained in some detail the origin, purpose and success of this organisation.[222] Leaders of various social circles and professional bodies met to discuss the development and future of the significant youth movement in France. The only question that was to be asked about the Compagnons, said the speaker, was this:

> By what means can we survive, so as to go back up the hill which we descended in a freefall in June 1940? What is the education system which should be rightly imposed on the youth? For the movement, the fatherland commands in absolute terms, unconditionally, with respect and dedication. It is therefore necessary to raise the young in this conviction, which they have to defend, safeguard, no matter what.[223]

The journalist continued his live presentation with military music in the background and emphasised the popularity of the Compagnons. At first, there had been 150 pioneers in the Forêt de Randan when the Maréchal visited them in August 1940; now, the Compagnons had 30,000 members across France and its empire, all imbued with enthusiasm.[224] Today, on 27 July, the second anniversary of the organisation was celebrated in its birthplace with a far greater number of participants: 3,000 Compagnons had been expected but 7,000 attended from all the provinces of France, Algeria and Tunisia, using all possible means of transportation, some even walking a long distance, all dressed up in blue. The occasion was marked with the informal visit of the Maréchal, who came as a 'neighbour', wearing a simple grey suit rather than his uniform. Both the head of state and Colonel de Tournemire watched the new youth of France marching along a big pathway in the forest, with the leader of each provincial delegation carrying a white urn containing some soil from their province. Later, the soil would be mixed and each group would bring back a bag containing this combined soil, which represented the land of France.

The demonstration was followed by a performance by folk groups, whose participants wore traditional costumes. Then the offerings were brought in, including a sheep, silk pieces, flowers and perfume. Offerings sessions such as this had become a custom during Pétain's visits, the gifts representing the respect of the population for the father figure through the hands of those who were – according to Vichy ideology – destined to rejuvenate France.

This spectacular parade lasted over 45 minutes. The Compagnons cheered when Pétain addressed his audience.[225] He declared that his message was essentially about honour and the accomplishment of one's duties, a message that was akin to a 'catechism' that one needed to embrace from an early age. Invariably, he repeated to the youth: 'try to do the tasks that you have to do in the best possible way … If you manage to do very well what you have to do, France will rise by itself'.[226] This concluded the broadcast, with applause, cheers and calls of 'Vive le Maréchal' from the crowd.[227]

The celebration of the anniversary of the Compagnons highlighted the ideology of the Vichy government that lay behind the creation of this youth group, and its perceived success and popularity. Pétain was open about the principles that he wanted young people to accept and reflect: follow his vision and messages, and France would rise up again. For youth, there was no room for creativity, imagination or space to choose their own destiny. They were asked to accept, not to discuss; to act, not to question. As stated in the *First Commandment for Good Compagnons*, a publication that was something of a bible for this youth organisation: 'Since we are not fully informed, we submit ourselves unreservedly to the Marshal and we refuse to discuss any decision taken by him in the political sphere. We follow the Marshal submissively in any political decision he may take' (26.7.41).[228]

The large number of attendees from both the provinces and the empire featured in the broadcast was intended to demonstrate to RN listeners that the French youth supported Vichy en masse; youth that Vichy had tried to reign in and control. Events like this were also an excellent opportunity for propagandists. After the event, censorship distributed a guidance note to the newspapers in the unoccupied zone so that they could report the event correctly.[229] One of the mandatory phrases to be included in the article was: 'The Randan gathering should be an opportunity to remember the hope that France places in its youth.'[230]

The colour of the clothes and the offerings were important. The Compagnons wore an alpine beret, a shirt with pockets and shoulder straps, and shorts. These three pieces of clothing were all in navy blue – a symbol for trust, loyalty and sincerity that also represents unity in faith. Blue is also one of the colours of the French flag, which makes it a symbol for nationalism and patriotism. In addition, Compagnons wore a grey or beige tie according to the company to which they belonged. On 15 August 1940, a rooster representing the movement's emblem was endorsed. This was a round design embroidered in white on a red background and was sewn on the left pocket of the shirt. Above it was a band bearing the name and number of the company.[231]

Pétain wore a grey suit as a civilian, which stood in contrast to the full military uniform he wore when he visited the Chantiers. This may be attributed to the fact that the Compagnons was a voluntary organisation and his participation in its anniversary event represented his acknowledgement and endorsement of the organisation as the head of state rather than as a high-ranked officer, although military music was played in the background, giving away the quasi-military nature of the event.

Although the broadcast depicted the Compagnons as an attractive and positive youth organisation, the perception of those who worked closely with the organisation or the members themselves could be very different. For instance, one Compagnon stated that 'in the Compagnons it's not very interesting because one doesn't learn much, and, what's more, one becomes more of a layabout than a worker'.[232] The Compagnons was described by an outsider as 'idle fellows, badly looked after, badly fed, not to mention the Compagnons's "exploits" – thefts, burglaries, etc … They couldn't care less'.[233] A report highlighted in some instances that 'fifty out of sixty Compagnons here are for de Gaulle'.[234] Despite Pétain and Vichy propagandists' efforts to keep the youth as close followers, there was an anti-Vichy undercurrent among the Compagnons themselves and in other youth camps.

Although the Compagnons largely disappeared after the war, one of the companies continued to exist and went on to become internationally renowned. The Compagnons de la Musique was created in September 1941. It toured France until it became the Compagnons de la Chanson, and travelled around the world. It exported a genre of music that was typically French, 'as ambassadors of good taste and finesse of expression'.[235] 'Their songs, their dances, their sketches, in a word their production, remain one of the intangible brands of the "*Compagnons*" style'.[236] The nine boys in the group excelled in their performance to such an extent that after the war, they toured and performed "Les trois cloches" with Edith Piaff,[237] and became the representatives of French songs which gained the reputation of "fresh, elegant and classic".'[238]

Teachers and the unofficial Vichy anthem

With the return of Laval as head of the government in April 1942, Jérôme Carcopino left his position as the Minister of National Education and returned to his permanent post as director of the École normale supérieure. His departure marked a turning point in Vichy's education policy towards young people, from constructive reform, the perseverance of political neutrality of schools and the pursuit of good faith under the ideology of the National Revolution, to hypocrisy and overt subservience to the Germans and their ideology. Carcopino was replaced by Abel Bonnard, who would remain in this function until August 1944.[239]

This change in educational ideology could be observed in the broadcasts and the written press. After April, there was a sea change in policy so that the propaganda addressed to teachers no longer sought merely to instil the ideology of the National Revolution but reconciliation and subtle conversion to the alliance of Germany's 'New Order' in Europe.[240] Instead of hostility and criticism, Bonnard publicly declared at Lille that 'teachers had *not* been responsible for the defeat'[241] of France. On 28 August, he made a 'Forgive and forget' broadcast, stating that he had no interest in teachers' former opinions.[242]

This policy of reconciliation was reflected in Pétain's address to teachers on 3 September in a broadcast that was aired at 13h45.[243] Champetier reported the visit, announcing that the Maréchal would be addressing the thousand teachers from both unoccupied and occupied zones waiting in the schoolyard of the Lycée Jules Ferry in Vichy. The Maréchal was accompanied by Laval, Bonnard and other high-ranking officials. A short while later, Pétain started his speech, declaring that the previous message from the Minister of National Education was remarkable and that they should read and meditate on it. Meanwhile, his thoughts for the teachers came back more often or more willingly,[244] because he himself had been a teacher for the soldiers when he was an officer. 'In all military commands that I presided, from *the most modest to the highest*, I have always had the desire and wish to join the men who depended on me, to make them understand me, and to gain their trust.'[245]

Pétain declared that trust could not be commanded, it had to be earned; no one would be better qualified to win the confidence of youth than their teachers. He knew this as he personally had fulfilled such a function in the army. Now, it was in this capacity as a former teacher that he allowed himself to give them some advice:[246]

> Teachers of France, it is you who, in the nation today, train the nation of tomorrow. You are both educators and *instructors*. You *take charge of* the child to form a man in him. Let them

grow for the health and the greatness of France; these little French that the *fatherland* puts in your hands.[247]

At the conclusion of his address, the children sang 'Maréchal, nous voilà!'[248] – a song dedicated to Pétain, expressing the affection of the people in the unoccupied zone towards him. The popularity of the song made it an unofficial anthem of Vichy and it was a powerful symbol of the support given to Pétain. Although the title of the song is addressed to the Maréchal, its lyrics played a role in indoctrinating the youth with the ideals of the National Revolution, reinforcing its popular slogans. It played a similar function to 'La Marseillaise'.[249] Everyone in the unoccupied zone knew 'Maréchal, nous voilà!', especially the children, who learned it at school and in youth organisations, and sang it in public ceremonies, especially when Pétain was present.[250] The song was also played on the radio on many occasions.[251]

At the address at Jules Ferry primary school on 3 September, Pétain was dressed in civilian clothes, although he referred extensively to his role in the military. To him, there was no difference between teaching soldiers and teaching children. The essence of education remained the same: trust from pupils was essential and could not be achieved unless the teachers had great affection and love for their pupils and for what they did. By using himself as an example, he implied that every teacher possessed the ability to command victory in their mission of educating the generation of the future. He urged the teachers to follow his example, attempting to convert them to become part of his alliance. This was a clear shift from blaming the teachers for the defeat of France to seeking their collaboration and allegiance as a new strategy necessitated by the low morality and apathy of the pupils.

A week after the address, Léon J. Gros wrote an article in *Radio National* commenting on the future duties of the teachers for educating young people.[252] Gros reproduced a segment of Pétain's speech to assert the shift in the official position regarding teachers: 'I am committed to returning to your profession the dignity it deserves. I want you to feel honoured, and that the conditions of your life be sufficiently assured so that you are able to forget about them and devote yourself to your job'.[253]

Gros wrote that this simple statement signalled an end to the intellectual and material injustice towards the teachers during the Third Republic, a gesture now endorsed by Laval. Gros interpreted the message contained in this broadcast: teachers were to be forgiven for their past mistakes and for allowing individualism to spread. The Third Republic was the real culprit for having created an oligarchy for the sole interest of their politics and money, and the teachers had been manipulated and betrayed by this politics.[254]

It was common practice for *Radio National* to reproduce and comment on important broadcasts in print so that their audience, whether they'd listened to the broadcast or not, could have the opportunity to comprehend the important message the leaders of the state wished to convey. In this case, the essence of the interpretation was that the failure in education was the failure of the regime, not the teachers. RN called for reconciliation, collaboration and acceptance of the new education ideology of Vichy.

Despite the shift in the attitude towards teachers, the material hardship endured by teachers and schools were not mentioned in either the broadcast or the written press. In early 1942, the situation for young teachers was desperate. For example, in Orléans, several teachers slept in a youth hostel and ate in the restaurant of the Secours National. At Biscarrosse (Landes), there was a case of a young teacher earning a mere 39F.70 a day, a sum that was clearly insufficient even to cover his room and board. The prefect of the Loiret estimated that a single 25-year-old teacher, who was not fully qualified, was earning a salary of 1,173F a month – a figure that had not changed since 1939. The prefect of the Gers reported that two primary teachers had already resigned from their posts to join the police, and were already earning twice as much by working as temporary inspectors. Given that the grossly overpriced black market was sometimes the only place to buy food, many urban teachers were poverty-stricken.[255]

A further broadcast was recorded on 13 September during Pétain's visit to Bourg-en-Bresse, where he met a number of officials and professionals, including a school inspector and two headteachers. When meeting with the inspector of the Academy of the *département* of Ain, Pétain reminded him of the admonition he had given to the teachers a few days earlier.[256] The inspector declared that the staff members accepted and followed his admonition with great interest; that pupils read his messages with the highest attention and learned them by heart so that they could put them into practice; and that the Maréchal's messages were regularly published in the newsletters of the primary schools.[257] 'So you are my best propagandist', Pétain said, to which the inspector responded, 'Yes, M. Maréchal, I believe so.'[258]

Pétain was then introduced to two headmasters, one from a secondary school for boys and one for girls. He asked them about the general spirit of the pupils. Before the headmasters could give an answer, Pétain expressed his disgust about the situation in some secondary schools in Paris, where some pupils misbehaved, and sometimes there was even a black market in school that was encouraged by parents. The headmistress promptly assured the Maréchal that such a practice did not exist here.[259] Pétain asserted that he would 'hit it on the head'[260] if he found out about it, because the black market was shameless and had to be stopped. To tolerate it would mean that general morality had become 'disgusting'.[261]

One observation that could be made from this broadcast is that Pétain both spoke over everybody else, as he usually did, and as if everyone agreed with him. His authority was never challenged in any reportage. In the conversation with the headmistress, Pétain asked her a question about her pupils but was not interested in her response. He was simply making a point expressing how displeased he was with the situation in Paris and was seeking reassurance that nothing of this kind would be tolerated in the unoccupied zone. There was never any disagreement between Pétain and any of the delegates to whom he spoke, and everyone was keen to show that they agreed with him.

Despite the positive images Vichy was presenting on the airwaves of RN about its politics and achievements regarding education, the real situation in schools was far from ideal. As reported by the prefect of the *Nord département* on 2 January and 2 March 1942, schoolchildren lacked moral sense because they skipped school to go to the cinema or took money from the café tills. Apathy was noticeable in the unoccupied zone, where the population had not suffered the same rigours as imposed by the occupiers in the occupied zone.[262]

Although there are only a few surviving broadcasts on the topic of schools and teachers, it could be observed that despite the fluctuation in public opinion about Pétain and Vichy in 1942, the propaganda style of the material delivered to the general public was very much 'business as usual'. Despite a departure from using the teachers as the scapegoat for the defeat of France, Vichy pursued a 'carrot and stick' policy to lure the teachers into collaboration. Only the most collaborative teachers and pupils were represented in the broadcasts and accompanying publication, while any contention or disagreement were swept under the carpet. There was no opportunity to discuss, debate or challenge the official position.

Mountain sports

Since its inception, the CGEGS had focused on the promotion of three specific types of sports: skiing, mountaineering and gliding. Mountaineering was considered an exemplary sport as it was particularly conducive to Vichy's education policy: it required strength, endurance and strong will, and cultivated teamwork and moral responsibility.[263] Thus mountaineering, with its strong values, became a tool at the service of the National Revolution, to which end all such new organisations were created. One of these was the Fédération Française de la Montagne (FFM), which was created in 1942.[264] At about the same time, skiing was emerging as another popular sport apart from mountaineering.[265]

The National Revolution gave sport its educational character to a large extent, an element that was lacking in the sport of the Popular Front.[266] Furthermore, if sport was a right under the Popular Front, it became a duty under Vichy.[267] In fact, this was the case to such an extent 'that one of the very first Vichy laws, the one of 7 November 1940, concerns the teaching of skiing'.[268]

The CGEGS considered the winter sport resorts of paramount importance in the development and practice of skiing. Some renowned resorts, such as Chamonix, Megève, Val d'Isère, etc. were already experiencing a certain growth and the CGEGS wanted to facilitate the creation and development of many others. It therefore continually acquired land through purchase and sometimes by expropriation to increase skiing or habitable areas. They also worked to safeguard these winter sport resorts by opposing certain works that might damage such sites, and under the law of 3 April 1942, they received a declaration of public utility. This law was significant in the history of mountain tourism because it was the first time that a specific legal category had been created for 'winter sport resorts and mountaineering'.[269]

The Information-propaganda Service of the CGEGS carried out an intense campaign to promote and raise awareness of the mountain's wonderful qualities. It seized all possible means at its disposal to promote the mountains as an arena for education and to more effectively influence the opinion and behaviour of the French public through the written press, radio programmes and the cinema – films such as *En cordée, Les Hommes dans la neige, Jeunesse et Montagne, Sports de neige, Trente jours au-dessus des nuages*, etc., which were shown in 1942.[270] Promotion of outdoor sports to the young people was made via a variety of means, including broadcasting on RN. The date and time of some of the broadcasts were announced in articles in *Radio National* before and/or after the event. Multiple articles were also written in *Radio National* that demonstrated Vichy's efforts to indoctrinate young people in the pursuit of sports and physical challenges to nurture their body and mind and prepare them for the future challenges of restoring France. Sufficient details are available for the following examples to exemplify how propagandists used sports to inspire youth.

Jeunesse et Montagne (JM), a new youth organisation and the mountain sports equivalent of the Chantiers, was created on 16 August 1940[271] by the French Air Force: long before the war, there were mountaineering internships for aircrew.[272] JM was set up outside the framework of the Chantiers, and was fully independent of it. The JM movement was originally created 'to welcome young aviation army specialists undergoing military training at the time of the armistice'.[273] It was 'open to volunteers aged eighteen to twenty-two, with priority to mountain professionals and those familiar with the mountain'.[274] For those who were eligible, a one-year service in the JM could be taken instead of the mandatory service in the Chantiers.[275]

By the end of 1941, JM included a commissariat in Grenoble, where a centre was established to provide the candidates with rope leader internship courses. In addition, there were three groups, two located in the Alps and one in the Pyrenees, with 1,300 volunteers divided into 50 teams, which included 130 executives and 160 instructors. The alpine instructors were among the elite mountaineers of the time and included Armand Charlet, Alexis Simond and Marcel Bozon. The organisation also went on to produce notable mountaineers such as Lionel Terray, Louis Lachenal and André Contamine.[276] The JM frequently participated in events and receptions of Vichy's officials and embodied 'the youth model desired by the National Revolution'[277] with their education programme.

In April, des Vallières wrote an article about Jeunesse et Montagne to showcase the success story of this youth organisation, including how young people acquired strength through the pursuit of mountaineering, and how other young people could develop their skills and strength by following their example. The article was written ahead of the broadcast that was scheduled for Tuesday 14 April at 07h20 on *Radio Jeunesse*[278] and served to raise interest and give background information. It was evident from the achievements of the JM in the previous winter championships, he wrote, that 'to be strong to serve' could be the motto of any pursuit of sport requiring energy and self-control. The pretentious theorists who taught with their slippers on had no right to command a group of young people; only those who had practical experience could lead and show the rest of the group how to cope when exposed to the elements.[279] If JM were to recruit new members, he said, they should address youth with the following statement:

> Young people, if you are disappointed by the banality of daily life, if you enjoy long winter hikes on the powdery snow or the difficult climbs of inaccessible rocks, come and breathe the mountain air with us; learn by facing the elements, by overcoming your fear, while accomplishing your compulsory national service.[280]

Des Vallières concluded that for the young people who were interested in mountains, alpine sports would provide an ideal environment for physical and moral education that could be practised all year long.[281]

Radio Jeunesse was a programme that specifically targeted youth. This article represents what Vichy was aiming to achieve by promoting sports to young people: sports allowed young people to enjoy the outdoors and to be physically engaged in a way that promoted a sense of discipline, something that was of critical importance when pursuing group activities in the mountains. JM was glorified and portrayed as a place where the young could gain physical and moral strength, as well as other qualities that were key to the resurrection of New France, although there was no mention of how this could help overcome the practical problems that they were facing at that time. What's more, alpine sports tended to involve small groups of people, meaning that the majority of the youth would not be able to participate.[282] The Comité d'études pour la France also warned that pupils were facing malnutrition and so it was necessary to cut down on their use of physical energy so as not to compromise their health.[283] Parents, meanwhile, complained about the lack of clothes for their children as well as the rapid wear and tear of their footwear, which hindered their participation in sport.[284]

A further article about mountaineering was written by Noël Vindry in the July issue of *Radio National*, advocating it as a sport that embraced danger and comradeship. The article was published prior to the broadcast, which was scheduled for 30 July at 07h50 in the programme *Pour la santé*.[285] Vindry described the sense of achievement one would acquire after conquering a summit thanks to your own efforts. The achievement was as concrete and tangible as that felt by an artisan after creating an object. To climb, one needed passion, the awareness and acceptance of danger, human solidarity and comradeship. To survive this expedition, a roped party was necessary at all times and death was part of the experience. If a climber fell, he must be held by the other two people on the rope to the limit of their strength, or else they would all fall together. There was no honour in surviving alone when your comrades had fallen. Hierarchy must also be respected in mountaineering, as the leader held absolute power in the organisation of the roped party. Experience and instinct were needed to climb up a mountain. Even the best athlete needed to be accompanied by a guide, even if he knew the way.[286] Vindry concluded that climbing was 'an admirable effort, made of courage, of perseverance, of energy, of intelligence, and of dedication'.[287]

It is evident that climbing represented, in many ways, the virtues that Vichy promoted as part of their National Revolution: Vichy actively propagated crafts-manship and a sense of community and climbing brought about the same sense of achievement whether the outcome was an object or an experience. The need to follow a leader who knew what was best for the nation was the same as following a leader who held absolute power in the course of climbing; solidarity and comradeship among participants as well as harmony with nature were key values that Vichy was keen to instil in youth.

As already discussed, *Radio National* was used to supplement the narratives of RN as it synchronised with the themes and topics being aired at any given time. *Radio National* was used extensively to support the theme of sports; on this occasion, it is possible to link the article with an announced broadcast, with the articles serving the purpose of either a 'taster' or supplementary information, making it possible for us to obtain a glimpse of how the propagandists used sports to cultivate the desired image of a renewed generation of youth.

In summary, Pétain promoted youth as the new force of France to enable the regeneration of the country. He dreamed of a healthy, strong and virile generation of young people to undertake this daunting task. Unfortunately, it was during his time as the leader of the Vichy government that the young generation's health was compromised: dietary deficiencies weakened children by making them more vulnerable to childhood diseases, hindering their physical development and ultimately compromising the future of the French 'race' that was so important to Vichy.[288] Vichy propaganda constantly sought to inspire the youth to devote themselves to youth movements, to follow Pétain's vision and guidance and to participate in sports.

Yet despite the surge in the popularity of youth movements and sports, it remains questionable how convinced and enthusiastic many of the young people remained at the end of his period in power. In the overwhelming majority of cases, those who practised sports heard the government's slogans without listening to them, and their goal was simply to momentarily escape reality.[289] Boredom and despair were among the reasons for the revival of sport activities, the cinema and reading.[290]

CHAPTER 5

Radio Paris Broadcasts

Radio Paris offered a good variety of programmes in different genres. As a French voice representing the German authority talking to the listeners, unsurprisingly, the broadcasts had a clear political agenda. They encouraged collaboration, tried to motivate the French to work in Germany, countered British propaganda and promoted anti-Semitism and anti-Communism. More covertly, from 1941 onwards, Radio Paris showed an increasing interest in French youth, not so much in the interests of the regeneration of France, as promoted by RN, but rather to sway them into collaboration with Germany and to establish a new identity as citizens of the New Europe that was being created and would guarantee a bright future.

Many historians see the creation of Vichy as the outcome of the pursuit of peace and resumption of normality that was given the highest priority after the French defeat, and that collaboration was a French proposal that offered an attractive alternative to total occupation by Hitler, at least in 1940.[1] What Vichy envisaged from collaboration, however, was very different to the terms that Hitler was willing to work with. When Pétain met Hitler in Montoire on 24 October 1940, a symbolic milestone in the politics of collaboration, his main expressed objectives were to keep France united and to reposition the country in the construction of the New European Order: collaboration would bring a reduction of the cost of occupation, the return of French POWs, less rigidity of the demarcation line and better treatment of France.[2] For Hitler, collaboration meant an amenable France, which gave him a secure base in western Europe against Britain and a rich source of supplies both in terms of materials and manpower.[3]

1940

The beginning of the new German order

The meeting of Montoire was explained to the French in Pétain's broadcast on 30 October 1940.[4] He declared that Montoire was a meeting in which a collaboration between France and Germany had been contemplated. He stressed that France's honour was safe and that his objective was to maintain French unity and to take up a position 'within the framework of the constructive activity of the New European Order'.[5] As France was now entering the path of collaboration, sincerity had to be established between both countries as France wanted to exclude any thought of aggression against Britain. Pétain had used the language of a 'father' up to that point, but now he was using the language of a 'Chef'. France now had numerous obligations towards Germany but would, at least, remain sovereign. France thus had the responsibility, as a sovereign nation, to defend her territory if attacked. France would also stamp out differences of opinion and curtail dissent in her colonies.[6]

Pétain's three directives defined his field of collaboration. First, the necessity of uniting the French in support of his policies to persuade Germany confidently. Second, the interests of France and Germany coincided regarding the project of defence of France's empire and the recapture of the Gaullist colonies. Finally, France had the 'advantage of restricting collaboration to a defensive framework'.[7] By protecting her own possessions or by reclaiming them from de Gaulle, France would show no aggression towards Britain, however, France would defend herself if Britain were to initiate an attack.[8]

By working with the German occupiers, Vichy was hoping for the New France to gain a privileged place and indeed a partnership status in Hitler's New Europe. Vichy defenders had argued that Pétain acted as a shield to protect France and its people from having the same fate as Poland, although others asserted that it was never Hitler's intention to destroy France; rather, he wanted to exploit it. This the Germans did pursue efficiently throughout the years of 1940–44, taking so much from the French economy that the calorie intake in France was the lowest in Western Europe. Vichy was credited with reducing the number of French workers being sent to Germany, however, others argue that Vichy facilitated the conscription of workers rather than deterring it, resulting in the French being the third largest group of workers in Germany after the Russians and the Poles.

Vichy had won some suboptimal concessions: it obtained a reduction in occupation costs between May 1941 and November 1942; the demarcation line disappeared in March 1943, although by that point, the whole of France had been occupied; and Vichy retained the right to equip its armed forces to a certain extent so that it could continue protecting France's colonies – something that worked in Germany's interest as well. Vichy enjoyed some success in getting POWs released from Germany at no cost to them, and they let the French believe that if they displayed good behaviour, more POWs would be released. Obviously, the release of French POWs did no harm to Germany either – these prisoners were more useful when working for them in France rather than rotting in camps:[9]

> Some prisoners were let out after Montoire, another 6,800 after the signing of the Protocols of Paris in June 1941, 1,075 after the sacking of Weygand, 90,747 under the terms of the *relève*. In total 600,000 prisoners came back during the war, about 220,800 thanks to Vichy's efforts (the others escaped or owed their release to illness).[10]

Pétain would not have known, in 1940, that the balance of power between Vichy and Germany was so disproportionate that many of his objectives for collaboration were simply unachievable. Hitler was not interested in working in partnership with France in this New European Order; he wanted the French to accept the superiority of German power.[11] The propaganda of Radio Paris served to demonstrate this aim very early on.

Radio Paris's propaganda emphasised the benefits of the New German Order in Europe to both families and the youth. Young people were addressed directly and indirectly to pressure the French into accepting Radio Paris's solution as the only viable answer to existing problems and as the guarantor of the future of the family. There is no shortage of examples of Radio Paris's propaganda aims; some of them will be discussed in more detail in this chapter. For example, Radio Paris targeted unemployed women with many children, with the speaker talking in a fatherly way. It attempted to legitimise collaboration by promoting employment in Germany as a means to support families, outlining the feasibility and benefits of doing so by interviewing youths who were already working in German factories. It also emphasised the civic duty of the youth to devote their hard work and love of the country to agriculture and to the 'return to the earth'.

The youth were encouraged to help distressed people through various charity organisations such as the Secours National and the Radio Paris Social Services. Radio Paris relentlessly aired the figures for civilian losses, especially the number of children who died in Paris and its suburbs as a result of British air raids, to raise hostility towards the Allies. It featured the enthusiasm of French youth in political meetings for the New Order, which saw a large number of interested young people visiting exhibitions or attending workshops to learn a trade in Paris in 1941 and 1942. Radio Paris also had a special programme dedicated to helping to locate children who had been separated from their parents, which had a practical benefit for the French.

There was both overt and covert propaganda towards the youth, sometimes under the guise of the authorities giving a helping hand to the distraught families. Here, we will focus on the narratives of the propaganda of Radio Paris targeting youth, as this makes it possible to compare this propaganda with the narratives of RN and the BBC.

The number of indexed broadcasts concerning youth in 1940 is extremely low. There were only three surviving broadcasts in the archives from July to September 1940. Following the incident in Dakar on 23 September[12] there was an increase in the number, with a total of 23 broadcasts from October to December 1940 available in the archives. A large number of these involved theatre, music, political affairs and the promotion of collaboration. Among the broadcasts of 1940, only two of them dealt with the youth: *Le Maréchal Pétain dans la forêt de Tronçais*, recorded on 8 November 1940, and *Importance de la veillée de cendres de l'Aiglon aux Invalides*, recorded on 15 December 1940.

Youth for France or Germany?

The first broadcast on the youth covered Pétain's visit to the Chantiers in the forest of Tronçais. It is interesting to take a closer look at the narratives of this broadcast because youth activities were curbed in the occupied zone from October 1940 onwards. Indeed, this is the only broadcast available from 1940 to 1942 regarding the Chantiers, one of the largest youth groups in the unoccupied zone. This reportage was recorded on 8 November 1940, the early days of the war, when the reportage of Radio Paris was conducted in a similar style to that of RN.

The reporter, Michel Ferry, justified why Radio Paris wanted to broadcast this event: the sound reported from the forest would enable the French to hear the words of the Maréchal, a familiar voice that everyone loved to hear.[13] This was, he continued, the advantage of a radio broadcast, as it gave the listeners the opportunity to feel the ambience of the event without being there in person. Ferry explained what was happening: the repeated '*Vive le Maréchal*' calls from the crowd and shouts of '*toujours prêt*', the motto of the young people of the Chantiers, similar to that of the Scout movement.[14] He then explained that the Maréchal talked to a few people working in different roles in the forest because he cared about the craftsmen in local industries. He also spent more than 20 minutes in the company of the young of the Chantiers. The Maréchal spoke in a familiar fashion to everyone and asked specific questions about their work, whether they had enough books, whether their food was adequate and if their living condition were good enough to allow them to spend the winter in the forest. He spoke with great kindness and simplicity and demonstrated a deep knowledge of things and people.[15]

There was a reason why Pétain asked these questions. At that time, life was particularly hard for the young people in such camps as they lacked everything, including stores and tools. They had to build their camps, 'helped only by mules whose fodder was often the bread ration issued to their drovers'[16] and everything was improvised. However, since the forest was one of the few abundant assets in the unoccupied zone, they could at least use wood from felled trees and charcoal in the ovens to keep them warm. It was a 24-hour activity just to keep the fire burning.[17] It is evident that life in the camps was not easy for the local craftsmen or the young people, and Pétain showed by his questions that he was aware of this.

The decision to set up camps for these young people in harsh conditions was, however, deliberate. First, it was an economic choice. The location of the camps was selected, in most cases, in agreement with the Water and Forests services, and the youth contributed to the work that needed to be done in that area. There was an ideological reason, too – the youth needed to be led away from the distractions of urban life and the moral deterioration associated with it. As written by the commissioner-general in an official periodical bulletin of September 1940, 'it was the cinemas, the cafes and among the bourgeoisie, the decadent social life that ruined traditional families.'[18] Moreover, it was an educational decision to reinvigorate the values of the earth and the experience of living an outdoor life. The aim was to break away from the materialistic and egoistic life, to take risks and to live a rough, active and athletic life without radio, cinemas or newspapers, so that there would be long-lasting effect on the moral value and physical strength of young people.[19]

The image of Pétain being surrounded by enthusiastic young people was one that could also be found in photos taken during his visits. Both the photos and the radio broadcasts of Pétain speaking to young people conveyed the message that an ageing Pétain, the father figure of the New France, who was stern but gentle, could communicate easily with the simple, honest and innocent youth, and was reinvigorated by their enthusiasm and vivacity.[20] Moreover, the same propaganda also sought to portray Pétain as an energetic old man whose quick and vigorous steps made other officials sweat, and whose good health and fitness made him an example to follow.[21]

Ferry continued his reportage by stressing that the majority of the young people of the Chantiers originated from Alsace and Lorraine, regions now attached to Germany.[22] It seems as though he wanted to highlight this to stress that despite being annexed to Germany, people from these regions were still considered French and participated in the activities of the Chantiers. This is a similar style to that used by RN reporters, who always made a point of presenting such information, especially in Pétain's presence, or when the opportunity arose. It also seems as though Ferry was keen to present Radio Paris as a 'French' station, despite it being under the control of the German authorities. Over the following months, this would change.

Ferry then reported the main activity of the day: the Oak Tree Ceremony. This was dedicated to a tall, strong and healthy oak tree of 270 years, which was chosen, as Pétain explained, because it had weathered the storms of all these years. Although Pétain denied that he could ever live as long or grow as tall as the tree, Ferry clearly drew an analogy between the strength of the tree and Pétain's contribution to the country. The tree was tall, solitary and pure, and stood in the middle of the forest, just like the Maréchal, who had to stand up tall in a forest of difficulties to lead France to its new future. The ceremony concluded with the tree being named the 'Oak Maréchal Pétain'.[23] This was an important message for the youth of France: they were being led by someone of the same strength as the oak tree, and it implied that Pétain was old but well connected with the young, with his roots deeply in the ground.

It was not explained why the reporter travelled to the unoccupied zone to report a symbolic and (what would become) a typical ceremony involving Pétain and young people. The Chantiers was already outlawed in the occupied zone so there was no benefit in promoting such an event. It may have been part of Radio Paris's German management gesture of support following the handshake between Hitler and Pétain in October, which sealed the agreement of collaboration between the occupier and Vichy and marked a new era during which Pétain would be acknowledged as the legitimate head of the French State, as opposed to the illegitimate government of de Gaulle in exile in Britain.

The second broadcast was presented by André Vauquelin des Yveteaux, who was in charge of a youth group called Jeunesses Populaires Françaises (JPF). In this live report, he announced that the gathering involving this youth group would take place from 20h30 to 08h00. He claimed that it was the first time that all the youth groups had been present together to guard the ashes of 'l'Aiglon' (the son of Napoleon I), the ashes that represented the past grandeur of France being guarded by the youth, who in turn represented the future grandeur of France. He then compared Napoleon I, the French hero who had sought to create a united Europe, with Hitler, who had the same vision. The purpose of both leaders was to make France rise again from the ashes as part of something honourable and 'grand', with youth on their side.[24]

This very short broadcast is a fine example of the propaganda strategy of Radio Paris, in which the youth was put at the heart of the efforts to regenerate France as part of a new empire governing Europe. The return of the ashes of l'Aiglon to Paris from Vienna was a gift from Hitler to win the support of the French. The role of youth was to protect the ashes of the only son of a French legend and take this opportunity to focus on the future of France by following Hitler in his quest for a New Europe.

1941

Wives of the POWs and employment under Vichy

Most families experienced separation from their loved ones at the outbreak of war. The structure and authority within households changed because of this and wives became the main provider of the family in the absence of the men. Although they qualified for some state benefits, quite often the amount was insufficient. There were additional state benefits linked to a working adult in the household and in the absence of the men, many women were better off taking up paid employment to qualify for this. The benefit system, therefore, achieved something that was rather contradictory to Vichy's policy intention that women should not work.[25]

The French economy suffered tremendously following the defeat and there was a rise in unemployment. To encourage women to remain at home, unemployment was used as a reason to create a new law on 11 October 1940, the Married Women's Work act, to forbid married women's employment in the public sector when their husbands could provide for their family. Women were also encouraged to retire at 50. The law did not apply to wives of POWs or unemployed men, just to women 'living in a shared household with a man'.[26]

There were 1,850,000 French POWs and some of them did not return home for up to five years, leaving their wives and families to deal with the situation without them. Despite Vichy's discourse and extensive visual propaganda celebrating the virtues of family life and motherhood, the families of POWs were not adequately provided for. In October 1941, a factory worker would be expected to earn between 1,200 and 1,800 francs a month, whereas a wife of a POW with one child would receive 630 francs a month in military benefit, 840 francs if there were two children and 1,060 francs if there were three. The Vichy Ministry of the Family claimed that financial difficulties led to demoralisation because the amount given to the families of POWs were insufficient and did not take into consideration the regional differences of people living in urban or rural areas,[27] or their ability to access food.[28]

There was a widespread belief in Vichy that the war would end soon and that the POWs would return home shortly. With this in mind, the officials were reluctant to make any changes. On 20 July 1942, a measure was finally introduced, known as the *délégation familiale*. The wives would receive a minimum of 600 francs a month for one child, 900 francs for two children or 1,200 francs for three children. This benefit had a different name, but the amount received was similar. This would remain the same until the end of the war, despite severe inflation. Apart from the monetary allowance, the wives also received other help, for example, many paid only 75 per cent of their rent (or, according to oral sources, rent was often waived by compassionate landlords), and they were exempt from paying tax.[29] Some wives also found ways to improve their chances of survival by moving into another household with a relative who would support them, or relocating to the country, where it was easier to obtain food. Women who found work on a farm quickly understood that they could supplement their income by selling food to city dwellers and by carrying out black market activities.[30]

As overall national unemployment gradually fell, women's unemployment jumped from 26 per cent in October 1940 to 54 per cent in July 1941 and 60 per cent in October 1942. This suggests that men were able to find work thanks to the ban on married women working in the public sector. On 12 September 1942, Vichy introduced a new law suspending the law of 11 October 1940 due to a notably different labour market situation in France. Women started to move back into the labour market to fill in for the men who were now forced to work in Germany. In December 1942, it was reported that women were now replacing men in some factories that were suffering from the departures of specialists under the La Relève scheme, whereby POWs were allowed to return home in exchange for labourers going to Germany to work.[31]

Employment matching as a social service

One of Radio Paris's political news programmes focused on 'crisis' and sought to address and alleviate various societal issues. Many of the crises concerned common issues such as 'Work, Family, Youth' – in similar fashion to RN[32] but not necessarily in the same contexts. Unemployment became a worry from 1941 onwards and young people were particularly vulnerable, especially young children who were dependent on their single mothers. Radio Paris had several programmes aimed at linking the unemployed to employers.

There were a few surviving recordings that featured employment matching initiated by the unemployed. The radio presenter would interview the unemployed on air and employers were encouraged to contact the radio to offer employment. The participants did not have to give their real names; instead, they were allocated a number, which was easier for the potential employer. As evidenced elsewhere, such programmes were broadcast regularly, some of them on a daily basis, as a social service to the general public. Employers who took up this opportunity were praised for caring about their social duties and were given free publicity.[33]

It was quite common for one broadcast to host several successive interviews, with the whole programme lasting 15–20 minutes. The reporter would ask a number of set questions – for example, locality, age, household situation, number of children, the trade and what the person was looking for. The interviewee would answer each of these questions in a very informal manner. The reporter would then summarise their situation, emphasising their number and plead with employers to respond and help the person in question. This style of interviewing was common in broadcasts regarding employment, including interviews of French workers in France and Germany.

One broadcast recorded on 10 January is a typical example of how these interviews were conducted. The interviewee was a woman of 36 years of age. She was allocated number 236. Her husband was a POW and she had a 13-year-old daughter. The reporter asked her to introduce her daughter to the listeners. The daughter took acting lessons at Châtelet because she wanted to pursue a career in theatre. She also took dance lessons, which were free, and a German course. The reporter wished the daughter success for her career; however, he thought that they were right not to consider the theatre as the only option for the future. In his words, the theatre was 'a job that one could learn by any means' – it was enough to be pretty to get a job at the theatre, and she was pretty. Now, a better use of her time would be to acquire general and technical knowledge. Of course, that would be expensive for her mother, he added. The reporter then turned to the mother's situation. She was having a difficult time supporting the family even with the military allowance. She explained that she had worked as a fabric sampler, an unskilled job, since the age of 15 but only intermittently since she had got married. She was hoping to find a job so that she could afford a small place in which to live and to raise and educate her daughter.[34]

Despite the main purpose of such a programme being to link the unemployed with employers, it was obvious that this reporter did not consider theatre to be of practical value and insisted that the young woman should acquire real knowledge that could lead to jobs in the future. The common view of women at the time was that their primary role was to take care of their family and children. If they had to work (which was often the case for working-class women), they would work in gender-specific roles; for example, in low-skilled 'womanly' jobs that could be performed at home, or in a profession that was considered suitable for women, such as the textile industry or teaching.

It is also worth highlighting that the fact that the daughter was studying German (which the mother possibly had to pay for) was mentioned in a neutral manner, without any negative undertones. Before the war, one in five French families would put their daughter down for a German language course. This increased to one in two families in 1941. What was most striking about this was that it was initiated by the parents themselves. Some of the French bourgeoisie seemed to have been resigned to Germany winning the war; learning German would improve the chances of their daughter bringing them a German son-in-law.[35] The reason the reporter spent quite some time exploring the daughter's situation was to urge employers to offer the mother employment to enable her daughter to continue with her education.

German courses mainly attracted an urban clientele and people from the tertiary sector. Peasants and workers were uncommon and the clergy was almost totally absent from the class lists. Probably about 100,000 people in France studied German language, in places ranging from secondary schools to German institutes, including language schools, special courses and private tuition. There were a number of reasons for taking up the German language. Schoolchildren and students might have needed to revise or catch up because German had not been their first choice at school. Employees, secretaries, shopkeepers and civil servants would either learn the language of their own accord because they came in contact with Germans through their work, or because their employers had suggested or put them under pressure to learn the language. The German Institute was an organisation created by Abetz in the autumn of 1940 and located in the Hotel de Sagan (the former building of the Polish embassy). The director, Karl Epting, was a zealous organiser who was knowledgeable about Parisian society. The German Institute was active until 1944, although its popularity declined from 1943. It organised things like language courses, concerts, theatre presentations, and public lectures in various locations which were all very well attended.[36] It was said that between May 1942 and July 1943, 7,600 people participated in various events such as receptions, parties and out of school activities. To supplement this, the German Institute also organised on average four or six cultural events per month, whose purpose was to communicate German culture and provide, little by little, a vision of the Nazi world. For example, in April 1941, the Paris Institute put on a screening of the film *Le Juif Süss*, an event attended by 3,600 pupils.[37]

The broadcast continued with the interview of another unemployed woman, number 107, who was raising six children on her own. She was a refugee in Paris who had no housing and lived alone with her children because her husband had recently abandoned her. When her husband had been around, she said, they had lived in a hotel. Since he had left, she and her children had moved to the barracks of the Boulevard de Port-Royal. Her children were eight, six, four, three, two and one years of age. The woman received no financial support and her children depended entirely on her. Luckily, they were fed at the barracks. The woman's skills were household jobs and sewing, as she used to work as a dressmaker. The reporter declared that she urgently needed a job so that she could house her little ones and feed them. Based on the reassuring voice of the reporter, there was no doubt that one of the employers listening to the programme would give her that chance.[38]

This broadcast is an example of how Radio Paris represented itself as a station with a social conscience that aimed at helping distressed wives and mothers, who were always welcome on this programme, or those with problems of a similar nature. Many jobseekers who appeared on this programme were women with children, although it was open to anyone in need of financial help through work. The radio presenter always had a few kind words, showed warmth and consideration and reassured the interviewees that someone out there would give them a job because solidarity was a value embraced by employers. The programme served to present the unemployed to the prospective employers, but it did not provide any update regarding whether the interviewees eventually found employment.

From 1941, *Le Trait d'Union du Travail* became a popular employment-matching programme initiated by employers, announcing available job opportunities. This was underpinned by political motives, as job opportunities dwindled in France while demand for labour increased in Germany.[39] In a broadcast recorded in August, a job numbered 5771 for an unmarried woman to work on a farm in Charente-Inférieure was announced. She had to be serious, honest and active; have knowledge of milking cows; and perform various household duties, including laundry for four people and helping the farmer in all aspects of farming life. In return, she would be fed, accommodated, given clean linen and would make a good living. The location of the farm was relatively isolated, about 1km from a main town.[40]

This broadcast is an example among many in which young women were required to work on a farm. It represented the common social expectation of an unmarried woman: to take care of household duties and the host family in exchange for lodging and a good salary. Such programmes were always presented in a neutral way and there was no overt propaganda promoting Radio Paris or German ideology. However, it is possible to detect a covert agenda: for example, by offering the service, Radio Paris sought to give itself the positive image of a station that genuinely cared. The practice of linking the unemployed to employers using radio, which was a fairly new technology for many households, also offered a new channel of job seeking, which had a unique advantage compared to traditional means.

Working in Germany

In 1940 and 1941, Germany pursued a policy of economic exploitation, although French manpower remained the most underutilised of all the factors of production for German purposes. The various methods of exploitation were duly pursued, and exploitation of French labour intensified from 1942, although opinions were divided as to where French workers should work.[41]

From January 1941 onwards,[42] interviews with French workers already in German factories became a regular feature on Radio Paris, with a clear political agenda of recruiting French labour to work in Germany to aid the war effort. Conditions of work and pay varied slightly from one employer to another but were generally fairly consistent. As early as September 1940, the German authorities had already publicised a clear and comprehensive outline of the French labour recruitment plan. In a typical example, whereby people would work for Ratal-Werke Company or with the suppliers of this company in Wernigerode, Cologne or Frankfurt, the wage for skilled workers would be 15 francs per hour for those over 23 years old, or 14 francs per hour for those aged between 20 and 23. Because the workers were paid for piecework, they could earn an average of additional 6 francs per hour. Each worker would also receive 300 francs as relocation subsidy when arriving in Germany; this would have to be repaid if the worker did not complete 12 weeks of work in Germany. For married workers who were separated from their families, an extra allowance of 30 francs a day would be paid during their stay in Germany. Each employee had to work an average of 50–60 hours per week. The employer would offer accommodation, which was charged weekly, and workers would be entitled to a few days of unpaid leave and travel expenses once their service duration had reached a threshold. A maximum of 125 Reichsmarks or 2,500 francs a month could be sent to their families in France.[43] This introduction to the benefits given to French workers, included in the September 1940 police report, gives an excellent overview of what the reporters of Radio Paris asked at every interview to lure potential French workers to work in Germany.

In a broadcast recorded on 25 February 1941,[44] several French workers in a noisy assembly plant in Berlin were interviewed. Radio Paris started the programme with the following announcement, which they did prior to the beginning of every interview:

> Dear listeners, please listen to a story about the life of French workers volunteering in Germany. These workers will be able to give you, through the intermediary of the microphone, news as well as their impressions of their lives in Germany. We are now in an assembly workshop in a factory for public transit. Needless to say, the plant is a modern establishment on all aspects, technical, hygiene, etc. Ah, let's get back to the basics. We are in an assembly workshop. I am going to talk to one of these young French who is working at a workbench at this time.[45]

In each case, the reporter would follow a similar interview structure using a question/answer style, asking the workers a number of set questions. In this broadcast, the second interviewee was a worker named Marcel who stated that he lived in the 15th *arrondissement* of Paris. He was married with three children. His wife was still in Paris and his children attended school there. He had now been in Germany for four months and worked as a milling machine operator. Marcel explained that he did not bring his family to Germany, despite his initial plan to do so, because they could not attend school there, and they were at an age when they could not be absent from school. The reporter expressed his regrets as it would have been more pleasant for Marcel to be with his wife and children while working in Germany; a statement gracefully acknowledged by Marcel. Marcel emphasised that his wife was from Alsace, spoke German very well and would have helped him and the whole family to adapt to and live in the new situation if she had come.[46]

The rest of the interview focused on standard questions that a reporter would ask each worker in such a programme; for example, the conditions in the dormitory, how many people lived with him, the type of food he ate, his work at the factory, his wages, including the amount sent to his wife, the number of hours he worked, his work schedule, hygiene at the factory, the kindness and warmth of the German workers towards the French workers at the factory, and the language spoken at work. At the end of his interview, the reporter asked the names of his children and Marcel replied, a girl, named Ginette, and boys named Jacques and Claude. The reporter ended the interview by asking Marcel to send a message to his wife, children, parents and friends, which he did.[47]

During the interview, the reporter showed considerable empathy and sympathy for Marcel being separated from his family. He was trying to create a real-life story with real people talking about their environment, work and feelings. He made the interview personal, as if he were speaking to an old friend, sending his greetings to his family, picking up on happy moments and obstacles that had to be overcome, making the information accessible to the listeners who might be interested to know what working in Germany was like. Marcel voluntarily pointed out that his wife was from Alsace and that she spoke German. Reporters in Radio Paris picked up such information that demonstrated a connection between France and Germany, to suggest that such connections would facilitate their building of a new life in Germany. Perhaps it was a way to confirm the importance of speaking German in the New Europe, or it might have been a way to reassert German ownership of Alsace and Lorraine through the language spoken by the wife. The fact that Marcel was working in Germany would have been reported with sarcasm or criticism by Anglo-friendly radio stations; however, the tone here was cheerful and neutral, as if it was the most natural thing for a Frenchman to do due to the increasing demand for French workers in Germany and the good working conditions. The fact that Marcel did not bring his family to Germany was presented as a legitimate and reasonable compromise, and it was stressed that given the choice, he would have willingly done so.

The interviews continued in this vein. The sixth one involved a law student from Paris who had arrived three weeks previously in Poppenberg/Papenburg,[48] Germany, as a volunteer worker. He was working as a locksmith, a job he had never done before but that he could cope with now. He had visited Berlin twice since his arrival, and had not found life in Berlin to be very different to that in Paris. Despite the war, the city remained vibrant. He would return to Paris in the middle of the year for a short break, the student continued. His mother was residing in Lille and he wrote to her whenever he wanted to. It would take about eight days for the letters to get to

Lille and eight days to return, so he knew that he would not hear from his mother for a little while. Regarding his language skills, he had never learned German but he hoped that in a few months, he would be able to get by.[49]

The broadcast sought to portray him as a young person with a prestigious status, which could be used as a reference by listeners. Throughout the interview, the student highlighted all the positive aspects of life in Germany, especially his visits to Berlin, which offered as much of a cultural and urban lifestyle as did Paris. Working in Germany did not prevent him from staying in contact with his mother as he could write as often as he wished. It also gave him the opportunity to learn German, which he thought would not be too difficult – this was a recurrent topic on Radio Paris, which promoted the learning of the German language.[50] As early as 1941, Radio Paris broadcasts had incorporated in their interview pattern discussions of points of practical concern for a French person considering working in Germany as part of the recruitment strategy for French labour.

The incentives to work in Germany were theoretically numerous, as pointed out by Radio Paris, especially in comparison to the limited availability of food in the occupied zone despite the price controls: the wage controls imposed on the French economy by the German authorities, the relatively higher salary that could be earned by working for the Germans, and the underemployment in many sectors in France meant that working in Germany was an attractive option.[51] And many French people did work in Germany. It was calculated that by 1943, the amount of money transferred by the French workers from Germany to France reached at least 277,046,200 Reichsmarks. The French Reparations Commission also estimated a total of 13 billion hours of work lost to the French economy due to French labourers working in Germany or for German agencies during the war years.[52]

Apart from interviews, there were also other programmes on Radio Paris that complemented the 'real-life story' approach from a different angle. Among them, the most prominent was perhaps the weekly talk show by Dr. Friedrich. From April 1941, Dr. Friedrich started his talk programme entitled *Les causeries du Dr. Friedrich*, '*Un journaliste allemand vous parle*'. These demonstrated the need and benefits of collaboration for the French as he presented them as partners of the European revolution, not enemies.[53]

On 15 June, Dr. Friedrich spoke about German socialism, explaining that socialist ideology was now deeply rooted in Germany. The German worker had understood that social problems would not be solved by opposing the state; they accepted that there was an eternal chain necessitated by nature,[54] the chain that bound 'the individual to his family, the family to his people, the people to their race, the race to humanity'.[55] German workers would seek to improve their lives according to the interests of the state, not against it.[56] Dr. Friedrich's position in his talks was borne out of the doctrine of Hitler's National Socialism, which aimed to unite all classes and workers in comradeship with the state, which, according to Friedrich, improved the worker's position and gave him social benefits. With the vision of the New Order in Europe, the same benefit rendered by National Socialism to German workers would be equally felt in France, especially by the French youth, who would in future form the backbone of the French workforce.

Dr. Friedrich's talk about National Socialism was followed by another announcement addressed specifically to French workers. On 2 July, he explained that he viewed himself as a passionate socialist who enjoyed conversing with the workers and peasants, whom he considered his brothers, and who formed the pillars of the nation. Despite his doctor title, he used to be a worker himself, just like the listeners; he worked hard every day in his overalls and old shoes, and he understood well the workers' plight and sorrow. His past working experience, he continued, enabled him to forge the ties that bound him to the working class, and he spoke in a language that the workers understood.[57] He saw a clear analogy of the social problems in Germany in the past and France today. He also said that French workers today had every reason to be pessimistic, when they:

> Live in a slum, with a wife and four children. To feed them, one works from morning to the evening and evening to the morning, in vile conditions; in the workshops or on dirty sites, poorly ventilated and poorly lit. When one feels like a beast of burden by those who make you work, one automatically loses all optimism, all confidence in human justice … One considers oneself as the damned of the earth and one becomes obviously proletarian with all that ensues … one throws oneself into the arms of international Marxism.[58]

However, Dr. Friedrich continued, the French workers should think for themselves and not fall for Communism or any enemy of the state that would only bring famine and chaos, and even poorer conditions for the workers. The French should not blindly copy the German model of socialism but rather take advantage of Germany's experience and achieve a social justice that was suitable for France. Dr. Friedrich recommended that France should implement a National Socialism similar to that in Germany to improve the people's situation.[59]

Dr. Friedrich's broadcasts linked very closely with the image that Radio Paris tried to project tirelessly through their interviews, namely that the French working in Germany had already been given the same privileges as German workers: they received better wages, had better working conditions and better occupational benefits; they had not lost their ties with France and yet could give their family members living in France the chance of a better life. The testimonies of the French workers served as evidence to back up this claim. Dr. Friedrich urged the listeners to 'think for themselves' what would benefit them: a better life in France brought by the same National Socialist politics as had been implemented in Germany in the era of the New Order, or to believe in those propagating Communism for an ideology that had only been preached and never materialised.

It is interesting to note that both Radio Paris and the BBC appealed to the everyday experience using affectionate language in their broadcasts to present their

LES "CAUSERIES" DU DOCTEUR FRIEDRICH

(Archives I. N. A.)

Une série de brochures nous retranscrivent les causeries au
micro de Radio-Paris du Dr FRIEDRICH du 20 Avril 1941 au 8 Août 1943

Voici la date et le thème de chacune de ces causeries &n *1941*

- 20.04. : - Français notre révolution est la vôtre.
- 27.04. - Vichy sert les intérêts de la France.
- 11.05 - "Mein Kampf" est-il méprisant pour la France ? Non, la France
  avait fait des erreurs.
- 18.05 - Il faut intensifier la collaboration à la suite de PETAIN et de
  DARLAN.
- 1.06 - L'Angleterre et l'Europe; elle abien mérité d'être chassée du
  continent.
- 22.06 - Explication de ce que fut le pacte germano-soviétique.
- 29.06 - Le bolchevisme est combattu maintenant par l'Allemagne, son idéo-
  logie est un faux socialisme.
- 15.06 - Développement de l'Allemagne malgré l'influence néfaste de la
  Juiverie marxiste.
- 24.06 - L'ouvrier allemand avant et depuis Adolf Hitler
- 2.07 - Ouvrier français, tu fus trompé par le communisme.
- 6.07 - Hitler n'est pas Napoléon, il ne sera pas écrasé en Russie.
- 8.07 - La communauté nationale allemande basée sur les ouvriers "sains".
- 13.07 - Le chantage britannique en Syrie.
- 15.07 - Liberté, égalité, fraternité sont encore des mots démunis de sens.
- 20.07 - V signe de la victoire allemande partout.
- 22.07 - Appel du P.C.F. à un front national commenté en se référant aux
  drames et horreurs de la guerre d'Espagne.
- 27.07. - La nouvelle conception européenne.
- 3.08. - Réponse à un contracteur de Radio-Londres.
- 10.08 - L'Angleterre parjure.
- 25.08 - L'assassinat d'un officier allemand, résultat de l'excitation
  judéo-anglaise.
- 28.08 - L'hypocrisie anglaise, l'influence des ragots sur les esprits
  faibles.
- 18.09 - Confiance dans les capacités du peuple allemand.
- 6.10 - Bilan du Secours d'Hiver.
- 19.10 - L'Angleterre et la Russie excitent la France à la guerre contre
  l'Allemagne.
- 2.11 - De GAULLE est le valet de l'impérialisme britannique (ap. tract
  P.C.F.)
- 16.11 - Le développement allemand depuis 1933.
- 30.11 - Les fauteurs de guerre, ce sont ROOSEVELT, CHURCHILL et les Juifs
  qui les dominent.
- 7.12 - ROOSEVELT est l'ennemi mortel de l'Europe nouvelle.
- 14.12 - ROOSEVELT saigne le peuple américain pour faire la guerre.

Dr. Friedrich's list of talks from 20 April 1941 to 14 December 1941. From CSA, *Cahiers d'Histoire de la Radiodiffusion*, No. 30 (September 1991), 53.

arguments but concluded by urging their listeners to 'think for themselves' using the evidence presented in their argument. This was a common propaganda strategy, adopted so that their points sounded compelling but less patronising or threatening.

The Rural Civic Service

There was a massive shortage of labour in France during World War II: 50,000 farmers died during the war and half a million more were taken prisoner, which was approximately a third of the entire agricultural workforce. To sustain agricultural output and avoid starvation, it was necessary to enlist young people to work in the fields. The Rural Civic Service was developed out of the law of 9 March 1941 that required young people, with the exception of Jews and foreigners, to perform civic duty.[60] This service was of significant importance for the occupied zone because youth movements had been outlawed the previous year and therefore there was no incentive or legal obligation for urban youth to participate in civic service. The service was under the administration of Vichy, with Lamirand playing a leading role in campaigning in the occupied zone for youth participation.

On 20 June, an appeal was made to French youth in the occupied zone via Radio Paris. The speaker began with a factual introduction of the Rural Civic Service and its practicalities: it was compulsory for young men and women between the ages of 17 and 21; there were benefits to early registration; and the youth participating in this service could save the crops and rescue France from starvation.

Lamirand's speech followed. Speaking on behalf of Pétain, he reminded listeners that the French had had to endure a painful period at the beginning of the previous winter, but he had faith in the French and in the land of France that a similar situation could be avoided this year. People could only rely on themselves, on their resources and the work of their sons. The land of France was rich, he continued, the peasants would soon begin to work in the fields because harvest was around the corner. However, there were one and a half million men who were prisoners of war and among them, farmers who would not be able to work in the fields. Eligible youth were now required to replace those absent, to ensure the return of the crops of France, for the people of France. Lamirand stated that he had no doubt that the youth would answer the call of the 'Chef',[61] 'the land, it doesn't lie, as the Maréchal said. You, the sons of this land, you will not fail your duty, or else you would make a liar out of France, and France, as the land, doesn't lie.'[62]

'France will become again what she should never have ceased to be: an essentially agricultural nation,' said Pétain in April 1941.[63] Agriculture had become a matter of survival for France. What was most important for the Vichy government was the return to the essential values of the past and a 'return to the earth'. What mattered for the Germans was a harvest that was essential for the war effort. Lamirand's call for French youth to participate in the Rural Civic Service not only reflected the urgency of the crisis in the fields, but also signified the willingness of the Germans to offer support to Vichy for a matter which, if not tackled, was detrimental to their interests.

It was generally known that the German authorities were behind Radio Paris. The BBC used this in its propaganda and produced a memorable slogan '*Radio-Paris ment*' ('Radio Paris lies'), which had been broadcast since September 1940.[64] Any direct messages to French youth that would have benefited the German authorities were therefore communicated by a member of a Vichy ministry, the 'official' governing body of France.[65] In this case, calling for the patriotism of French youth to contribute to a service for the nation was more effective when it came from a French minister rather than the German authority.

Lamirand referred to Pétain as 'Chef' as it was a term frequently used by Pétain himself in his speeches in the elitist and hierarchic regime of Vichy. He presented himself many times as 'the chef of the French, the chef of the State, the chef of the government and the chef of the army',[66] although it was used much less frequently after Laval returned to power in April 1942, when Pétain's role became more an honorary one.[67]

Five days after Lamirand's speech, another talk ensued in a broadcast to promote the Rural Civic Service. The speaker first explained in more detail the legal requirement of this service, stressing the benefits and the compelling reasons for young people to participate. Two students from Paris were then interviewed to give their views: Gérard Brasseur, a student of political science, and an anonymous student of business studies.

Brasseur stated that he had signed a commitment with his colleagues in political science to spend his holidays in Touraine. They intended to go in teams of six or eight. Two teams were planned: one would go from 15 July to 15 August and the second from 15 August to 15 September. The other student's situation was simpler, as he was already living in the countryside near Guingamp, at Plouisy, where his uncle ran a small farm of 15 hectares. He arranged everything with his uncle as his uncle would be happy to have him on his farm. Nonetheless, he acknowledged that he might not be that useful as he did not know how to drive a mower or handle horses. The reporter assured him that he would do very well at the farm and that all he needed was good will. The student agreed that he would quickly learn how to handle a fork and mower. At the end of the interview, the reporter concluded that these two students, alongside others, would give effective help to the farmers.[68] Their work 'will be, for the whole nation, an example and the assured promise of bread'.[69]

The interview with the two university students sought to show their great enthusiasm for their patriotic mission, even if they did not know much about farming. The important message was that if they could do it, then nobody should be discouraged due to a lack of skills, and everyone should try their best to participate, in the general interest of the country. Radio Paris was an ideal platform for such calls, as it could be heard throughout France due to its powerful transmitters.

In reality, though, despite the vast number of young people working the fields and the unmarried women who were brought into the agricultural workforce, the Rural Civic Service and the youth organisations did not save France's agricultural output as these young people were largely unskilled. There was a dramatic fall in production, caused by German occupation and hefty requisitions.[70]

Both Radio Paris and RN emphasised tirelessly the importance of working in the agricultural sector, because it was for the common good. In the unoccupied zone, Claude Roy explained in *Radio National* the instrumental role played by *Radio Jeunesse* programmes in reporting the various achievements of French youth in terms of solving the problem of labour shortage in agriculture. *Radio Jeunesse* painted a rosy picture demonstrating the enthusiasm of young people for working in the fields, and the willingness of youth from urban and rural areas to work together. This, coupled with the articles published in *Radio National*, served as a powerful propaganda tool to showcase success and encourage participation.[71] Radio Paris followed a similar pattern in its efforts to motivate young people in their attempt to address labour shortages in agriculture.

During the summer vacation, schools became the 'centre of workforce' for certain types of farm work. The youth who would carry out their Rural Civic Service had to first undergo a medical check-up, during which they were examined without any clothes on to detect any obvious defects on their body. They would then be classified 'according to the state of their musculature, heart and lungs, into three categories: suitable for heavy agricultural work, temporarily unfit for heavy work, or permanently unfit for heavy work'.[72] After the medical examination, groups of eight to 10 would be formed according to their physical affinity and assigned to labour centres. They would perform a variety of tasks, including haymaking, potato grubbing, harvesting, grape harvesting and bean picking. Monitors and representatives from their school would be on site to check students' behaviour.

The Rural Civic Service, which operated between 15 June and 15 October, had a 'carrot and stick' system. Youth were encouraged to apply as volunteers and those who did so were given certain benefits: their service would last five weeks instead of the three months 'non-volunteers' were forced to serve; they had the right to choose the region and the farm; they were entitled to bring home 25kg of potatoes for every two weeks of work; they were fed and accommodated; and they would receive an allowance of 10 francs per working day for the first 10 days, 15 francs per working day for the subsequent 10 days, and 20 francs per working day for the last 10 days. Performance bonuses were also available. On the other hand, there were 'sticks'; for example, sanctions would be enforced when deemed necessary and workers could be moved from one farm to another; the allowance could be removed partially or entirely; and the duration of the service could be extended to a maximum of three months, etc. Although many young people attempted to escape from their Rural Civic Service duties by providing false medical certificates, 12,000 students were mobilised in 1941, increasing to 700,000 in 1943.[73]

Some young people were delighted with their experience at the farm. One of them wrote to the Comité Sully, the organiser of the Rural Civic Service:

You have showed me a new life, made up of hard work sometimes, but it is always accomplished with joy and with a song on my lips. So, I come back enchanted from this first period; that is why I immediately ask to return.[74]

However, there were also numerous testimonies denigrating the Rural Civic Service. 'According to the head of the Student Service, the rural civic service would have been an operation which was "poorly engaged and poorly mastered", which took place in "great confusion"'.[75] A report from the general inspection indicated that some students had found the farmers gave them 'a reserved and even defiant welcome'.[76] Their accommodation was often poor as they slept on straw in a stable, while others were mixed with convicted criminals and unemployed people. The lack of hygiene on the farms worried them – it would likely lead to a degeneration of the race, which would explain the desertion of the countryside. The amount of food received was also sometimes insufficient 'for young people still in training and making abnormal physical efforts for them'.[77] They had to work long hours in the field, putting in 11–14 hours of work per day, which wiped them out in the evenings. There was often a lack of suitable clothing for work in the fields, especially shoes. Finally, the salary was not always paid, or it was below what was promised to them.[78]

There was an additional problem for some students. The Parents' Association, in 1942, protested to the rector of Paris because the Rural Civic Service made it difficult for those students who had failed the baccalaureate in July. These students would not have had enough time to prepare for the re-sit, especially after a period of intense physical work that had rendered them exhausted. They had already suffered poor nutrition during their education in the past year, they lamented, and now, Rural Civic Service would affect their performance in the following year as well.[79]

A common interest: skilled and submissive youth

In terms of propaganda aimed at young people, Radio Paris had an ingenious approach. Despite banning youth movements in the occupied zone, there were elements that were of interest to the German authorities: the large number of skilled workers both for immediate use and for the purpose of rebuilding their New Europe. As early as 1941, the Germans sought to inspire youth leadership in the name of a New France through the broadcast of Lamirand from Paris.

Radio Paris reported on Lamirand's speech to French youth workers at the Salle Wagram, Paris in a major youth event, speaking on behalf of Pétain, who could not attend. As reported at the beginning of the programme, there were well over 3,000 young enthusiasts present to talk about the foundation of youth today.[80]

Lamirand stated that France had lacked managers in recent years and that that trend would continue in the future. He expressed the absolute necessity for French youth to become educated in order to be trained as future executives and to become part of the elite.[81] 'You have the opportunity, you have the duty to learn your craft and learn it thoroughly,'[82] declared Lamirand. Speaking to those present and to the radio audience, he stated, 'I want you to understand the overwhelming responsibilities that you will have – tomorrow you will be the leaders of this country'.[83] He argued that a few diplomas were not sufficient to manage a factory; one must know the craft inside out through hands-on training to become a good manager. Speaking as someone with 20 years of experience, he stated that a true leader was difficult to find.[84]

Lamirand continued by stressing the necessity of a united and coordinated youth movement across the country. This was why a leader was needed and trust had to be placed in the Maréchal. Next, Lamirand explained that the term 'collaboration' had been mistakenly taken as a synonym for treason.[85] He stated that 'when the Maréchal speaks of collaboration, as you well know, it is for France to have its place in the New Europe. He did not pronounce the word to the vanquished; he pronounced it as the chef of the country that wants France to live'.[86]

The reporter summarised that collaboration was meant to further both French and European unity. Then four young men walked up to the podium; they were the sons of Frenchmen killed during the Great War and they would now testify their thoughts about the Maréchal individually. One of them stated: 'And yes, we must have a simple faith; we must follow the leader blindly. Do not try to understand. You have nothing to understand, we have wasted enough time talking, he gives orders, let's obey!'[87] Loud applause could be heard after each youth had spoken to the audience.[88]

Lamirand's speech was similar to Pétain's, as if Pétain himself were speaking to the young people in Paris. This was not in conflict with the German interests either: to create a New France that was part of the New Europe, both Pétain and the German authorities needed new and skilled young people who believed in this New Europe and had the skills and aspirations to lead others. Germany also needed skilled French workers, including young people, to fill the places in factories and workshops, and encouraged the youth to learn a trade.

Lamirand defended collaboration vigorously in his speech. This was in accordance with what the German authorities would have expected from the Vichy government. Lamirand wanted to convince the youth that the future of France lay in the willing integration of France into the New Europe. Pétain and Lamirand presented it as the best path for the country, and so the youth should follow their leadership rather than questioning it.

However, what the Germans would like French youth to think and believe is fundamentally different to Vichy's vision. While Radio Paris did broadcast speeches and talks from the Vichy administration targeting French youth, they did not hesitate to attack Vichy when they felt Vichy's call for youth was getting out of hand. As observed by a BBC intelligence report, in addition to labelling the youth movement a miserable failure, Radio Paris also attacked Vichy policy on youth, which they saw as reactionary. For example, Déat announced on Radio Paris on 14 March 1941 that:

As a result of eight months of reactionary fanaticism, schools have been wrecked ... we need a young France, and we are offered an old and doddering France. We want a France turned towards the New Europe, and this is the France they are trying to smash. It is a sordid attempt, it is also a risky attempt, and France will not allow it to be done.[89]

Despite the tension, there remained striking similarities in the narratives of the speakers from RN and Radio Paris in terms of the future for French youth. For Pétain, the key to making the French happy again lay in the pursuit of the National Revolution, in which young people should have complete faith; they should embrace and act upon it wholeheartedly. As Lamirand said in December 1941 when addressing a group of 6,000 young people standing on the lawn of the Stade de la Pépinière in Nancy, Lorraine, France was in trouble, but the French should not lose trust. The new generation should not despair; they needed to fully trust their heritage for the sake of France. Obstacles would have to be overcome but French youth was ready and willing to make the required effort and sacrifices, especially after years of compromises, domestic conflict and hatred. He referred here to the French Republic. The National Revolution meant a complete and definitive break with the past to regain control and join together the forces of the whole country to rebuild France; a New France where justice would prevail, and more brotherhood would coexist between the French. The Maréchal, asserted Lamirand, had a fierce determination to bring more happiness in France, which could only be accomplished by asking everyone to participate in this joint effort. All this would require the youth to work, put in some effort and make sacrifices.[90]

The speech of Lamirand was of a similar style to Pétain; it was filled with the rhetoric of abstract ideal but little substance. He did not address anything that would be of practical value to the youth; he talked about collaboration as a means to revive France but nothing about the hardship the young people had to endure as the result of collaboration.

The idea of happiness expressed in Lamirand's speech mirrored what Dr. Friedrich expressed in his broadcast of 18 May. The wait-and-see policy was now outdated as France had to work for the European cause, Dr. Friedrich declared. He stressed that the French should not look for immediate happiness without pain in the eventuality of a Franco-German agreement, nor should any individual seek happiness to the detriment of the community. It would be illusory or utopian to think otherwise.[91] He assured the listeners that 'it is by working for Europe, that you will be closer than ever to the happiness of your children'.[92] To bring happiness to the future of France, today's hardship and suffering was inevitable.

Both Lamirand and Dr. Friedrich addressed the need for the workforce, of adults and young people, to make decisions now. Both argued for the cause of a New France, which would find its place among the great countries again as part of a New Europe. Both acknowledged that it would not be an easy path and would require effort and sacrifices on the behalf of the whole population, including the youth.

As further events unfolded in 1942, there was a shift in the narratives of the speakers regarding French youth on Radio Paris, as exploitation of French labour became a key element in the German policy from 1942 onwards. A burden fell on the shoulders of the youth; the matter 'which eventually affected the majority of young men aged between eighteen and twenty-four, was conscription for industrial work in Germany'.[93]

1942

The bombing of Paris

Following the RAF bombing of Paris on 3 March – one of the largest air raids, which killed hundreds of civilians – Radio Paris seized the opportunity and increased the intensity of radio broadcasts about the aftermath. There were numerous interviews with people who had been affected by the bombing in an attempt to stir up anti-British sentiment among the French. One tactic was to highlight the gruesome aspect of children killed, injured or orphaned to pinpoint the cruelty of the British, who had showed no mercy even to children.

On 4 March, a reporter interviewed some local people residing in the area of rue de Seine of Boulogne-Billancourt. He began the broadcast by quoting a short text from a leaflet dropped by British aircraft over Paris the previous day, stating that 'in France, as elsewhere, our targets are chosen after specific intelligence. And to provide the most immediate results, we will also aim as accurately as possible – we know our business.'[94] He then described his impression of the streets of Boulogne-Billancourt to see how 'precise' the bombing had been. He stated that the British had assaulted this quiet neighbourhood in a cowardly manner, destroying houses and leaving homeless people wandering through the streets trying to retrieve whatever household items remained after the bombing. The reporter emphasised that there was very little left of this peaceful working-class neighbourhood. He had just now seen a bicycle that used to belong to a girl aged 15, who was killed in her bed as a wall collapsed on her. Her mother, who was only 40 years old, had also died. Her father and her brother had been injured and taken to hospital. The bicycle was the only thing left to remind the people how life used to be in this peaceful neighbourhood.[95]

From the angle of the reportage there can be little doubt that the reporter was seeking to emphasise and amplify the drama, the death and the suffering of this quiet neighbourhood of Paris. The reporter used an everyday object, a girl's bicycle, which is associated with the normality of life, to highlight the tragic death of the young girl and her mother, thus creating a compelling contrast between life before and after the bombing to shock the listeners and evince a sentiment of hatred towards the British. Not only was their 'accuracy' pathetic, but they were also ruthless in killing innocent civilians.

After giving this emotional account of the girl's bicycle, the reporter interviewed a few people living in the neighbourhood, enquiring about their experiences in the bombing, the damage to their properties, and whether there had been any children injured or killed in the incident. Among the several interviews he conducted, one stood out as particularly emotional as the radio transmitted the innocent voices of a mother and her child.

The interviewee was a woman living at rue de Meudon, a victim of the bombing. She gave an account of her story in a matter-of-fact fashion: her house had not been completely destroyed in the raid; however, no one could enter the house because it had been structurally damaged, and there was still an unexploded bomb in it. When the raid started at bedtime, she said, she and her nine-year-old boy had gone to hide in the cellar. The reporter asked the boy if he had been scared, to which he replied 'no'. The family had lost everything in the raid, she continued, and they were now on the street with no shoes. They had not expected the raid so they had only had time to put on their slippers. They did not know where to find food, either. The reporter explained that they would be directed to an accommodation centre where they could spend the night. Tomorrow, they would see what to do next. He concluded his interview by wishing her good luck.[96]

His vivid reportage continued with a visit to a room where coffins were lined up, where corpses were found with stunned and distorted faces, and where entire families rested in peace, including a family of 11 who had all died together. There were women, children and unknown people whom parents and friends anxiously attempted to recognise. The reporter wrapped up his broadcast by declaring that the war brought to French soil by the British was covered with women's and children's blood. This was the same soil that the British had not been willing to fight for or defend two years ago. He asked, where had the RAF and its bombs been when the Germans were near Paris in 1940? Boulogne-Billancourt was the vision of war brought by the British to France.[97]

References to women's and children's suffering appealed to the emotions of ordinary people and led to an outcry from the public. A propaganda film was made to illustrate the damage caused by the British air raid over Boulogne-Billancourt in March 1942.[98] Radio Paris's reportage following the air raid focused mainly on the people: the suffering of those who had lost their houses, food, jobs and income, and how the authorities had been quick in providing aid, practical help and advice. The fact that key military production facilities such as the Renault plant had been destroyed, which would be detrimental to the German war effort, was deliberately omitted by the reporter. Throughout the reportage, only one man who was a worker at Renault plant was interviewed but the reporter did not ask any specific questions relating to his workplace.[99] With the bombing of Paris, the reporter had clearly found it easier to blame the British directly as perpetrators of these actions, thus radiating anger through the airwaves.

In early March, the RAF was equipped with a new generation of bomb-carriers and Air Marshal Arthur Harris, chief of RAF Bomber Command, became determined to carry out raids over medium-sized industrial cities with a large number of bombers.[100] This raid was the first large-scale air offensive in the West; it was met with mixed responses from the public, and left Britain vulnerable to German propaganda. For example, one Frenchman wrote to the BBC stating that 'some English people found they were "not looked upon with a very friendly eye"' (Monte Carlo, 7.3).[101] In the summary of the BBC report dated 6 May, most of the excerpts of letters from the unoccupied zone reflected a similar opinion: the British should have left the French alone and the attack was unnecessary. However, excerpts of two letters from the occupied zone were much more sympathetic to the British, stating that the reasons for the bombing were understood, despite the damage, the cost of human life (Switzerland 23.3) and the sadness for the innocent victims (Paris, undated, via Tangiers, 4.4).[102]

It may be that for the French living in the occupied zone, the presence of the Germans in their day-to-day life made it easier for them to accept the bombing as a necessity to destroy German military production; however, for the French living in the unoccupied zone, having little German presence meant that they did not feel the acuteness of the invasion and were more inclined to focus on the casualties and death rather than the reason for the air raid. The air raid was well publicised in the unoccupied zone with *Radio National* dedicating a full page to it, featuring five photos taken after the raid, although the description of each photo was written in a seemingly neutral tone.[103] This demonstrates that while Radio Paris had become completely overt in its anti-British propaganda after the bombing, *Radio National* remained more covert and subtle, preserving its neutrality in its reporting at this point, although this neutrality proved to be short-lived as British bombing continued.[104]

The BBC broadcast two programmes on 4 March defending the reasons behind the bombing of Boulogne-Billancourt and the Renault factory, in particular. The speaker declared that the delivery of trucks from the Renault factory to Germany amounted to 85 per cent of its total production, with only 15 per cent staying in France but then mainly being used to supply factories working for Germany. This meant that the entire French production of trucks was benefiting Germany either directly or indirectly. The speaker added that during the year 1941, Renault had delivered up to 1,000 trucks per month to Germany. By providing these trucks to the German army, Renault provided a great relief to the factories in Germany, meaning that they could focus on the manufacture of tanks. In addition, Renault built gasogenes, tanks and aircraft engines for Germany. One should not forget that the Renault repair shop had been used since the Armistice for the repair of tanks and other vehicles belonging to the German army.

The speaker concluded that the German army's setbacks in Russia with its huge loss of vehicles meant that Hitler needed French industry more than ever because

German workers were on the Eastern Front and German factories were short of manpower. The Armistice was a deceit. The French workers of the industrial belt of Paris were condemned to forced labour and were the victims of the war that the Allies were waging to liberate France from Nazi oppression.[105] A second broadcast was put on air with similar content the same day.[106]

The police report stated on 9 March that there was some serious criticism from the public of the occupation authorities, who were accused for not having warned the public that there was an imminent danger over Paris.[107] On March 7, a message from Pétain declared that 'History has already judged the criminal aggression of a former ally who did not let our soldiers die alone, but throw into it, two years later, our innocent civilians with the coldest resolution'.[108]

There were subsequent air raids by the British over Paris and its suburbs, accompanied by extensive coverage on air by Radio Paris following each one. The broadcasts were very similar in reportage style, and in the questions asked and answers given in interviews. The aim of Radio Paris was to portray a broad but clear picture that the British were responsible for murdering a large number of innocent people among the civilian population, including women, children and the elderly. Presenting miserable pictures of the French who suffered from the air raids repeatedly served to reinforce hatred towards Britain. All aspects of a particular air raid were exploited to serve this purpose, as illustrated in the broadcast dated 1 May, which focused on the bombing of the hospital in Argenteuil, a suburb of Paris.

The reporter interviewed the director of the hospital who stated that the alert had sounded at 23h00. Thirty minutes later, they had heard the cracking of the building. Fortunately, the maternity service had been evacuated some time ago, and there were only a handful of people in the hospital due to the persistent threat over Paris. However, the reporter continued, five people had lost their lives, including a nurse on duty who was killed at her battle station by an isolated piece of shrapnel. Another victim was a three-year-old boy who had just had an operation for a hernia. He was supposed to have left the hospital that very morning but he had been killed in the raid at night. Three more bombs had exploded in the garden, leaving a few buildings intact, including the children's ward, where about 50 children had gone into hiding in the cellars. The reporter declared in a sympathetic tone that it was pure luck that the children's ward had not been hit as it would have seriously increased the number of deaths among the children at the hospital. At the end of his report, he concluded that there could be no doubt that the aim of the RAF was twofold: to destroy the French population's morale and to systematically destroy French industrial facilities. The real intention of Britain was to remove a future industrial competitor. Who could believe that Britain could win the war by attacking Paris suburbs, he questioned? He continued to emphasise that France was the real target; that the bombing was symbolic because it had taken place the day before 1 May (Labour Day), implying that this was done to undermine French workers. For this reason, French workers had to unite against Britain because their future was directly threatened.[109]

This broadcast represents a typical reporting style that involved the amalgamation of the grave consequences of the military attack on the civilian French population and the condemnation of the perpetrators. In this context, the reporter was making an overt attempt to insert logic into his conclusion about the reasons for the air raid. Using the symbolic importance of Labour Day, he was trying to make the French workers resent Britain for destroying their workplaces. It was important for the Germans to obtain the support of French workers because at that time, French workers had already started having suspicions about whether the recruitment of French labour for work in Germany would remain voluntary. In fact, a decree made in Belgium on 6 March 1942 became one of the first indications that the recruitment of labour to Germany would become compulsory.[110] French workers would soon find out that this suspicion was not unfounded when Laval announced on the radio the start of La Relève on 22 June.[111]

The police report of 4 May stated that the recent bombardment in the north-western suburbs of the Paris region by the RAF did not evince as much emotion as the raid on the factories of Boulogne-Billancourt. Still, the population deplored the number of victims and the losses suffered by the families. Most of the public had, however, now accepted the need to destroy the factories working for Germany.[112]

A coordinated approach for crisis relief

Following the bombing of Paris and its suburbs by the RAF in March, in addition to the propaganda to instil hatred and resentment towards the British, there was extended coverage on both Radio Paris and in Les Ondes of the charitable work Radio Paris had initiated and implemented to provide immediate aid to the victims. This shed light on the paradoxical nature of Radio Paris as both a propaganda tool of the German occupying force and a highly efficient medium to promote solidarity and charity, and how the messages from Radio Paris were perceived by the audience.

Within days of the bombing of 3 March, Radio Paris announced in the first part of its programme, Le quart d'heure du travail, the results of a collection to provide immediate aid to the victims. The reporter stated that this was a follow-up to the discussions held the previous evening regarding the amount of donations received. The campaign for donations was a total success because 100,000 francs had now been collected. Moreover, since the previous afternoon, Radio Paris had already hired a truck and brought the first load of clothes for women, men and children as well as food for those in need. As that was not sufficient, the reporter continued, he would now like to make another urgent appeal to the public to donate shoes, clothes, blankets, towels and food. He gave clear instructions about how to make different kinds of donations: the address where gifts, postal order and cheques should be sent; any donation to be clearly marked as 'Secours Rapide' on the envelope or package so that it could be easily identified and sorted; that the Radio Paris premises would be open from 09h00 to 20h00 and people could drop their packages there; and that if they could not come, they could phone Elysées 1382, stations 312 and 313, where the staff would arrange to collect the packages from people's homes. At the end, he expressed his heartfelt gratitude to the audience.[113]

Radio Paris's campaign for donations was supported by *Les Ondes* to promote the charitable work of its aid agency, the Centre d'Initiatives Sociales de Radio Paris (CIS). An article published on 15 March stated that Radio Paris was working closely with the CIS to provide relief to the victims of the bombing in the Paris suburbs. Radio Paris was able to mobilise its services immediately, calling for donations through the airwaves and arranging efficient collection and distribution; its listeners responded with a moving spontaneity. As announced on air, 600,000 francs had now been received along with thousands of parcels of clothes, shoes, baby clothes, blankets, sheets etc., as well as foodstuffs such as sugar, coffee, pasta, biscuits, jams and chocolate, etc. The French also brought all kinds of items, ranging from bedding, dishes, toys and coal. One of the most remarkable aspects of these collective efforts was demonstrated by the sheer number of applications made to adopt child victims: over 500 requests were received on the first evening alone. It was also noted that at that point, 800 families were still homeless. *Les Ondes* praised Radio Paris for its magnificent initiative and the dedication shown by its staff to help the Parisians along with all the French people who fulfilled their duty in these difficult times. The article concluded that these were examples of selfless acts that would lead to hope in the future of France.[114]

Thus, Radio Paris, *Les Ondes* and the CIS were mobilised immediately and provided material relief alongside warm messages expressing empathy and devotion to the victims. The extensive promotion and efficient distribution of aid for the victims was presented in stark contrast to the cause of the crisis: the British who had inflicted the suffering and death of innocent workers and families, and this clearly served the political agenda of Radio Paris. Despite its dubious motive, the charitable work of Radio Paris did capture the hearts of many French, who provided swift and vital help that could make a real difference to the victims, especially the children. As observed elsewhere, the sympathy and generosity of the adults for French children never faltered. The work of the numerous relief organisations that sought to improve the daily lives of children should not be underestimated, despite the mixed motives of some of them.[115]

Following the RAF bombing, the work of the CIS became better known due to the publicity on air. A broadcast in April featured a reportage highlighting the achievements and future plans of the CIS. The reporter first announced an update of the accomplishment of the charitable collections following the bombing: 280,000 pieces of clothing and 2 tons of groceries, worth a total value of 10 million francs, had been collected. He praised the generosity and fraternity of the listeners of Radio Paris who had voluntarily deprived themselves of food and clothing to bring a little comfort to those who had lost everything. The most striking fact, he highlighted, was that most donations were very modest, but they came in great quantity. This meant that the vast majority of donations most certainly came from people who were themselves in a difficult situation – people who had POWs in their families or were badly affected by the war. A ceremony ensued in front of the press, with the head of the CIS presenting a cheque for 1,885,930 francs to M. Yvetot, the head of the Comité ouvrier de secours immédiat (COSI). This was the amount of donations received so far by the CIS, and more would follow as some were being logged and more donations continued to arrive. The reporter explained that to remember the beautiful solidarity shown by the public, a certificate would be given to all the donors with the statement 'small donations have relieved the greatest miseries',[116] and this should never be forgotten.

There could be little doubt that the aid agency of Radio Paris was considered part of the solidarity movement and played an active role in fostering it among its listeners. Radio Paris was notorious for its anti-British propaganda, but it also served to some extent a social function that provided practical aid to alleviate the suffering of the victims of the war, complementing the efforts of a number of French charitable organisations.

Despite an overt attempt to sway the French public into the mindset of collaboration it would be too simplistic to label the radio station as a pure German propaganda machine. Likewise, it would be far too simplistic to divide the French into categories of collaborators and members of the resistance; the fact that the French public participated en masse in the initiatives of Radio Paris in giving aid to the victims of the bombing does not necessarily represent their allegiance to the political stance and aims of the station. The complexity of the inter-relationship between the French and the occupier, as well as those speaking on its behalf, should not be underestimated. The practical sense of many French and the widely embraced value of solidarity to help the vulnerable often led to acts that may be labelled as collaboration, but in fact went beyond any political allegiance to serve humanitarian causes. It was remarkable that 'the French formed new relationships, built new networks and discovered new forms of solidarity in order to deal with the challenges and crises inflicted by the Occupation'.[117]

The second part of this reportage was dedicated to M. Perrot, the manager of the CIS, showcasing the organisation's extensive range of activities and future plans. Thanks to the generosity of the listeners, said the reporter, the CIS was able to give practical items such as prams, wireless sets, books and clothing, among other things, to those in need every day. Their job placement office also helped unemployed people find jobs: within one year, it had aided 35,000 unemployed people to find jobs, including 4,500 wives of POWs, thus helping to make some improvements in their daily lives. M. Perrot went on to explain the CIS's plan to launch several joint projects with the Secours National. These included the opening of new beaches in the Paris area, where many children would be able to get the fresh air and space that were too often missing in their poor neighbourhoods; sending a large number of children on holiday; and, most importantly,[118] opening 'two temporary shelters for the poor children, preferably war orphans, children of prisoners, children of unemployed, children whose mothers cannot provide care'[119] in the Paris region. The CIS had also organised two magnificent children's festivals at the end of the previous year, which were attended by more than 3,000 children and offered a great choice of activities and toys that most of the children had not seen for a long time. These efforts had to be continued, which was why the press had been invited to learn more about the social activities of Radio Paris so that the print media would help them promote their activities and attract donations.[120]

The CIS focused on immediate relief at great speed – something that was often lacking in the actions of the Secours National, which contributed to the relief of the victims of a disaster but at a much slower pace as its aim was to alleviate long-term misery.[121] The activities that the CIS organised for young people were similar to those offered by Secours National, although the latter was far more influential and had a wider coverage in both the occupied zone and the unoccupied zone.[122] One example was *Croisade de l'air pur,* a documentary about the action of the Secours National and the Entraide d'Hiver, for the children living in cities. The aim of this documentary was to show the benefit of fighting back against the lack of pure air, sun and hygiene in poor neighbourhoods of big cities. It depicted how happy the children were when they were away from the city and could sing, play outside, eat well and have normal relationships with other children, showcasing the success of this attractive and joyous experience.[123]

Despite being much smaller in scale, the CIS was keen to tap into the activities of the Secours National and to involve more young people in its various activities and initiatives. Using the opportunity of presenting the donation, the CIS managed to secure more media coverage by using press involvement. Both CIS and Radio Paris obviously had much to gain from having public support and by presenting themselves as working for the French in distress and the well-being of French children.

Selling employment in Germany to French youth

As compared to 1941, there was a sharp increase in the efforts to promote the employment centres for the French to work in Germany, with much reportage featuring a wide range of interviews with jobseekers, French people already working in Germany, and spokesmen from French authorities clarifying the incentives, training opportunities, employment conditions and social welfare while working in Germany. *Travailleurs français en Allemagne* (French workers in Germany) were introduced to Radio Paris's programmes as early as October 1940 specifically for this purpose.[124] Among the French already working in Germany, quite often the testimonies were given by workers, foremen, worker representatives and managers; people in favour of collaboration who were willing to make a public commitment to showcase their success and to normalise the idea that French workers should work in Germany.

The frequency of TFA programmes intensified significantly in 1942: out of the 34 surviving broadcast scripts involving the TFA, four were aired in 1941 and 30 in 1942. As TFA programmes appeared regularly on Radio Paris (in 1942, this programme was aired bi-weekly, each broadcast lasting 15 minutes),[125] the total number of broadcasts would certainly have been much greater than those available at the INA.

Some interviews were with French people who had already been working in Germany for a while. This type of interview continued to be presented in the familiar format of question/answer; however, there was now a marked shift in the focus of the interview from the rhetoric about the superior pay and benefits (although this aspect continued to be present) to the modern and clean working environment in German factories, the broadening and enriching personal experiences people gained through working abroad, the opportunities to travel, which appealed to young people, and the emergence of a French workers' community in Germany.

This shift is well illustrated in the reportage of an interview with a 19-year-old Frenchman who had been working in Germany for five months. The interview appeared to have taken place in a factory in Germany. The young man explained that he was originally from Rouen in Normandy and had previously worked in an office in Paris. He had decided to go to Germany because he was unemployed. He had read about the possibilities of working in Germany in *Paris-Soir*. Within a week of sending his application for a labourer position, he was sent to a factory on the outskirts of Berlin, where he worked as a spray painter and then as an assistant fitter for two months before he was allocated to a different factory in a different town, where he worked in various workshops. In the second factory, there was a large French community with over a hundred French workers. He gave an account of his salary, number of hours worked, provisions for time off and food in the canteen.[126]

The young Frenchman then started talking about what he did on his days off with much greater enthusiasm. The workers were free in the evenings and from noon on Saturdays and the whole of Sundays, and they were allowed to travel in Germany. He had visited Berlin, a city he now knew well. The reporter commented that it must have been a very interesting experience for a young man like him. He agreed wholeheartedly, stating that his taste for travelling was one of the reasons why he decided to work in Germany. He enjoyed going to the cinema because he understood a bit of German. He visited the town, played cards and went to the café with his French mates, just like he did while in France. He explained that ArbeitsFront, a German organisation, had created a magazine for the French workers with the purpose of giving workers news about France. Moreover, travel opportunities in Germany were being thought through and would be introduced from spring. He stated that the work and living conditions in his factory were excellent. The workshops were both hygienic and clean. During the winter, the temperature in the workshops was mild and workers were entitled to regular breaks. He thought that it was the duty of all Frenchmen with families to work in Germany so that they could provide for their families, especially as he had recently learned that the workers could now bring their wives and children with them. He was going back to Berlin on Wednesday to work in a different factory.

The reporter concluded that this young Frenchman was interested in working in Germany for two reasons: the opportunity to travel and the excellent conditions of employment. He added that this was a simple and direct testimony that should inspire young unemployed people from France to work in Germany, where factories ran at full capacity, even for a short period. This man represented the audacity of the youth and proved himself a role model for many young French to follow his example.[127]

This interview highlighted how easy it was to obtain a job in Germany, with or without technical skills. This was an important message because many unemployed young French people did not have any technical skills. The reporter repeatedly contrasted the poor working conditions in France with those of the superior modern factories in Germany. Travelling was something that appealed to the young but was restricted in France. However, when working in Germany, travelling in the local area and to Berlin became a possibility. French people working in Germany had access to a variety of entertainment and leisure activities and had money to spare. The Germans even acknowledged the emergence of a French community and fostered its growth by publishing a magazine in French and creating opportunities for them to meet more Frenchmen outside of work. All these portrayed the normality of life among the French community in Germany.

Other interviews focused on the French who expressed an interest in working in Germany. The reportage of this type of interviews is quite often very detailed and covered French people in different situations and age groups. There is no evidence that Radio Paris targeted any specific categories of people. Interviews with jobseekers appeared to be ad hoc, spontaneous and without prior arrangement, and were commonly aired with their names and residential addresses. Naturally, this would make listeners feel as if they were listening to real people and their stories, whether credible or not.

Throughout the month of July, police reports noted that the recent appeal made by Laval to the French workers did not seem to have been followed with enthusiasm. The number of people visiting the employment offices and the number of registrations were quite low. The workers remained sceptical about the return of the POWs. Nervousness reigned among the workers, who expected to travel in organised groups to Germany, which was less anxiety-inducing than having to go individually. Workers feared that coercion could be used against those who refused to go, and there were rumours that food cards could be withdrawn for those who appeared reluctant.[128]

A broadcast of 12 August in the TFA programme is a typical example of an interview at an employment centre. The reporter began by stating that this was his fourth interview taking place in a different employment centre in Paris, having previously reported from the centres of Courbevoie, Issy-Les-Moulineaux and Vincennes. He was now at 1, rue Scribe in the district of Opéra, a former bank, and he was going to interview the jobseekers in the office. This employment centre had recruited more than 4,000 workers for Germany since its opening. One section of the office was reserved for the recruitment of female labour to Germany.

The first interviewee was a 15-year-old girl. The centre employee told her that she was too young as no one under the age of 18 could be sent to work in Germany. Between the ages of 18 to 21, she would need to present a parental authorisation paper legalised by the commissioner. The employee added that once she had reached the legal age, she could come back to the office and they would help her find a place, an easy job in a factory that would not require many skills, as training would be provided if required. The whole procedure would go quite fast. She would earn 10 francs per hour at the beginning, but when she became sufficiently competent to earn by the piece, her salary would increase naturally. The young girl appeared disappointed because she wanted to make a living now; she already had some work experience as an apprentice tailor. Apprentice tailors were needed in Germany, the reporter was told, as they could work in fashion design. The employee concluded the interview by telling her to grow up quickly so that she could go to Germany. After the interview, the employee said to the reporter that they had placed such young women mainly in families, where they were well treated and highly regarded in their work.[129]

Even though the employee did not place the underage girl, she did not hesitate to encourage her to come back when she turned 18, and to reassure her that she did not need any particular skills. This was meant to inspire other young women, with or without skills, to approach the employment office. Underage girls asking to work in Germany also appeared in *Les Ondes*. In the section '*Le courrier des "Ondes"*', a question was asked by a 17-year-old girl who introduced herself as Nostalgie as to whether she could work in Germany without the authorisation of her parents. The response was negative, as the legislative provision regarding minors were still in force in 1942.[130] This was a recurring question in both *Les Ondes* and the various programmes of Radio Paris for jobseekers, highlighting the vulnerability of these young women as their only alternative would be to seek employment illegally if they could not obtain help through official channels. As evidenced elsewhere, this rule about minors and parental authorisation was often disregarded and minors were sent to work in Germany on numerous occasions.[131]

The second interviewee was Miss Bernal, an 18-year-old Parisian who was going to Vienna the following Thursday. Her father had died four years earlier from a work accident, and she lived with her mother, who was a kitchen assistant. Despite never having worked in her life, she decided to go to the employment centre at 129, rue La Fayette, where she was offered a job in a Viennese family, helping in the household and keeping the young girls of the family company. She admitted that she didn't speak much German because the pronunciation was difficult, but this would not be too much of a problem as the daughters knew a bit of French – they could teach each other. She confessed that she was happy to go but she was sad at the same time because she had never undertaken such a long journey before.[132]

It was, in fact, not uncommon for young men and women to work in the German Reich voluntarily. As evidenced elsewhere, those who volunteered to work in Germany would start as young as 20, quite often due to family circumstances or the lack of job opportunities in France thanks to all the restrictions imposed by the occupying authorities. There was also the omnipresent fear in occupied France, which resulted in young French people having very little opportunity to experience life outside the home. This was a common feature of the young generation.[133]

There was thus a steady flow of women who went to work in Germany from across France, especially those from the south, where job shortages were most severe. The number of women moving to Germany reached 23,000 by July 1942. Most of these women worked in factories, but also as cleaners or shop assistants. Some went to Germany to find employment and a salary, others to be close to their POW husband under a deal called 'spouse's contract' – a one-year arrangement promoted by Laval on 21 October 1942. It is difficult to know how many of these women were coerced, but it is plausible that some were sent to Germany forcibly.[134]

There were other reasons for women to go work in Germany, too. For example, there was a case of a woman who had been beaten by her husband and decided to leave him when he joined the German police in Bordeaux. Another example was a 16-year-old girl, who at the time claimed that her mother had coerced her into volunteering to work in Germany so she could have affairs with German soldiers. Her sister was already in Germany.[135]

The propaganda did not stop there. The press also promoted the departure of couples and targeted above all women who wanted to join their husbands in Germany. To facilitate this, Radio Paris announced on 9 October 1942 the opening of a home near Rouen whose aim was to take care of children of workers who were going to Germany.[136] Usually, though, mothers would make all the necessary arrangements with extended family, such as grandparents and aunts. Children also often stayed with family in the countryside – where they would often be better fed and safer. For those who needed help, the municipality had also organised a system whereby parents could apply for their children to be placed in families. As one woman explained, her daughter was sent 'to the peasants who boarded children'.[137]

During the interview, there was again a reinforcement of the language barrier, which was a common feature in broadcasts promoting employment in Germany;

interviewees were always happy to state that they could get around it thanks to the help given by the host family.

The last interviewee was M. Morel, a Parisian who had worked in Germany previously but wanted to return for another six months. He was married with three children. He said that he had worked for a year and a half in the suburbs of Berlin, and now he was going to Stuttgart. He went to work in Germany because the wages were much higher there than in France. By working in Germany, he could send money to his wife to raise the children and even save some for the future. The only thing he complained about was the payslip, which was not written in French. The interview continued with standard questions regarding the weekly living costs for a worker, the cost of meals in the canteen and how they dealt with their evening meals; how they got along with the German workers; useful tips to give to new joiners to improve their daily life – for example, the difference in wages depending on skill levels and qualifications, and how to transfer money quickly and reliably from Germany to France, especially if the beneficiary lived in the provinces. The reporter added that the issue of money transfer from Germany to France was studied very seriously by the department of French Workforce in Germany, which had been recently created at 18, rue de Madrid, and which would benefit the French workers in Germany tremendously. This service was known to M. Morel because he had already received a visit from a delegate of this department in Berlin, who helped him resolve some issues and enabled him to help many of his colleagues with similar concerns. The service also provided support for the workers' families who remained in France. The reporter concluded by reiterating that this programme was for the benefit of French listeners by giving them as much information as they might desire. Listeners could also help improve the programme by writing to Radio Paris.[138]

This reportage featuring three interviews is a typical example of Radio Paris's campaign to promote the employment centres in Paris that arranged for French people to work in Germany. Throughout the interviews, the desire of the French jobseekers to work in Germany and the positive feedback of their previous experience dominated the tone of the broadcast, making working in Germany both an attractive opportunity for the skilled or unskilled, and a positive experience that did not need to be feared. M. Morel's circumstances would perhaps attract the attention of many French people with big families. The detailed account of the economic benefits, as well as the existence of a dedicated office to assist both the French working in Germany and their families living in France with practical issues, would be both valuable information and an attractive alternative for those who struggled to make ends meet in France.

In addition to financial details, the reporter also sought positive feedback about living and working in Germany, and the personal satisfaction this brought about. In this case, M. Morel liked changing location so the opportunity to work in different parts of Germany was an advantage to him. In the conclusion to the broadcast, the reporter made an appeal to the listeners of Radio Paris to provide feedback and suggestions, which could be used to monitor the popularity of the programme.

It also became apparent that the opportunity to travel was promoted regularly to potential young workers as an advantage of working in Germany; the exposure to other cultures was presented as a valuable new experience; and learning German appeared frequently in the interviews – the reporter never failed to compliment the willingness and desire of the French workers to learn German to facilitate communication and friendship between the two communities.

The Speer Report, written by Albert Speer who served as Reich Minister of Armaments and War Production in Nazi Germany, was about the output of foreign workers in Germany. His report found that the French workforce was the most efficient of all the various foreign nationalities working in Germany, although they were less efficient than their German counterparts. Speer's optimistic view originated from a survey by the Reichswirtschaftskammer (Reich Chamber of Commerce) in 1944, which concluded that the productivity of Russian women and French men was roughly between 90 and 100 per cent of that of their German counterparts.[139]

The propagated glorious opportunities of working in Germany are contradicted by evidence elsewhere. For example, a girl named Charlotte wrote a letter to the BBC on 29 September 1942 saying that at the end of August, at the Blériot Aéronautique factory at Puteaux, two workers had been killed and numerous others injured by the French police who attempted to force the workers to go to Germany. She also claimed that French workers did not want to return to Germany once they had completed their contract.[140] The extent of the brutality, cruelty and arbitrariness embedded in the familiar day-to-day life of the foreign labourers in Nazi Germany could only be understood in the context of a social order built on repression and terror against such foreign labourers.[141] In this case, Radio Paris sugar-coated working in Germany by presenting the opportunities and advantages but disregarding the risks and disadvantages.

The difficulty in recruiting French workers was also substantiated by the testimony of Leonidas Savinos, a Greek merchant who arrived in England in 1942 (and who was subsequently interviewed on 16 September). He stated that there had been no increase in the number of French workers going to Germany since Laval had returned to power because those willing to do so had already left. Furthermore, a German director had told him that working conditions in Germany were terrible and that foreign workers were absolutely hopeless because of the length of time needed to train them in the usage of German machinery. Unfortunately, he could not remember the name of the director or his factory.[142]

The Greek merchant's account offers a glimpse of the suspicion that might well have been the underpinning cause of the failure to recruit French workers: the distrust in German propaganda despite numerous testimonies from French workers that sounded credible. The opinion of the anonymous 'German director' towards foreign workers might not be completely baseless, either, as the employment centres cared more about recruiting French workers but far less about their skills.

This may be why Radio Paris tirelessly promoted technical education to young people, so that they could develop specific practical skills for the future, perhaps in a German factory. For example, one broadcast was about the training centre of Pantin, the purpose of which was to train young unemployed people from the ages of 14 to 17 on courses such as carpentry, general machinery, sheet metal, foundry, electrical matters and masonry for a period of three years. The apprentice would then receive his certificat d'aptitude professionnelle (CAP).[143]

Another broadcast was about the aircraft manufacturing workshops of Issy-les-Moulineaux, where labourers of 18 to 48 years of age, including hairdressers and bakers, could attend the on-site training. The German director stated that the workers would receive training for a period of eight to 10 weeks prior to being sent to Germany and they would be given a similar position and wage to those trained workers. Most importantly, the sketches given to the trainees would be written in both French and German.[144] These broadcasts demonstrated that the Germans were systematically rounding up young French people, using technical training as an excuse to give them some basic but often inadequate training, the ultimate goal being to send them off to work in Germany.

La Relève

On 4 September 1942, a new law stipulated that 'any male over the age of 18 and under the age of 50, as well as any unmarried female over the age of 21 year and under the age of 35, may be subject to do any work that the Government deems useful in the higher interest of the nation.'[145] This marked the formalisation of La Relève of French prisoners in Germany. To counter the negative reception of this law, Radio Paris broadcast the visit of François Chasseigne, from the Ministry of Industry to the workers of the factory of Manurhin, in Cusset.[146] At the beginning of this visit, Chasseigne declared that he had come to Cusset to explain what the government expected from the French working class regarding La Relève of the prisoners. He had brought with him two former POWs who lived in the region; both of them wanted to challenge the false perception that was widespread among the French workers that only those prisoners who were in poor health or were no longer wanted were returned to France. These two men wanted to make an appeal to their fellow French workers that their comrades were still in Germany, eagerly waiting for the decision of the workers of France.

Chasseigne went on to explain that this operation, La Relève of the prisoners, requested by the Germans, was simply asking for more skilled workers. He urged the workers to leave for Germany in groups so they would continue working together in Germany under similar conditions as in their current job. He addressed young workers in particular, stressing that they had a duty to work in Germany: French

POWs had fulfilled their duty by fighting for France so now it was the duty of young French people to work in Germany so that the POWs could return to their families. Chasseigne urged the wives of POWs to talk to the young people and encourage them to act so that their husbands might return. He warned that if the recruitment target weren't reached by 15 October, there would be repercussions for the whole of France.[147] 'I am afraid that even this zone, which believes itself to be free, is only free in appearance. Other measures will follow',[148] he said, ending his address.

The law of 4 September was seen by those concerned as an attack on the principles of freedom and a total requisition of French industrial manpower to meet the massive and pressing needs of the German war industry. Hostility grew among the workers in Paris and in some factories and there was a noticeable slowdown in the productivity of the workers. In some places, work even stopped.[149] The workers showed little enthusiasm for the call of the government as they continued to be sceptical about the return of the POWs from Germany. Families were concerned about sending French workers to the factories of the Reich, especially those in the industrial areas, which would likely be bombarded by the RAF. To avoid their eventual departure for Germany, some young people decided to voluntarily join the French army. The law of 19 September was passed quickly to counter the effect of the law of 4 September by prohibiting the hiring and termination of contracts for workers in France without authorisation from the Ministry of Labour. As a result, the number of employees in French industries, such as Renault, Citroën and Alsthom, did not undergo any major change in numbers.[150]

Chasseigne's visit was part of an extensive campaign staged by Vichy officials in a bid to reach the recruitment target – a task in which they were failing miserably: Germany had imposed a quota of 150,000 skilled workers to Germany by 15 October, but two-thirds were missing by the deadline, despite Chasseigne addressing the French six times on RN in the first two weeks of October.[151] He also spoke on Radio Paris, where he continued to appear keen to eliminate the fear and distrust among French workers by asserting that healthy POWs were being repatriated as well as the sick ones, and that French workers leaving in a group would continue to work together. He sought to create an obligation for the 'free' French workers to help the 'unfree' POWs, making it a patriotic duty to bring back the POWs.

The threatening undertone was apparent: France had no other option but to comply with the requests of the occupier, and French workers had to volunteer to save the country from severe penalties and to end the suffering of the POWs. On the other hand, there were multiple police reports that highlighted that large numbers of sick POWs had arrived in France by train, alongside normal POWs. For example, the police report dated 24 August recorded that a train from Germany arrived on 14 August, bearing 401 sick POWs destined for Paris and 125 sick POWs destined for Lyon.[152]

The following broadcast supported Chasseigne in his quest to get more skilled French workers to work in Germany. This time, Schueller spoke on Radio Paris to express his views about La Relève to factory employees, targeting in particular the young people who had escaped the fate of the battlefield and who should now take responsibility for the country as their older peers had done in 1940. Schueller started his broadcast with the following statement:

> Some prisoners, since the beginning of the war, have been there for 37 months … They are the ones who are out there, away from their country, from their family, from their friends; they are the ones who could be in your place, here, with their family, among their friends. Do you not feel a great injustice? You could make some of them come back.[153]

Schueller elaborated his argument along similar lines as Chasseigne but emphasised to a greater extent the patriotic duty of young people, who had so far been spared by the war. 'Do you not feel you have a duty to fulfil, a debt to pay and now it is time for you to do so,' Schueller questioned.[154] It would now be up to the young people to achieve this act of national fraternity. Schueller stressed that at the present time, many did not want to volunteer to work in Germany unless they were conscripted. However, going forward, there would only be three possibilities: to volunteer, to be conscripted or to be taken at random; both latter scenarios would mean that the workers would lose control of their destiny.[155]

He then moved on to talk about the incentives and his personal experience of working in Germany. He had gone to Germany 30 years previously because he wanted to learn and experience a new life. He had had to save up for the trip and pay for his own living expenses. Today, everything was given to the workers: travelling expenses and a guaranteed job. He appealed to their sense of adventure. Had the French forgotten their taste for travel, he asked, the excitement of going abroad and meeting other people to learn about their customs? French workers would gain both personal and technical skills if they had this important experience.[156]

Both broadcasts labelled La Relève as 'a necessary and sacred duty'[157] and commended those who were volunteering to work in Germany as having fulfilled 'their civic and moral responsibility'.[158] As in the previous broadcast by Chasseigne, Schueller used a similar rhetoric in an attempt to make the workers feel compelled to volunteer to work in Germany. His speech placed on the French a sense of guilt for not helping a countryman when they could, and a sense of losing out on an exciting adventure. Furthermore, to ensure that French workers would go to Germany, the authorities had prohibited French employers from employing new workers unless special authorisation had been given.[159]

Despite the increasingly patronising message and pressure put on French workers, many chose not to work in Germany. Jean, a French electric engineer who left Bordeaux on 23 October 1942, stated that the workers were all against the idea of working in Germany and that they would only go if they were forced to. The method used by the authorities to counteract this reluctance and incite the French to work in Germany was a simple yet powerful one: they lowered the salary for working in France significantly as compared to working in Germany. Jean, however, ascertained that the pressure put on French workers to work in Germany only served to increase their discontent and resentment towards the Germans.[160]

Faced with the failure to gather the sufficient number of specialists demanded by the occupier, Laval spoke on air on 20 October and threatened the public that 'the government is determined not to tolerate the resistance of individuals or groups of bosses or workers who, in defiance of the national interest, remain deaf to the call that I address to them'.[161] In response to the slow take-up, Radio Paris increased the number of programmes designated to this purpose, a fact that demonstrates that the exploitation of French labour had become a key element of German policy from 1942 onwards. This was largely due to the military situation in Russia.

In the end, a total of 32,530 La Relève volunteers went to work in Germany of their own free will between June and October 1942.[162] For most POWs' wives, 'the Relève brought misinformation, false hopes, bitterness, and jealousy'.[163] This was because by July 1942, many families thought that a POW would be returned if his family member volunteered to work in Germany. However, that was not the case, because La Relève was a collective action and not an individual exchange of labour.[164] As one of the disgruntled family members wrote, 'At times we are very unhappy to see returning young men without family responsibilities while those who have children remain behind barbed wires.'[165]

On the other hand, the state of affairs in France in 1942 was far more complex than a clear trajectory of German domination of Europe. Two elements in particular could have flooded the youth with a sense of freedom rather than shame: the entry of America in the war in December 1941, signalling that Germany would not be able to win the war so easily in the long run; and the sustained suspicion that the Vichy doctrines would not last, not least because of the lack of moral examples from Vichy leaders.[166]

It is not at all surprising that young people were not convinced of the permanence of collaboration – even a devoted collaborator had doubts. As the author Drieu La Rochelle wrote in his journal on 22 April 1942, he did not believe in collaboration any longer, and thought the French would 'rather stay faithful to the sentiment of shame than to take control of this sentiment.[167] Equally, many French workers rejected working in Germany despite the repeated calls of Radio Paris. La Relève was the last attempt by Vichy to compel French workers to go to Germany on a voluntary basis before the total occupation of France in November 1942, giving way shortly afterwards to a compulsory labour scheme from 15 February 1943, under the name Service du travail obligatoire (STO), which specifically concerned young people born between 1920 and 1922.[168]

Conclusion

The experience of propaganda to the French between 1940–1942 seems to confirm the belief, to a certain extent, that propaganda has the capacity to shape minds. The BBC had gone to great lengths to collect intelligence regarding the day-to-day situation and events in France. Sources included correspondence from listeners of both zones, French and foreign press, interviews with people arriving in the UK and the monitoring of radio stations in France, all with the aim of gauging public opinion.[1] The BBC was credited both by historians and listeners with providing accurate and timely news and information to its listeners.

The information collected from listeners' correspondence and interviews was based on personal accounts and observations that were subjective and opinionated, but nevertheless important; the lived experience of ordinary French people could not be understood merely from official reports and figures. The BBC trusted these kaleidoscopic and disparate sources of information when compiling their Monthly Intelligent Reports about listeners' responses and public opinion, and this played an important role in ensuring that the content of their daily broadcast to France stayed relevant.

When compared to the BBC, there is little evidence that an equivalent level of monitoring of public opinion was conducted by either RN or Radio Paris. There were letters from listeners to RN and Radio Paris, but they were mainly addressed to specific broadcasts. The Vichy government had censorship in place, which involved opening and vetting private letters and tapping telephone lines; however, there is little evidence that the intelligence obtained was passed on to the radio stations.[2] Radio Paris compiled reports of listeners' responses to the popular programme *La Rose des Vents*, for example, but it used the correspondence mainly to create a network of supporters of collaboration.[3]

Both RN and Radio Paris made their presence felt among the listeners in France as they broadcast from Vichy and Paris respectively. Their reporters could report from any corner of France, using a variety of formats, such as reportage, coverage of sporting events, concerts and interviews with artists and professionals, while cleverly promoting their political views and propaganda messages.

Compared to RN and Radio Paris, the BBC had an inherent disadvantage when broadcasting to France because of its overseas location. Most of the programmes were made in the studio, and there could be no live broadcasting of events taking place in France. In fact, the BBC had to wait until mid-1942 to be able to broadcast news about events occurring in the unoccupied zone with only a few hours' delay; for example, the coverage of the 14 July celebration, which was the first for the BBC since the war had started.[4]

It was, therefore, no small achievement that the BBC managed to broadcast to both zones of France[5] and to stay relevant to their listeners throughout the period 1940–42. Moreover, despite jamming and synchronisation issues, the retention of their listeners in the early months of the war[6] and the increase of their popularity as the war progressed were crucial to the later success of the BBC. By 1942, it had firmly established its credibility among the French[7] and was well received across France.[8]

As for RN, among surviving material there are many live broadcasts focusing on Pétain's visits, his political addresses to the French and his participation in live public events, showcasing his popularity and promoting Vichy's ideology in the unoccupied zone. The broad coverage of these events also served to demonstrate the public's enthusiasm for Pétain's leadership. By broadcasting live events, the listeners could easily immerse themselves in the scene with its background noise and were transcended by Pétain's presence. The response of the crowd to Pétain's presence was always boisterous, and the passionate display of enthusiasm at that moment was captured faithfully by the recording of RN and could be broadcast at will by the radio. This was a unique feature of the programmes of RN, which could be heard clearly within the borders of the unoccupied zone.[9]

RN inherited problems with its distribution of transmitters, largely due to the French politicians' lack of vision prior to the war. National synchronisation in the unoccupied zone was only achieved on 1 December 1941.[10] In the occupied zone, its programmes were not heard properly due to the lack of sufficiently powerful relays, and this remained the case throughout the years of 1940–42. RN's programmes were, at first, met with a marked disaffection by the public. At the beginning of 1941, it became apparent that there was a lack of interest among the public for its radio programmes, including its artistic and musical programmes and variety shows, which were of mediocre quality. The public was irritated by its lack of timely news, and the programmes surrounding the themes of the youth, work, school, etc., which were often broadcast at peak time.[11] A reform was initiated from May 1941, resulting in the news department being reorganised and a marked improvement in the quality of its artistic programmes,[12] making it an attractive alternative to the jammed BBC broadcasts. By the end of 1942, it had shifted from a radio station promoting an idealised and abstract motion associated with the National Revolution with mediocre quality, to a station aimed at maintaining the efficiency of the Vichy government and providing light and vivid artistic and entertainment programmes.[13]

However, it remained a radio station operating within the shadow and constraints of the German authorities. In 1942, its propaganda aimed more and more at facilitating the relationship between Laval and the occupiers, and not so much at shaping French public opinion.[14]

Radio Paris was clearly a German station by organisation and management but presented itself as a French station in terms of the programmes broadcast to the public.[15] Its programming was completely overhauled after the German take-over, using new support and frontline staff,[16] with the most modern technical studio facilities in Paris.[17] Although it could reach the whole of France, the programmes were intended for listeners in and around Paris. The German management carefully balanced the various programmes to appeal to the audience at large and to maintain its propaganda purpose. The programme schedule remained more or less the same from 1940 to 1944, with built-in flexibility to broadcast unplanned events.[18] This was an approach that was similar to that of the BBC, where the programme schedule remained practically unchanged from 18 July 1940 until 1944.[19]

As with RN, Radio Paris often reported from outside the studio; for example, it broadcast live recordings of entertainment as well as interviews conducted in public spaces or employment offices, etc. However, the style was more formal and there was little appetite for showcasing Pétain's visits. Many of Radio Paris's programmes reflected the political aims and social issues of the time. Their propaganda messages could be crude and repetitive, although they often engaged authoritative figures and used examples to indoctrinate the French or to evoke fear. Radio Paris's entertainment programmes occupied more than two-thirds of the broadcasting schedule.[20] These served to glue the radio schedule together and to lighten the listening experience. These artistic programmes were popular, interesting and of good quality, and therefore reached a wide audience.

Radio Paris had five powerful transmitters located in the occupied zone, enabling it to cover Paris and its suburbs, as well as much of Vichy France, making it a more powerful station than RN in terms of geographic coverage.[21] Synchronisation of the transmitters was also a problem for Radio Paris, however. As the war progressed, it became imperative for Radio Paris to extend its broadcasting hours late into the night so that the BBC would not become the default choice for the listeners,[22] but this was not achieved until June 1942, when the broadcasting of programmes was extended beyond midnight.[23]

The BBC French Service did not have a magazine to illustrate its radio programmes to its target audience in France, due to the very nature of it being an overseas station. In contrast, the messages and narratives of RN were supplemented by its in-house magazine, *Radio National*, which was published weekly and contained a detailed daily schedule. *Radio National* was more than a magazine for radio programmes; it was also a very effective propaganda tool that was used to reach out to the general public, who were not necessarily listeners, in order to revive patriotism, with its numerous articles on Pétain, the youth movement, sports, etc. It was also regularly supplemented by photos, commentaries and illustrated pictures.

Radio Paris also had a magazine, *Les Ondes,* which played a similar role to *Radio National,* promoting the weekly programmes of Radio Paris and other affiliated radio stations, giving information about the numerous Parisian shows, and using commentaries, columns, articles and photos to illustrate its political position.

In terms of the narratives of the broadcasts of the three radio stations, the BBC reported events taking place in France according to their intelligence, picking up issues that seemed insignificant in isolation, but portrayed a societal tendency when they took place often and spontaneously. The women's demonstrations against food shortage in France is a good example. The narratives of the BBC with a focus on food were discussed in broad terms, encompassing the reality of food supply, the underlying military and political reasons for food shortages, the public's reaction to them, and the physical and psychological consequences. It thus portrayed a realistic image of the food situation in France. By doing so, it maintained a link between the Allies and the population in France, communicating what was happening and why, and this served to counteract the organised propaganda of RN and Radio Paris.

Of course, the French were already largely aware of what the BBC reported regarding the food situation: the food rationing, the requisitions and levies, the presence of the occupiers, the empty grocery stores, etc. In fact, the French were the ones reporting these details to the BBC. One could argue that the role of the BBC, in this sense, was to join the dots, to enable the French to have a fuller picture of the extent of the persistent requisitions and levies imposed by both the occupier and the Vichy government, to appreciate the devastating effects of food shortages on the ordinary French people and to voice their discontent. By doing so, they fostered a sense of solidarity against the occupiers and Vichy as their puppet government. The narratives served a dual purpose of 'agitation' and 'integration': agitation against the occupier and Vichy, and unity among the people. It was not until September 1941 that the BBC started giving advice on how to counteract German and Vichy's food exactions,[24] moving further along the path of resistance.

It also became evident that as the war dragged on, food became one of the major concerns for the French. This was also one of the lasting war memories of the French population: a film made in 1956, *La Traversée de Paris,* which portrays two men carrying the meat of a pig that had been illegally slaughtered in a suitcase through the city of Paris quickly became a classic as it caught the imagination of the public regarding the black market.[25]

To revive the patriotic flame of the French, the BBC spoke regularly about what it meant to be French and the importance of French grandeur. As time went by, the speakers started talking more and more about the practical problems of the French people, who had to face difficult times ahead. To win the hearts and minds of the people, the BBC started to cleverly blend in their broadcasts things that made France great with solid and detailed information depicting people's feelings and concerns about what France would look like after the war was over.

Although propaganda could convince people and even make them believe stories, the question of 'to what extent could propaganda make people act?' remained. Général de Gaulle did not have any illusions about this but he was certain that the French themselves had to contribute to their own liberation. 'What mattered most was creating an environment in which the 3 per cent of the population involved in active resistance in France could successfully execute their mission "like fish in the water"'.[26]

As for RN, among the surviving broadcasts available to researchers, the youth stood out as a theme occupying a significant place as it was central to the government's political agenda. The discussion of the narratives surrounding the youth encompassed children, young people, family, women, education, etc. RN's narrative about the youth was conveyed in a completely innocuous way: the youth was presented as a positive and promising force for the reconstruction of France. RN's narratives were more focused on Vichy's political and ideological aspirations than on the everyday problems of the population. Vichy was more concerned with how youth should think, talk and behave and how they would be involved in the making of the New France. Vichy's political and ideological aspirations concerning the youth were achieved through the development of youth groups, the reform of the education system, the emphasis on sports but also by repeatedly calling, appealing, coaching and indoctrinating young people via radio.

In a way, Vichy largely emulated the German policy with regard to young people and women, demonstrating a certain level of similarity in their ideology. However, Germany did not want Vichy to replicate the German model to strengthen French youth, as this could potentially be turned against Germany. Therefore, a successful development of the youth movements in Vichy was against the interest of the Germans: they wanted to use French youth as a source of labour for German war efforts and for the ideology of New Europe, not for the rise of France.

The context and purpose of the narratives is what made the broadcasts of RN appealing and dangerous at the same time. They reflected the rhetoric of the Vichy government, promoting Pétain's ideology of National Revolution, but for the people who lived in Vichy France during the war years, it would have been difficult to contest the narratives of the broadcasts. For example, how could any French person contest the merits of a high standard of behaviour among pupils at school, a love of the country, the importance of hard work and learning a practical skill to be successful in life, the encouragement of sport to allow the development of friendship, comradeship, teamwork, courage and tenacity, or the necessity to maintain local and regional traditions? Even today, the moral values promoted by RN still seem to largely mimic modern conservative moral values.

RN was never going to be an independent or neutral radio station, as it claimed itself to be. Although the stance and rhetoric of RN changed little in the period covered, especially those associated with the youth movement and the National Revolution, it became inevitable that it would gradually lose its self-perceived neutrality due to the pressure exerted by German authorities. As time went on, it began using to a greater extent the language of the occupier, making it possible for the public to see through Vichy's hypocrisy. Thus, the station lost credibility with the listeners,[27] particularly after Laval's return to power in April 1942.

The Germans invested more time and effort in Radio Paris than in any other European radio station.[28] It provided an entertainment package of superior quality, with its state-of-the-art studio facilities and experienced French presenters. It is also evident from the broadcasting narratives that it presented itself as a French radio station for Parisians, promoting solidarity and fulfilling its social duty by promoting practical skills, providing employment information for jobseekers, and encouraging the young to assist the elderly and the vulnerable and to help with the harvest.

French youth was of common interest for Vichy and the German occupiers. Therefore, some elements of collaboration between the radio stations could be observed. For example, Radio Paris broadcast the speech of a minister of the Vichy government about education, the future of youth, practical training for young people, etc., all of which reflected the ideology of the National Revolution. However, despite sharing a common focus on 'Work, Family … Youth' in many of their daily broadcasts,[29] the youth had a different meaning for RN and Radio Paris. RN portrayed the youth as a means to rejuvenate and repopulate France and create new families, youth being one of the pillars of the New France, and work being synonymous with the reconstruction of France. In contrast, the German occupier, as discussed, was not interested in the National Revolution; they were interested in having a pool of indoctrinated and trained young people who could help the German war efforts and support their vision for a New Europe. By 1942, the narratives presented in Radio Paris's broadcasts about the youth became overtly pro-collaboration and anti-British. The focus shifted to a renewed vision for French youth, their obligation to engage in charitable work for France, and the recruitment of youth labour to work in Germany. The exploitation of French labour became a key element in German policy from 1942 onwards due to the situation in Russia.[30] By February 1943, with mandatory conscription to work in Germany, French youth had to choose between collaboration or fighting against the occupier. Being neutral with a 'wait-and-see' attitude became an impossible option for youth to contemplate.

It is conceivable that the listeners enjoyed Radio Paris's high-quality entertainment programmes while rejecting many of the propaganda messages, which many loathed.[31] However, less evidence could be found in terms of how many people actively listened to its programmes and how widely *Les Ondes* circulated. This is because following the defeat of the Germans in 1944, many documents were destroyed, deliberately or otherwise.[32] Moreover, until 1942, the Germans were winning the war and Radio Paris's programmes and styles more or less reflected this fact: it was more about entertainment and laughter; about normalising the Parisian way of life and glorifying collaboration and the New Order in Europe.

There were limitations to what propaganda could achieve. During the period 1940–42, the changes in the military landscape from rapid and sustained Germany victories to a period of stagnation helped comfort the people, who now believed that German rule might not last and that there was hope for the Allies' final victory. Landmark events were the British victory of the Battle of Britain in 1940, the entry of the USA into the war on 6 December 1941 and the problems the German army encountered against the Soviet Union in 1942. The military setbacks of Germany and the increasing hope for its defeat contributed much more to the flourishing of the French resistance movement after 1942 than the BBC's repeated calls for patriotism and resistance.

Nonetheless, BBC propaganda contributed to the prosecution of the war by asking the audience to gather information; by asking them to disrupt the German war effort; and by asking them to obey the instructions given by the Allies. The year 1942 was marked with an explosion of civil resistance in France and listening to the BBC was a widespread phenomenon. 'For many people […] listening to the BBC was the first act of resistance'.[33] This was the achievement of the BBC radio propaganda as practical concerns were discussed and direct appeals were made on the airwaves to bring the French together to fight the occupier.[34]

As for Radio Paris, although its entertainment programmes were known for their quality, the remaining content, which contained overt and covert political messages, was often frowned upon and considered unpalatable, especially the direct anti-Semitic and anti-British rhetoric. It also tried too hard to convince the French to work in Germany, so much so that many turned away from listening to its political messages in 1942. Radio Paris and its attempt to present itself as the true voice of French were discredited from as early as September 1940 when the BBC put on air the slogan 'Radio-Paris ment'.[35]

The narratives of radio broadcasts and their magazines are valuable sources for the understanding of the social history of France. Radio as a relatively new technology penetrated the households of millions of people, redefining the landscape of national and transnational communication. The French lived through the war accompanied by these three main radio stations (and their attendant magazines): they heard news, commentaries, reportage, music and entertainment. They heard views and opinions expressed by each radio station, fighting for their ground in an attempt to indoctrinate the listeners and steer public opinion for their own political gain. The narratives of the radio broadcasts and their magazines gave an authentic account of how each radio station interacted with and attempted to impact society, and to convey its political messages in the execution of a psychological battle. These narratives offer another dimension to the construction of the experiences of wartime France using retrospective testimonies and contemporary documents. Therefore, they contribute to the understanding of the social history of France just as much as official reports, personal diaries, published memoires and autobiographies.[36]

The propaganda techniques demonstrated in the context of France during World War II remain relevant to propaganda in modern warfare and conflicts as well; for example, the conflict in Ukraine or the war in Syria, where mass media is used extensively to communicate and spread political messages to rally support from allies and spread fear among the enemy. We can now appreciate the evolution of technology from radio broadcasting to the use of TV broadcasting, the internet and social networking tools such as Facebook, Twitter, etc., as well as the evolution of the narratives in propaganda messages, from simple, repetitive, formal, lengthy communication to the short, snappy, fast-flowing messages to which the new generation has increasingly grown accustomed.

Despite these changes, the essence of propaganda remains similar: to strive to be the first to release new information, accurate or not, and to present one's interpretations as the voice of truth to sway, persuade and indoctrinate the targeted audience. As with RN and Radio Paris, the media of today continue to be concerned with projecting legitimacy and disseminating information using the voices of authorities and celebrities. The rapid development of technology since World War II has made it much easier and quicker to penetrate households and to enable public participation via a variety of channels, but the foundations of this technique were laid back when radio was the modern medium of communication.

Endnotes

Introduction

1 Gerd Horten, *Radio Goes to War: The Cultural Politics of Propaganda during World War II* (Berkeley: University of California Press, 2002), 1.

2 Susan Jeanne Douglas, *Listening In: Radio and the American Imagination* (Minneapolis: University of Minnesota Press, 2004), 9.

3 Ibid.

4 Ibid, 7.

5 Asa Briggs, *The History of Broadcasting in the United Kingdom 1896–1927: Volume I: The Birth of Broadcasting* (Oxford University Press, 1995), 5, 19.

6 Ibid, 3–4.

7 Christian Delporte, 'The Image and Myth of the "Fifth Column" during the Two World Wars', in Valerie Holman and Debra Kelly (eds), *France at War in the Twentieth Century: Propaganda, Myth and Metaphor* (New York, Oxford: Berghahn Books, 2000), 50; Stephanie Seul and Nelson Ribeiro, 'Revisiting Transnational Broadcasting', *Media History*, Vol. 21, No. 4 (2015): 367.

8 Douglas, *Listening In*, 10.

9 Ibid, 11.

10 Horten, *Radio Goes to War*, 3.

11 Jason Loviglio, *Radio's Intimate Public: Network Broadcasting and Mass Mediated Democracy* (Minneapolis: University of Minnesota Press, 2005), xviii–xix.

12 Ibid, xix.

13 Aurélie Luneau, *Radio Londres: Les Voix de la Liberté (1940–1944)* (Paris: Editions Perrin, 2005), 22.

14 Tim Brooks, *British Propaganda to France, 1940–1944: Machinery, Method and Message* (Edinburgh: Edinburgh University Press, 2007), 55.

15 Laurence Thibault (dir.), *Les femmes et la Résistance* (Paris: La documentation Française, 2006), 11.

16 Paul J. Kingston, 'Broadcasts in French from Moscow February 1940–August 1941: An evaluation of the reorientation of radio propaganda', *Cahiers du monde russe et soviétique*, XXV (2–3), avr.–September 1984: 201; Jean-Louis Crémieux-Brilhac and Georges Bensimhon, 'Les propagandes radiophoniques et l'opinion publique en France de 1940 à 1944', *Revue d'histoire de la deuxième guerre mondiale*, No. 101 (January 1976): 1–18; Ernst Kris and Hans Speier, *German Radio Propaganda: Report on Home Broadcasts during the War* (London, New York, Toronto: Oxford University Press, 1944), 89–90.

17 Brooks, *British Propaganda to France*, 142–6.

18 Julian Jackson, *France: The Dark Years 1940–1944* (Oxford: Oxford University Press, 2003), xxi (map 2 Occupied France), 246. To be precise, France was divided into six zones: the unoccupied zone (Vichy); the occupied zone; the zone attached to the German command in Brussels, Belgium (Nord-Pas-de-Calais *départements*); the 'forbidden' or 'reserved' zone, which included six

départements and part of four others, stretching north to south from the mouth of the Somme to the Swiss border in the Jura; the annexed zone (Alsace and Moselle in Lorraine); and the Italian zone from June 1940 to November 1942. The coastal zone was added from October 1941 (the zone stretching from Spain to the forbidden zone along the coastal line).

19 Asa Briggs, *The History of Broadcasting in the UK, Vol. 3, The War of Words* (London, New York, Toronto: Oxford University Press, 1970).

20 Brooks, *British Propaganda to France*, 2007.

21 Martyn Cornick, 'The BBC and the Propaganda War against Occupied France: The Work of Emile Delavenay and the European Intelligence Department', *French History*, 8:3 (Oxford University Press 1994: Sept): 316–54.

22 Jean-Louis Crémieux-Brilhac, 'Le rôle de la radio, 1940–1944', *Espoir*, No. 66 (1989): 1–6; Jean-Louis Crémieux-Brilhac, 'La France libre et la radio', *Mélanges de l'Ecole française de Rome. Italie et Méditerranée*, T. 108, No. 1 (1996): 73–81; Jean-Louis Crémieux-Brilhac, 'Information, propagande et opinion publique durant la deuxième Guerre mondiale. Réflexions en guise de conclusions', *Mélanges de l'Ecole française de Rome. Italie et Méditerranée*, T. 108, No. 1 (1996): 147–54; Crémieux-Brilhac and Bensimhon, 'Les propagandes radiophoniques': 1–18.

23 Edward Tangye Lean, *Voices in the Darkness: The Story of the European Radio War* (London: Secker and Warburg, 1943), 3.

24 Hélène Eck (dir.), *La guerre des ondes: Histoire des radios de langue française pendant la Deuxième Guerre Mondiale* (Paris: Editions Payot Lausanne et Armand Colin, 1985).

25 Cécile Méadel, 'Pauses musicales ou les éclatants silences de Radio-Paris', in M. Chimènes (ed.), *La Vie musicale sous Vichy* (Brussels: Editions Complexe, 2001).

26 Seul and Ribeiro, 'Revisiting Transnational Broadcasting': 366.

27 Ibid, 365; Brooks, *British Propaganda to France,* 121–2.

28 Siân Nicholas, *The Echo of War: Home Front Propaganda and the Wartime BBC, 1939–45* (Manchester, New York: Manchester University Press, 1996), 6.

29 Arthur Ponsonby, *Falsehood in War-Time* (London: Kimble & Bradford, 1940), 16.

30 David Welch, *Nazi Propaganda: The Power and the Limitations* (London, Canberra: Croom Helm, 1983), 2; Jacques Ellul, *Propaganda: The Formation of Men's Attitudes* (New York: Vintage Books, 1973), v.

31 Ellul, *Propaganda*, v–vi.

32 Ibid, 52–3.

33 BBC Written Archives Centre (BBC WAC), E2/186/4, 21 February 1941 (European Intelligence Papers).

34 BBC WAC, E2/186/2, 8 July 1940 (European Intelligence Papers).

35 Welch, *Nazi Propaganda*, 2.

36 Ibid.

37 Ellul, *Propaganda,* v.

38 Ibid, 71–6.

39 Ibid, vii.

40 Ibid.

41 Ibid, 295.

42 Ibid, 295–6.

43 Ibid, 296.

44 Richard Taylor, 'Goebbels and the Function of Propaganda', in David Welch (ed.), *Nazi Propaganda: The Power and the Limitations* (London and Canberra: Croom Helm, 1983), 39.

45 BBC WAC, E2/186/2, 8 July 1940 (European Intelligence Papers).

46 Brooks, *British Propaganda to France,* 38–41.

47 Jean Louis Crémieux-Brilhac and Hélène Eck, (avec le concours de Charles Louis Foulon), 'France', in Hélène Eck (dir.), *La guerre des ondes: Histoire des radios de langue française pendant la Deuxième Guerre Mondiale* (Paris: Editions Payot Lausanne et Armand Colin, 1985), 39.

48 Welch, *Nazi Propaganda*, 7.

49 Taylor, 'Goebbels and the Function of Propaganda', 38.

50 Collections du Service Archives écrites et Musée de Radio France (CSA), Jacques Chardonnier, 'Radio-Paris, un foyer artistique très actif', *Cahiers d'Histoire de la Radiodiffusion*, No. 34 (September–November 1992): 55; Méadel, 'Pauses musicales', 237–8.

51 Crémieux-Brilhac and Eck, 'France', 149.

52 BBC WAC, 'La chasse', 17 September, 20h30–21h00.

53 BBC WAC, Jacques Duchesne, 'Réflexion de Jacques Duchesne', samedi 22 March 1941, *Les Francais parlent aux Français*, Service Français, 20h30–21h00 BST.

54 BBC WAC, Jean Marin, 'Dépêche', Thursday 20 August 1942, *Quart d'Heure Français de Midi*, French Service, 12h00–12h15 BST.

55 Jacques Pessis (ed.), *Les Français parlent aux Français 1940–1941* (Paris: Edition Omnibus, 2010); Jacques Pessis (ed.), *Les Français parlent aux Français 1941–1942* (Paris: Edition Omnibus, 2011); Maurice Schumann, *Honneur et Patrie* (Paris: Editions du Livre Français, 1946).

56 Lobenberg, 'Punitions', 27 September 1942, in *Les Français parlent aux Français 1941–1942*, 1450; Maurice Schumann, 'Manifestez le 11 novembre!', 7 November 1942, in *Les Français parlent aux Français 1941–1942*, 1571; BBC WAC, 'Le Faust de Berlioz', 21 September 1940, *Les Français parlent aux Français*, 20h30–21h00; BBC WAC, Mme. Paris, MM. Bonifas, Brunius, 'Courrier de France', Friday 2 May 1941, *Les Français parlent aux Français*, French Service. 20:30–21:00; BBC WAC, 'La Savoie', Sunday, 29 March 1942, *Demi-Heure Française du Matin*, French Service. 11:45–12:15 BST. Mme. Paris is the pseudonym of a speaker whose real name is unknown.

57 BBC WAC, Jacques Duchesne, 'Réflexions de Jacques Duchesne, 2 novembre 1941', *Les Français parlent aux Français*, Service Français, 20:30–21:00 BST.

58 The number of audio recordings of the wartime BBC French Service available at the BBC Sound Archives dated between 22.6.40 and 11.11.42 amounts to 27.

59 Jean-Claude Barbas (ed.), *Philippe Pétain, Discours aux Français 17 June 1940–20 août 1944* (Paris: Albin Michel, 1989).

60 Ibid, 19.

61 Dr. Friedrich, *Un journaliste allemand vous parle …* (Paris: Editions LE PONT, 1942).

62 See some examples, Institut national de l'audiovisuel (INA), Fonds Vichy, disques de la BDIC, *Pétain: visite de l'Hôtel-Dieu de Lyon, déjeuner avec les soeurs*, recorded on 28.09.1941, on Radio Etat Français-Radiodiffusion Nationale; INA, Fonds Vichy, disques de la BDIC, *Prise d'otages après l'assassinat d'officiers allemands*, recorded on 22.10.1941, on Radio Etat Français-Radiodiffusion Nationale; INA, Fonds Vichy, disques de la BDIC, *Discours aux scouts de France*, recorded on 15.08.1942, on Radio Etat Français-Radiodiffusion Nationale; INA, Inventaire Disques, *Offres d'emplois pour chômeurs*, recorded on 17.08.1941, on Radio Paris (RP), 1941; INA, Inventaire Disques, *Discours de Georges LAMIRAND à la jeunesse*, recorded on 01.12.1941, on Radio Paris (RP), 1941; INA, Inventaire Disques, *Reportage au centre d'apprentissage de Pantin*, recorded on 01.01.1942, on Radio Paris (RP), 1942; INA, Inventaire Disques, *Propagande en faveur de la relève*, recorded on 20.10.1942, on Radio Paris (RP), 1942.

63 Christopher Barker and Dariusz Galasinski, *Cultural Studies and Discourse Analysis: A Dialogue on Language and Identity* (London: SAGE Publications, 2001), 63.

64 Douglas, *Listening In*, p. 9.

65 For example, INA, Inventaire Disques, *Interviews d'ouvriers français travaillant dans une usine à Berlin*, recorded on 25.02.1941, on Radio Paris (RP), 1941.

66 Barbas, *Pétain, Discours aux Français*, 21.
67 When such a situation arises, I have noted it in an endnote.
68 Wilfred Douglas Halls, *The Youth of Vichy France* (Oxford: Clarendon Press, 1981), 312. The school moved from the château de la Fauconnière (Gannat) to the château d'Uriage (Grenoble) in October 1940. The château d'Uriage is a castle associated with Bayard.
69 CSA, *Radio National*, 28 September–4 October 1941.
70 I have also highlighted such errors to the archivists to enable corrections to be made for future researchers.

Chapter 1

1   Seul and Ribeiro, 'Revisiting Transnational Broadcasting': 367–8; Briggs, *The History of Broadcasting in the UK, Vol. 3*, 6, 81.
2   Briggs, *The History of Broadcasting in the UK, Vol. 3*, 6, 81.
3   Sir Samuel Hoare quoted in Briggs, *The History of Broadcasting in the UK, Vol. 3*, 91.
4   Briggs, *The History of Broadcasting in the UK, Vol. 3*, 92.
5   Ibid, 92–3.
6   Ibid, 82.
7   Ibid, 100.
8   Ibid, 101–2.
9   Luneau, *Radio Londres*, 27.
10 Seul and Ribeiro, 'Revisiting Transnational Broadcasting': 368.
11 Papers of Douglas E. Ritchie and Noel Newsome, GBR/0014/NERI. Biographical data. Churchill Archives Centre.
12 Briggs, *The History of Broadcasting in the UK, vol. 3*, 425; Crémieux-Brilhac, 'Le rôle de la radio': 2.
13 Brooks, *British Propaganda to France*, 29, 185.
14 Briggs, *The History of Broadcasting in the UK, Vol. 3*, 196.
15 Ibid, 197.
16 Ibid.
17 Ibid.
18 Ibid.
19 Ibid, 198.
20 Ibid, 204.
21 Ibid, 203.
22 BBC WAC, E2/186/2, 8 July 1940 (European Intelligence Papers).
23 Ibid.
24 Crémieux-Brilhac, 'Le rôle de la radio': 3.
25 Ibid.
26 Crémieux-Brilhac and Eck, 'France',65.
27 Pierre Bourdan, *1940–1944: Pierre Bourdan vous parle* (Paris: Editions Magnard, 1990), 3.
28 Ibid, 367.
29 Crémieux-Brilhac, 'La France libre et la radio': 74.
30 Jacques Pessis, *La Bataille de Radio Londres 1940–1944* (Paris: Edition Omnibus, 2010), 62.
31 Crémieux-Brilhac, 'La France libre et la radio': 74.
32 Michael Stenton, *Radio London and Resistance in Occupied Europe British Political Warfare 1939–1943* (Oxford: Oxford University Press, 2000), 133.

33 Crémieux-Brilhac and Eck, 'France', 65.

34 Briggs, *The History of Broadcasting in the UK, Vol. 3*, 342; Seul and Ribeiro, 'Revisiting Transnational Broadcasting': 368.

35 Briggs, *The History of Broadcasting in the UK, Vol. 3*, 417–18.

36 Ibid, 418.

37 Ibid.

38 Ibid, 260.

39 Ibid, 418–21.

40 Crémieux-Brilhac, 'La France libre et la radio': 78; BBC WAC, Anonymous letters from France (521–693), Limoges, 26 July 1941 (526); BBC WAC, Anonymous letters from France (827–952), Oullins, 24 August 1941 (845); BBC WAC, Anonymous letters from France (953–1150) 27 June 1942 (999); Henri Hauck, 'Nazification', 26 June 1941, in *Les Français parlent aux Français 1941–1942*, 43–4; 'Alsace et Lorraine, régions très prisées', 3 July 1941, in *Les Français parlent aux Français 1941–1942*, 81; Maurice Schumann, 'Ici habite un traître', 5 August 1941, in *Les Français parlent aux Français 1941–1942*, 151.

41 Maurice Schumann, 'L'homme qui "souhaite la victoire de l'Allemagne"', 22 June 1942, in *Les Français parlent aux Français 1941–1942*, 1170.

42 Crémieux-Brilhac, 'Le rôle de la radio': 3.

43 'Imposant et sanglant 14 juillet à Marseille', 16 July 1942, in *Les Français parlent aux Français 1941–1942*, 1242–3.

44 Luneau, *Radio Londres*, 207; Crémieux-Brilhac, 'La France libre et la radio': 77.

45 For example, 'Le 11 novembre 1940', 17 March 1941, in *Les Français parlent aux Français 1940–1941*, 834–6; Pierre Bourdan, 'Les fusillades d'otages', 20 September 1941, in *Les Français parlent aux Français 1941–1942*, 250–1; 'Des résistances fusillées', 22 September 1941, in *Les Français parlent aux Français 1941–1942*, 255–6; Louis Aragon, 'Les martyrs de Châteaubriant', 22 May 1942, in *Les Français parlent aux Français 1941–1942*, 1074–9; Jacques Duchesne, 'Les 27 martyrs de Châteaubriant', 25 May 1942, in *Les Français parlent aux Français 1941–1942*, 1091–2; Jacques Duchesne-Pierre Lefèvre, 'Nouvelles mesures contre les juifs', 12 June 1942, in *Les Français parlent aux Français 1941–1942*, 1139–43; 'Massacre de 700 000 juifs en Pologne', 1 July 1942, in *Les Français parlent aux Français 1941–1942*, 1210–1; Henri Hauck, 'Laval et les juifs étrangers de France, ou la leçon de solidarité', 10 August 1942, in *Les Français parlent aux Français 1941–1942*, 1328–30, etc.

46 INA, Fonds Vichy, disques de la BDIC, *Après le bombardement de Brest par la RAF*, recorded on 01.01.1941, sur la Radio Etat Français-Radiodiffusion Nationale; INA, Fonds Vichy, disques de la BDIC, *Prise d'otages après l'assassinat d'officiers allemands*, recorded on 22.10.1941, on Radio Etat Français-Radiodiffusion Nationale.

47 INA, Fonds Vichy, disques de la BDIC, *Prise d'otages après l'assassinat d'officiers allemands*, recorded on 22.10.1941, on Radio Etat Français-Radiodiffusion Nationale.

48 INA, Inventaire Disques, *Conférence du Docteur Schlottmann sur la politique anglaise*, recorded on 01.12.1941, on Radio Paris (RP), 1941.

49 Briggs, *The History of Broadcasting in the UK, Vol. 3*, 455.

50 BBC WAC, Maurice Schumann, 11 November 1942, French Service.

51 Brooks, *British Propaganda to France*, 59.

52 Crémieux-Brilhac, 'La France libre et la radio': 73.

53 Brooks, *British Propaganda to France*, 5.

54 Ibid, 4.

55 BBC WAC, E2/186/2, 8 July 1940 (European Intelligence Papers).

56 Brooks, *British Propaganda to France*, 4–5.

57 Crémieux-Brilhac, 'Le rôle de la radio': 2.

58 Brooks, *British Propaganda to France*, xvii.
59 BBC WAC, E2/186/2, 5 August 1940 (European Intelligence Papers).
60 Briggs, *The History of Broadcasting in the UK, Vol. 3*, 257.
61 BBC WAC, E2/186/3, 30 September 1940 (European Intelligence Papers).
62 Brooks, *British Propaganda to France*, 4.
63 Briggs, *The History of Broadcasting in the UK, Vol. 3*, 176.
64 Ibid, 64; Brooks, *British Propaganda to France*, 53.
65 Brooks, *British Propaganda to France*, 53; Briggs, *The History of Broadcasting in the UK, Vol. 3*, 65.
66 Brooks, *British Propaganda to France*, 53.
67 BBC WAC, E2/186/3, 30 September 1940 (European Intelligence Papers).
68 Ibid.
69 Brooks, *British Propaganda to France*, 54.
70 Briggs, *The History of Broadcasting in the UK, Vol. 3*, 64.
71 Brooks, *British Propaganda to France*, 121.
72 Tangye Lean, *Voices in the Darkness*, 174.
73 Ibid.
74 BBC WAC, E2/186/4, November 1940 (European Intelligence Papers).
75 Luneau, *Radio Londres*, 22.
76 BBC WAC, E2/186/2, 10 June 1940 (European Intelligence Papers).
77 CSA, Box 1682W90 'Commission Consultative des Dommages et des Réparations. Emprise Allemande sur la Pensée Française. Monographie P. F. 4 'Radiodiffusion', Imprimerie nationale, 1947.
78 Brooks, *British Propaganda to France*, 55–7.
79 Ibid, 28.
80 Ibid.
81 Pessis, *Les Français parlent aux Français 1941–1942*, I.
82 Crémieux-Brilhac, 'Le rôle de la radio': 3.
83 Stenton, *Radio London and Resistance*, 130.
84 Jackson, *France: The Dark Years*, 128–9.
85 Crémieux-Brilhac, 'Le rôle de la radio': 2.
86 Crémieux-Brilhac, 'La France libre et la radio': 74.
87 CSA, Bernard Lauzanne, 'Ici Londres', *Cahiers d'Histoire de la Radiodiffusion*, No. 27 (December 1990): 56; Crémieux-Brilhac, 'Le rôle de la radio': 2.
88 Pessis, *La Bataille de Radio Londres*, 60.
89 Brooks, *British Propaganda to France*, 60.
90 Pessis, *La Bataille de Radio Londres*, 61.
91 Ibid, 59.
92 Pessis, *Les Français parlent aux Français 1941–1942*, VI.
93 Cornick, 'The BBC and the Propaganda War': 342.
94 Pessis, *La Bataille de Radio Londres*, 62; BBC WAC, E2/188/1, 23 January 1942 (European Intelligence Papers).
95 BBC WAC, E2/188/1, 23 January 1942 (European Intelligence Papers).
96 Pessis, *La Bataille de Radio Londres*, 62; Luneau, *Radio Londres*, 66; Martyn Cornick, 'Fighting Myth with Reality: The Fall of France, Anglophobia and the BBC', in Valerie Holman and Debra Kelly (eds), *France at War in the Twentieth Century: Propaganda, Myth, and Metaphor* (New York, Oxford: Berghahn Books, 2000), 65–87.
97 BBC WAC, E2/185, 8 April 1941 (European Intelligence Papers).
98 Pessis, *La Bataille de Radio Londres*, 59.
99 Ibid, 60.

100 Cornick, 'The BBC and the Propaganda War': 329.

101 Ibid: 322.

102 Henri Hauck and William Pickles, 'Aux travailleurs français: message d'un socialiste anglais', 7 August 1940, in *Les Français parlent aux Français 1940–1941*, 101–2.

103 Pessis, *La Bataille de Radio Londres*, 62.

104 Ernest Bevin, 'Pas de pain', 2 May 1941, in *Les Français parlent aux Français 1940–1941*, 1001–3.

105 Pessis, *Les Français parlent aux Français 1941–1942*, VI–VII.

106 BBC WAC, E2/188/1, 23 January 1942 (European Intelligence Papers).

107 Ibid.

108 'Des prisonniers s'évadent et rejoignent les FFL. Entretien avec le commandant Billotte', 15 September 1941, in *Les Français parlent aux Français 1941–1942*, 221–5.

109 BBC WAC, E2/188/1, 23 January 1942 (European Intelligence Papers).

110 Ibid.

111 Cornick, 'The BBC and the Propaganda War': 320–1.

112 Ibid: 322–3; Cornick, 'Fighting Myth with Reality', 84.

113 Brooks, *British Propaganda to France*, 108.

114 Richard Vinen, *The Unfree French: Life under the Occupation* (London: Penguin Group, 2006), 86.

115 Brooks, *British Propaganda to France*, 108.

116 Ibid, 111.

117 Cornick, 'The BBC and the Propaganda War': 329.

118 Brooks, *British Propaganda to France*, 109.

119 For example, in BBC WAC, E2/186/3, 2 September 1940 (European Intelligence Papers).

120 For example, BBC WAC, Anonymous letters from France (1361–1496), Saint-Etienne, 25 September 1942 (1373).

121 Emile Delavenay, *Témoignage d'un village Savoyard au village mondial (1905–1991)* (La Calade: Edition EDISUD, 1992), 231.

122 Nicholas Atkin, *The Forgotten French Exiles in the British Isles, 1940–44* (Manchester: Manchester University Press, 2003), 48; Cornick, 'Fighting Myth with Reality', 78.

123 Cornick, 'The BBC and the Propaganda War': 323.

124 Ibid: 343.

125 Ibid: 324.

126 Crémieux-Brilhac and Eck, 'France', 17.

127 CSA, Bernard Lauzanne, 'De la drôle de guerre à la défaite et à l'occupation', *Cahiers d'Histoire de la Radiodiffusion*, No. 27 (December 1990): 1.

128 Pierre Sorlin, 'The Struggle for Control of French Minds, 1940–1944', in K. R. M. Short (ed.), *Film & Radio Propaganda in World War II* (Knoxville: The University of Tennessee Press, 1983), 247.

129 Luneau, *Radio Londres*, 22.

130 Crémieux-Brilhac and Eck, 'France', 24.

131 Luneau, *Radio Londres*, 22.

132 CSA, Lauzanne, 'De la drôle de guerre': 2.

133 Luneau, *Radio Londres*, 22–3.

134 CSA, Lauzanne, 'De la drôle de guerre': 1.

135 Ibid; Crémieux-Brilhac and Eck, 'France', 19.

136 Crémieux-Brilhac and Eck, 'France', 19–20.

137 Ibid, 20.

138 Ibid.

139 Luneau, *Radio Londres*, 28.

140 Crémieux-Brilhac and Eck, 'France', 20–1; Ponsonby, *Falsehood in War-Time*, 16, 28.
141 Crémieux-Brilhac and Eck, 'France', 21.
142 CSA, Lauzanne, 'De la drôle de guerre': 2–3.
143 Ibid.
144 Sorlin, 'The Struggle for Control of French Minds', 248.
145 Crémieux-Brilhac and Eck, 'France', 21.
146 CSA, Lauzanne, 'De la drôle de guerre': 3.
147 Tangye Lean, *Voices in the Darkness,*104–5.
148 Anatole De Monzie, *Ci-devant* (Paris: Flammarion, 1941), 279.
149 CSA, Lauzanne, 'De la drôle de guerre': 3.
150 Luneau, *Radio Londres,* 23.
151 Rémy Pithon, 'French Film Propaganda July 1939–June 1940', in K. R. M. Short (ed.), *Film & Radio Propaganda in World War II* (Knoxville: The University of Tennessee Press, 1983), 87.
152 CSA, Lauzanne, 'De la drôle de guerre': 4.
153 Sorlin, 'The Struggle for Control of French Minds', 249.
154 Kay Chadwick, 'Our Enemy's Enemy: Selling Britain to Occupied France on the BBC French Service', *Media History*, Vol. 21, No. 4 (2015): 428.
155 CSA, Box 1682W90 'Radiodiffusion'.
156 CSA, Lauzanne, 'De la drôle de guerre': 4.
157 Luneau, *Radio Londres*, 56; Crémieux-Brilhac and Eck, 'France', 43.
158 Pierre Giolitto, *Histoire de la jeunesse sous Vichy* (Paris: Librairie Académique Perrin, 1991), 116; CSA, Bernard Lauzanne, 'La radio de Vichy', *Cahiers d'Histoire de la Radiodiffusion*, No. 27 (December 1990): 49.
159 Crémieux-Brilhac and Eck, 'France', 41–2.
160 Ibid, 39.
161 Sorlin, 'The Struggle for Control of French Minds', 249.
162 Jacques Polonski, *La Presse La Propagande et l'Opinion Publique sous l'Occupation* (Paris: Editions du Centre, 1946), 57–8.
163 Ellul, *Propaganda*, 102.
164 Polonski, *La Presse La Propagande et l'Opinion Publique*, 58.
165 CSA, Box 1682W89 'COPIE transmise à Monsieur Le CORBEILLER pour exécution'.
166 Crémieux-Brilhac and Eck, 'France', 39.
167 Ibid.
168 François Garçon, 'Nazi Film Propaganda in Occupied France' in David Welch (ed.), *Nazi Propaganda: The Power and the Limitations* (London and Canberra: Croom Helm, 1983), 168.
169 Crémieux-Brilhac and Eck, 'France', 43.
170 Ibid, 40.
171 Vinen, *The Unfree French*, 62.
172 Polonski, *La Presse La Propagande et l'Opinion Publique*, 80–1.
173 Sorlin, 'The Struggle for Control of French Minds', 253–4.
174 CSA, Bernard Lauzanne, 'De la bataille d'Angleterre au conflit planétaire', *Cahiers d'Histoire de la Radiodiffusion*, No. 30 (September 1991): 5.
175 CSA, Box 1682W90 'Radio Méditerranée, Antibes, le 5 février 1941'.
176 CSA, Box 1682W89 'Exposé d'ensemble de la situation de la Radiodiffusion Nationale'.
177 Crémieux-Brilhac and Eck, 'France', 41.
178 Ibid.
179 CSA, Box 1682W89 'Exposé d'ensemble'.
180 Crémieux-Brilhac and Eck, 'France', 41.

181 CSA, *Radio National*, 25–31 May 1941.

182 Ibid, 6–12 July 1941.

183 Ibid, 5–11 October 1941.

184 Ibid, 7–13 December 1941; Crémieux-Brilhac and Eck, 'France', 46.

185 CSA, *Radio National*, 8–14 November 1942.

186 CSA, Box 1682W89 'Exposé d'ensemble'.

187 Briggs, *The History of Broadcasting in the UK, Vol. 3*, 101–2.

188 CSA, Box 1682W89 'Exposé d'ensemble'.

189 Ibid.

190 Crémieux-Brilhac and Eck, 'France', 48–9.

191 Ibid, 46.

192 Ibid, 79.

193 Ibid.

194 CSA, Bernard Lauzanne, 'Un double tournant: Stalingrad et Alger', *Cahiers d'Histoire de la Radiodiffusion*, No. 34 (September–November 1992): 5.

195 CSA, Bernard Lauzanne, 'Radio-Paris et Radiodiffusion Nationale: une semaine de programmes', *Cahiers d'Histoire de la Radiodiffusion*, No. 34 (September–November 1992): 81–5.

196 CSA, Hélène Eck, 'Création du Service des dramatiques', *Cahiers d'Histoire de la Radiodiffusion*, No. 30 (September 1991): 66.

197 CSA, Lauzanne, 'Un double tournant': 5.

198 BBC WAC, E2/185, 17 August 1942 (European Intelligence Papers).

199 Crémieux-Brilhac and Eck, 'France', 80–1; CSA, Box 1682W89 'France: loi No. 994 du 7 novembre 1942 portant réorganisation de la radiodiffusion nationale'.

200 CSA, Lauzanne, 'La radio de Vichy': 50; Lauzanne, 'De la bataille d'Angleterre': 5.

201 Crémieux-Brilhac and Eck, 'France', 51; CSA, Lauzanne, 'La radio de Vichy': 50.

202 Crémieux-Brilhac and Eck, 'France', 88.

203 Ibid, 51; Bernadette Lespinard, 'Le répertoire choral des mouvements de jeunesse', in Myriam Chimènes (ed.), *La Vie musicale sous Vichy* (Bruxelles: Editions Complexe, 2001), 272.

204 Crémieux-Brilhac and Eck, 'France', 51.

205 BBC WAC, E2/188/1, 23 January 1942 (European Intelligence Papers).

206 Ibid.

207 BBC WAC, E2/193/2, 4 June 1941 (European Intelligence Papers).

208 CSA, Lauzanne, 'De la bataille d'Angleterre': 5.

209 BBC WAC, E2/188/1, 23 January 1942 (European Intelligence Papers).

210 CSA, Lauzanne, 'De la bataille d'Angleterre': 5.

211 BBC WAC, E2/188/1, 23 January 1942 (European Intelligence Papers).

212 Ibid.

213 Ibid.

214 Ibid.

215 Ibid.

216 Ibid.

217 Ibid.

218 Brooks, *British Propaganda to France*, 117, 148.

219 BBC WAC, E2/188/1, 23 January 1942 (European Intelligence Papers).

220 Ibid.

221 CSA, Bernard Lauzanne, 'L'année radiophonique 1941 au jour le jour', *Cahiers d'Histoire de la Radiodiffusion*, No. 30 (September 1991): 37.

222 BBC WAC, E2/188/1, 23 January 1942 (European Intelligence Papers).

223 CSA, Lauzanne, 'De la bataille d'Angleterre': 4–5.

224 Jackson, *France: The Dark Years,* 256.

225 France, Archives nationales (FAN), F/43/59 Speakers on Radio Paris.

226 CSA, *Radio National,* 20–26 July 1941.

227 Nathalie Dompnier, 'Entre La Marseillaise et Maréchal, nous voilà! Quel hymne pour le régime de Vichy?', in Myriam Chimènes (ed.), *La Vie musicale sous Vichy* (Bruxelles: Editions Complexe, 2001), 70.

228 CSA, *Radio National,* 25–31 May 1941.

229 Crémieux-Brilhac and Eck, 'France', 47.

230 CSA, *Radio National,* 25–31 May 1941.

231 Ibid, 12–18 July 1942; ibid, 19–25 July 1942.

232 Ibid, 15–21 June 1941.

233 Ibid, 13–19 July 1941.

234 Ibid, 10–16 August 1941; CSA, Bernard Lauzanne, 'Extraits des programmes', *Cahiers d'Histoire de la Radiodiffusion,* No. 30 (September 1991): 58.

235 CSA, *Radio National,* 3–9 August 1941.

236 Ibid, 9–15 August 1942.

237 Ibid, 24–30 May 1942.

238 Ibid, 13–19 July 1941.

239 Ibid, 24–30 August 1941.

240 Ibid, 31 August–6 September 1941.

241 Ibid, 10–16 August 1941.

242 Ibid, 28 December 1941–3 January 1942. This list reflects the key figures of entertainment at the time: Mistinguett, Maurice Chevalier, Fernandel, Sacha Guitry, Albert Préjean, Yvonne Printemps, Raimu and Tino Rossi, among other artists.

243 Ibid, 16–22 November 1941; ibid, 23–29 November 1941; ibid, 30 November–6 December 1941; ibid, 7–13 December 1941.

244 Ibid, 16–22 November 1941.

245 Ibid.

246 CSA, Box 1682W89 'Exposé d'ensemble'.

247 BBC WAC, E2/185, 8 April 1941 (European Intelligence Papers).

248 CSA, Lauzanne, 'De la bataille d'Angleterre': 4.

249 Crémieux-Brilhac and Eck, 'France', 47.

250 Ibid.

251 Ibid, 48.

252 Luneau, *Radio Londres,* 22.

253 Tangye Lean, *Voices in the Darkness,* 142; CSA, Box 1682W90 'Radiodiffusion'.

254 Tangye Lean, *Voices in the Darkness,* 142–3.

255 Crémieux-Brilhac and Eck, 'France', 38–9; CSA, Box 1682W90 'Radiodiffusion'; 'Première écoute de Radio Paris', 5 July 1940, in *Les Français parlent aux Français 1940–1941,* 37–40.

256 René Gustave Nobécourt, *Les Secrets de la propagande en France occupée* (Paris: Librairie Arthème Fayard, 1962), 25; Méadel, 'Pauses musicales', 236.

257 Manuela Schwartz, 'La musique, outil majeur de la propagande culturelle des Nazis', in Myriam Chimènes (ed.), *La Vie musicale sous Vichy* (Bruxelles: Editions Complexe, 2001), 89–90.

258 Méadel, 'Pauses musicales', 237.

259 Ibid.

260 Ibid; Crémieux-Brilhac and Eck, 'France', 53.

261 Schwartz, 'La musique', 89–90; Méadel, 'Pauses musicales', 236–7.

262 CSA, Chardonnier, 'Radio-Paris': 71; Luneau, *Radio Londres*, 52.

263 Méadel, 'Pauses musicales', 237–9.

264 CSA, Box 1682W90 'Radiodiffusion'.

265 Ibid.

266 Ibid.; Méadel, 'Pauses musicales', 237.

267 Méadel, 'Pauses musicales', 237.

268 CSA, Box 1682W90 'Radiodiffusion'.

269 FAN, F/43/59 Speakers on Radio Paris. The end of programming on the radio varied throughout the year as detailed in the Radio Paris logbook.

270 CSA, Claude Lévy, '1942: Radio-Paris prend le tournant de la guerre totale', *Cahiers d'Histoire de la Radiodiffusion*, No. 34 (September–November 1992): 48.

271 FAN, F/43/59 Speakers on Radio Paris. A gap exists in the logbook covering the period ranging from September 1941 to July 1942 inclusive and *Les Ondes* is only obtainable from January 1942 at the Collections du Service Archives écrites et Musée de Radio France.

272 CSA, Lévy, '1942: Radio-Paris': 48.

273 CSA, *Les Ondes*, 21 June 1942.

274 Méadel, 'Pauses musicales', 240.

275 Ibid, 238.

276 CSA, Chardonnier, 'Radio-Paris': 55.

277 For example, INA, Inventaire Disques, *Les grands travaux entrepris dans la région parisienne*, recorded on 22.08.1941, on Radio Paris (RP), 1941.

278 For example, INA, Inventaire Disques, *Interview de Jean VIGNAUD, sur l'aide apportée aux prisonniers*, recorded on 11.02.1942, on Radio Paris (RP), 1942.

279 For example, INA, Inventaire Disques, *Charles DULLIN, nouveau directeur du Théâtre Sarah BERNHARDT*, recorded on 30.07.1941, on Radio Paris (RP), 1941.

280 Sorlin, 'The Struggle for Control of French Minds', 254.

281 CSA, Bernard Lauzanne (with the collaboration of Philippe Modol), 'Radio-Paris', *Cahiers d'Histoire de la Radiodiffusion*, No. 27 (December 1990): 51.

282 CSA, Lauzanne, 'De la bataille d'Angleterre': 7.

283 CSA, Lauzanne, 'Radio-Paris': 51.

284 CSA, Lévy, '1942: Radio-Paris': 49.

285 FAN, F/43/59 Speakers on Radio Paris.

286 INA, Inventaire Disques, *Hommage aux morts allemands de la guerre 14–18*, recorded on 09.11.1940, on Radio Paris (RP), 1940; INA, Inventaire Disques, *Alfred Rosenberg: cérémonie nazie au Palais Bourbon*, recorded on 28.11.1940, on Radio Paris (RP), 1940; INA, Inventaire Disques, *Hitler dans un meeting de travailleurs de l'armement*, recorded on 10.12.1940, on Berlin: Reichsrundfunk (ARD), 1940; INA, Inventaire Disques, *Attentat contre LAVAL*, recorded on 27.08.1941, on Radio Paris (RP), 1941.

287 CSA, Chardonnier, 'Radio-Paris': 73.

288 Ibid: 66.

289 Méadel, 'Pauses musicales', 242.

290 Ludovic Tournès, 'Le jazz: un espace de liberté pour un phénomène culturel en voie d'identification', in Myriam Chimènes (ed.), *La Vie musicale sous Vichy* (Bruxelles: Editions Complexe, 2001), 316.

291 CSA, Chardonnier, 'Radio-Paris': 59.

292 Tournès, 'Le jazz', 316.

293 CSA, Chardonnier, 'Radio-Paris': 60.

294 Normal here implies the normalisation of the occupation and that people were getting on with their lives under occupation.
295 Les archives de la Préfecture de police de Paris (PP), Box JB 37 'Rapport d'activité sur 10 mois des radio-actualités'.
296 CSA, Lévy, '1942: Radio-Paris': 49.
297 CSA, Lauzanne, 'Radio-Paris': 51–2.
298 Méadel, 'Pauses musicales', 241.
299 Ibid, 242.
300 PP, Box JB 37 'Rapport d'activité'.
301 Ibid.
302 CSA, Bernard Lauzanne, 'Deux hebdomadaires de programmes', *Cahiers d'Histoire de la Radiodiffusion*, No. 30 (September 1991): 83; PP, Box JB 37 'Rapport d'activité'.
303 PP, Box JB 37 'Rapport d'activité'.
304 PP, Box JB 37 'Rapport zg du 28 février au 30 avril 1941'.
305 PP, Box JB 37 'Rapport d'activité'.
306 PP, Box JB 37 'Rapport zg'.
307 PP, Box JB 37 'Rapport d'activité'.
308 CSA, Lauzanne, 'Deux hebdomadaires': 83.
309 PP, Box JB 37 'Rapport d'activité'.
310 There is a discrepancy to be noted in the report as *La Rose des Vents* seems to appear for the first time in February 1941; information obtained in the radio logbook at FAN, F/43/59 Speakers on Radio Paris.
311 Crémieux-Brilhac and Eck, 'France', 55.
312 PP, Box JB 37 'Collaborateurs de la *Rose des Vents*'. For example, Arlette Carlys (comedian), Max Delty (comedian and collaborator of the *Rose des Vents* from 1940 to 1944), Pierre Ducornoy (nine programmes only), Yves Furet (Comédie-Française), Jacques Marin (comedian-speaker), etc.
313 PP, Box JB 37 'Rapport d'activité'.
314 PP, Box JB 37 'Rapport zg'.
315 BBC WAC, E2/193/2, 4 June 1941 (European Intelligence Papers).
316 Ibid.
317 Tangye Lean, *Voices in the Darkness*, 182.
318 Crémieux-Brilhac and Eck, 'France', 55.
319 PP, Box JB 37 'Rapport d'activité'.
320 Ibid.
321 This is not necessarily the 'National Revolution' of Vichy. From the context of the report, this term seems to refer to the New Order envisaged by Germany.
322 PP, Box JB 37 'Rapport d'activité'.
323 Ibid.
324 Ibid.
325 Jackson, *France: The Dark Years*, 256.
326 PP, Box JB 37 'Rapport d'activité'.
327 PP, Box JB 37 'Rapport zg'.
328 Crémieux-Brilhac and Eck, 'France', 55.
329 BBC WAC, E2/188/1, 23 January 1942 (European Intelligence Papers).
330 Ibid.
331 Ibid.
332 Ibid.

333 Ibid
334 Ibid.
335 Ibid.
336 CSA, Lauzanne, 'Deux hebdomadaires': 83.
337 CSA, *Les Ondes*, 1 February 1942.
338 Ibid, 15 March 1942.
339 Ibid, 21 June 1942.
340 Ibid, 16 August 1942.
341 Ibid, 17 May 1942.
342 CSA, Chardonnier, 'Radio-Paris': 56.
343 CSA, Lauzanne, 'Un double tournant': 4; CSA, *Les Ondes*, 18 January 1942; his columns appear in almost every issue of *Les Ondes* in 1942.
344 CSA, Chardonnier, 'Radio-Paris': 56.
345 CSA, *Les Ondes*, 5 April 1942.
346 For example, CSA, *Les Ondes*, 25 January 1942; ibid, 8 February 1942; ibid, 12 April 1942; ibid, 7 June 1942; ibid, 21 June 1942; ibid, 19 July 1942; ibid, 16 August 1942; ibid, 18 October 1942.
347 CSA, *Les Ondes*, 12 April 1942.
348 Ibid, 19 July 1942.
349 Ibid, 15 March 1942.
350 CSA, Lauzanne, 'Deux hebdomadaires': 83.
351 CSA, *Les Ondes*, 27 September 1942.
352 Ibid, 8 February 1942.
353 For example, INA, Inventaire Disques, *Inauguration d'une exposition anti-maçonnique au Petit Palais*, recorded on 15.10.1940, on Radio Paris (RP), 1940; INA, Inventaire Disques, *L'exposition 'le Juif et la France' au Palais Berlitz*, recorded on 20.10.1941, on Radio Paris (RP), 1941; INA, Inventaire Disques, *Responsabilité des juifs américains dans la guerre*, recorded on 12.11.1941, on Radio Paris (RP), 1941; INA, Inventaire Disques, *L'ordre donné aux juifs de porter l'étoile jaune*, recorded on 29.05.1942, on Radio Paris (RP), 1942.
354 Sorlin, 'The Struggle for Control of French Minds', 254.
355 Crémieux-Brilhac and Eck, 'France', 53.
356 Méadel, 'Pauses musicales', 239.
357 Ibid, 241.
358 Ibid, 250.
359 CSA, Chardonnier, 'Radio-Paris': 70.
360 Ibid: 67–9.
361 Ibid: 58.
362 Méadel, 'Pauses musicales', 250.
363 INA, Inventaire Disques, *Commentaires d'Hérold PAQUIS sur publication des discours de DE GAULLE*, recorded on 01.01.1942, on Radio Paris (RP), 1942.
364 CSA, Lévy, '1942: Radio-Paris': 50.
365 Jean-Louis Jeannelle, 'Les Mémoires à l'épreuve du burlesque: Céline ou la chronique des Grands Guignols', *Revue d'Histoire littéraire de la France*, No. 3 (July–September 2009): 686.
366 Ibid: 687.
367 Crémieux-Brilhac and Eck, 'France', 369.

Chapter 2

1   Jean Dujardin, 'Belgique', in Hélène Eck (dir.), *La guerre des ondes: Histoire des radios de langue française pendant la Deuxième Guerre Mondiale* (Paris: Editions Payot Lausanne et Armand Colin, 1985), 160, 167.
2   Dujardin, 'Belgique', 160.
3   Ibid, 162.
4   Ibid, 162–4.
5   Ibid, 165.
6   Ibid, 167–8.
7   Ibid, 203.
8   Ibid, 206.
9   Ibid, 203.
10 Ibid, 204.
11 Ibid, 205.
12 Ibid.
13 Ibid, 206–7.
14 Ibid, 207–9.
15 Ibid, 211–12.
16 Ibid, 212.
17 Ibid, 213–14.
18 Ibid, 214.
19 Kew National Archives, Richmond (TNA), WO 208 3673, February/March 1942 (Royal Victoria Patriotic School).
20 Brooks, *British Propaganda to France*, 142.
21 Ibid, 145.
22 TNA, WO 208 3690, November 1942 (Royal Victoria Patriotic School).
23 TNA, WO 208 3685, September 1942 (Royal Victoria Patriotic School).
24 Brooks, *British Propaganda to France*, 143.
25 Ibid, 144.
26 Jackson, *France: The Dark Years*, 175. Halls, *The Youth of Vichy France*, 32.
27 Jackson, *France: The Dark Years*, 213.
28 Brooks, *British Propaganda to France*, 144.
29 Ibid, 145.
30 Ibid, 143.
31 Ibid, 144.
32 Ibid.
33 Ibid.
34 Ibid, 145.
35 Ibid, 146.
36 Ibid, 143.
37 Ibid, 144.
38 Ibid, 144–5.
39 Ibid, 143.
40 Ibid, 145.
41 Ibid.
42 TNA, WO 208 3688, October 1942 (Royal Victoria Patriotic School).
43 Brooks, *British Propaganda to France*, 143.

44 Ibid, 145.
45 CSA, Box 1682W90 'Radiodiffusion'.
46 CSA, Bernard Lauzanne, 'Guerre des ondes et radios noires', *Cahiers d'Histoire de la Radiodiffusion*, No. 27 (December 1990): 38.
47 TNA, WO 208/3684, September 1942 (Royal Victoria Patriotic School).
48 Dujardin, 'Belgique', 177.
49 Ibid, 174.
50 Ibid, 177.
51 Ibid, 182–3.
52 Ibid, 177.
53 Ibid.
54 Ibid, 179–80.
55 Ibid, 184.
56 Ibid, 182–3.
57 Ibid, 184.
58 Ibid, 184–5.
59 Ibid, 192.
60 Ibid, 191.
61 Ibid, 194.
62 Ibid, 197.
63 Ibid, 199.
64 Ibid, 200.
65 TNA, WO 208/3684, September 1942 (Royal Victoria Patriotic School).
66 Dujardin, 'Belgique', 178.
67 Crémieux-Brilhac and Eck, 'France', 106.
68 Ibid, 106–7.
69 Ibid, 108.
70 Ibid.
71 Ibid, 106.
72 Ibid.
73 Ibid, 107.
74 Ibid, 108.
75 Luneau, *Radio Londres*, 217–20.
76 Dujardin, 'Belgique', 215.
77 The official journal publishing the laws and other regulatory texts of the Belgian State.
78 Dujardin, 'Belgique', 216–17.
79 Ibid, 217.
80 Geneviève Billeter, 'Suisse', in Hélène Eck (dir.), *La guerre des ondes: Histoire des radios de langue française pendant la Deuxième Guerre Mondiale* (Paris: Editions Payot Lausanne et Armand Colin, 1985), 232–3.
81 Billeter, 'Suisse', 233.
82 Ibid, 234.
83 Ibid.
84 Ibid, 234–5.
85 Ibid, 235.
86 Ibid, 236.
87 Ibid, 237.
88 Ibid, 238.
89 Ibid.

90 Ibid, 260.
91 Ibid, 238.
92 Ibid, 251.
93 Ibid, 252–3.
94 Ibid, 253.
95 Ibid, 254–7; CSA, Lauzanne, 'L'année radiophonique 1941': 39.
96 Billeter, 'Suisse', 257, 259.
97 Robert J. Clements, 'Foreign Language Broadcasting of 'Radio Boston'', *The Modern Language Journal*, Vol. 27, No. 3, (1943): 175–6, 178.
98 Clements, 'Foreign Language Broadcasting': 176.
99 Ibid.
100 Ibid: 176–7.
101 Ibid: 177.
102 TNA, WO 208/3688, October 1942 (Royal Victoria Patriotic School).
103 Clements, 'Foreign Language Broadcasting': 179.
104 BBC WAC, E2/185, 8 April 1941 (European Intelligence Papers).
105 BBC WAC, E2/193/3, 1 July 1942 (European Intelligence Papers).
106 TNA, WO 208 3689, October 1942 (Royal Victoria Patriotic School).
107 Clements, 'Foreign Language Broadcasting': 177.
108 Ibid: 178.
109 Mark D Winek, 'Radio as a Tool of the State: Radio Moscow and the Early Cold War', *Comparative Humanities Review*, Vol. 3, Article 9 (2009): 100.
110 Ibid.
111 Ibid.
112 Ibid: 100–1.
113 Ibid: 101.
114 Ibid.
115 Ibid: 101–2.
116 Kingston, 'Broadcasts in French': 201–2.
117 Ibid: 203.
118 Ibid.
119 Ibid: 203–4.
120 Ibid: 204.
121 Ibid: 209.
122 Ibid: 202.
123 Ibid: 203.
124 Ibid: 205.
125 Ibid: 206–7.
126 Ibid: 207.
127 Ibid: 208.
128 Ibid.

Chapter 3

1 Fabrice Grenard, 'Les implication politiques du ravitaillement en France sous l'Occupation', *Vingtième Siècle. Revue d'histoire*, No. 94 (2007/2): 199.
2 Ibid: 199, 215.
3 Kris and Speier, *German Radio Propaganda*, 217.

4   Ibid, 220.
5   Adolph Hitler, *Mein Kampf* (Boston: The Houghton Mifflin Company, 1971), 617–18.
6   Jacques Delarue, *Trafics et crimes sous l'occupation* (Paris: Librairie Arthème Fayard, 1968), 77.
7   Ibid, 78.
8   Ibid, 79–80; Kenneth Mouré, 'Food rationing and the black market in France (1940–1944)', *French History*, Vol. 24, No. 2 (2010): 275.
9   Fabrice Grenard, *La France du marché noir (1940–1949)* (Paris: Editions Payot & Rivages, 2012), 48.
10 Maurice Schumann, 'La guerre continue', 3 September 1940, in *Honneur et Patrie* (Paris: Editions du Livre Français, 1946), 23.
11 PP, 220W1, 22 July 1940 (police report).
12 Michel Cépède, *Agriculture et Alimentation en France durant la IIe Guerre Mondiale* (Paris: Editions M.-TH. GENIN, 1961), 255.
13 Cépède, *Agriculture et Alimentation en France*, 257.
14 Ibid, 260.
15 Robert Gildea, *Marianne in Chains: In Search of the German Occupation of France 1940–45* (London: Pan Books, 2003), 112.
16 Mouré, 'Food rationing and the black market in France': 272.
17 Delarue, *Trafics et crimes sous l'occupation*, 79.
18 Don and Petie Kladstrup, *Wine and War* (New York: Broadway Books, 2001), 49.
19 Jackson, *France: The Dark Years,* 169.
20 François Quilici, 'La Haute Cour', 1 August 1940, in *Les Français parlent aux Français 1940–1941*, 80.
21 Ibid, 81.
22 PP, 220W1, 26 August 1940 (police report).
23 Ibid.
24 I François Quilici, 'La Haute Cour', 1 August 1940, in *Les Français parlent aux Français 1940–1941*, 81.
25 PP, 220W1, 22 July 1940 (police report).
26 PP, 220W1, 26 August 1940 (police report).
27 PP, 220W1, 16 September 1940 (police report).
28 PP, 220W1, 21 October 1940 (police report).
29 George Boris, 'Les privations: blocus ou pillage Allemand?', 16 September 1940, in *Les Français parlent aux Français 1940–1941*, 215.
30 BBC WAC, E2/186/3, 2 September 1940 (European Intelligence Papers).
31 BBC WAC, E2/186/3, 28 October 1940 (European Intelligence Papers).
32 George Boris, 'Les privations: blocus ou pillage Allemand?', 16 September 1940, in *Les Français parlent aux Français 1940–1941,* 215.
33 Cépède, *Agriculture et Alimentation en France,* 53–4.
34 Dominique Veillon, *Vivre et Survivre en France 1939–1947* (Paris: Editions Payot & Rivages, 1995), 82; George Boris, 'Les privations: blocus ou pillage Allemand?', 16 September 1940, in *Les Français parlent aux Français 1940–1941,* 215.
35 George Boris, 'Les privations: blocus ou pillage Allemand?', 16 September 1940, in *Les Français parlent aux Français 1940–1941,* 216.
36 Pierre Laborie, *L'opinion française sous Vichy: Les Français et la crise d'identité nationale 1936–1944* (Paris: Editions du Seuil, 2001), 249.
37 BBC WAC, E2/186/4, November 1940 (European Intelligence Papers).

38 Jean Marin, 'Que les Anglais gagnent, nous mangerons après', 25 October 1940', in *Les Français parlent aux Français 1940–1941,* 322.

39 BBC WAC, E2/186/3, 28 October 1940 (European Intelligence Papers).

40 BBC WAC, E2/186/4, November 1940 (European Intelligence Papers).

41 Mouré, 'Food rationing and the black market in France': 272.

42 Veillon, *Vivre et Survivre en France,* 66.

43 Grenard, 'Les implication politiques du ravitaillement': 200.

44 George Boris, 'Le nouveau rationnement', 27 September 1940, in *Les Français parlent aux Français 1940–1941,* 238–9; George Boris, 'Les privations: blocus ou pillage Allemand?', 16 September 1940, in *Les Français parlent aux Français 1940 –1941,* 215.

45 Kingston, 'Broadcasts in French': 211.

46 CSA, *Radio National,* 27 July–2 August 1941.

47 PP, 220W1, 23 September 1940 (police report).

48 PP, 220W1, 21 October 1940 (police report).

49 PP, 220W1, 23 September 1940 (police report).

50 George Boris, 'Le nouveau rationnement', 27 September 1940, in *Les Français parlent aux Français 1940–1941,* 239.

51 Ibid.

52 See for example, PP, 220W1, 9 September 1940 (police report).

53 Veillon, *Vivre et Survivre en France,* 113 and 116; BBC WAC, Anonymous letters from France (241–249), 16 March 1941 (247).

54 Hanna Diamond, *Women and the Second World War in France 1939–1948: Choices and Constraints* (Harlow: Editions Pearson Education Limited, 1999), 52.

55 George Boris, 'Le nouveau rationnement', 27 September 1940, in *Les Français parlent aux Français 1940–1941,* 239.

56 Grenard, 'Les implication politiques du ravitaillement': 202.

57 Georges Boris, 'Le pillage organisé', 4 October 1940, in *Les Français parlent aux Français 1940–1941,* 250.

58 Ibid.

59 I did not find any evidence of Darré's speech in secondary literature printed in English or French. Darré was a high-ranking Nazi official. It is conceivable that he may have made a speech that was detected by British intelligence, although the BBC speaker did not disclose the source of their information and so it is not possible to verify the content.

60 Georges Boris, 'Mensonges aux Français', 17 December 1940, in *Les Français parlent aux Français 1940–1941,* 514.

61 Ibid.

62 'Les auditeurs écrivent', 21 December 1940, in *Les Français parlent aux Français 1940–1941,* 535.

63 Grenard, 'Les implication politiques du ravitaillement': 207.

64 Briggs, *The History of Broadcasting in the UK, Vol. 3,* 446.

65 Grenard, 'Les implication politiques du ravitaillement': 207; 'Vous nous écrivez', 4 February 1941, in *Les Français parlent aux Français 1940–1941,* 694; BBC WAC, Mme. Paris, MM. Bonifas, Brunius, 'Courrier de France', Friday 2 May 1941, *Les Français parlent aux Français,* French Service, 20:30–21:00.

66 Léon Werth, *Déposition: Journal de guerre 1940–1944* (Paris: Editions Points, 2007), 115.

67 William Pickles, 'Les colis de la Croix-Rouge', 13 January 1941, in *Les Français parlent aux Français 1940–1941,* 607–8.

68 BBC WAC, E2/193/3, 27 August 1941 (European Intelligence Papers).

69 Mme. Paris, 'Les raisons d'un blocus', 6 February 1941, in *Les Français parlent aux Français 1940–1941,* 699; Jacques Duchesne, 'Darlan remplace Laval', 1 April 1941, in *Les Français parlent aux Français 1940–1941,* 883.

70 Jackson, *France: The Dark Years,* 177.

71 Ibid.

72 Ibid, 152.

73 Ibid, 177.

74 Ibid.

75 PP, 220W4, 9 June 1941 (police report).

76 BBC WAC, E2/193/3, 27 August 1941 (European Intelligence Papers).

77 PP, 220W5, 25 August 1941 (police report).

78 PP, 220W6, 29 December 1941 (police report).

79 Mouré, 'Food rationing and the black market in France': 263.

80 Ibid.

81 Ibid.

82 William Pickles, 'Les colis de la Croix-Rouge', 13 January 1941, in *Les Français parlent aux Français 1940–1941,* 607–8.

83 Leila J. Rupp, *Mobilizing Women for War: German and American Propaganda 1939–1945* (Princeton: Princeton University Press, 1978), 102.

84 Jill Stephenson, 'Propaganda, Autarky and the German Housewife', in David Welch (ed.), *Nazi Propaganda: The Power and the Limitations* (London and Canberra: Croom Helm, 1983), 120.

85 Ibid, 137–8.

86 Georges Boris, 'Le pillage Allemand en Europe', 14 January 1941, in *Les Français parlent aux Français 1940–1941,* 614–15.

87 Alan. S. Milward, *The New Order and the French Economy* (Oxford: Clarendon Press, 1970), 162.

88 Georges Boris, 'Le pillage allemand en Europe', 14 January 1941, in *Les Français parlent aux Français 1940–1941,* 616.

89 Ibid.

90 Mme. Paris, 'Les raisons d'un blocus', 6 February 1941, in *Les Français parlent aux Français 1940–1941,* 699.

91 Ibid, 700.

92 Halls, *The Youth of Vichy France,* 203.

93 Ibid.

94 This is a discrepancy of spelling of this name from different sources. The spelling is Dr. Bézançon in Georges Boris's pamphlet but Besançon in the broadcast.

95 Georges Boris, *French Public Opinion Since the Armistice* (Oxford: Oxford University Press, 1942), 12.

96 PP, 220W5, 6 October 1941 (police report).

97 Robert. O. Paxton, *Vichy France: Old Guard and New Order 1940–1944* (New York: Columbia University Press, 2001), 361.

98 Boris, *French public opinion,* 12.

99 'Se nourrir', 30 September 1941, in *Les Français parlent aux Français 1941–1942,* 286.

100 Grenard, 'Les implication politiques du ravitaillement': 207.

101 German Propaganda Archive. "Zeitschriften-Dienst Issue 126 — 26 September 1941." 5 June 2013. https://research.calvin.edu/german-propaganda-archive/.

102 Harold Nicolson, *Peacemaking 1919* (Safety Harbor: Simon Publications, 2001), 14; Hitler, *Mein Kampf,* 675.

103 TNA, FO 115/3448 France foreign policy 1941.

104 Jacques Duchesne, 'Darlan remplace Laval', 1 April 1941, in *Les Français parlent aux Français 1940–1941,* 882–3.

105 Richard Overy, *Why the Allies Won* (New York and London: W. W. Norton & Company, 1997), 248–9.

106 BBC WAC, E2/186/4, 25 March 1941 (European Intelligence Papers).

107 BBC WAC, Mme. Paris, MM. Bonifas, Brunius, Dumonceau, 'Courrier de France', Friday 4 July 1941, in *Les Français parlent aux Français*, 21:30–22:00 DBST.

108 TNA, WO208/3664 A.B.149, July 1941 (Royal Patriotic School).

109 Georges Boris, 'Bourrage de Crâne', 1 April 1941, in *Les Français parlent aux Français 1940–1941*, 888.

110 Maurice Schumann, 'Des V dessinés au bâton de rouge', 17 April 1941, in *Les Français parlent aux Français 1940–1941*, 955.

111 Ibid.

112 Jean-Marie Guillon, 'Les manifestations de ménagères: protestation populaire et résistance féminine spécifique', in Mechtild Gilzmer, Christine Levisse-Touzé, Stefan Martens (eds), *Les Femmes dans la Résistance en France* (Paris: Editions Tallandier, 2003), 130; Danielle Tartakowsky, *Les Manifestations de rue en France (1918–1968)* (Paris: Publications de la Sorbonne, 1997), 463.

113 Ernest Bevin, 'Pas de pain', 2 May 1941, in *Les Français parlent aux Français 1940–1941*, 1001–3.

114 'Razzia', 5 September 1941, in *Les Français parlent aux Français 1941–1942*, 185–6.

115 Ibid, 186.

116 Ibid, 185–6.

117 Ibid, 186.

118 Thibault, *Les femmes et la Résistance*, 64.

119 Tartakowsky, *Les Manifestations de rue*, 461; Thibault, *Les femmes et la Résistance*, 62.

120 Dominique Veillon, 'Les Femmes Anonymes dans la Résistance', in Mechtild Gilzmer, Christine Levisse-Touzé, Stefan Martens (eds), *Les Femmes dans la Résistance en France* (Paris: Editions Tallandier, 2003), 96.

121 Tartakowsky, *Les Manifestations de rue*, 461.

122 Guillon, 'Les manifestations de ménagères', 120–1.

123 Tartakowsky, *Les Manifestations de rue*, 462.

124 Maurice Schumann, 'La guerre pour l'affameur', 21 February 1941, in *Les Français parlent aux Français 1940–1941*, 750.

125 Boris, *French public opinion*, 11–12.

126 Mme. Paris, 'Manifestation à propos du lait', 2 March 1941, in *Les Français parlent aux Français 1940–1941*, 785.

127 Ibid, 785–6.

128 Ibid, 786.

129 Guillon, 'Les manifestations de ménagères', 127–9; Thibault, *Les femmes et la Résistance*, 64.

130 For example, PP, 220W4, 9 June 1941 (police report); PP, 220W5, 4 August 1941 (police report); PP, 220W5, 11 August 1941 (police report); PP, 220W5, 18 August 1941 (police report); PP, 220W5, 13 October 1941 (police report); PP, 220W5, 20 October 1941 (police report); PP, 220W5, 27 October 1941 (police report); PP, 220W6, 8 December 1941 (police report); PP, 220W6, 22 December 1941 (police report), etc.

131 Crémieux-Brilhac, 'La France libre et la radio': 81.

132 Georges Boris, 'Régime sans pain', 9 September 1941, in *Les Français parlent aux Français 1941–1942*, 201.

133 'La Récolte des pommes de terre', 25 September 1941, in *Les Français parlent aux Français 1941–1942*, 274; 'Se Nourrir', 30 September 1941, *Les Français parlent aux Français 1941–1942*, 287.

134 Grenard, *La France du marché noir*, 126.

135 Veillon, *Vivre et Survivre en France*, 208–9.

136 Jackson, *France: The Dark Years*, 291.

137 PP, 220W6, 1 December 1941 (police report), etc.

138 PP, 220W7, 5 January 1942 (police report); PP, 220W7, 12 January 1942 (police report), etc.

139 PP, 220W7, 19 January 1942 (police report); PP, 220W7, 26 January 1942 (police report), etc.

140 Georges Boris, 'Disette dans deux départements', 31 January 1942, in *Les Français parlent aux Français 1941–1942*, 681.

141 PP, 220W7, 23 February 1942 (police report).

142 Tartakowsky, *Les Manifestations de rue*, 462–3.

143 Ibid, 465–7.

144 Cépède, *Agriculture et Alimentation en France*, 279–80.

145 Marcel Baudot, *L'Opinion Publique sous l'Occupation* (Paris: Presses Universitaires de France, 1960), 22.

146 Diamond, *Women and the Second World War*, 62.

147 Vinen, *The Unfree French*, 227.

148 Ibid.

149 PP, 220W7, 26 January 1942 (police report).

150 PP, 220W7, 16 February 1942 (police report).

151 Diamond, *Women and the Second World War*, 64.

152 Ibid.

153 Ibid.

154 CSA, *Radio National*, 21–27 September 1941.

155 PP, 220W7, 5 January 1942 (police report).

156 Diamond, *Women and the Second World War*, 63–4.

157 'Laval censure Goering', 7 October 1942, in *Les Français parlent aux Français 1941–1942*, 1481; Maurice Schumann, 'J'ai faim', 12 November 1941, in *Les Français parlent aux Français 1941–1942*, 362; Boris, *French Public Opinion*, 12.

158 'Laval censure Goering', 7 October 1942, in *Les Français parlent aux Français 1941–1942*, 1481.

159 Ibid, 1481–2.

160 Ibid.

161 PP, 220W10, 21 September 1942 (police report); Halls, *The Youth of Vichy France*, 208.

162 Halls, *The Youth of Vichy France*, 208 and 450.

163 Ibid, 209.

164 PP, 220W10, 19 October 1942 (police report).

165 BBC WAC, E2/193/3, 21 October 1942 (European Intelligence Papers).

166 Halls, *The Youth of Vichy France*, 211.

167 BBC WAC, Anonymous letters from France (1077–1100), Bâle, 27 July 1942 (1077).

168 Jacques Duchesne, 'Un Troisième Hiver', 21 September 1942, in *Les Français parlent aux Français 1941–1942*, 1432.

169 Ibid.

170 Ibid.

171 Veillon, *Vivre et Survivre en France*, 174–5; Cépède, *Agriculture et Alimentation en France*, 380.

172 Grenard, 'Les implication politiques du ravitaillement': 209.

173 Grenard, *La France du marché noir*, 138.

174 Ibid, 137.

175 Ibid, 138.

176 Veillon, *Vivre et Survivre en France*, 176.

177 Jacques Duchesne, 'L'Organisation de la Famine', 24 September 1942, in *Les Français parlent aux Français 1941–1942*, 1443–4.

178 BBC WAC, 'Courrier de France', Friday 17 July 1942, in *Les Français parlent aux Français*, 20:30–21:00 DBST.

179 The term '*marché rose*' or 'rose market' is used in the archival document.

180 TNA, WO208/3682 829, August 1942 (Royal Patriotic School).

181 Grenard, *La France du marché noir*, 132–6.

182 Ibid, 152.

183 Ibid, 89.

184 Ibid, 175.

185 TNA, WO208 3682 848, August 1942 (Royal Patriotic School).

186 BBC WAC, 'Courrier de France', Friday 17 July 1942, in *Les Français parlent aux Français*, 20:30–21:00 DBST.

187 Ibid.

188 TNA, WO208/3682 847, August 1942 (Royal Patriotic School).

189 Ibid.

190 'Amis Paysans', 28 October 1942, in *Les Français parlent aux Français 1941–1942*, 1549–50.

191 Kay Chadwick, 'Radio Propaganda and Public Opinion Under Endgame Vichy: The Impact of Philippe Henriot', *French History*, Vol. 25, No. 2 (2011): 239.

192 TNA, WO208/3690 1088, November 1942 (Royal Patriotic School).

193 Cépède, *Agriculture et Alimentation en France*, 357.

194 Telegram from the President of the United States, Franklin Roosevelt, to WSC explaining his proposal to resume limited economic assistance to North Africa, 23 Mar 1942, Churchill Archives Centre (CHAR 20/72/69–71, biographical data, 4–5). The term 'United Nations' is used by Roosevelt in his telegraph to represent the nations that were united against the Axis powers.

195 Nobécourt, *Les Secrets de la propagande*, 44.

196 BBC WAC, E2/193/3, 1 July 1942 (European Intelligence Papers).

197 Ibid.

198 Aux Femmes françaises', 21 June 1942, in *Les Français parlent aux Français 1941–1942*, 1168–9.

199 Maurice Schumann, 'L'homme qui "souhaite la victoire de l'Allemagne"', 22 June 1942, in *Les Français parlent aux Français 1941–1942*, 1170.

200 Jean Marin, 'Le Reich Hitlérien est aux abois', 23 June 1942, in *Les Français parlent aux Français 1941–1942*, 1172.

201 Jacques Borel, 'Laval embauche pour Hitler', 23 June 1942, in *Les Français parlent aux Français 1941–1942*, 1173.

202 Pierre Bourdan, 'Laval renouvelle son appel à aider l'Allemagne', 23 June 1942, in *Les Français parlent aux Français 1941–1942*, 1175.

203 Georges Boris, 'Laval le négrier', 23 June 1942, in *Les Français parlent aux Français 1941–1942*, 1177.

204 BBC WAC, E2/193/3, 26 August 1942 (European Intelligence Papers).

205 Ibid.

206 André Labarthe, 'Le laboratoire de Dieppe', 27 August 1942, in *Les Français parlent aux Français 1941–1942*, 1380.

207 BBC WAC, E2/193/3, 21 October 1942 (European Intelligence Papers).

208 CSA, *Radio National*, 30 August–5 September 1942.

209 CSA, *Les Ondes*, 20 September 1942.

210 'La récolte des pommes de terre', 25 September 1941, in *Les Français parlent aux Français 1941–1942*, 273–4.

Chapter 4

1   Barbas, *Pétain, Discours aux Français,* 31.
2   Giolitto, *Histoire de la jeunesse,* 73.
3   Ibid, 81.
4   Ibid, 73–4.
5   Ibid, 74.
6   Ibid, 74–5.
7   Ibid, 75.
8   Ibid.
9   Ibid, 75–6.
10 Halls, *The Youth of Vichy France,* xi.
11 Giolitto, *Histoire de la jeunesse,* 76.
12 Ibid, 77.
13 Halls, *The Youth of Vichy France,* 186.
14 Giolitto, *Histoire de la jeunesse,* 77, 78, 84.
15 Ibid, 84.
16 Ibid, 77.
17 Ibid.
18 Ibid, 77–8.
19 Ibid, 78.
20 Halls, *The Youth of Vichy France,* 6. The italics are in the original quote.
21 Ibid, 7.
22 Cécile Desprairies, *Sous l'oeil de l'occupant: La France vue par l'Allemagne 1940–1944* (Paris: Armand Collin, 2010), 12; INA, Fonds Vichy, disques de la BDIC, *Pétain: sa prise de fonctions,* recorded on 17.06.1940, on Radio Bordeaux Sud-Ouest; INA, Fonds Vichy, disques de la BDIC, *Pétain: La demande d'armistice,* recorded on 20.06.1940, on Radio Bordeaux Sud-Ouest; INA, Fonds Vichy, disques de la BDIC, *Philippe PETAIN conteste les propos de Churchill sur l'armée,* recorded on 23.06.1940, on Radio Bordeaux Sud-Ouest; INA, Fonds Vichy, disques de la BDIC, *Philippe PETAIN: les deux armistices avec l'Allemagne et l'Italie,* recorded on 25.06.1940, on Radio Bordeaux Sud-Ouest; INA, Fonds Vichy, disques de la BDIC, *Philippe PETAIN: les pleins pouvoirs constituants et Mers-el-Kébir,* recorded on 11.07.1940, on Radio Etat Français-Radio Nationale; INA, Fonds Vichy, disques de la BDIC, *La collaboration après l'armistice,* recorded on 24.07.1940, on Radio Etat Français-Radio Nationale; INA, Fonds Vichy, disques de la BDIC, *Violente critique des querelles des gaullistes,* recorded on 01.09.1940 on Radio Etat Francais-Radiodiffusion Nationale.
23 Jackson, *France: The Dark Years,* 31; Laborie, *L'opinion française sous Vichy,* 83; Jean Giraudoux, *Pleins Pouvoirs* (Paris: Gallimard, 1939), 46, 55–8.
24 Christophe Pecout, *Les Chantiers de la Jeunesse et la revitalisation physique et morale de la jeunesse française (1940–1944)* (Paris: L'Harmattan, 2007), 27.
25 Halls, *The Youth of Vichy France,* 10–11.
26 Thibault, *Les femmes et la Résistance,* 12.
27 Jackson, *France: The Dark Years,* 149.
28 Sarah Fishman, *We Will Wait: Wives of French Prisoners of War, 1940–1945* (New Haven: Yale University Press, 1991), 45; Jackson, *France: The Dark Years,* 329.
29 Fishman, *We Will Wait,* 43.
30 Dr. Goebbels, Joseph. "Deutsches Frauentum." German Propaganda Archive. 5 June 2013. https://research.calvin.edu/german-propaganda-archive/.
31 Ibid.

32 Jean Pierre Bertin-Maghit, *Les documenteurs des Années Noires. Les documentaires de propagande, France 1940–1944* (Paris: Nouveau Monde Editions, 2004), 223, 242; Jean Pierre Bertin-Maghit 'Le documentaire de propagande dans la France de l'Occupation', in Jacky Evrard and Jacques Kermabon (eds), *Une encyclopédie du court métrage français* (Crisnée: Editions Yellow Now, 2004), 273–5.

33 Giolitto, *Histoire de la jeunesse*, 124.

34 Ibid, 125; Marc Bloch, *Strange Defeat: A Statement of Evidence Written in 1940* (New York, London: W. W. Norton & Company, 1968), 136.

35 Giolitto, *Histoire de la jeunesse,* 125.

36 Ibid, 126.

37 Halls, *The Youth of Vichy France,* 9.

38 Ibid, 186.

39 Judith K. Proud, *Children and Propaganda* (Bristol: Intellect European Studies Series, 1995), 12.

40 Proud, *Children and Propaganda*, 7–8.

41 Paxton, *Vichy France*, 160–1.

42 Halls, *The Youth of Vichy France,* 401.

43 Pierre Drieu La Rochelle, *Journal 1939–1945* (Paris: Editions Gallimard, 1992), 36.

44 Giolitto, *Histoire de la jeunesse,* 181.

45 Ibid.

46 Hitler, *Mein Kampf,* 409–14.

47 Giolitto, *Histoire de la jeunesse,* 181.

48 Pecout, *Les Chantiers de la Jeunesse,* 33.

49 Ibid.

50 Jean-Louis Gay-Lescot, *Sport et Education sous Vichy (1940–44)* (Lyon: Presses universitaires de Lyon, 1991), 192–3; Halls, *The Youth of Vichy France,* 186.

51 Halls, *The Youth of Vichy France,* 199.

52 Ibid.

53 Ibid, 189.

54 Ibid.

55 Ibid, 186; Gay-Lescot, *Sport et Education sous Vichy*, 192.

56 Giolitto, *Histoire de la jeunesse,* 182.

57 Gay-Lescot, *Sport et Education sous Vichy,* 199.

58 INA, Fonds Vichy, disques de la BDIC, *Philippe PETAIN: les deux armistices avec l'Allemagne et l'Italie*, recorded on 25.06.1940, on Radio Bordeaux Sud-Ouest; Barbas, *Pétain, Discours aux Français*, 63.

59 Barbas, *Pétain, Discours aux Français,* 66.

60 Ibid.

61 Jackson, *France: The Dark Years,* 129.

62 Robert Gaillard, *Jours de Pénitence. Mes Evasions* (Paris: René Debresse, 1942), 29–30.

63 INA, Fonds Vichy, disques de la BDIC, *La collaboration après l'armistice*, recorded on 24.07.1940, on Radio Etat Français-Radio Nationale.

64 Brett Bowles, 'Newsreels, Ideology, and Public Opinion under Vichy: The Case of La France en Marche', *French Historical Studies*, Vol. 27, No. 2 (Spring 2004): 429.

65 Ibid.

66 Giolitto, *Histoire de la jeunesse,* 10.

67 Ibid, 18; Proud, *Children and Propaganda,* 4.

68 Giolitto, *Histoire de la jeunesse,* 18.

69 Benoîte and Flora Groult, *Journal à quatre mains* (Paris: Editions Denoël, 1962), 123–4.

70 Barbas, *Pétain, Discours aux Français,* 67–71.

71 Ibid, 71. The italics are in the original quote.

72 Groult, *Journal à quatre mains,* 133.

73 PP, 220W1, 26 August 1940 (police report).

74 INA, Fonds Vichy, disques de la BDIC, *Pétain pose la première pierre du tunnel de la Croix-Rousse,* recorded on 19.11.1940, on Radio Etat Français-Radiodiffusion Nationale.

75 Ellul, *Propaganda,* 292.

76 Proud, *Children and Propaganda,* 5–7.

77 INA, Fonds Vichy, disques de la BDIC, *Pétain visite une ferme dans le Limousin,* recorded on 19.06.1941, on Radio Etat Français-Radiodiffusion Nationale.

78 Ibid.

79 Ibid.

80 Ibid.

81 Jackson, *France: The Dark Years,* 338; Jean-Paul Cointet, *La Légion Française des Combattants, 1940–1944. La tentation du fascisme* (Paris: Albin Michel S. A., 1995), 143.

82 Halls, *The Youth of Vichy France,* 284.

83 Pecout, *Les Chantiers de la Jeunesse,* 51.

84 Halls, *The Youth of Vichy France,* 285, 291.

85 Ibid, 291.

86 Ibid, 289–92.

87 Ibid, 286–7.

88 Pecout, *Les Chantiers de la Jeunesse,* 53.

89 Ibid, 59.

90 Ibid, 59–60.

91 Barbas, *Pétain, Discours aux Français,* 25.

92 Ibid, 76.

93 Ibid. The italics are in the original quote.

94 Halls, *The Youth of Vichy France,* 284.

95 Barbas, *Pétain, Discours aux Français,* 77. The italics are in the original quote.

96 Ibid.

97 Ibid. The italics are in the original quote.

98 Halls, *The Youth of Vichy France,* 398.

99 TNA, WO208/3677 717, May 1942 (Royal Patriotic School).

100 Barbas, *Pétain, Discours aux Français,* 85.

101 Ibid, 97.

102 Halls, *The Youth of Vichy France,* 208.

103 Barbas, *Pétain, Discours aux Français,* 96.

104 INA, Fonds Vichy, disques de la BDIC, *Campagne du Secours National d'hiver,* recorded on 15.11.1940, on Radio Etat Français-Radio Nationale.

105 Halls, *The Youth of Vichy France,* 208.

106 Paxton, *Vichy France,* 165.

107 Halls, *The Youth of Vichy France,* 312.

108 Paxton, *Vichy France,* 165.

109 In the archival record of INA, this broadcast was filed under October 1941, but I listed it as October 1940 because it became apparent after listening to the content of the recording that the event took place in 1940. See Halls, *The Youth of Vichy France,* 312.

110 INA, Fonds Vichy, disques de la BDIC, *Après la visite de Pétain à l'école de cadres de Gannat*, recorded on 20.10.1941, on Radio Etat Français-Radiodiffusion Nationale.

111 Ibid.

112 These are broadcasts linked to the youth: INA, Fonds Vichy, disques de la BDIC, *La collaboration après l'armistice*, recorded on 24.07.1940, on Radio Etat Français-Radio Nationale; INA, Fonds Vichy, disques de la BDIC, *Après la visite de Pétain à l'école de cadres de Gannat*, recorded on 20.10.1941, on Radio Etat Français-Radiodiffusion Nationale; INA, Fonds Vichy, disques de la BDIC, *Voyage du Maréchal Pétain à Chambéry (Savoie)*, recorded on 01.01.1941, on Radio Etat Français-Radiodiffusion Nationale; INA, Fonds Vichy, disques de la BDIC, *Serment de la ligue de loyauté des écoliers d'Algérie*, recorded on 01.01.1941, on Radio Etat Français-Radiodiffusion Nationale; INA, Fonds Vichy, disques de la BDIC, *Pétain: discours aux écoliers de France*, recorded on 13.10.1941, on Radio Etat Français-Radiodiffusion Nationale; INA, Fonds Vichy, disques de la BDIC, *Deuxième journée à Bourg-En-Bresse*, recorded on 13.09.1942, on Radio Etat Français-Radiodiffusion Nationale.

113 INA, Inventaire Disques, *Attentat de Paul Collette contre Pierre Laval et de Marcel Déat*, recorded on 27.08.1941, on Etat Français-Radiodiffusion Nationale (RN), 1941.

114 INA, Inventaire Disques, *Conférence 'Révolution nationale et Révolution sociale'*, recorded on 24.01.1942, on Etat Français-Radiodiffusion Nationale (RN), 1942.

115 INA, Inventaire Disques, *Réunion politique organisée par le mouvement 'le Feu'*, recorded on 01.01.1941, on Radio Paris (RP), 1941.

116 INA, Inventaire Disques, *Cardinal Emmanuel Suhard: concert de musique religieuse donné au profit des prisonniers de guerre*, recorded on 08.03.1941, on Radio Paris (RP), 1941.

117 INA, Inventaire Disques, *Fernand de Brinon: l'attentat de Paul Collette contre Pierre Laval*, recorded on 28.08.1941, on Radio Paris (RP), 1941.

118 INA, Inventaire Disques, *Discours prononcé par Fernand de BRINON*, recorded on 01.03.1942, on Radio Paris (RP), 1942.

119 For example, INA, Inventaire Disques, *Fernand de Brinon: l'attentat de Paul Collette contre Pierre Laval*, recorded on 28.08.1941, on Radio Paris (RP), 1941.

120 Dompnier, 'Entre La Marseillaise et Maréchal, nous voilà!', 75–6.

121 Halls, *The Youth of Vichy France*, 308.

122 INA, Fonds Vichy, disques de la BDIC, *Voyage dans la région de Toulouse: Pétain visite une école viticole*, recorded on 19.11.1940, on Radio Etat Français-Radiodiffusion Nationale.

123 Giolitto, *Histoire de la jeunesse*, 313.

124 BBC WAC, E2/185, 16 December 1940 (European Intelligence Papers).

125 BBC WAC, E2/186/4, 23 December 1940 (European Intelligence Papers).

126 There a total of four broadcasts among these 13 that are dated 1.1.1941; as explained in the Introduction, these are not necessarily the actual dates of the broadcasts.

127 BBC WAC, E2/193/2, 4 June 1941 (European Intelligence Papers).

128 INA, Fonds Vichy, disques de la BDIC, *Pétain visite une ferme dans le Limousin*, recorded on 19.06.1941, on Radio Etat Français-Radiodiffusion Nationale.

129 Ibid.

130 INA, Fonds Vichy, disques de la BDIC, *Voyage de Pétain à Limoges*, recorded on 20.06.1941, on Radio Etat Français-Radiodiffusion Nationale.

131 CSA, *Radio National*, 29 June–5 July 1941.

132 Barbas, *Pétain, Discours aux Francais*, 146.

133 INA, Fonds Vichy, disques de la BDIC, *Voyage de Pétain à Limoges*, recorded on 20.06.1941, on Radio Etat Français-Radiodiffusion Nationale; Barbas, *Pétain, Discours aux Français*, 147.

134 Proud, *Children and Propaganda*, 10.
135 Dompnier, 'Entre La Marseillaise et Maréchal, nous voilà!', 70, 80–1; Barbas, *Pétain, Discours aux Français*, 146; INA, Fonds Vichy, disques de la BDIC, *Voyage de Pétain à Limoges*, recorded on 20.06.1941, on Radio Etat Français-Radiodiffusion Nationale; See CSA, *Radio National*, 29 June–5 July 1941 for more details.
136 Jackson, *France: The Dark Years*, 129.
137 For example, CSA, *Radio National*, 29 June–5 July 1941.
138 Robert Hervet, *Les Compagnons de France* (Paris: Editions France-Empire, 1965), 59–60; Bertin-Maghit, *Les documenteurs des Années Noires*, 233.
139 Barbas, *Pétain, Discours aux Francais*, 205. It was broadcast at 18h00.
140 Ibid, *206*.
141 Ibid, 206–7.
142 INA, Fonds Vichy, disques de la BDIC, *Campagne d'hiver du Secours National*, recorded on 19.11.1941, on Radio Etat Français-Radiodiffusion Nationale. This programme was broadcast on 22.11.1941.
143 INA, Fonds Vichy, disques de la BDIC, *Message d'un instituteur pour le Secours National*, recorded on 19.11.1941, on Radio Etat Français-Radiodiffusion Nationale. This programme was broadcast on 22.11.1941.
144 Barbas, *Pétain, Discours aux Francais*, 207.
145 Ibid, 208.
146 Ellul, *Propaganda*, 18–19.
147 Hervet, *Les Compagnons de France*, 60–1.
148 Giolitto, *Histoire de la jeunesse*, 283–4.
149 Barbas, *Pétain, Discours aux Francais*, 194–6.
150 INA, Fonds Vichy, disques de la BDIC, *Pétain: discours aux écoliers de France*, recorded on 13.10.1941, on Radio Etat Français-Radiodiffusion Nationale.
151 Proud, *Children and Propaganda*, 11; De Monzie, *Ci-devant*, 253.
152 Halls, *The Youth of Vichy France*, 146.
153 Ibid, 182.
154 Ibid, 184; Micheline Bood, *Les années doubles: Journal d'une lycéenne sous l'Occupation* (Paris: Editions Robert Laffont, 1974), 83, 91.
155 INA, Fonds Vichy, disques de la BDIC, *Serment de la ligue de loyauté des écoliers d'Algérie*, recorded on 01.01.1941, on Radio Etat Français-Radiodiffusion Nationale. The exact date of recording and broadcasting are unknown.
156 Ibid.
157 Ibid.
158 Ibid.
159 Halls, *The Youth of Vichy France*, 12; Marcel Déat, *Mémoires Politiques* (Paris: Editions Denoël, 1989), 625–6.
160 Gay-Lescot, *Sport et Education sous Vichy*, 128.
161 Halls, *The Youth of Vichy France*, 179.
162 Ibid.
163 INA, Fonds Vichy, disques de la BDIC, *Pétain reçoit des enfants en vacances à Vichy*, recorded on 01.01.1941, on Radio Etat Français-Radiodiffusion Nationale. The actual date of the broadcast is unknown and was archived as 01.01.41 but it could be gauged from the content of the broadcast that it was recorded around the month of September.
164 Ibid.
165 Ibid.
166 Halls, *The Youth of Vichy France*, 15.

167 PP, 220W9, 27 July 1942 (police report).

168 Bernard Prêtet, *Sports et sportifs français sous Vichy* (Paris: Nouveau Monde éditions, 2016), 41.

169 Prêtet, *Sports et sportifs français*, 30 and 41.

170 Ibid, 41.

171 Ibid.

172 Ibid, 47.

173 Pecout, *Les Chantiers de la Jeunesse*, 34.

174 Ibid, 35–6.

175 Ibid, 36.

176 Alice Travers, *Politique et représentations de la montagne sous Vichy. La Montagne Educatrice, 1940–1944* (Paris: L'Harmattan, 2001), 179.

177 Pecout, *Les Chantiers de la Jeunesse*, 36–7; Bertin-Maghit, *Les documenteurs des Années Noires*, 226, 228, 233, 246.

178 Pecout, *Les Chantiers de la Jeunesse*, 41–2.

179 For example, it was announced in CSA, *Radio National*, 7–13 September 1941 that Georges Briquet would present sports in *Radiodiffusion* from 18h05–18h10 on 13 September.

180 INA, Fonds Vichy, disques de la BDIC, *Epreuves d'éducation physique relais inter-armes à Ambérieux*, recorded on 12.09.1942, on Radio Etat Français-Radiodiffusion Nationale; INA, Fonds Vichy, disques de la BDIC, *Relais inter-armes à Ambérieux*, recorded on 12.09.1942, on Radio Etat Français-Radiodiffusion Nationale.

181 Halls, *The Youth of Vichy France*, 398; Gay-Lescot, *Sport et Education sous Vichy*, 192–3.

182 CSA, *Radio National*, 31 August–6 September 1941.

183 Ibid, 20–26 July 1941.

184 Ibid, 31 August–6 September 1941.

185 Ibid, 7–13 September 1941.

186 Ibid.

187 Ibid.

188 Ibid, 21–27 September 1941.

189 Ibid.

190 Gay-Lescot, *Sport et Education sous Vichy*, 128; Prêtet, *Sports et sportifs français*, 84–5.

191 Cointet, *La Légion Française des Combattants,* 132.

192 Ibid, 179.

193 BBC WAC, E2/188/1, 23 January 1942 (European Intelligence Papers).

194 INA, Fonds Vichy, disques de la BDIC, *Courrier du Maréchal dépouillé par les jeunes des Chantiers*, recorded on 28.01.1942, on Radio Etat Français-Radiodiffusion Nationale. No broadcasting date available.

195 Pecout, *Les Chantiers de la Jeunesse*, 134.

196 Ibid.

197 INA, Fonds Vichy, disques de la BDIC, *Courrier du Maréchal dépouillé par les jeunes des Chantiers*, recorded on 28.01.1942, on Radio Etat Français-Radiodiffusion Nationale.

198 Ibid.

199 Ibid.

200 Halls, *The Youth of Vichy France*, 14. In this case, Halls consulted the newspaper *La Croix* of February 1941 as primary source to substantiate the veracity of such a claim.

201 Ibid.

202 CSA, *Radio National*, 4–10 January 1942; Pecout, *Les Chantiers de la Jeunesse*, 251–5. Pecout gives a list of all the *Chantiers* groups with their creation and dissolution dates.

203 Halls, *The Youth of Vichy France,* 199; CSA, *Radio National,* 10–16 May 1942.

204 Halls, *The Youth of Vichy France*, 288–9.
205 Ibid, 199; Giolitto, *Histoire de la jeunesse*, 181–2.
206 Pecout, *Les Chantiers de la Jeunesse*, 172.
207 Ibid, 43.
208 Halls, *The Youth of Vichy France*, 294.
209 INA, Fonds Vichy, disques de la BDIC, *PETAIN dans les Chantiers de jeunesse de RANDAN*, recorded on 01.01.1942, on Radio Etat Français-Radiodiffusion Nationale. This recording date is 1 January, and the broadcasting date is 28 July 1942.
210 Pecout, *Les Chantiers de la Jeunesse*, 108.
211 INA, Fonds Vichy, disques de la BDIC, *PETAIN dans les Chantiers de jeunesse de RANDAN*, recorded on 01.01.1942, on Radio Etat Français-Radiodiffusion Nationale.
212 Pecout, *Les Chantiers de la Jeunesse*, 107–8.
213 Paxton, *Vichy France*, 163; Hervet, *Les Compagnons de France*, 23.
214 Hervet, *Les Compagnons de France*, 23.
215 Halls, *The Youth of Vichy France*, 267.
216 Hervet, *Les Compagnons de France*, 135.
217 Ibid, 23.
218 Paxton, *Vichy France*, 161.
219 Hervet, *Les Compagnons de France*, 51.
220 Paxton, *Vichy France*, 161; Barbas, *Pétain, Discours aux Français*, 183.
221 Paxton, *Vichy France*, 161–2.
222 INA, Fonds Vichy, disques de la BDIC, *Discours aux Chantiers de jeunesse de RANDAN*, recorded on 26.06.1942, on Radio Etat Français-Radiodiffusion Nationale. From the context of broadcast, it seems it was recorded on 26.07.1942 instead.
223 Ibid.
224 Ibid; CSA, *Radio National*, 28 June–4 July 1942.
225 At this point, the recording is of poor quality and some parts of the speech were inaudible.
226 INA, Fonds Vichy, disques de la BDIC, *Discours aux Chantiers de jeunesse de RANDAN*, recorded on 26.06.1942, on Radio Etat Français-Radiodiffusion Nationale.
227 Ibid.
228 BBC WAC, E2/188/1, 23 January 1942 (European Intelligence Papers).
229 Hervet, *Les Compagnons de France*, 192.
230 Ibid, 193.
231 Ibid, 47–8.
232 Halls, *The Youth of Vichy France*, 270.
233 Ibid.
234 Ibid.
235 Hervet, *Les Compagnons de France*, 76–7.
236 Ibid, 77.
237 Ibid, 75.
238 Ibid.
239 Halls, *The Youth of Vichy France*, 32–3.
240 Ibid, 127.
241 Ibid, 128.
242 Ibid.
243 Barbas, *Pétain, Discours aux Francais*, 272–5. The speech was made at 11h00 and broadcast at 13h45 the same day.

244 INA, Fonds Vichy, disques de la BDIC, *Message aux instituteurs de France*, recorded on 03.09.1942, on Radio Etat Français-Radiodiffusion Nationale.

245 Barbas, *Pétain, Discours aux Francais,* 272–3; The italics are in the original quote.

246 Ibid, 273.

247 Ibid, 273–4; The italics are in the original quote.

248 INA, Fonds Vichy, disques de la BDIC, *Message aux instituteurs de France*, recorded on 03.09.1942, on Radio Etat Français-Radiodiffusion Nationale.

249 Dompnier, 'Entre La Marseillaise et Maréchal, nous voilà!', 70–1.

250 Ibid, 73, 84–8.

251 See for example, INA, Fonds Vichy, disques de la BDIC, *Aubusson accueille Pétain*, recorded on 20.06.1941, on Radio Etat Français-Radiodiffusion Nationale; INA, Fonds Vichy, disques de la BDIC, *Pétain à Aix-les-Bains*, recorded on 22.09.1941, on Radio Etat Français-Radiodiffusion Nationale; INA, Fonds Vichy, disques de la BDIC, *Maréchal PETAIN: voyage à Clermont-Ferrand*, recorded on 22.03.1942, on Radio Etat Français-Radiodiffusion Nationale; INA, Fonds Vichy, disques de la BDIC, *Construction d'un centre socio-culturel à Châteauroux*, recorded on 28.05.1942, on Radio Etat Français-Radiodiffusion Nationale; INA, Fonds Vichy, disques de la BDIC, *Toulouse: offices protestant et catholique*, recorded on 14.06.1942, on Radio Etat Français-Radiodiffusion Nationale; INA, Fonds Vichy, disques de la BDIC, *Message aux instituteurs de France*, recorded on 03.09.1942, on Radio Etat Français-Radiodiffusion Nationale; INA, Fonds Vichy, disques de la BDIC, *Relais inter-armes à Ambérieux*, recorded on 12.09.1942, on Radio Etat Français-Radiodiffusion Nationale.

252 CSA, *Radio National*, 13–19 September 1942.

253 Ibid.

254 Ibid.

255 Halls, *The Youth of Vichy France,* 117–18.

256 The date and content of the admonition were unknown. From the context of the broadcast, it seems to be linked to the poor behaviour of pupils in some schools.

257 INA, Fonds Vichy, disques de la BDIC, *Deuxième journée à Bourg-En-Bresse*, recorded on 13.09.1942, on Radio Etat Français-Radiodiffusion Nationale.

258 Ibid.

259 Ibid.

260 Ibid.

261 Ibid.

262 Halls, *The Youth of Vichy France,* 184.

263 Gay-Lescot, *Sport et Education sous Vichy,* 44–5.

264 Pecout, *Les Chantiers de la Jeunesse,* 174–5.

265 Gay-Lescot, *Sport et Education sous Vichy,* 44–5.

266 Travers, *Politique et représentations de la montagne,* 34.

267 Ibid, 36.

268 Ibid, 46.

269 Ibid, 85.

270 Ibid, 123; Bertin-Maghit, *Les documenteurs des Années Noires,* 239, 241, 242, 246, 248.

271 Pecout, *Les Chantiers de la Jeunesse,* 257.

272 Travers, *Politique et représentations de la montagne,* 164.

273 Ibid, 165.

274 Ibid.

275 Ibid.

276 Ibid, 165–6.

277 Ibid, 169.
278 CSA, *Radio National*, 12–18 April 1942.
279 Ibid.
280 Ibid.
281 Ibid.
282 Gay-Lescot, *Sport et Education sous Vichy*, 174.
283 Giolitto, *Histoire de la jeunesse*, 206; Halls, *The Youth of Vichy France*, 211.
284 Giolitto, *Histoire de la jeunesse*, 207.
285 CSA, *Radio National*, 26 July–1 August 1942.
286 Ibid.
287 Ibid.
288 Giolitto, *Histoire de la jeunesse*, 359.
289 Gay-Lescot, *Sport et Education sous Vichy*, 213.
290 Ibid, 201.

Chapter 5

1 Paxton, *Vichy France*, 51.
2 Philippe Burrin, *Living with Defeat: France under the German Occupation 1940–1944* (London, Sydney, Auckland: Arnold, 1996), 101.
3 Paxton, *Vichy France*, 51; Eberhard Jäckel, *La France dans l'Europe de Hitler* (Paris: Edition Librairie Arthème Fayard, 1968), 18.
4 Barbas, *Pétain, Discours aux Français*, 94–6.
5 Burrin, *Living with Defeat*, 101; Barbas, *Pétain, Discours aux Français*, 95–6.
6 Ibid.
7 Burrin, *Living with Defeat*, 101.
8 Ibid.
9 Jackson, *France: The Dark Years*, 233–5.
10 Ibid, 233.
11 Jäckel, *La France dans l'Europe de Hitler*, 18–19.
12 The battle of Dakar was a confrontation between Vichy France and the Anglo-Free French from 23 to 25 September 1940. It ended in failure for the British and Free French.
13 INA, Inventaire Disques, *Le Maréchal Pétain dans la forêt de Tronçais*, recorded on 08.11.1940, on Radio Paris (RP), 1940. It would seem that the main part of this broadcast was recorded on 8 November, but it was broadcast on 9 November according to Michel Ferry.
14 Halls, *The Youth of Vichy France*, 286; Pecout, *Les Chantiers de la Jeunesse*, 128.
15 INA, Inventaire Disques, *Le Maréchal Pétain dans la forêt de Tronçais*, recorded on 08.11.1940, on Radio Paris (RP), 1940.
16 Halls, *The Youth of Vichy France*, 290.
17 Ibid, 290–1.
18 Pecout, *Les Chantiers de la Jeunesse*, 121.
19 Ibid, 121–2.
20 Proud, *Children and Propaganda*, 6.
21 Pecout, *Les Chantiers de la Jeunesse*, 37–38.
22 INA, Inventaire Disques, *Le Maréchal Pétain dans la forêt de Tronçais*, recorded on 08.11.1940, on Radio Paris (RP), 1940.
23 Ibid.

24 INA, Inventaire Disques, *Importance de la veillée de cendres de l'Aiglon aux Invalides*, recorded on 15.12.1940, on Radio Paris (RP), 1940.

25 Diamond, *Women and the Second World War*, 20–1.

26 Ibid, 32.

27 Ibid, 23.

28 Ibid, 26.

29 Ibid, 23–4.

30 Ibid, 27.

31 Ibid, 33–5.

32 CSA, Lauzanne, 'L'année radiophonique 1941': 37.

33 Tangye Lean, *Voices in the Darkness*, 144.

34 INA, Inventaire Disques, *Plusieurs interviews de personnes au chômage*, recorded on 10.01.1941, on Radio Paris (RP), 1941.

35 Burrin, *Living with Defeat*, 300.

36 Ibid, 296–302.

37 Ibid, 303–5.

38 INA, Inventaire Disques, *Plusieurs interviews de personnes au chômage*, recorded on 10.01.1941, on Radio Paris (RP), 1941.

39 Crémieux-Brilhac and Eck, 'France', 55.

40 INA, Inventaire Disques, *Offres d'emplois pour chômeurs*, recorded on 17.08.1941, on Radio Paris (RP), 1941.

41 Milward, *The New Order*, 110.

42 INA, Inventaire Disques, *Interview d'un ouvrier français revenu d'Allemagne*, recorded on 29.01.1941, on Radio Paris (RP), 1941.

43 PP, 220W1, 9 September 1940 (police report).

44 INA, Inventaire Disques, *Interviews d'ouvriers français travaillant dans une usine à Berlin*, recorded on 25.02.1941, on Radio Paris (RP), 1941. This is one of the few broadcasts that has both a recording date (25 February) and a broadcasting date (28 February).

45 Ibid.

46 Ibid.

47 Ibid.

48 Due to the French pronunciation of the German town, it was not possible to identify clearly which town the interviewee talked about because both cities' names exist, and both are far away from Berlin.

49 INA, Inventaire Disques, *Interviews d'ouvriers français travaillant dans une usine à Berlin*, recorded on 25.02.1941, on Radio Paris (RP), 1941.

50 Burrin, *Living with Defeat*, 305.

51 Milward, *The New Order*, 114.

52 Ibid, 274–5.

53 Crémieux-Brilhac and Eck, 'France', 57; a collection of Dr. Friedrich's talks in Dr. Friedrich, *Un journaliste allemand vous parle …* (Paris: Editions LE PONT, 1942).

54 Dr. Friedrich, 'Le socialisme allemand', 15 June 1941, in *Un journaliste allemand vous parle*, 46.

55 Ibid.

56 Ibid.

57 Dr. Friedrich, 'Aux ouvriers de France', 2 July 1941, in *Un journaliste allemand vous parle*, 56.

58 Ibid, 57.

59 Ibid, 57–8.

60 Giolitto, *Histoire de la jeunesse*, 388.

61 INA, Inventaire Disques, *Georges Lamirand: appel en faveur du service civique rural*, recorded on 20.06.1941, on Radio Paris (RP), 1941.
62 Ibid.
63 Jackson, *France: The Dark Years*, 149.
64 Cornick, 'Fighting Myth with Reality', 83.
65 Although the legitimacy of Vichy government remains contested from 1940 to 1942, it maintained its function as a governing body for social and civic matters for both the occupied zone and the unoccupied zone, as long as the politics in place were not in conflict with the interests of the Germans.
66 Barbas, *Pétain, Discours aux Français*, 34.
67 Ibid, 34–5.
68 INA, Inventaire Disques, *Appel en faveur du service civique rural*, recorded on 25.06.1941, on Radio Paris (RP), 1941.
69 Ibid.
70 Harry Roderick Kedward, *Occupied France: Collaboration and Resistance 1940–1944* (Oxford, New York: Basil Blackwell, 1985), 25.
71 CSA, *Radio National*, 10–16 August 1941.
72 Giolitto, *Histoire de la jeunesse*, 389.
73 Ibid, 389–90.
74 Ibid, 390–1.
75 Ibid, 392.
76 Ibid.
77 Ibid.
78 Ibid.
79 Ibid, 392–3.
80 INA, Inventaire Disques, *Georges Lamirand: appel aux jeunes ouvriers*, recorded on 16.06.1941, on Radio Paris (RP), 1941.
81 Ibid.
82 Ibid.
83 Ibid.
84 Ibid.
85 Ibid.
86 Ibid.
87 Ibid.
88 Ibid.
89 BBC WAC, E2/188/1, 23 January 1942 (European Intelligence Papers). In this report, the BBC recognises the originality of this German propaganda targeted at youth by promising them a place in the New Europe, and the danger their appeal to the youth would entail if German dominance over Western Europe were to remain unchanged for a long period of time.
90 INA, Inventaire Disques, *Discours de Georges LAMIRAND à la jeunesse*, recorded on 01.12.1941, on Radio Paris (RP), 1941.
91 Dr. Friedrich, 'L'avenir se dessine', 18 May 41, in *Un journaliste allemand vous parle*, 21–2.
92 Ibid, 22.
93 Halls, *The Youth of Vichy France*, 357.
94 INA, Inventaire Disques, *Reportage et interviews après le bombardement de Boulogne-Billancourt*, recorded on 04.03.1942, on Radio Paris (RP), 1942.
95 Ibid.
96 Ibid.

97 Ibid.

98 Bertin-Maghit, *Les documenteurs des Années Noires,* 235.

99 INA, Inventaire Disques, *Reportage et interviews après le bombardement de Boulogne-Billancourt,* recorded on 04.03.1942, on Radio Paris (RP), 1942.

100 John Keegan, *The Second World War* (New York: Penguin Books USA Inc., 1990), 415, 422.

101 BBC WAC, E2/193/3, 6 May 1942 (European Intelligence Papers).

102 Ibid.

103 CSA, *Radio National,* 15–21 March 1942.

104 INA, Fonds Vichy, disques de la BDIC, *Après le bombardement de Brest par la RAF,* recorded on 01.01.1941, sur la Radio Etat Français-Radiodiffusion Nationale. In this reportage, which is estimated to be recorded a month later, the tone was much more aggressive, accusing the RAF of killing civilians.

105 'Les usines Renault bombardées', 4 March 1942, in *Les Français parlent aux Français 1941–1942,* 834–5.

106 Jacques Duchesne, 'Le bombardement de Billancourt', 4 March 1942, in *Les Français parlent aux Français 1941–1942,* 835–6.

107 PP, 220W7, 9 March 1942 (police report).

108 Barbas, *Pétain, Discours aux Français,* 240.

109 INA, Inventaire Disques, *Reportage après un bombardement à Argenteuil,* recorded on 01.05.1942, on Radio Paris (RP), 1942.

110 Milward, *The New Order,* 113.

111 Ibid, 115.

112 PP, 220W8, 4 May 1942 (police report).

113 INA, Inventaire Disques, *Résultats d'une collecte en faveur des sinistrés d'un bombardement,* recorded on 06.03.1942, on Radio Paris (RP), 1942.

114 CSA, *Les Ondes,* 15 March 1942.

115 Halls, *The Youth of Vichy France,* 211.

116 INA, Inventaire Disques, *La collecte du centre d'initiative sociale de Radio-Paris,* recorded on 02.04.1942, on RP, 1942.

117 Gildea, *Marianne in Chains,* 16.

118 INA, Inventaire Disques, *La collecte du centre d'initiative sociale de Radio-Paris,* recorded on 02.04.1942, on Radio Paris (RP), 1942.

119 Ibid.

120 Ibid.

121 Déat, *Mémoires Politiques,* 665.

122 Barbas, *Pétain, Discours aux Français,* 96.

123 Bertin-Maghit, *Les documenteurs des Années Noires,* 237.

124 Tangye Lean, *Voices in the Darkness,* 144; Crémieux-Brilhac and Eck, 'France', 55.

125 CSA, Lévy, '1942: Radio-Paris': 49.

126 INA, Inventaire Disques, *Interview d'un travailleur français en Allemagne,* recorded on 30.05.1942, on Radio Paris (RP), 1942.

127 Ibid.

128 PP, 220W9, 13 July 1942 (police report); PP, 220W9, 27 July 1942 (police report).

129 INA, Inventaire Disques, *Au centre de recrutement pour TFA,* recorded on 12.08.1942, on Radio Paris (RP), 1942.

130 CSA, *Les Ondes,* 16 February 1942.

131 Vinen, *The Unfree French,* 170.

132 INA, Inventaire Disques, *Au centre de recrutement pour TFA*, recorded on 12.08.1942, on Radio Paris (RP), 1942.

133 Vinen, *The Unfree French*, 272.

134 Diamond, *Women and the Second World War*, 78–9.

135 Vinen, *The Unfree French*, 162.

136 Diamond, *Women and the Second World War*, 78.

137 Ibid, 47.

138 INA, Inventaire Disques, *Au centre de recrutement pour TFA*, recorded on 12.08.1942, on Radio Paris (RP), 1942.

139 Milward, *The New Order*, 274.

140 BBC WAC, Anonymous letters from France (1276–1308), 29 September 1942 (1291).

141 Ulrich Herbert, *Hitler's Foreign Workers: Enforced Foreign Labor in Germany under the Third Reich* (Cambridge University Press, 1997), 383.

142 TNA, WO208/3684 982, September 1942 (Royal Patriotic School).

143 INA, Inventaire Disques, *Reportage au centre d'apprentissage de Pantin*, recorded on 01.01.1942, on Radio Paris (RP), 1942.

144 INA, Inventaire Disques, *Aux ateliers de construction aéronautique d'Issy-les-Moulineaux*, recorded on 01.07.1942, on Radio Paris (RP), 1942.

145 PP, 220W10, 21 September 1942 (police report).

146 Bertin-Maghit, *Les documenteurs des Années Noires*, 69.

147 INA, Inventaire Disques, *Discours de François Chasseigne en faveur de la relève*, recorded on 05.10.1942, on Radio Paris (RP), 1942.

148 Ibid.

149 PP, 220W10, 5 October 1942 (police report).

150 PP, 220W10, 19 October 1942 (police report).

151 Crémieux-Brilhac and Eck, 'France', 94.

152 For example, PP, 220W5, 11 August 1941 (police report); PP, 220W8, 18 May 1942 (police report); PP, 220W9, 8 June 1942 (police report); PP, 220W10, 24 August 1942 (police report), etc.

153 INA, Inventaire Disques, *Propagande en faveur de la relève*, recorded on 20.10.1942, on Radio Paris (RP), 1942.

154 Ibid.

155 Ibid.

156 Ibid.

157 Crémieux-Brilhac and Eck, 'France', 91.

158 Ibid, 92.

159 Ibid, 94.

160 TNA, WO208/3695 1217, January 1943 (Royal Patriotic School).

161 Crémieux-Brilhac and Eck, 'France', 94.

162 Burrin, *Living with Defeat*, 284.

163 Fishman, *We Will Wait*, 37.

164 Ibid, 37–8.

165 Ibid, 38.

166 Halls, *The Youth of Vichy France*, 185; 'Privations', 11 May 1942, in *Les Français parlent aux Français 1941–1942*, 1046–8.

167 Drieu La Rochelle, *Journal 1939–1945*, 294.

168 Crémieux-Brilhac and Eck, 'France', 94–5.

Conclusion

1   Cornick, 'The BBC and the Propaganda War': 321–3.
2   Vinen, *The Unfree French*, 86; Bowles, 'Newsreels, Ideology, and Public Opinion under Vichy': 438; Guillon, 'Les manifestations de ménagères', 111; Jackson, *France: The Dark Years*, 259; Cépède, *Agriculture et Alimentation en France*, 51.
3   PP, Box JB 37 'Rapport zg'; PP, Box JB 37 'Rapport d'activité'. From the available evidence it is unclear if such a report was compiled on an ad hoc or regular basis.
4   Pessis, *Les Français parlent aux Français 1941–1942,* iv.
5   Brooks, *British Propaganda to France,* 54.
6   Crémieux-Brilhac, 'La France libre et la radio': 74.
7   Pessis, *Les Français parlent aux Français 1941–1942,* vi–vii.
8   Brooks, *British Propaganda to France,* 54.
9   Crémieux-Brilhac and Eck, 'France', 41.
10   Ibid, 46.
11   CSA, Box 1682W89 'Exposé d'ensemble'.
12   Crémieux-Brilhac and Eck, 'France', 48–9.
13   CSA, Lauzanne, 'Un double tournant': 5.
14   Crémieux-Brilhac and Eck, 'France', 79.
15   Méadel, 'Pauses musicales', 238.
16   Ibid, 240.
17   CSA, Chardonnier, 'Radio-Paris': 71.
18   Ibid: 55–6.
19   CSA, Lauzanne, 'Ici Londres': 56.
20   Méadel, 'Pauses musicales', 241.
21   CSA, Box 1682W90 'Radiodiffusion'.
22   CSA, Lévy, '1942: Radio-Paris': 48.
23   CSA, *Les Ondes*, 21–27 June 1942.
24   'La récolte des pommes de terre', 25 September 1941, in *Les Français parlent aux Français 1941–1942,* 273–4.
25   Vinen, *The Unfree French,* 3.
26   Crémieux-Brilhac, 'La France libre et la radio': 80–1.
27   Crémieux-Brilhac and Eck, 'France', 149.
28   CSA, Lévy, '1942: Radio-Paris': 47.
29   CSA, Lauzanne, 'L'année radiophonique 1941': 37.
30   Milward, *The New Order,* 110.
31   Méadel, 'Pauses musicales', 251.
32   Crémieux-Brilhac and Eck, 'France', 369.
33   Brooks, *British Propaganda to France*, 160.
34   Ibid, 5.
35   Cornick, 'Fighting Myth with Reality', 83.
36   Vinen, *The Unfree French*, 6–7.

Bibliography

Source Material

Archival and museum holdings

The British Broadcasting Corporation Written Archives Centre, Caversham, Reading (BBC WAC)

BBC European Department, (Bi-) Monthly Intelligence Report from the BBC Written Archives Centre, Caversham (June 1940–November 1942).
Files drawn from the following file series:
BBC WAC E2/185, Intelligence Reports, 1941–1943.
BBC WAC E2/186/2, Intelligence Reports Europe, June–August 1940.
BBC WAC E2/186/3, Intelligence Reports Europe, September–October 1940.
BBC WAC E2/186/4, Intelligence Reports Europe, November 1940–January 1941.
BBC WAC E2/188/1, Studies of European Audiences, May 1941–September 1942.
BBC WAC E2/193/2, Surveys of European Audiences France, May–July 1941.
BBC WAC E2/193/3, Surveys of European Audiences France, August 1941–April 1942.
Boxes of anonymous letters:
A collection of anonymous letters from France (numbered 1–1373).
Boxes of broadcasts from the BBC French Services:
A collection of various narratives of the BBC French Service (June 1940–November 1942).

Kew National Archives, Richmond (TNA)

FO 115/3448 France foreign policy 1941.
Royal Patriotic School: interrogation of civilians arriving in UK from abroad (May 1941–March 1943).
Files drawn from the following file series:
WO 208/3664, July 1941.
WO 208 3673, February/March 1942.
WO 208/3677, May 1942.
WO 208/3682, August 1942.
WO 208/3684, September 1942.
WO 208 3685, September 1942.
WO 208/3688, October 1942.
WO 208/3689, October 1942.
WO 208/3690, November 1942.
WO 208/3695, January 1943.

Collections du Service Archives écrites et Musée de Radio France (CSA)

Magazines
  Revue Nationale – Radio National – Organe officiel de la Radiodiffusion Nationale. 1941 No. 1 to
    Radio National 1942 No. 79.
  Les Ondes CD ROM Disc 1 1942 (Nos. 37 to 83).
Thematic files: Fonds Christian Brochand.
Box 1682W89 La Radio en France 1940–1944.
Box 1682W90 Radio Normandie 1940–1944 /Radio Méditerranée 1940–1944.
Periodicals
  'La radiodiffusion en France en 1940', Cahiers d'Histoire de la Radiodiffusion, No. 27 (December
    1990).
  'La radiodiffusion en France en 1941', Cahiers d'Histoire de la Radiodiffusion, No. 30 (September
    1991).
  'L'année radiophonique 1942', Cahiers d'Histoire de la Radiodiffusion, No. 34 (September–
    November 1992).

Institut national de l'audiovisuel (INA)

Fonds Vichy, disques de la BDIC (June 1940–November 1942).
Inventaire Disques, Radio Paris (June 1940–November 1942).

Les archives de la Préfecture de police de Paris (PP)

Situation de Paris 1940–1944: Période Occupation 1940/1944. Rapports hebdomadaires ou de
  quinzaine au préfet de police émanant de la Direction des renseignements généraux.
Files drawn from the following file series:
  220W1, June to October 1940.
  220W4, April to July 1941.
  220W5, August to October 1941.
  220W6, November to December 1941.
  220W7, January to March 1942.
  220W8, April to May 1942.
  220W9, June and July 1942.
  220W10, August to December 1942.
Box JB 37 Presses et organes de presse, théâtres, cabarets.

France, Archives nationales (FAN)

F/43/59 Speakers on Radio Paris.

Churchill College Archive Centre

The catalogue of the Papers of Douglas E. Ritchie and Noel Newsome, Churchill Archives Centre
  (GBR/0014/NERI).
Telegram from the President of the United States, Franklin Roosevelt, to WSC explaining his proposal
  to resume limited economic assistance to North Africa, 23 Mar 1942, Churchill Archives Centre
  (CHAR 20/72/69-71).

German Archives (Calvin University)

Dr. Goebbels, Joseph. 'Deutsches Frauentum.' German Propaganda Archive. 5 June 2013. https://research.calvin.edu/german-propaganda-archive/
German Propaganda Archive. 'Zeitschriften-Dienst Issue 126: 26 September 1941.' 5 June 2013. https://research.calvin.edu/german-propaganda-archive/

Published broadcasts

Barbas, J.C. (ed.), *Philippe Pétain, Discours aux Français 17 juin 1940–20 août 1944*, Paris: Albin Michel, 1989.
Dr. Friedrich, *Un journaliste allemand vous parle ...*, Paris: Editions LE PONT, 1942.
Pessis, J. (ed.), *Les Français parlent aux Français 1940–1941*, Paris: Edition Omnibus, 2010.
Pessis, J. (ed.), *Les Français parlent aux Français 1941–1942*, Paris: Edition Omnibus, 2011.
Schumann, M. *Honneur et Patrie*, Paris: Editions du Livre Français, 1946.

Secondary Sources

Books

Atkin, N. *The Forgotten French Exiles in the British Isles, 1940–44*. Manchester: Manchester University Press, 2003.
Barker, C. and Galasinski, D. *Cultural Studies and Discourse Analysis: A Dialogue on Language and Identity*. London: Sage Publications, 2001.
Baudot, M. *L'Opinion Publique sous l'Occupation*. Paris: Presses Universitaires de France, 1960.
Bertin-Maghit, J. P. *Les documenteurs des Années Noires. Les documentaires de propagande, France 1940–1944*. Paris: Nouveau Monde Editions, 2004.
Bloch, M. *Strange Defeat: A Statement of Evidence Written in 1940*. New York-London: W. W. Norton & Company, 1968.
Bood, M. *Les Années doubles: Journal d'une lycéenne sous l'Occupation*. Paris: Editions Robert Laffont, 1974.
Bourdan, P. *1940–1944: Pierre Bourdan vous parle*. Paris: Editions Magnard, 1990.
Briggs, A. *The History of Broadcasting in the United Kingdom 1896-1927: Volume I: The Birth of Broadcasting*. Oxford: Oxford University Press, 1995.
Briggs, A. *The History of Broadcasting in the UK, Vol. 3, The War of Words*. London, New York, Toronto: Oxford University Press, 1970.
Brooks, T. *British Propaganda to France, 1940–1944: Machinery, Method and Message*. Edinburgh: Edinburgh University Press, 2007.
Burrin, P. *Living with Defeat: France under the German Occupation 1940–1944*. London, Sydney, Auckland: Arnold, 1996.
Cépède, M. *Agriculture et alimentation en France durant la IIeme guerre mondiale*. Paris: Editions M.-TH. Génin, 1961.
Chimènes, M. *La Vie musicale sous Vichy*. Bruxelles: Editions Complexe, 2001.
Cointet, J. P. *La Légion Française des Combattants, 1940–1944. La tentation du fascisme*. Paris: Albin Michel S. A., 1995.
Déat, M. *Mémoires Politiques*. Paris: Editions Denoël, 1989.
Delarue, J. *Trafics et crimes sous l'occupation*. Paris: Librairie Arthème Fayard, 1968.
Delavenay, E. *Témoignage d'un village Savoyard au village mondial (1905–1991)*. La Calade: Edition EDISUD, 1992.
De Monzie, A. *Ci-devant*. Paris: Flammarion, 1941.

Desprairies, C. *Sous l'oeil de l'occupant: La France vue par l'Allemagne 1940–1944*. Paris: Armand Collin, 2010.

Diamond, H. *Women and the Second World War in France 1939–1948: Choices and Constraints*. Harlow: Pearson Education Limited, 1999.

Douglas, S. J. *Listening In: Radio and the American Imagination*. Minneapolis: University of Minnesota Press, 2004.

Dricu La Rochelle, P. *Journal 1939–1945*. Paris: Editions Gallimard, 1992.

Eck, H. (dir.) *La guerre des ondes: Histoire des radios de langue française pendant la Deuxième Guerre mondiale*. Lausanne, Paris: Editions Payot et Armand Colin, 1985.

Ellul, J. *Propaganda: The Formation of Men's Attitudes*. New York: Vintage Books Edition, 1973.

Evrard, J. and Kermabon, J. *Une encyclopédie du court métrage français*. Crisnée: Editions Yellow Now, 2004.

Fishman, S. *We Will Wait: Wives of French Prisoners of War, 1940–1945*. New Haven: Yale University Press, 1991.

Gaillard, R. *Jours de pénitence. Mes évasions*. Paris: René Debresse, 1942.

Gay-Lescot, J. L. *Sport et Education sous Vichy (1940–44)*. Lyon: Presses universitaires de Lyon, 1991.

Gildea, R. *Marianne in Chains: In Search of the German Occupation of France 1940–45*. London: Pan Books, 2003.

Gilzmer, M. Levisse-Touzé, C. and Martens, S. *Les Femmes dans la Résistance en France*. Paris: Editions Tallandier, 2003.

Giolitto, P. *Histoire de la jeunesse sous Vichy*. Paris: Librairie Académique Perrin, 1991.

Giraudoux, J. *Pleins Pouvoirs*. Paris: Gallimard, 1939.

Grenard, F. *La France du marché noir (1940–1949)*. Paris: Editions Payot & Rivages, 2012.

Groult, B. and F. *Journal à quatre mains*. Paris: Editions Denoël, 1962.

Halls, W. D. *The Youth of Vichy France*. Oxford: Clarendon Press, 1981.

Herbert, U. *Hitler's Foreign Workers: Enforced Foreign Labor in Germany under the Third Reich*. Cambridge: Cambridge University Press, 1997.

Hervet, R. *Les Compagnons de France*. Paris: Editions France-Empire, 1965.

Hitler, A. *Mein Kampf*. Boston: The Houghton Mifflin Company, 1971.

Holman, V. and Kelly, D. *France at War in the Twentieth Century: Propaganda, Myth, and Metaphor*. New York, Oxford: Berghahn Books, 2000.

Horten, G. *Radio Goes to War: The Cultural Politics of Propaganda during World War II*. Berkeley: University of California Press, 2002.

Jäckel, E. *La France dans l'Europe de Hitler*. Paris: Edition Librairie Arthème Fayard, 1968.

Jackson, J. *France: The Dark Years 1940–1944*. Oxford: Oxford University Press, 2003.

Kedward, H. R. *Occupied France: Collaboration and Resistance 1940–1944*. Oxford, New York: Basil Blackwell, 1985.

Keegan, J. *The Second World War*. New York: Penguin Books USA Inc., 1990.

Kladstrup, D. and P. *Wine and War*. New York: Broadway Books, 2001.

Kris, E. and Speier, H. *German Radio Propaganda: Report on Home Broadcasts during the War*. London, New York, Toronto: Oxford University Press, 1944.

Laborie, P. *L'opinion française sous Vichy: Les Français et la crise d'identité nationale 1936–1944*. Paris: Editions du Seuil, 2001.

Loviglio, J. *Radio's Intimate Public: Network Broadcasting and Mass-Mediated Democracy*. Minneapolis: University of Minnesota Press, 2005.

Luneau, A. *Radio Londres: Les Voix de la Liberté (1940–1944)*. Paris: Editions Perrin, 2005.

Milward, A. S. *The New Order and the French Economy*. Oxford: Clarendon Press, 1970.

Nicholas, S. *The Echo of War: Home Front Propaganda and the Wartime BBC, 1939–45*. Manchester, New York: Manchester University Press, 1996.

Nicolson, H. *Peacemaking 1919*. Safety Harbor: Simon Publications, 2001.

Nobécourt, R. G. *Les Secrets de la propagande en France occupée*. Paris: Librairie Arthème Fayard, 1962.

Overy, R. *Why the Allies Won*. New York, London: W. W. Norton & Company, 1997.

Paxton, R. O. *Vichy France: Old Guard and New Order 1940–1944*. New York: Columbia University Press, 2001.

Pecout, C. *Les Chantiers de la Jeunesse et la revitalisation physique et morale de la jeunesse française (1940–1944)*. Paris: L'Harmattan, 2007.

Pessis, J. *La Bataille de Radio Londres 1940–1944*. Paris: Edition Omnibus, 2010.

Polonski, J. *La Presse La Propagande et l'Opinion Publique sous l'Occupation*. Paris: Editions du Centre, 1946.

Ponsonby, A. *Falsehood in War-Time*. London: Kimble & Bradford, 1940.

Prêtet, B. *Sports et sportifs français sous Vichy*. Paris: Nouveau Monde éditions, 2016.

Proud, J. K. *Children and Propaganda*. Bristol: Intellect European Studies Series, 1995.

Rupp, L. J. *Mobilizing Women for War: German and American Propaganda 1939–1945*. Princeton: Princeton University Press, 1978.

Short, K. R. M. *Film & Radio Propaganda in World War II*. Knoxville: The University of Tennessee Press, 1983.

Stenton, M. *Radio London and Resistance in Occupied Europe British Political Warfare 1939–1943*. Oxford: Oxford University Press, 2000.

Tangye Lean, E. *Voices in the Darkness: The Story of the European Radio War*. London: Secker and Warburg, 1943.

Tartakowsky, D. *Les Manifestations de rue en France (1918–1968)*. Paris: Publications de la Sorbonne, 1997.

Thibault, L. (dir.) *Les femmes et la Résistance*. Paris: La Documentation Française, 2006.

Travers, A. (dir.) *Politique et représentations de la montagne sous Vichy. La Montagne Educatrice, 1940–1944*. Paris: L'Harmattan, 2001.

Veillon, D. *Vivre et Survivre en France 1939–1947*. Paris: Editions Payot & Rivages, 1995.

Vinen, R. *The Unfree French: Life under the Occupation*. London: Penguin Group, 2006.

Welch, D. *Nazi Propaganda: The Power and the Limitations*. London and Canberra: Croom Helm, 1983.

Werth, L. *Déposition: Journal de guerre 1940–1944*. Paris: Editions Points, 2007.

Chapters in edited books

Bertin-Maghit, J. P. 'Le documentaire de propagande dans la France de l'Occupation', in J. Evrard and J. Kermabon (eds), *Une encyclopédie du court métrage français*, Crisnée: Editions Yellow Now, 2004.

Billeter, G. 'Suisse', in H. Eck (ed.), *La guerre des ondes: Histoire des radios de langue française pendant la Deuxième Guerre Mondiale*, Paris: Editions Payot Lausanne et Armand Colin, 1985.

Cornick, M. 'Fighting Myth with Reality: The Fall of France, Anglophobia and the BBC', in V. Hollman and D. Kelly (eds), *France at War in the Twentieth Century: Propaganda, Myth, and Metaphor*, New York, Oxford: Berghahn Books, 2000.

Crémieux-Brilhac, J. L. and Eck, H. (with Charles Louis Foulon) 'France', in H. Eck (ed.), *La guerre des ondes: Histoire des radios de langue française pendant la Deuxième Guerre Mondiale*, Paris: Editions Payot Lausanne et Armand Colin, 1985.

Delporte, C. 'The Image and Myth of the "Fifth Column" during the Two World Wars', in V. Holman and D. Kelly (eds), *France at War in the Twentieth Century: Propaganda, Myth and Metaphor*, New York, Oxford: Berghahn Books, 2000.

Dompnier, N. 'Entre La Marseillaise et Maréchal, nous voilà! Quel hymne pour le régime de Vichy?', in M. Chimènes (ed), *La Vie musicale sous Vichy*, Bruxelles: Editions Complexe, 2001.

Dujardin, J. 'Belgique', in H. Eck (ed.), *La guerre des ondes: Histoire des radios de langue française pendant la Deuxième Guerre Mondiale*, Paris: Editions Payot Lausanne et Armand Colin, 1985.

Garçon, F. 'Nazi Film Propaganda in Occupied France', in D. Welch (ed.), *Nazi Propaganda: The Power and the Limitations*, London, Canberra: Croom Helm, 1983.

Guillon, J.-M. 'Les manifestations de ménagères: protestation populaire et résistance féminine spécifique', in M. Gilzmer, C. Levisse-Touzé and R. Martens (eds), *Les Femmes dans la Résistance en France*, Paris: Editions Tallandier, 2003.

Lespinard, B. 'Le répertoire choral des mouvements de jeunesse', in M. Chimènes (ed.), *La Vie musicale sous Vichy*, Bruxelles: Editions Complexe, 2001.

Méadel, C. 'Pauses musicales ou les éclatants silences de Radio-Paris', in M. Chimènes (ed.), *La Vie musicale sous Vichy*, Bruxelles: Editions Complexe, 2001.

Pithon, R. 'French Film Propaganda July 1939–June 1940', in K. R. M. Short (ed.), *Film & Radio Propaganda in World War II*, Knoxville: The University of Tennessee Press, 1983.

Schwartz, M. 'La musique, outil majeur de la propagande culturelle des Nazis', in M. Chimènes (ed.), *La Vie musicale sous Vichy*, Bruxelles: Editions Complexe, 2001.

Sorlin, P. 'The Struggle for Control of French Minds, 1940–1944', in K. R. M. Short (ed.), *Film & Radio Propaganda in World War II*, Knoxville: The University of Tennessee Press, 1983.

Stephenson, J. 'Propaganda, Autarky and the German Housewife', in D. Welch (ed.), *Nazi Propaganda: The Power and the Limitations*, London, Canberra: Croom Helm, 1983.

Taylor, R. 'Goebbels and the Function of Propaganda', in D. Welch (ed.), *Nazi Propaganda: The Power and the Limitations*, London, Canberra: Croom Helm, 1983.

Tournès, L. 'Le jazz: un espace de liberté pour un phénomène culturel en voie d'identification', in M. Chimènes (ed.), *La Vie musicale sous Vichy*, Bruxelles: Editions Complexe, 2001.

Veillon, D. 'Les Femmes Anonymes dans la Résistance', in M. Gilzmer, C. Levisse-Touzé et S. Martens (eds), *Les Femmes dans la Résistance en France*, Paris: Editions Tallandier, 2003.

Articles in journals

Bowles, B. 'Newsreels, Ideology, and Public Opinion under Vichy: The Case of La France en Marche', *French Historical Studies*, Vol. 27, No. 2 (2004): 419–63.

Chadwick, K. 'Our Enemy's Enemy: Selling Britain to Occupied France on the BBC French Service', *Media History*, Vol. 21, No. 4 (2015): 426–42.

Chadwick, K. 'Radio Propaganda and Public Opinion Under Endgame Vichy: The Impact of Philippe Henriot', *French History*, Vol. 25, No. 2 (2011): 232–52.

Clements, Robert J. 'Foreign Language Broadcasting of "Radio Boston"'. *The Modern Language Journal*, Vol. 27, No. 3 (1943): 175–9.

Cornick, M. 'The BBC and the Propaganda War against Occupied France: The Work of Emile Delavenay and the European Intelligence Department', *French History*, Vol. 8, No. 3 (1994): 316–54.

Crémieux-Brilhac, J.-L. 'Information, propagande et opinion publique durant la deuxième Guerre Mondiale. Réflexions en guise de conclusions', *Mélanges de l'Ecole française de Rome*, T. 108, No. 1 (1996): 147–54.

Crémieux-Brilhac, J.-L. 'La France libre et la radio', *Mélanges de l'Ecole française de Rome*, T. 108, No. 1 (1996): 73–81.

Crémieux-Brilhac, J.-L. 'Le rôle de la radio, 1940–1944', *Espoir*, No. 66 (1989): 1–6.

Crémieux-Brilhac, J.-L. and Bensimhon, G. 'Les propagandes radiophoniques et l'opinion publique en France de 1940 à 1944', *Revue d'histoire de la deuxième guerre mondiale*, No. 101 (January 1976): 1–18.

Grenard, F. 'Les implication politiques du ravitaillement en France sous l'Occupation', *Vingtième Siècle Revue d'histoire*, No. 94 (2007): 199–215.

Jeannelle, J. L. 'Les Mémoires à l'épreuve du burlesque: Céline ou la chronique des Grands Guignols', *Revue d'Histoire littéraire de la France*, No. 3 (July-September 2009): 681–98.

Kingston, P. J. 'Broadcasts in French from Moscow February 1940–August 1941: An evaluation of the reorientation of radio propaganda', *Cahiers du monde russe et soviétique*, Vol. 25, No. 2–3 (April–September 1984): 201–18.

Mouré, K. 'Food Rationing and the Black Market in France (1940–1944)', *French History*, Vol. 24, No. 2 (2010): 262–82.

Seul, S. and Ribeiro, N. 'Revisiting Transnational Broadcasting', *Media History*, Vol. 21, No. 4 (2015): 365–77.

Winek, Mark D. 'Radio as a Tool of the State: Radio Moscow and the Early Cold War', *Comparative Humanities Review*, Vol. 3, Article 9 (2009): 99–113.

Pamphlets

Boris, G. *French Public Opinion since the Armistice*. Oxford: Oxford University Press, 1942.

Index